MACRO FEDERALISM AND LOCAL FINANCE

Introduction to the Public Sector Governance and Accountability Series

Anwar Shah, Series Editor

A well-functioning public sector that delivers quality public services consistent with citizen preferences and that fosters private market-led growth while managing fiscal resources prudently is considered critical to the World Bank's mission of poverty alleviation and the achievement of the Millennium Development Goals. This important new series aims to advance those objectives by disseminating conceptual guidance and lessons from practices and by facilitating learning from each others' experiences on ideas and practices that promote *responsive* (by matching public services with citizens' preferences), *responsible* (through efficiency and equity in service provision without undue fiscal and social risk), and *accountable* (to citizens for all actions) public governance in developing countries.

This series represents a response to several independent evaluations in recent years that have argued that development practitioners and policy makers dealing with public sector reforms in developing countries and, indeed, anyone with a concern for effective public governance could benefit from a synthesis of newer perspectives on public sector reforms. This series distills current wisdom and presents tools of analysis for improving the efficiency, equity, and efficacy of the public sector. Leading public policy experts and practitioners have contributed to this series.

The first 14 volumes in this series, listed below, are concerned with public sector accountability for prudent fiscal management; efficiency, equity, and integrity in public service provision; safeguards for the protection of the poor, women, minorities, and other disadvantaged groups; ways of strengthening institutional arrangements for voice, choice, and exit; means of ensuring public financial accountability for integrity and results; methods of evaluating public sector programs, fiscal federalism, and local finances; international practices in local governance; and a framework for responsive and accountable governance.

Fiscal Management

Public Services Delivery

Public Expenditure Analysis

Local Governance in Industrial Countries

Local Governance in Developing Countries

Intergovernmental Fiscal Transfers: Principles and Practice

Participatory Budgeting

Budgeting and Budgetary Institutions

Local Budgeting

Local Public Financial Management

Performance Accountability and Combating Corruption

Tools for Public Sector Evaluations

Macro Federalism and Local Finance

Managing Natural Resources and the Environment

PUBLIC SECTOR
GOVERNANCE AND
ACCOUNTABILITY SERIES

MACRO FEDERALISM AND
LOCAL FINANCE

Edited by ANWAR SHAH

THE WORLD BANK
Washington, D.C.

ISBN: 978-0-8213-6326-3
eISBN: 978-0-8213-6327-0
DOI: 10.1596/978-0-8213-6326-3

Library of Congress Cataloging-in-Publication Data
Macro federalism and local finance / Anwar Shah, editor.
    p. cm.
  Includes bibliographical references and index.
  ISBN 978-0-8213-6326-3 — ISBN 978-0-8213-6327-0 (electronic)
    1. Intergovernmental fiscal relations—Case studies. 2. Federal government—Case studies. 3. Local finance—Case studies. 4. Decentralization in government—Case studies. 5. Finance, Public—Case studies. I. Shah, Anwar.

HJ197.M33 2008
336—dc22

                                                                  2008006103

Contents

Foreword   xi

Preface   xiii

Acknowledgments   xv

Contributors   xvii

Abbreviations   xxi

Overview   1
Anwar Shah

Part I Macro Federalism

CHAPTER

Macro Federalism: An Introduction with Principal Reference to the Canadian Experience   9
Thomas J. Courchene
Globalization, Confederalism, and the
    Information-Knowledge Revolution   11
Defining *Macro Federalism*   18
Outline of the Analysis   19
Internal Economic Integration   20
Transfer Dependency: A Macro Federalism Approach
    to Regional Policy and Fiscal Federalism   34
Monetary Policy and Central Banking   47

Fiscal Policy   53
Miscellaneous Macro Federalism Issues   57
Overall Conclusions   68
Notes   74
References   75

Globalization, the Information Revolution, and Emerging Imperatives for Rethinking Fiscal Federalism   77

Anwar Shah

Governance Implications of Globalization and the
     Information Revolution   78
Localization   84
Emerging Jurisdictional Realignments: Glocalization   85
Emerging Imperatives for Rethinking Fiscal Federalism   86
Federalism and Regional Equity: Reflections on Alternative
     Approaches to Reducing Regional Disparities   93
Conclusions: The New Vision of Multicentered
     Governance   103
Notes   104
References   104

Federalism and Macroeconomic Performance   107

Anwar Shah

Institutional Environment for Macroeconomic
     Management   109
Fiscal Decentralization and Fiscal Performance:
     Some Conclusions   136
Notes   137
References   137

Regional Income Disparities and Convergence: Measurement and Policy Impact Evaluation   143

Raja Shankar and Anwar Shah

Measures of Regional Inequality   144

Regional Disparities: A Cross-Country Snapshot   149
Regional Income Disparities and Convergence   157
Regional Inequalities and Convergence: A Scorecard
    on National Policies for Regional Development   169
Annex 4A: Regional Disparity Trends   171
Annex 4B: Data Sources   188
Notes   189
References   189

5 Harmonizing Taxation of Interstate Trade under a Subnational VAT: Lessons from International Experience   193

Mahesh C. Purohit

Brazil   194
Canada   196
European Union   198
The Little Boat Model   200
India   202
The Recommended Options   208
Conclusion   210
Notes   210
References   212

6 Subnational Borrowing, Insolvency, and Regulation   215

Lili Liu and Michael Waibel

Benefits and Risks of Subnational Borrowing   217
Rationales for Regulating Subnational
    Borrowing   221
Frameworks for Subnational Borrowing:
    Ex ante Regulation   223
Regulatory Frameworks for Subnational Borrowing:
    Insolvency Mechanisms   226
Conclusions   231
Notes   234
References   239

Part II Local Finance

7 **A Local Perspective on Fiscal Federalism: Practices, Experiences, and Lessons from Industrial Countries**   245
Melville L. McMillan
Expenditure Responsibilities of Local Government   246
Local Government Revenue   263
Summary, Conclusions, and Lessons   283
Notes   287
References   288

8 **Decentralized Governance in Developing and Transition Countries: A Comparative Review**   291
Sebastian Eckardt and Anwar Shah
The Building Blocks of Citizen-Centered Governance
    in Decentralized Systems   292
A Simple Scorecard to Measure Decentralized
    Citizen-Centered Governance   301
Conclusion   314
Annex: Country Sample   316
Note   318
References   318

Index   323

BOXES

2.1   Emerging Rearrangements of Government Assignments:
      Glocalization   85
3.1   Legislated Fiscal Rules: Do They Matter for
      Fiscal Outcomes?   124

FIGURES

1.1   The Economic Integration Continuum   24
1.2   A Geometry of Regional Dependence   37
4.1   Regional Disparities in Industrial Countries   151
4.2   Regional Disparities in Nonindustrial Countries   155
4.3   Regional Disparity Trends in Federal Countries   158
4.4   Regional Disparity Trends in Unitary Countries   162
4A.1 Regional Disparity Trends in Canada   171

4A.2   Regional Disparity Trends in the United States   172
4A.3   Regional Disparity Trends in Brazil   173
4A.4   Regional Disparity Trends in India   174
4A.5   Regional Disparity Trends in Mexico   175
4A.6   Regional Disparity Trends in Pakistan   176
4A.7   Regional Disparity Trends in the Russian Federation   177
4A.8   Regional Disparity Trends in Chile   178
4A.9   Regional Disparity Trends in China   180
4A.10 Regional Disparity Trends in Indonesia   181
4A.11 Regional Disparity Trends in the Philippines   182
4A.12 Regional Disparity Trends in Romania   183
4A.13 Regional Disparity Trends in Sri Lanka   184
4A.14 Regional Disparity Trends in Thailand   185
4A.15 Regional Disparity Trends in Uzbekistan   186
4A.16 Regional Disparity Trends in Vietnam   187
8.1   Political Freedom and Bureaucratic Quality: Partial
       Correlation Controlling for Per Capita GDP Log   293
8.2   Accountability   303
8.3   Fiscal Responsibility   310

TABLES

1.1   Globalization and the Information-Knowledge Revolution:
       Variations on the New Technoeconomic Paradigm   12
1.2   Selected Institutional Features of Mature Federations   21
1.3   Comparison of Constitutional Provisions   22
1.4   Central Bank Structure   48.
2.1   Governance Structure: 20th versus 21st Century   87
3.1   Fiscal Decentralization and Fiscal Performance:
       Selected Regressions   114
3.2   Fiscal Rules at a Glance   123
3.3   Fiscal Decentralization and Fiscal Performance:
       A Summary of Empirical Results   136
4.1   Regional Disparities in Industrial Countries   150
4.2   Regional Disparities in Nonindustrial Countries   153
4.3   Regression Results   156
4.4   Spearman Rank Correlation   157
4.5   Beta Convergence Results in Federal Countries   159
4.6   Beta Convergence Results in Unitary Countries   164
4.7   Regional Inequalities and Convergence: A Summary View   170
4A.1   Regional Disparity Trends in Canada   171

4A.2   Regional Disparity Trends in the United States   172
4A.3   Regional Disparity Trends in Brazil   173
4A.4   Regional Disparity Trends in India   174
4A.5   Regional Disparity Trends in Mexico   175
4A.6   Regional Disparity Trends in Pakistan   176
4A.7   Regional Disparity Trends in the Russian Federation   177
4A.8   Regional Disparity Trends in Chile   178
4A.9   Regional Disparity Trends in China   179
4A.10   Regional Disparity Trends in Indonesia   181
4A.11   Regional Disparity Trends in the Philippines   182
4A.12   Regional Disparity Trends in Romania   183
4A.13   Regional Disparity Trends in Sri Lanka   184
4A.14   Regional Disparity Trends in Thailand   185
4A.15   Regional Disparity Trends in Uzbekistan   186
4A.16   Regional Disparity Trends in Vietnam   187
5.1   Cascading Effects of Central Sales Tax in Consuming States   206
5.2   Distribution of Revenue from CST among Indian States   207
7.1   Local Government Expenditures by Function, 2003   247
7.2   Relative Government Expenditures for Selected Countries   251
7.3   Social Programs in Local Government Finance, 2003   253
7.4   Local Government Expenditures by Function as a Percentage
        of GDP, 2003   256
7.5   Local Government Consumption of Fixed Capital and
        Debt, 2004   262
7.6   Main Taxes and Selected Other Own-Source Revenues of
        Local Governments in OECD Member Countries as a
        Percentage of GDP, 2003   264
7.7   Composition of Local Government Tax Revenue in
        OECD Countries, 2003   267
7.8   Tax, Nontax, and Grant Revenue of Local
        Governments, 2003   274
7.9   Sources of Nontax Own-Source Revenue, 2003   275
7.10   Local Government Tax Autonomy, 1995   277
7.11   Types of Grants Received by Local Governments   279
8.1   Accountability Indicators   302
8.2   Accountability Scores   304
8.3   Fiscal Responsibility Indicators   308
8.4   Fiscal Responsibility Scores   311
8A.1   Country Sample   316
8A.2   Sources for Country Sample   317

Foreword

In Western democracies, systems of checks and balances built into government structures have formed the core of good governance and have helped empower citizens for more than two hundred years. The incentives that motivate public servants and policy makers— the rewards and sanctions linked to results that help shape public sector performance—are rooted in a country's accountability frameworks. Sound public sector management and government spending help determine the course of economic development and social equity, especially for the poor and other disadvantaged groups, such as women and the elderly.

Many developing countries, however, continue to suffer from unsatisfactory and often dysfunctional governance systems that include rent seeking and malfeasance, inappropriate allocation of resources, inefficient revenue systems, and weak delivery of vital public services. Such poor governance leads to unwelcome outcomes for access to public services by the poor and other disadvantaged members of society, such as women, children, and minorities. In dealing with these concerns, the development assistance community in general and the World Bank in particular are continuously striving to learn lessons from practices around the world to achieve a better understanding of what works and what does not work in improving public sector governance, especially with respect to combating corruption and making services work for poor people.

The Public Sector Governance and Accountability Series advances our knowledge by providing tools and lessons from practices in improving efficiency and equity of public services provision and strengthening institutions of accountability in governance. The series highlights frameworks to create incentive environments and pressures for good governance from within and beyond governments. It outlines institutional mechanisms to empower citizens to demand accountability for results from their governments. It provides practical guidance on managing for results and prudent fiscal management. It outlines approaches to dealing with corruption and malfeasance. It provides conceptual and practical guidance on alternative service delivery frameworks for extending the reach and access of public services. The series also covers safeguards for the protection of the poor, women, minorities, and other disadvantaged groups; ways of strengthening institutional arrangements for voice and exit; methods of evaluating public sector programs; frameworks for responsive and accountable governance; and fiscal federalism and local governance.

This series will be of interest to public officials, development practitioners, students of development, and those interested in public governance in developing countries.

Rakesh Nangia
Acting Vice President
World Bank Institute

Preface

During the past two decades, two prominent influences—globalization and the information revolution—have brought about profound changes in the division of powers within nations as well as beyond nation-states. As a result, the world has gradually but steadily moved from closed-economy centralized governance to open-economy globalized and localized governance—sometimes called "glocalized" governance. International security concerns in recent years have somewhat dampened this change process. Nevertheless, these rearrangements have had profound implications for the roles of and relations among various orders of government. They also have implications for democratic choice and citizen voice and exit. Nevertheless, they have received only scant attention in the fiscal federalism literature.

Even ignoring these newer developments, past analyses of federal systems have usually focused on inward-looking, static-efficiency considerations to the neglect of important dynamic internal and external economic influences. The dynamic-efficiency and growth implications of federal systems are critical for holding a federal country together but have not received adequate attention in the economics literature. This book takes a first step toward addressing these important yet relatively neglected policy areas by (a) examining the effect of globalization and the information revolution on multiorder governance structures, (b) reviewing the dynamic-efficiency and growth implications of intergovernmental fiscal relations, and (c) providing a comparative review of local government organization and finances and their consistency with a changing role of local government in the new economic era.

The book is divided into two parts. The first part, "Macro Federalism," provides a fresh look at emerging constitutional challenges arising from globalization and the information revolution, as well as the dynamic-efficiency and growth implications of existing federal constitutions. Several aspects of these systems are examined: (a) institutional design to achieve internal economic union; (b) policies for regional development; (c) conduct of monetary policy; (d) coordination of fiscal policies, with a special emphasis on tax harmonization; and (e) management of risks of insolvency from subnational borrowing. The second part of the book, "Local Finance," provides a comparative perspective on local finances and measures the progress of decentralized governance reforms in developing countries.

The book is the outgrowth of a partnership between the Canadian International Development Agency and the World Bank Institute. It is hoped that the book will assist policy makers and practitioners in realigning responsibilities of various orders of government to adapt to a changing world and to serve their citizens better.

Roumeen Islam
Manager, Poverty Reduction and Economic Management
World Bank Institute

Acknowledgments

This book brings together selected learning modules on fiscal federalism and local finance. The modules were prepared for the World Bank staff training programs and World Bank Institute learning programs on fiscal decentralization that were conducted by the editor over the past two decades. The book was initially planned for publication in 1995, but because of circumstances beyond the editor's control, its publication was indefinitely delayed. Most chapters from the original manuscript have been either updated or rewritten to make current publication possible. The chapters by Courchene and McMillan published in this volume represent abridged versions of original manuscripts; the full versions have been posted on the Web site http://www.worldbank.org/wbi/publicfinance.

The learning modules and their publication in the current volume were financed primarily by the Canadian International Development Agency through its Intergovernmental Fiscal Relations and Local Governance partnership program with the World Bank Institute—a program that is directed by the editor. The editor is grateful to Walter Bernyck, Baljit Nagpal, and Jeff Nankivell of the Canadian International Development Agency and Kent Smith of the Canadian Embassy in Beijing for their support of the partnership program.

The book has benefited from contributions to World Bank Institute learning events by senior policy makers and scholars from Australia, Brazil, Canada, Central Asia, China, India, Indonesia, Pakistan, the Russian Federation, South Africa, Switzerland, Thailand, the United States, and elsewhere. In particular, thanks are due to Allan Morris, chairman of the Commonwealth Grants Commission,

Australia; Walter Moser, Federal Department of Finance, Switzerland; Almos Tassonyi, Government of Ontario, Canada; Paul Boothe, Glen Campbell, and Munir Sheikh, Ministry of Finance, Canada; Raoul Blindenbacher, Forum of Federations, Canada; George Kopits, National Bank of Hungary; and Neil Cole and Ismail Momoniat, South Africa National Treasury. Special thanks are also due to Professors Robin Boadway, Thomas J. Courchene, Bev Dahlby, Harry Kitchen, Harvey Lazar, Melville L. McMillan, Enid Slack, and Paul Bernd Spahn.

The editor is grateful to the leading scholars who contributed chapters and to the distinguished reviewers who provided comments. Theresa Thompson helped during various stages of preparation of this book and provided comments and editorial revisions of individual chapters. Blair Ann Corcoran provided excellent administrative support for this project.

The editor is also grateful to Stephen McGroarty for ensuring a fast-track process for publication of this book. The quality of this book was enhanced by excellent editorial inputs provided by a team of exceptionally qualified editors from Publications Professionals LLC under the direction of Janet Sasser. Andres Meneses is to be thanked for the excellent print quality of this book.

Contributors

THOMAS J. COURCHENE is the Jarislowsky-Deutsch Professor of Economic and Financial Policy at Queen's University. He is also a senior scholar at the Institute for Research on Public Policy in Montreal. Courchene is the author of some 250 books and articles on Canadian policy issues, and his book *Social Canada in the Millennium* was awarded the Doug Purvis Prize for the best Canadian economic policy contribution in 1994. His 1998 book with Colin Telmer, *From Heartland to North American Region State*, won the inaugural Donner Prize for the best book on Canadian public policy. His ongoing research interests include financial deregulation, the political economy of Canadian federalism, and comparative federal systems. Courchene was chair of the Ontario Economic Council of Canada from 1982 to 1985, has been a senior fellow of the C. D. Howe Institute since 1980, was a former member of the Economic Council of Canada, is a fellow of the Royal Society of Canada, and is a past president of the Canadian Economics Association.

SEBASTIAN ECKARDT is an extended term consultant at the World Bank office in Jakarta, Indonesia. He holds a PhD in political science from the University of Potsdam, Germany. He previously served at the University of Potsdam and the German Business Foundation. His current research blends quantitative and qualitative forms of evidence in an attempt (a) to understand public finance and fiscal decentralization reforms in developing countries and (b) to discover links to public service outcomes, growth, and poverty reduction. He has previously worked as a consultant on governance and decentralization reforms for various donor agencies, including the

German Agency for Technical Cooperation and the U.S. Agency for International Development.

LILI LIU is a lead economist at the World Bank's Department of Economic Policy and Debt. She cochairs the Decentralization and Subnational Regional Economics Thematic Group, a Bankwide network focusing on subnational finance, decentralization, and regional development. She leads policy research on subnational finance, reform, and sustainability and their links to macroeconomic management, intergovernmental fiscal systems, capital market development, and infrastructure finance. She has led policy dialogues, large lending operations, preparations of major economic reports, and reviews of country assistance strategies for India and other countries. Liu has a PhD in economics from the University of Michigan, Ann Arbor.

MELVILLE L. MCMILLAN is a professor in the Department of Economics and a fellow of the Institute of Public Economics at the University of Alberta, Canada. He has served on the faculty of the University of Wisconsin at Madison and has held research appointments at the Australian National University, Canberra, and the University of York, England. He has served on the editorial board of various journals—mostly recently the *Canadian Tax Journal*. He has published extensively in public economics, particularly urban and local economics, fiscal federalism, and demand and supply of public goods and services. He has also provided policy advice to governments in both industrial and developing countries in those areas.

MAHESH C. PUROHIT is director of the Foundation for Public Economics and Policy Research. Previous appointments included member-secretary of the Empowered Committee of State Finance Ministers to Monitor Sales Tax Reforms, secretary of the Committee of State Finance Ministers, secretary of the Committee of Chief Ministers on Value Added Tax and Incentives to Backward Areas, and member-secretary of the Committee of Finance Secretaries on Backward Area Incentives. Purohit has been a professor at the National Institute of Public Finance and Policy, New Delhi; a senior research fellow at the Centre for Advanced Studies in Industrial Economics and Public Finance, University of Bombay; and a postdoctoral fellow at the Department of Economics, University of California. Purohit has authored several books and numerous journal articles in the areas of public finance, industrial economics, and environmental protection. His special interests include tax reforms, capacity building for tax administration, corruption in tax administration, e-commerce and e-governance, and information and communication technology.

ANWAR SHAH is lead economist and program leader of the Public Sector Governance Program at the World Bank Institute, Washington, D.C. He is also a member of the Executive Board of the International Institute of Public Finance, Munich, Germany, and a fellow of the Institute for Public Economics, Edmonton, Alberta. He has served the government of Alberta, the government of Canada, the U.S. Agency for International Development, and the United Nations Intergovernmental Panel on Climate Change. He has coordinated the global dialogue on fiscal federalism. He has advised the governments of Australia, Argentina, Brazil, Canada, China, Germany, India, Indonesia, Mexico, Pakistan, Poland, South Africa, and Turkey on fiscal system reform issues. He has published books and articles in refereed journals on governance issues and has coauthored with Robin Boadway *Fiscal Federalism*, forthcoming from Cambridge University Press.

RAJA SHANKAR is a researcher at Oxford University in the United Kingdom and a consultant to the World Bank in Washington, D.C. He has a PhD in economic development and planning from the Massachusetts Institute of Technology. He has served as a project leader at the Boston Consulting Group, Washington, D.C., and as a program executive at Development Alternatives, New Delhi. He also worked as a research associate at the Massachusetts Institute of Technology and at the Asian Development Bank, Tokyo. His research interests are political economy, regional development, industrial policy, and project finance.

MICHAEL WAIBEL, a lawyer and an economist, is currently completing a graduate law degree at Harvard Law School. He also serves as a teaching fellow in Harvard's Economics Department. His doctoral thesis deals with how international courts and tribunals respond to sovereign defaults. Broader research interests include international finance and trade, investment and monetary law, and public finance and economic history. His work experiences include the European Central Bank, the International Monetary Fund, and the World Bank. He holds law degrees from the University of Vienna, Austria, and an MSc in Economics from the London School of Economics.

Abbreviations

BANDEPE	Banco do Estado de Pernambuco, or State Bank of Pernambuco (Brazil)
BANEB	Banco do Estado da Bahia, or State Bank of Bahia (Brazil)
BANERJ	Banco do Estado do Rio de Janeiro, or State Bank of Rio de Janeiro (Brazil)
BANESPA	Banco do Estado de São Paulo, or State Bank of São Paulo (Brazil)
BANESTADO	Banco do Estado do Paraná, or State Bank of Paraná (Brazil)
BEA	Banco do Estado do Amazonas, or State Bank of Amazonas (Brazil)
BEG	Banco do Estado de Goiás, or State Bank of Goiás (Brazil)
BEMGE	Banco do Estado de Minas Gerais, or State Bank of Minas Gerais (Brazil)
CenVAT	central value added tax (India)
CONFAZ	Conselho Nacional de Politica Fazendária, or National Public Finance Council
CST	central sales tax (India)
CV	coefficient of variation
CVAT	compensating value added tax
CVD	countervailing duty (India)
DBCPT	destination-based central purchase tax
ECB	European Central Bank
ECJ	European Court of Justice
EMU	European Monetary Union
EU	European Union

FRG	Federal Republic of Germany
FTA	free trade agreement
GATT	General Agreement on Tariffs and Trade
GDP	gross domestic product
GNP	gross national product
GRDP	gross regional domestic product
GST	goods and services tax (Canada)
HST	harmonized sales tax (Canada)
ICMS	*imposto sobre circulação de mercadorias e prestação de serviços*, or tax on the circulation of goods and services (Brazil)
IMF	International Monetary Fund
IPI	*imposto sobre produtos industrializados*, or tax on industrial products (Brazil)
LRF	Lei de Responsibilidade Fiscal, or Law of Fiscal Responsibility (Brazil)
MASH	municipalities, academic institutions, schools, and hospitals
MBB	municipal bond bank
MMR	minimum-to-maximum ratio
MNC	multinational corporation
Modvat	modified value added tax (India)
NAFTA	North American Free Trade Agreement
OECD	Organisation for Economic Co-operation and Development
PARAIBAN	Banco do Estado da Paraíba, or State Bank of Paraíba (Brazil)
PBC	People's Bank of China
PST	provincial sales tax (Canada)
QST	Quebec sales tax
SOE	state-owned enterprise
TINXSYS	tax information exchange system (India)
TNC	transnational corporation
UED	union excise duty (India)
VAT	value added tax
ZFM	Zona Franca de Manaus, Manaus Free Zone (Brazil)

Overview

ANWAR SHAH

In recent years, federalism has been advanced as a form of government that can provide safeguards against the threats of centralized exploitation and decentralized opportunistic behavior while bringing decision making closer to the people. But federal systems in recent decades have come under increased strain from domestic and external factors. Two prominent influences, globalization and the information revolution, are bringing about profound changes in the division of powers within nations as well as beyond nationstates. The overwhelming influence of these twin forces is moving the world from centralized governance structures to globalized and localized structures, sometimes called *glocalized governance*. In the past, analysts typically have examined federal systems using inward-looking, static-efficiency considerations. Dynamic internal and external influences have not received the attention they deserve. The dynamic-efficiency and growth implications of federal systems are critical for holding a federal country together but have not received adequate attention in the economics literature. This book takes a first step in that direction by (a) examining the effect of globalization and the information revolution on multiorder governance structures, (b) reviewing the dynamic-efficiency and growth implications of fiscal arrangements, and (c) providing a comparative evaluation of local government organization and finances.

The book addresses *glocalization*, a term that embodies globalization and two additional distinct yet interconnected concerns: (a) macro federalism, or the institutional dimensions of macroeconomics

1

in a federal system, including the division of powers within and beyond nation-states, and (b) decentralized local governance. The first part of this book provides a fresh look at the strains federal constitutions face from globalization and the information revolution as well as the dynamic-efficiency and growth implications of federal constitutions. Several aspects of these systems are reviewed: (a) institutional design to achieve internal economic union; (b) policies for regional development; (c) conduct of monetary policy; (d) coordination of fiscal policies, with special emphasis on tax harmonization; and (e) management of risks of insolvency from subnational borrowing. Emerging challenges to constitutional federalism arising from globalization and the information revolution are also explored. The second part of this book is concerned with providing a comparative perspective on local finances and the progress of decentralized governance reforms in developing countries. Following are highlights of each chapter.

Part I: Macro Federalism

In chapter 1, Thomas J. Courchene is concerned with the institutional dimensions of macroeconomics in a federal system. He provides a fresh look at the dynamic-efficiency and growth implications of federal constitutions. Three aspects of these systems are reviewed: (a) institutional design to achieve internal economic union, (b) policies for regional development, and (c) conduct of monetary policy and coordination of fiscal policies. He also explores emerging challenges to constitutional federalism arising from globalization and the information revolution.

The chapter concludes that constitutional design does matter for ensuring an internal common market. Protectionist policies and fiscal transfer regimes that undermine the free flow of factors retard the dynamic adjustment process and negatively affect the convergence of regional incomes. Federal nations are more likely to support independent central banks with price stability as the principal mandate. Fiscal rules are needed to isolate monetary policy from fiscal influences. Institutional arrangements for fiscal policy coordination are important in federal countries. Globalization and the information revolution are forcing a continuous realignment of the division of powers within and across nations, which implies that all nations are federal now; that is, all economic relations between governments are increasingly federal or confederal.

Chapter 2, by Anwar Shah, carries the theme of chapter 1 on jurisdictional realignment further. The chapter reflects on the governance implications of globalization and the information revolution and draws implications for the divisions of power in multicentered governance. The chapter posits that as a result of globalization and the information revolution, nation-states are fast losing control of some of their areas of traditional control and regulation, such as macroeconomic policy, regulation of external trade, telecommunications, and financial transactions. Globalization is also making small open economies vulnerable to the whims of the large hedge funds and polarizing the distribution of income in favor of regions with skilled workers and against regions with lower skills and less access to information, thus widening income disparities within nations. With the information revolution, governments are experiencing a diminished ability to control the flow of goods and services, ideas, and cultural products. These changes are strengthening localization, which is simultaneously leading to citizen empowerment in some areas while strengthening local elites in others. The chapter analyzes the potentials and perils associated with the effect of these mega changes on governance structures in the 21st century. It highlights emerging challenges and local responses to those challenges, followed by a discussion of policy options to deal with the regional economic divide within nations. The chapter argues that policies that secure an internal common market by removing barriers to factor and goods mobility and that level the playing field by ensuring common minimum standards in merit public services and infrastructure offer the best hope for overcoming the economic divide within nations. The chapter concludes with a bold new vision of a globalized and localized world where citizens reassert their roles as governors and principals and, in the process, local governments and "beyond-government" entities at the local level assume a pivotal role in improving economic and social outcomes for their residents.

Chapter 3, by Anwar Shah, poses a central question in fiscal federalism: whether fiscal decentralization implies serious risks for fiscal discipline and macroeconomic management for the nation as a whole. The chapter addresses this important issue by drawing on the existing evidence regarding macro management and fiscal institutions in federal and unitary countries. This analysis is supplemented by cross-country regression analysis plus two case studies: the Brazilian federation and the unitary regime in China. The chapter's main conclusion is that decentralized fiscal systems offer a greater potential for improved macroeconomic governance than centralized fiscal regimes because the former recognize the challenges posed by fiscal decentralization and these challenges shape the design of countervailing institutions to overcome adverse incentives associated with incomplete contracts, "common property" resource management problems, or rent-seeking behaviors.

Regional inequalities represent an ever-present development challenge in most countries, especially those with large geographic areas under their jurisdiction. Globalization heightens these challenges because it places a premium on skills. With globalization, skills rather than the resource base of regions determine regions' competitiveness. Skilled workers gain at the expense of unskilled ones. Because, typically, rich regions also have better-educated and better-skilled labor, the gulf between rich and poor regions widens. In chapter 4, Raja Shankar and Anwar Shah provide an empirical perspective on the effect of regional policies. Large regional disparities represent serious threats in federal states because the inability of the state to deal with such inequities creates the potential for disunity and, in extreme cases, for disintegration. Although reducing regional disparities presents serious policy challenges, the division of powers in a federation curtails federal flexibility in the choice of policy instruments. In contrast, central governments in unitary states are relatively unconstrained in their choice of appropriate policies and instruments. Under these circumstances, a presumption exists in development economics that a decentralized fiscal constitution would lead to ever-widening regional inequalities. This chapter provides an empirical test of that hypothesis. The chapter concludes that regional development policies have failed in almost all countries—federal and unitary alike. Nevertheless, federal countries do better in restraining regional inequalities because widening regional disparities pose a greater political risk in federal countries. In such countries, inequalities beyond a certain threshold may lead to calls for separation by both the richest and the poorest regions. The chapter also reflects on the causes of regional convergence and divergence and observes that countries experiencing divergence generally focus on interventionist policies for regional development. Countries experiencing convergence, in contrast, have a hands-off approach to regional development policies and instead focus on policies to promote a common economic union by removing barriers to factor mobility and by ensuring minimum standards of basic services across the nation. This finding leads to the conclusion that, paradoxically, creating a level playing field is more helpful to disadvantaged regions than following paternalistic protectionist policies.

Harmonization of value added taxes (VATs) is considered critical to the efficiency of the internal common market in federal countries. Although a large number of countries have introduced VAT, no country has been able to successfully implement a fully harmonized VAT. Chapter 5, by Mahesh C. Purohit, reviews experiences with subnational VATs to discover what issues have affected VAT implementation in a federal system and how various countries have tried to resolve those issues. Purohit reviews experiences in Brazil, Canada, India, and the European Union to draw some lessons of general interest. The chapter concludes that VAT should be based solely on the destination principle. Coordination of subnational VAT with central VAT is also critical. One way of achieving such coordination is through a prepaid destination-based VAT.

The success of fiscal decentralization critically depends on enhanced accountability to local residents through responsible expenditure, tax, and borrowing policies. In chapter 6, Lili Liu and Michael Waibel propose a regulatory framework for subnational borrowing. They review world experiences with subnational capital finance and risks of insolvency, and then draw lessons for the design of ex ante and ex post subnational borrowing frameworks. They suggest that a subnational borrowing framework should require fiscal transparency and have ex ante rules on the purpose and process of borrowing and any limitations as well as ex post insolvency mechanisms to resolve financial distress. They conclude that subnational borrowing regulations alone are not sufficient for sustainable credit-market access and must be accompanied by complementary institutional reforms in intergovernmental finance and regulation of capital markets.

Part II: Local Finance

Globalization and the information revolution are motivating a large and growing number of countries worldwide to reexamine the roles of various orders of government and their partnership with the private sector and civil society. These reforms typically involve shifting responsibilities to local governments and "beyond-government" providers, with the objective of moving government functions and services closer to the people. This movement has generated interest in learning from historical and current practices on local government organization and finance across countries. Chapter 7, by Melville L. McMillan, reviews the experiences of industrial nations with fiscal structures of local governments to draw lessons of interest to other nations aiming to reform their local governments. The chapter concludes that (a) effective performance by local government is determined not by size but by design; (b) property taxes and user charges can cover core local government activities but should not be expected to finance social services; (c) local own-source revenues from property taxes, personal income tax surcharges, and user fees should be used to finance local services for which the residents are willing to pay; (d) transfers are best provided through formal arrangements agreed on by the grantor and recipients; (e) higher-level government assistance for expanding local access to capital finance is important in dealing with infrastructure deficiencies;

and (f) democratic accountability and local autonomy are central to successful local government operations.

The ultimate goal of improving government architecture is to create responsive, responsible, fair, and accountable governance. The extent to which governments in developing countries meet these criteria is examined in the final chapter of this volume by Sebastian Eckardt and Anwar Shah. Chapter 8 develops a simple diagnostic tool that has been designed to analyze selected aspects of governance in decentralized fiscal systems. Comparing governance systems across countries is a complex task. It requires identification of political and bureaucratic incentives and of countervailing institutions that restrain governments, as well as assessments of the result orientation that prevails in public organizations. The tool combines a mix of qualitative indicators and specific descriptive features regarding properties of both organizational procedures and governance outcomes. The framework encapsulates the fiscal and administrative incentives that governments and bureaucracies face as well as the overarching political environment in which they operate. The tool is used to compare developing countries on three aspects of good governance: political accountability, fiscal responsibility, and service delivery orientation. The chapter concludes that although developing countries have made significant progress in implementing reform of their governance systems, the progress is uneven, and without further fundamental reforms, a large majority of these countries will not realize the fruits of their initial progress. Regarding decentralization, the chapter notes that both administrative decentralization and fiscal decentralization remain unrealized goals.

One

Macro Federalism

1

Macro Federalism: An Introduction with Principal Reference to the Canadian Experience

THOMAS J. COURCHENE

Much of the systematic literature relating to the economics of federal systems falls into what has come to be known as *fiscal federalism*. In general, this literature relates to the allocative and distributive functions of Musgrave's (1959) celebrated trilogy. The purpose of this paper is to engage in some exploratory research relating to the third function (growth and stabilization) or, more generally, to the macroeconomic design of federal systems—hence

Editor's note: This chapter is a much abridged version of an unpublished monograph, "Macrofederalism: Some Exploratory Research Relating to Theory and Practice," written by Professor Courchene for the World Bank in 1995 (Courchene 1995a). Because the monograph represents a classic and pioneering piece of work on this subject, the editor has prepared this abridged version from the original with permission from the author. Although the original manuscript focused rather evenly on the five mature federations, the abridged version in much more directed toward the Canadian experience. Readers should take into account the historic context of the work, which has not been updated for the purposes of this volume.

the term *macro federalism*. Macro federalism is not well defined, perhaps with good reason, because no set of analytical principles or "best practices" may exist that can support an attempt to systematize aspects of the literature. Nonetheless, one of the objectives of this chapter is to search for patterns of best practice, if not analytical principles. Although this framework will inform aspects of the ensuing analysis, application becomes difficult because the boundary between what is macro and what is allocative or distributive is likewise ill defined. Perhaps this problem should not be surprising, because there are bound to be macro implications for many of the areas that one would normally associate with the core of the existing fiscal federalism literature, particularly as it relates to intergovernmental transfers and the allocation of taxing and expenditure competencies. No doubt the reverse is true as well.

However, the dilemma is even greater: these macro implications tend, in many cases, to be ignored by the existing fiscal federalism literature. Rather, the emphasis has been tilted toward distributional or redistributional concerns. And where allocative or efficiency aspects do come to the fore, they are frequently couched in terms of considerations of local preference or economies of scale. In other words, the emphasis is on redistribution, on static efficiency, and on accommodation of spillovers. Inadequate attention is directed to dynamic efficiency, to competitive federalism à la Breton (1985) and others, and (perhaps not surprisingly) to concepts associated with endogenous growth—path dependence, positive feedbacks, and Schumpeterian creative destruction. Thus, a good deal of traditional fiscal federalism merits a second look in terms of dynamic efficiency or growth. Providing this comprehensive second look is well beyond the intent or design of this chapter. However, because concerns about dynamic efficiency and growth are legitimate issues in an overview of macro federalism, occasions will arise when one can lend a macro federalism perspective to selected areas that heretofore have been dealt with primarily from a redistributive and static-efficiency framework. Regional policy within a federal system is a case in point.

However, there is a second approach to macro federalism that will be featured in parts of the chapter—namely, one that embraces aspects of the emerging nature of the national and global economies on the one hand and the resultant emerging changes in the nature of federalism itself on the other. The purpose of the next section is to highlight aspects of these trends in terms of how they may relate to macro federalism.

Globalization, Confederalism, and the Information-Knowledge Revolution

Globalization

Globalization or international economic integration comes in many varieties. Table 1.1 contains a range of definitions or conceptions of globalization—or the *new technoeconomic paradigm*, as Freeman and Perez (1988) and Lipsey (1994) refer to it. Several of the conceptions of globalization have implications for what lies ahead in terms of the macro design of federal systems and, equally important, for the necessity of rethinking and reworking much of the existing fiscal federalism literature. Although the task of perusing table 1.1 will be left to the reader, attention is now directed to the implications for federalism of two of the conceptions of globalization.

Federalism and the internationalization of production

In its most basic form, globalization is the internationalization of production. Firms can source from and sell anywhere in the world, so they are no longer constrained by the endowments of resources, physical capital, and human capital in their home country. Incentives in the modern welfare state have typically been geared to the nature and characteristics of domestic production. But what are the characteristics of an optimal welfare state when production is international? Although this challenge applies to federal and unitary states alike, it becomes a federalism issue for nations such as Canada, where much of the social envelope is designed and delivered by the provinces.

The regional-international interface

Among the more profound implications of the new technoeconomic paradigm is the way in which it is altering the economics of political and geographic space. Again, consider Canada. With trade increasingly going north-south and with evolving north-south institutional links under the Canada–U.S. Free Trade Agreement and the North American Free Trade Agreement (NAFTA), it is no longer appropriate to view Canada as a single national economy. Rather, Canada is a series of quite distinct north-south (cross-border) economies. Hence, the policy focus should shift from the traditional national-national conception of Canadian policy and its relation to the global economic order to one that embodies a regional-international interface, even to the point of viewing comparative advantage more in regional than in national terms.

TABLE 1.1 Globalization and the Information-Knowledge Revolution: Variations on the New Technoeconomic Paradigm

Variation	Definition	Features or characteristics	Policy implications or challenges
a. "Nothing is 'overseas' any longer" (Ohmae 1990: vii)	This quotation refers to the increasing internationalization of production, initially in manufacturing but progressively in services as well.	This definition decouples firms from the factor endowments of any single nation.	This definition wreaks havoc with national welfare states that have geared incentives to national production systems. What is the nature of a welfare state when production is international?
b. Shift from multinational corporations (MNCs) to transnational corporations (TNCs)	TNCs are no longer subject to host-country controls, unlike MNCs.	This definition reflects two polar models: "national treatment" under the free trade agreement (FTA) and North American Free Trade Agreement (NAFTA) and the single-passport (home-country rule) model in the European Union (EU). In theory at least, the former is sovereignty enhancing and the latter implies policy homogenization.	Canadians will eventually recognize that the genius of the FTA lies in the sovereignty-enhancing "national treatment" principle. It is the international private sector that is globalizing, not the public sector. Pressures mount for governments to transfer powers upward so that political space is more contiguous with economic space.
c. Globalization as the internationalization of cities	Economies of scale and scope associated with the information explosion imply that international	This definition represents one way in which the institutional structure is globalizing. It may be a temporary phenomenon	This definition identifies an integral part of the process by which power is being transferred downward from nation-states—especially because, in

	cities have become the outward connectors to the Londons, New Yorks, and Tokyos and inward connectors to their regional hinterlands.	as the spread of the information revolution allows for a greater dispersion of economic power and activity.	Canada at least, international cities are "constitutionless." A distinct society needs an international city. Part of Quebec's independence challenge is that Montreal is in decline.
d. Globalization as the information-knowledge revolution: knowledge	Knowledge is increasingly at the cutting edge of competitiveness.	Skilled labor is more like capital than like traditional labor. The middle class is disappearing. For resources to remain important, they must embody knowledge (or high-value-added techniques).	This definition has dramatic implications in all nations with respect to the distribution of incomes. Even resource-rich economies must make the transition to an economy and society based on human capital. Social policy, as it relates to human capital and skills formation, is indistinguishable from economic policy.
e. Globalization as the information-knowledge revolution: information	The information revolution compresses both time and distance in terms of economic activity and, therefore, enhances global integration.	This definition privileges individuals in the sense that they now have the ability to access, transmit, and transform information in ways that governments of all types are powerless to prevent.	Arguably, the information revolution is inherently decentralizing. It will also serve to redraw the boundary between what is feasible in the public and private sectors (for example, the information revolution will ultimately relegate telecommunication regulators to the sidelines, just as faxes have marginalized the post office).

(continued)

TABLE 1.1 Globalization and the Information-Knowledge Revolution: Variations on the New Technoeconomic Paradigm (*continued*)

Variation	Definition	Features or characteristics	Policy implications or challenges
f. Globalization as consumer sovereignty (Ohmae 1990)	Ohmae (1990: dust jacket) argues that "performance standards are now set in the global marketplace by those that buy the products, not those that make or regulate them."	This definition is a variant of the information revolution in panel e in that it implies that "receptors" rather than "transmitters" are in the driver's seat.	Obviously, this definition transfers power from governments to consumers. Of more interest to this chapter, however, is the fact that though the information revolution privileges citizens as consumers, it may tend to disenfranchise them as citizens, because an important set of decisions relating to them are beyond the purview of the nation-state.
g. Globalization as regime theory	In a sense, this is the oldest form of globalization. Regimes are the formal or information international institutional devices through which economic and political actors organize and manage their interdependencies.	Regimes have long been with us—in energy, airlines, minerals, and so on. Their activities run the gamut from setting standards, performing allocation functions, monitoring compliance, reducing conflict, and resolving disputes.	Regimes restrict the autonomy of nation-states. What is occurring now, however, is the spread of regimes into hitherto "soft" areas, such as nontariff barriers, the environment, social charters, and rights for indigenous peoples.

| h. Globalization as ultramobility | Enhanced mobility is generic in that it underpins all conceptions of globalization as well as virtually all conceptions of a technoeconomic paradigm shift. | Because taxation or regulation of mobile factors becomes more difficult and because globalization or ultramobility implies an increase in the number and range of factors and commodities that are mobile, this aspect of globalization constrains the instrument set available to policy authorities. In tandem with the spread of the free trade arrangements, it constrains policy authorities from using allocative instruments to deliver distributional goals. | Arguably, the optimal jurisdictional space for taxation has increased relative to the optimal jurisdictional space for spending. Thus, one now speaks of EU-wide corporate taxes or carbon taxes, for example. Yet the optimal spending jurisdiction has not (yet) become EU-wide. This aspect creates the specter of EU financial transfers to member states (that is, an internationalization of Canadian-type fiscal federalism). |

Source: Based on Courchene 1992, 1994b.

Confederalism

Another trend associated with globalization relates to the transformation of the economic nation-state. One need not go as far as Reich (1991) and proclaim the death knell of the economic nation-state, but certainly one must take seriously the observation of Daniel Bell (1987) that nation-states are becoming too small to tackle the large things in life and too large to address the small things. Paquet (1995) puts this comment more colorfully, referring to it as the "Gulliver Effect": the traditional economic nation-states are finding it difficult to deal with both the dwarfs of Lilliput and the giants of Brobdingnag. Translated, this remark implies that the economic power is being transferred upward, downward, and probably outward from nation-states and from the central governments of federal states. Aspects of this phenomenon appear in the various entries of table 1.1, especially panel b.

The passing-powers-upward aspect is rather straightforward: economic space is transcending political space. Whether this trend has to do with the advent of transnational corporations (panel b of table 1.1), the information revolution (panel e), or enhanced mobility (panel h), the message is the same: supranational regulatory regimes are emerging in the form of explicit trade agreements (such as NAFTA and the Europe 1992 program); international regulatory and supervisory bodies (such as the Bank for International Settlements); and other exemplars of the "vast growth of institutions, organizations, and regimes which have laid the basis for global governance" (Held 1991: 146). In political economy terms, what is occurring is a process of "jurisdictional realignment" or "jurisdictional mapping," as it were—namely, an attempt on the part of nation-states to ensure that the jurisdictional reach of this supranational authority roughly coincides with the expanded economic space. But in strictly political or quasi-constitutional terms, nation-states themselves are "federalizing" or, perhaps more appropriately, "confederalizing." To the extent that there are "constitutions" in this new environment, they are in the nature of economic constitutions, not the sort of political constitutions that govern federal states. Moreover, though confederal arrangements have long been with us, their nature is changing. Daniel Elazar (1994: 12) notes that the "difference between earlier and contemporary confederations is that the primary purpose of earlier confederations was military security, while in postmodern society it is economic."

In terms of macro federalism, at least three implications merit attention. First, states, provinces, *Länder*, or cantons can now leapfrog the economic nation-state and attempt to attach themselves to these supranational regulatory structures. The 1989 Belgian federation is probably the best example:

power has been significantly decentralized to the three regions, which, in turn, are latching on to the European Union (EU) infrastructure and are bypassing or eclipsing the traditional role for the federal government.

Second, decisions made at the supranational level (or even the supranational agreements themselves) can have quite dramatic implications for the division of powers within federal systems. The ensuing analysis will focus on recent developments in the German federation that are designed to ensure that the EU principle of subsidiarity will carry through to subnational levels of government. More generally, as these trade pacts broaden and deepen, federations are likely to undergo quite substantial institutional—even constitutional—changes internally. How have federations accommodated this integration-driven alteration in the effective division of powers? This aspect may not be a new dimension of macro federalism as much as it is a change in the structure of existing federations.

The third implication is quite different. Consider the Europe 1992 program. The focus on the single market within confederal Europe rekindled interest in the single market within existing federations. Moreover, the EU's principle of home-country rule (alternatively, the concept of a "designated jurisdiction" and "mutual recognition") provided a new perspective and a new set of instruments with the potential for freeing up the internal markets of federal nations. Relatedly, the proposed debt-deficit guidelines for entry into the European Monetary Union (EMU) also had a significant influence on the thinking about the fiscal leeway of subnational governments in other federations.

In effect, then, the advent of Europe 1992 and the Maastricht Treaty has not only created enhanced awareness of macro federalist issues in various federations, but also provided new analytical insights that are already having an effect. Australia is among the leaders in adopting the designated-jurisdiction mutual-recognition model for enhancing aspects of its internal economic union. One might refer to these as pure "information" or "demonstration" aspects of macro federalism, because they have a direct influence—one that need not involve trade flows. In that sense, they may well fall into the category of principles that can underpin aspects of macro federalism.

The Information-Knowledge Revolution

Panels d and e of table 1.1 highlight yet another feature of the new techno-economic paradigm—the information-knowledge revolution. One does not have to believe that the ongoing revolution will do for human capital what the industrial revolution did for physical capital to recognize that the world is in the throes of a truly epic transformation. With knowledge increasingly at the cutting edge of competitiveness, aspects of what used to be viewed as social policy now are indistinguishable from economy policy. Whereas issues related to physical capital formation and mobility were traditionally part of macro policy, issues related to human capital formation generally were not. The information-knowledge revolution is altering this situation and, therefore, will also alter aspects of the way that these areas have been addressed in the existing fiscal federalism literature. In particular, the reference in EU circles to "social dumping" and the presence of the social policy "rider" to NAFTA indicate that aspects of social policy are now an integral part of competition policy for trade purposes. This situation not only changes the perception of these policy areas but also has obvious feedbacks in terms of the manner in which these areas interact with the existing distribution of competencies in federal nations.

Defining *Macro Federalism*

With the above analysis as an illustrative but hardly exhaustive backdrop, one can begin to make some inroads into a definition of *macro federalism*. The most obvious components relate to the manner in which a federal system interacts with the structure and processes of the "traditional" macro areas, such as monetary policy, fiscal policy, and trade and commercial policy. Beyond these components, it is clear that the emergence of the new technoeconomic paradigm (defined to incorporate globalization, confederalism, and the information-knowledge revolution) is having profound effects on nation-states—in particular, federal nation-states. These effects include the following:

- The directing of attention toward the free flow of goods, services, labor, and enterprise within federal states, given the dramatic increase in the ability of these flows to cross international boundaries.
- The effect of economic integration (that is, of supranational agreements) on the actual or de facto assignment of powers in federal systems.
- Relatedly, the quite dramatic shift in the conception of selected policy areas. For example, social policy was traditionally viewed largely as a set of domestic programs and transfers. With the information-knowledge revolution, aspects of social policy have become critical to a nation's competitiveness (and, hence, have become macro variables), and social policy has more recently become caught up in trade agreements and become a component— almost as in the General Agreement on Tariffs and Trade (GATT)—

of international competition policy. This shift affects all nations, but it poses special problems and challenges for federal nations, particularly those that relegated much or most of their social policy design to subnational governments.

■ The rise of supranational integration, regulation, and coordination bodies has, in effect, federalized or confederalized most industrial nation-states. This trend has two effects. First, it highlights in a special way some issues that were masked by the fact that, unlike these supranational "constitutions," which are largely economic in nature, traditional federal constitutions are primarily political rather than economic documents. As already noted, among these are the characteristics of a single market (Europe 1992) and the principles relating to the behavior of member EU states with regard to their fiscal positions under the Maastricht Treaty. Second, these developments dramatically increase the relevance and scope of macro federalism, because many of the same principles could apply both to the Canadian provinces in relation to the Canadian federal government and to the EU member states in relation to Brussels. Phrased differently, the realm of the economic theory of federalism is now expanding well beyond the traditional federal nation-state.

Although these developments are admittedly exciting and far reaching, and although they probably call for a rethinking of much of fiscal federalism (because they are driven largely by dynamic-efficiency concerns that are largely ignored in the fiscal federalism literature), it is not clear that they can, in any meaningful analytic way, be brought under the umbrella of macro federalism.

Nonetheless, selected aspects of all of these issues are dealt with in this chapter. The final section will give an overall assessment of whether these aspects are quite distinct macro policy areas or whether some underlying principles can be identified that are capable of integrating parts of the analysis within a macro federalism framework.

Outline of the Analysis

The analysis proceeds as follows. The next section focuses on internal economic integration, with special attention to the manner in which the five mature federations (Australia, Canada, Germany, Switzerland, and the United States) achieve their internal economic unions. Included also is a subsection on the relationships of globalization and the securing of the internal economic union. The analysis then shifts to the macroeconomics of regional policy in federal systems, where the emphasis is on transfer dependency at the subnational level. Toward the end, attention is directed to a "geometry" of regional balance, where the transfer system essentially plays the role of increasing the subnational regions' dependence on transfers. The section concludes with a brief focus on subnational stabilization policy.

The following two sections deal, in turn, with monetary policy and fiscal policy, respectively, and their relationship with federalism. In terms of the former, the issue addressed is the nature of the structure and mandate of the central banks in federal systems. For the latter, the issue is whether the Maastricht guidelines are an appropriate defense in terms of ensuring that central banks of federal nations can achieve their monetary policy goals.

The final substantive section addresses a range of miscellaneous macro federalism issues: the environment, the regional-international interface in terms of the deployment of subnational diplomats in other nation-states, the role of international agreements in altering the de facto division of powers within federations, and the challenge arising from the creation of "democracy deficits" as powers are transferred upward from nation-states.

An integrative conclusion completes the chapter. With this as backdrop, the chapter now turns to the first macro policy area: securing the internal market for goods, services, labor, and capital.

Internal Economic Integration

With the advent of the Europe 1992 program and its 300 or so integration directives, attention has been focused on the degree to which the national markets of federal nations (and even unitary states) are integrated. For example, Canadian politicians and business leaders are fond of claiming that goods and capital can flow more freely across member states of the EU than across the Canadian provinces. Presumably, this claim can also be made of the U.S. states and the Australian states and territories, among others, at least in terms of selected types of goods and capital (see tables 1.2 and 1.3 for a comparative institutional and constitutional perspective on these issues for mature federations).

However, this observation should not be surprising: federal constitutions are essentially political blueprints, whereas Europe 1992 is primarily an economic blueprint. Thus, the overwhelming rationale for Europe 1992 is to free up European markets or, more positively, to create a single market where disputes with respect to adherence to the directives are largely a matter to be settled in the arena of administrative law. However, though all federations have constitutional provisions related to securing their internal

TABLE 1.2 Selected Institutional Features of Mature Federations

| Federation | Nature of executive | Elected? | Nature of upper chamber | | Legislative or administrative federalism? |
			Representation	Powers relative to lower chamber	
Australia	Parliamentary	Direct election	Equal by state	Most powerful second chamber of parliamentary federations	Legislative
Canada	Parliamentary[a]	Appointed for life (to age 75) by the federal government	Equal by region (not by province)	Except for money bills, equal in principle, but not in practice	Legislative
Germany	Parliamentary	Delegates from *Länder* government	Population more than 6,000,000—5 seats; population 4,000,001–6,000,000—4 seats; population less than 4,000,000—3 seats	Suspensive veto over ordinary legislation; absolute veto over legislation affecting *Länder*	Administrative
Switzerland	Pluralist	Direct election, but often members of the Council of States are also members of a cantonal government	Full canton—2 representatives; half canton—1 representative	Equal	Administrative
United States	Pluralist	Direct election	Equal—2 per state	Equal[b]	Legislative

Source: Hayes 1982.

a. The adoption of a constitutional bill of rights in 1982 has introduced an aspect of checks and balances into Canada's parliamentary federation.

b. The U.S. Senate also ratifies federal appointments (for example, Supreme Court appointments).

TABLE 1.3 Comparison of Constitutional Provisions

Federation	What is the scope of mobility rights for individuals?	(a) What is the scope of the free trade guarantee? and (b) is the federal authority bound by the guarantee?	What is the scope of powers directly affecting trade and mobility?	(a) What is the scope of federal powers indirectly affecting mobility compared with Canada? and (b) what are some examples?
Australia	Moderate	(a) Wide; (b) yes, it is bound by the guarantee, for example, in agricultural marketing and nationalization.	Interstate: they are concurrent with federal paramountcy, and wider federal powers exist than in Canada. Intrastate: they are exclusively a state jurisdiction.	(a) Somewhat wider; (b) corporations, industrial disputes, treaties, and conditional grants
Canada	Rights of moderate scope are planned	(a) Narrow, supplemented by narrow exclusive federal trade jurisdiction; (b) yes, it is bound by the guarantee.	Scope is exclusively federal, but narrowly interpreted. Courts have reserved intraprovincial authority for the provinces.	n.a.

Germany	Wide	Exclusive federal jurisdiction is equivalent to a guarantee, insofar as the *Länder* only are concerned.	No inter-intra distinction exists. There is exclusive federal authority, much wider than in Canada.	(a) Much wider; (b) the economy, labor, and civil law, securities
Switzerland	Wide	(a) Wide; (b) in principle, it is bound by the guarantee, but there is broad authority to override the guarantee.	No inter-intra distinction exists; they are concurrent with federal paramountcy. Wider federal powers exist than in Canada. State trade powers are largely confined to "police" regulations.	(a) Wider; (b) civil law, labor, and social security
United States	Moderate	Exclusive federal interstate jurisdiction is equivalent to a guarantee, insofar as the states only are concerned.	Exclusive federal powers over interstate trade extend well into intrastate. State trade powers are largely confined to "police" regulations.	(a) Wider; (b) labor, securities, and conditional grants

Source: Hayes 1982: 24.
Note: n.a. = not applicable.

economic unions, disputes related to barriers or impediments to the internal economic union tend to be resolved, initially at least, in the political arena, although resort to the courts is also an option. In this sense, achieving a single or unified market for certain goods or factors may well be more difficult in federal systems than in arrangements such as Europe 1992 that were explicitly designed for this purpose. More interesting, perhaps, is that the types of instruments capable of delivering unified markets are likely to differ between economic unions and federal nations.

At the most general level, one can speak of two types of integration: negative integration and positive integration (Leslie 1991). *Negative integration*, an admittedly awkward term, refers to the imposition of a series of constraints—or if one prefers, a set of "thou shalt nots"—on the behavior of governments. In other words, negative integration facilitates the creation of a single market by removing the ability of governments to impede the flow of goods, services, and factors of production across political boundaries. Beyond some point, however, more is needed to secure a unified market. Thus, positive integration relates to legislative or regulatory action designed to coordinate or harmonize policy across boundaries, for example, to ensure full portability of social benefits across jurisdictions. Although, as noted, federal systems may well fall short of the European Union in selected aspects of negative integration, they are typically well ahead of the EU in terms of positive integration.

To incorporate these concepts in a more analytical—or at least formal—manner, the chapter now turns to the economic integration continuum.

The Economic Integration Continuum

Figure 1.1 presents a stylized version of the economic integration spectrum. At the left end of the spectrum is autarky; at the other end (the highly integrated end) is a unified socioeconomic space in which there are no jurisdictional or policy distinctions across the geographic space.

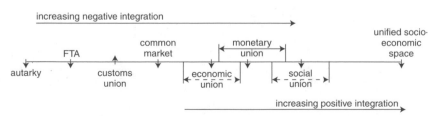

Source: Author's representation.

FIGURE 1.1 The Economic Integration Continuum

Identifying the first three points on the spectrum is relatively easy:

- The first is a free trade agreement (FTA), which ensures the free movement of goods and (perhaps only a specified set of) produced services.
- The second is a customs union, which is an FTA with the added condition that the partners in the FTA agree to maintain a common set of tariffs with regard to third countries.
- The third is a common market, which represents an enhanced degree of integration in that the free movement of labor and capital is also provided for.

These three integration stages are depicted as progressive points along the spectrum in figure 1.1, implying that the degree of integration increases in lockstep, as it were.

In the typical version of this schema, the only stage in the spectrum between "common market" and "unified economic space" was that of an "economic union," which was defined to extend mobility rights not only to labor but also to people (including access to core public goods and social programs) wherever they reside in the union. Figure 1.1 modifies this spectrum by disaggregating this economic union stage into three components—economic union (which in terms of figure 1.1 now relates to economic union in the sense of Europe 1992 or the European single market), monetary union, and social union. To conform to the nature of the evolution that is occurring in Europe (that is, the EU is an economic union without—as of 1995—a monetary union or a social union), figure 1.1 depicts these three stages as overlapping intervals with the integration progression going from an economic union to a monetary union and then to a social union.

If one is viewing figure 1.1 from the vantage point of a single nation-state, then all nation-states fall at least into the "monetary union" stage of the integration. (Admittedly a few nation-states do not have their own separate currency, but they are still monetary unions in that a single currency applies within their political boundaries.) Because of the overlaps, the spectrum still allows for the possibility that federal states may have a less developed economic union than some political structures that are not characterized by a monetary union (such as the EU). More likely, however, nation-states would also embody sufficient integration to put them in the social union stage. Admittedly, others would have drawn figure 1.1 somewhat differently, for example, allowing all three stages (economic, monetary, and social unions) to overlap.

However, many nations are now becoming part of supranational trading blocs; hence, the integration spectrum can be viewed as proceeding at two levels: one internal and one international. For example, with the Canada–U.S.

free trade agreement and, more recently, NAFTA, Canada is in the "economic union" category in terms of its international integration. Moreover, for some specific goods and services (such as beer), Canada's international integration is more thorough than its internal integration (that is, there is more mobility of beer across the Canada–U.S. border than there is across provincial borders). Indeed, it is the pressures arising from international integration that, in many cases, are serving to free up the internal markets.

Figure 1.1 further stylizes the economic integration process by indicating that negative integration will likely be uppermost the further left one is on the continuum. Phrased differently, as one moves forward toward greater economic integration, more reliance will have to be placed on positive integration. Nonetheless, it is probably the case that both positive integration and negative integration exist in varying degrees at each point along the spectrum. For example, even in an FTA, which is largely an exercise in negative integration, the existence of a dispute resolution mechanism would qualify as positive integration. Economic union, à la Europe 1992, can be seen to embody healthy doses of both negative and positive integration, with the latter reflected in the requirement that member nations coordinate regulatory regimes. Once one enters the social union space in figure 1.1, further integration requires proactive legislation that harmonizes, enhances, and otherwise promotes the social union, and most, if not all, of this integration would fall under the rubric of positive integration.

Obviously, where one is located along the economic integration continuum is not independent of the degree of political integration. For example, it is highly unlikely that the EU could advance to the social union (or, in European jargon, "social cohesion") stage of figure 1.1 without political deepening (that is, without embracing federalism and, in the process, remedying the so-called democracy deficit). In more general terms, increasing economic integration entails increasing political integration. Yet this observation may be in the nature of an elastic generalization in the sense that few students of politics or economics would have predicted (from the vantage point of, say, the 1970s) that European economic integration could have proceeded as far as it has, even to the point of contemplating monetary union, without much in the nature of political deepening.

As a final comment on figure 1.1, it might appear that one could identify the unified economic space with a unitary state. Hence, federal systems would be to the left of a unitary state in terms of the integration spectrum (that is, a federal system would be somewhat inferior to a unitary state when it comes to the integration spectrum). The problem with this interpretation is that it mixes up economic and political integration. There is no presumption that a federal system is in any way a stepping-stone to a unitary state. Thus, for federal states in terms of figure 1.1, the unified economic space would relate to full socioeconomic integration of these federal systems. There is another, perhaps preferable, way of viewing this issue. The rationale for progressing along the economic integration spectrum is that the economic benefits also increase. In this sense, the end point of the spectrum—namely, unified economic space—should be where net economic benefits are maximized. Now if economic benefits were measured entirely in terms of output, then one could make a case that a unitary state could constitute the appropriate end point, because all relative prices and tradeoffs (labor-leisure, private sector–public sector) would be identical across the political-geographic space. However, if, as is appropriate, economic benefits are cast in terms of welfare rather than output, a unitary state would maximize welfare only if preferences were identical across all citizens. But the potential for the maximization of welfare is one of the principal rationales for federal nations. In this sense, it is wrong to assume that a unified economic space coincides with a unitary state.

One can take this argument further. Even for federal nations, one can visualize quite different versions of what might constitute a unified economic space. It is convenient to focus initially on a comparison between Europe 1992 and the Canada–U.S. Free Trade Agreement. The integration principle underlying the latter is *national treatment*, which means that a U.S. firm can do in Canada exactly what a Canadian firm can do. Contrast this principle with what is referred to as *home-country rule*, which holds sway in certain areas of Europe 1992. This principle means that a German firm can do in France what it can do in Germany. Although both of these approaches are filtered through health, safety, and other regulations, they embody very different conceptions of integration and sovereignty. Specifically, national treatment maximizes national sovereignty. Canada is free to legislate its own priorities, subject only to the provision that it cannot discriminate between Canadian and U.S. firms. However, a thorough home-country rule approach would tend to homogenize national policies.

Transferred to the federal level, a unified economic space within Canada, for example, could embody either *provincial treatment* or *home-province rule*. The former concept is far more likely to characterize the decentralized federations than the centralized ones. In other words, the political nature of federations will likely place parameters on—or define— what is possible in terms of a unified economic space.

With this discussion as a backdrop, the analysis now turns to the variety of arrangements by which federal nations attempt to secure their economic unions.

Comparative Constitutional Approaches to Securing the Economic Union

Barriers to an internal economic union arise for a multitude of reasons. However, principal among these reasons is the nature of the legislative, financial, and political powers that attach to subnational governments. At one end of the spectrum are "administrative federalisms" such as Germany, where most legislation is federal and where there is a broad reach to the federal powers over the economy. In an important sense, this type of constitutional arrangement essentially ensures that internal markets will be largely free. At the other end of the spectrum are federations such as Canada, where the provinces have a long list of exclusive powers—especially if the federation is relatively old, because areas such as communications and the securities industry could have been viewed, before the turn of the 20th century, as matters of a local nature so that provincial legislation over these matters became firmly established.

Beyond these influences on division of powers, however, there is a broad range of other factors that will play a major role in the degree to which economic space is integrated. Countries such as Switzerland and, to a lesser extent, the United States, which take a dim view of government intervention in economic matters, are more likely to have free internal markets. Countries that have a small geographic space, where the probability of living in one province or state and working in another is relatively high, will also presumably strive to ensure full individual and occupational mobility. Germany and Switzerland fall into that category. In contrast, large landmasses such as Australia with great distances between the populated areas will, other things being equal, tend to develop policies that reflect their regional identities. If one adds to this picture the Canadian reality, where the various provinces have quite different economies, the temptation for mounting protective barriers is enhanced. Finally, but hardly exhaustively, the existence of cultural or linguistic differences across federations will presumably make achieving an integrated economic market more difficult.

As Hayes (1982: 26) notes (and as represented in table 1.3), the constitutions of the mature federations have attempted to cope with the internal economic union challenge in terms of three approaches or categories:

- In the first category are Germany and the United States, which depend mainly on exclusive federal trade powers and on mobility rights.
- In the second category are Australia and Switzerland: in both federations there are concurrent federal trade powers supplemented by a mobility rights and strong free trade guarantees.

■ In the third category is Canada, in which narrowly interpreted exclusive federal trade powers are combined with a narrow free trade guarantee and, until 1982, an absence of mobility rights. The scope for provincial barriers is wider than in any of the other federations.

The Canadian case can probably be ignored in terms of a precedent for the future because some of the areas that have the potential for creating economic union problems in Canada (such as provincial control of securities regulation and telecommunications) would unlikely be assigned to the subnational governments of emerging federations. And even for those emerging nations that may require considerable decentralization, the Europe 1992 initiative ensures that decentralization and an economic union are not incompatible. The other tendency in recent federations (such as Germany) is for many more powers to be concurrent with an economic union override. For truly decentralized federations, an iron-clad free trade guarantee that is binding on both levels of government may be appropriate. For other federations, the more likely approach would presumably be to vest the power to enforce the internal market at the federal level.

However, this (largely) negative integration flowing from constitutional provisions can go only so far. Except perhaps in federations such as Germany, where the legislative power is concentrated at the federal level, constitutional provisions will not generate a unified economic space. This observation harkens back to figure 1.1, which implied that the further one is along the economic integration spectrum, the more likely it is that additional progress must embody positive integration or deliberately harmonizing initiatives. Here the Canadian case may provide useful role models: creative use of the federal spending power to enhance economic or social integration; resorting to the designated-jurisdiction, mutual-recognition approach (although this approach is probably European in origin and has also been adopted in Australia for certain areas); and interprovincial agreements to ensure mobility of the good or service in question. In terms of this last approach, an important message is that policies need not be federal to be national. This message is certainly true in Canada in terms of the securities industry, and it resonates in selected areas in terms of the progress that Australia is making in moving toward a unified economic space.

At least in part, this discussion relates back to the introductory section, which emphasized that federal constitutions were, at base, political documents, whereas agreements such as Europe 1992 were economic blueprints. There is little doubt that contravening one of the European directives will land one before the administrative courts or tribunals. However, contravention of the economic union provisions of a constitution may not end up in the courts. For example, the United States probably has the constitutional authority, but not the political will or backing, to ride herd on state purchasing preferences. Likewise, the Swiss federal authority could tidy up the "tax jungle," but the politics of doing so are not tenable. Moreover, there is a cost for one level of government to challenge the other in the courts, because the resolution will likely be in binary form—yes or no. It is far better for both parties to work through the political process (positive integration) to address the issue in a way that satisfies everyone. This point would seem to call for some sort of federal-provincial or interprovincial commission or task force on the internal economic union. Although such an initiative could well be superfluous in Germany, it could serve an important role in the other federal systems.

International Integration and the Internal Economic Union

It is instructive once again to refer to the economic integration continuum (figure 1.1) and, in particular, the observation that for most federal systems integration is now progressing on both the domestic and the international fronts. As was emphasized in the earlier discussion of the Canadian case, this international integration may well be the catalyst for enhancing the internal economic union. What is occurring can be viewed, conceptually, as a process by which these international agreements—NAFTA, Europe 1992, GATT (now the World Trade Organization)—are assuming part of the role of the constitutional provisions related to the free trade clause and the federal regulatory power. In other words, power is being passed "upward," as it were, in terms of important aspects of securing domestic economic unions. One potential advantage of this development from the perspective of enhancing internal markets is that economic union measures that could not be introduced within a federation because of, say, political reasons can now be implemented more easily under the umbrella of international integration. For example, it would have been political dynamite for Ottawa to force the Canadian provinces (through the courts) to abandon their protectionist policies against out-of-province beer. Yet this change is now occurring, almost naturally, as a result of the Canada–U.S. free trade area. On a related front, it is politically difficult for any federation to attempt to eliminate subnational purchasing preferences. But if the removal of purchasing preferences is part of a multinational trade deal, then the internal politics may become much easier.

Two other important issues arise in the context of the international-national nexus. The first is that several new areas are being brought not only under the umbrella of these agreements but, just as important, under the umbrella of competition policy. Foremost among these areas are the environment and the social policy. There is now considerable discussion of "environmental dumping" and "social dumping." NAFTA contained side agreements with respect to both of these areas. In the European arena, comparative social policies (including wages, fringe benefits, and working conditions) will emerge as a major comparative advantage issue (Courchene 1994b). The Europeans hope that social policies will be "leveled up" rather than forced to the lowest common denominator. But what transpires will depend on many factors that need not be discussed here. The relevant point is that these supranational agreements will of necessity influence the manner in which these policies play out in federal systems. In general, one should be able to assume that the result will be an enhanced internal social union. What is not yet evident is whether this integrated socioeconomic space will be the result of leveling all policies up to the top level or whether a leveling down will dominate.

The second and final point is somewhat related. Given that a unitary state approach to an economic union—or to an integrated economic space—is such a "centralizing" instrument (since almost any differences across provinces can be viewed as impinging in some way or another on the unified economic space), what is the future for federal systems as global economic integration proceeds? Will they be converted into effective unitary states? Presumably, the future for administrative federalism is ensured, because the issues here relate to economies of scale and the addressing of local preferences. Not so clear are the implications for legislative federations such as Canada.

To this point in the analysis of internal economic integration, the focus has been on the manner in which the five mature federations have attempted to secure, through constitutional provisions, their internal economic unions. At one level of analysis, constitutions obviously matter: administrative federalisms such as Germany will obviously have more unified economic spaces than legislative federations such as Canada. Moreover, among legislative federalisms, those with far-reaching federal internal-market powers—either as interpreted by the courts or in terms of the structure of the constitution (for example, whether there is a separate listing of provincial powers)—will also have more integrated markets. Yet the written constitutional word may not carry the day. Other features of federations are important. If one did not know the constitutional provisions of Canada or

Switzerland, one could probably guess that the portability across cantons of professional and skills accreditation in Switzerland would be greater than that across the provinces in Canada simply because of geography: the likelihood of living in one canton or province and working in another is much greater in Switzerland than in Canada, so this reality would presumably be reflected regardless of the nature of the constitutional provisions.

The point is that in federations such as Canada (or Australia and the United States), further progress toward a unified economic space will likely require new sorts of instruments and arrangements.

Conclusion

Are there lessons in the above analysis relating to either principles or best practices that can advance the concept of macro federalism? At the most general level, the answer is yes. Although all federal systems have provisions in their constitutions pertaining to internal economic union, there is little doubt that Europe 1992 has rekindled interest in preserving and promoting the internal economic unions in all federations. Beyond this observation, it is not clear that the evidence from the five mature federations points toward a set of best practices. Indeed, it does not. Among the results of the above analysis are the following:

- Administrative federalisms are likely to have more thorough internal economic unions than do legislative federalisms.
- Likewise, intrastate federalisms (that is, those where the subnational units are effectively represented in national decision making) will likely have freer internal flows than interstate federalisms.
- Both these points demonstrate that the broad constitutional design does matter.
- In terms of the specific constitutional provisions, similarly worded provisions appear to be given quite different interpretations by the courts. As the forces of globalization take hold, the courts in the respective federations are likely to interpret the economic union provisions more expansively.
- Nonetheless, because the constitutions of four mature federations (all except Germany) date from long ago (the constitution of the youngest of these four federations, Australia, dates from 1901), they are probably not particularly helpful in terms of how one might design a modern federation to ensure an effective internal economic union. Indeed, some of these federations have had to resort to "modern" instruments (mutual

recognition as in the EU, formal internal free trade agreements as in Canada) to enhance their internal markets.

■ Beyond these issues relating to constitutional design or specific internal economic union provisions, other factors undoubtedly influence the free flow of goods, services, capital, and labor across subnational boundaries. Size of the country is one such variable. Even decentralized federations such as Switzerland are likely to have effective labor and skills mobility if geography dictates that many citizens reside in one canton but work in another. Obviously, linguistic and cultural diversity is another factor that conditions the degree of internal mobility.

In summary, therefore, different federations face quite different challenges in terms of promoting an internal economic union. This statement will probably be true of emerging federations, although constitutional design for federations in the 21st century will probably place more emphasis on internal-market issues than was the case for some of the earlier federations.

Finally, this section turns to a reconsideration of the importance of ensuring a full-blown internal economic union. There are two facets to this counterperspective. The first falls under the earlier-mentioned rubric of the regional-international interface. Canada is the obvious example here. With trade in goods and services increasingly going north-south rather than east-west, one cannot state that it is optimal to "force" some centrally determined vision relating to east-west trade. What economic sense would it make to enforce a uniform approach to corporate taxation across the provinces if the result were that energy-rich Alberta would be unable to match the corporate tax provisions of the Texas Gulf, its major competitor? One suspects that this degree of flexibility in terms of internal trade is likely to be appropriate for European federations and even Australia. In terms of Australia, it is not obvious that the manner in which Sydney integrates with the Pacific West will call for the same policy parameters that are required for a successful integration of Perth with the Pacific East. The point is that internal economic unions should be tempered by the manner in which subnational governments or regions interact with their international neighbors.

The second facet is related. No doubt uniformity is desirable with respect to some aspects of the internal economic union. However, uniformity everywhere (that is, a full-blown economic union) is likely to undermine the economic rationale for federations—namely, the exercise of competitive federalism (which is defined as the ability of subnational governments to experiment with alternative design and delivery mechanisms for public goods and services).

In other words, a thoroughgoing internal economic union emanating from the center would emasculate competitive federalism and, in the process, undermine the dynamic-efficiency rationale for federal systems. Thus, there are some important limits to how far federal systems should strive for effective internal economic unions, and as noted, these limits probably depend on the geoeconomic situations of the various federations.

Transfer Dependency: A Macro Federalism Approach to Regional Policy and Fiscal Federalism

Fiscal federalism approaches regional policy largely in terms of its focus on intergovernmental transfers. Most of this literature is motivated by fiscal equity concerns. However, the regional science literature, at least until recently, was predominantly micro driven, particularly in terms of its location-theory focus. And the recent growth literature addresses subnational regions largely in terms of "convergence." Although this methodology is admittedly a macro approach, the analysis tends to be very aggregative and typically does not embody the manner in which regional policy influences the degree of convergence or nonconvergence, as the case may be.

The purpose of this section is to attempt to provide a macro perspective on regional policy. Obviously, central governments in both unitary and federal states can and do engage in regional policies that have macro, growth, or dynamic-efficiency effects. What makes regional policy a macro federalism issue, however, is the ability of subnational governments to counter these central initiatives with their own arsenal of policies and instruments and, in the process, potentially create significant regional problems for federal countries. Indeed, the emphasis in this section is on the potential for dysfunctional result—hence the title "Transfer Dependency."

Transfer dependency, as used in this chapter, has a specific meaning. Because transfers exist in virtually all nations, it does not refer to regions or persons within these regions that are dependent on transfers. Rather, the term relates to various ways in which the incentives within—and the magnitude of—these transfers serve to counteract the natural forces of adjustment or to lead the recipient governments or individuals to undertake decisions that are not in their own economic interests (but do make sense in the presence of the transfers). The evidence of transfer dependency would include persistently high regional unemployment rates relative to the national average; wages that are well above productivity levels; and, in severe cases like those in Canada, provinces that have, in terms of national accounting definitions, personal income in excess of gross domestic product (GDP).

The mature federations differ greatly in their tendency to fall into transfer dependency. Canada probably best exemplifies the problems that can beset a federation in this regard. Thus, most of the analysis will focus on Canada. However, further research and documentation are clearly warranted for the other federations. Not surprisingly, this issue also looms large in the European Union, because the per capita wage and income differentials of the member states are far greater than the comparable within-country differentials in the mature federations (with the possible exception of Germany just before unification). In particular, the EU concern with respect to "wage demonstration effects" in the context of a single currency is essentially equivalent to the concept of transfer dependency.

To motivate the macro-cum-federal aspects of regional policy, the following two subsections present analytical treatments of regional transfers.[1] Although these analyses are cast largely in the context of the Canadian regional transfer system, the analytical implications are not country specific.

Transfers and Macro Federalism: A Gold-Standard Analogy

Assume, for present purposes, that Canada is the "world." In this stylized world, there are 10 "countries" (provinces) linked together by a single currency—the Canadian dollar. By definition of a federal nation, the exchange rates between these "countries" are fixed, irrevocably, at parity (that is, a Nova Scotia "dollar" can be traded, one-for-one, for a British Columbia "dollar"). Hence, in effect, the gold standard has been transferred by analogy to the Canadian federation.

Now assume that the Atlantic region of Canada (which comprises the four easternmost provinces) runs a balance-of-payments deficit on current account.[2] Under the gold-standard equilibrating mechanism, gold (dollars) has to flow out in order to pay for this balance-of-payments deficit. The resulting decrease in the Atlantic money supply would trigger declines in wages and domestic prices. In reality, though wages are lower in the Atlantic region than in the rest of Canada, they are not falling on an annual basis. Indeed, the opposite has been true since the mid-1980s: Atlantic wages are moving toward the national average. The question at issue here is what mechanism is at work to allow the Atlantic provinces to run these substantial balance-of-payments deficits year in and year out?

To a degree, the current-account deficit could be financed by purchases of Atlantic assets by the rest of Canada, by a drawing down of savings of Atlantic residents, or by borrowing on the part of Atlantic governments and citizens. No doubt all of these factors come into play from time to time. But these sources cannot come anywhere near to accounting for the magnitude of the annual current-account deficits.

Hence, one cannot escape the conclusion that the (dis)equilibrating mechanism at work here is the federal tax, expenditure, and transfer system. Ottawa effectively rechannels these funds back into the Atlantic region through the comprehensive interregional and intergovernmental transfer system (equalization, unemployment insurance, operations of the personal income tax system, and so forth). In effect, this "sterilization" of the gold (dollar) outflows allows the Atlantic region to run deficits in perpetuity. It is as if the Atlantic region has latched onto the fabled "widow's cruse" or, equivalently, has an "annuity" from the rest of Canada that permits it to escape the rigors of the gold-standard adjustment mechanism.

All states, federal and unitary alike, engage in internal regional distribution, if only through the operations of the income tax system. For the most part, this redistribution goes unnoticed in unitary states because it typically does not leave an easily identifiable statistical trail. (Countries such as Italy, where the redistribution is clearly geographic, may be an exception.) In contrast, federations tend to identify this redistribution in the context of publishing data on provinces, states, cantons, or *Länder*, as the case may be. And three of the mature federations (Australia, Canada, and Germany) engage in active equalization, so aspects of the gold-standard analogy clearly operate in those countries. Thus, subnational units in those countries depend on transfers. But as already noted, the term *transfer dependency* goes well beyond this definition: it depicts a situation in which the incentives in the transfer system impede the natural adjustment mechanism, lead to the entrenchment of existing income or unemployment disparities, and perhaps even exacerbate those disparities. It is instructive to focus on an alternative way of approaching the macro effects of regional transfers. Again the context will be Canada, but the analysis generalizes to all federations.

A Geometry of the Macro Region Problem

The starting point of the transfer dependency analysis is the assumption that the federal government's goal is to minimize the variation in unemployment rates across regions. This is not quite Ottawa's goal, but it is close enough to reality that the analysis will lead to useful implications. For convenience, Canada is viewed as being composed of two regions—the Maritimes and Ontario, where Ontario can be viewed as the rest of Canada. The diagrammatic representation of the analysis is presented in figure 1.2. The vertical axis represents "numbers of people." Equal distances along this axis, whether

A geometry of regional dependence

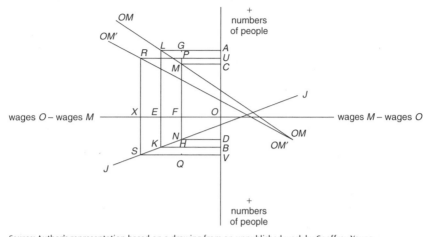

Source: Author's representation based on a drawing from an unpublished work by Geoffrey Young.
Note: JJ = job-creation function; OM – OM = outmigration function; wages M = wages in Maritime region; wages O = wages in Ontario.

FIGURE 1.2 A Geometry of Regional Dependence

above and below the origin (or, for that matter, straddling the origin), represent correspondingly equal numbers of people. The horizontal axis depicts relative wage rates. To the right of the origin, wages are higher in the Maritimes (M) than they are in Ontario (O); that is, wages M – wages O is positive—and increasingly so the farther right one goes. To the left of the origin, the opposite prevails: wages O – wages M is positive; that is, wage rates are higher in Ontario. Obviously, at the origin wages O = wages M.

Curve *JJ* represents new jobs created for the Maritimes. For convenience, it is drawn as a straight line. The positive slope of *JJ* is intuitively plausible: the lower the wages are in the Maritimes (relative to Ontario), the greater the number of new jobs that will be created there. For example, where wages O – wages M = OF, the number of new jobs in the Maritimes will be OD. At a relatively lower Maritime wage (OE), job creation will rise to level OB. Curve *JJ* is drawn so that even when relative wages are equal (at the origin), there is still some positive Maritime job creation.

Curve *OM* (also drawn as a straight line for convenience) is designed to represent the probability of outmigration from the Maritimes. An increase in Ontario wages relative to Maritime wages will lead to a greater outflow of people to Ontario; for differential OF, the outmigration flow is OC, and for wage differential OE, it is OA. The *OM* function is drawn so that even where wage rates are identical, there is some outmigration, but this aspect is of no special significance to the analysis.

The starting assumption is that the two economies are currently in equilibrium, and the task at hand is to allocate the new entrants into the Maritime labor force between new jobs and outmigration. Let the number of new entrants in the Maritime job market be equal to the vertical distance *AB* in the diagram. (Note that this distance represents an exogenously determined number of people. Although it is represented thus far by the vertical distance *AB*, it can also be represented by any other equivalent vertical distance in the diagram, such as *UV*.)

The separate currency area solution

If the Maritimes had a separate currency, the system would, in the absence of government intervention, settle down at an effective wage differential equal to *OE* in figure 1.2. This effective wage differential is obtained by taking the vertical distance representing the numbers of new entrants into the labor force and sliding it between the curves *OM* and *JJ* until it fits exactly (that is, distance *KL* = distance *AB*). At this effective wage differential, *OA* new entrants would migrate, and *OB* new entrants would find jobs in the Maritimes. Because *OA* + *OB* = *AB*, this effective wage differential "looks after" all the new entrants, so to speak. If the actual wage differential were equal only to *OF*, then *OC* people would migrate, *OD* people would get new jobs, and the remainder (*AC* + *DB*) would be unemployed, which would put downward pressure on the effective wage rate and move the differential back toward *OE*.

The analysis has been conducted in terms of the effective wage rate. What would presumably generate this effective wage differential is a movement in the exchange rate between the Maritimes and Ontario (assuming for the moment that the regions have their own currencies). If the actual wage differential is, say, *OF*, the currency of the Maritimes will depreciate until the effective wage differential equals *OE*.

Even though regions and provinces do not have their own currencies, this assumption has value as the starting point for the present analysis because it provides a useful benchmark for comparing other solutions to the regional problem. In particular, the next subsection will demonstrate that this "flexible exchange rate" solution to figure 1.2 can be reproduced by means of a set of subsidies. Hence, even though the two levels of government in a federation are normally constrained in certain actions by, say, the provisions of the constitution, frequently other policy instruments can accomplish much the same result. For example, provinces are not allowed to mount tariffs against goods from other provinces. However, provincial purchasing preferences have the same effect as a tariff for the goods in question. Indeed, these purchasing preferences can be viewed as altering the province's exchange rate for the protected goods.

The optimal subsidy scheme

To breathe a bit of reality into figure 1.2, assume that the Maritimes does not have its own currency. Moreover, assume that although wage rates are lower in the Maritimes, the differential is only OF, which is less than the "separate currency" effective wage differential OE. As noted in the previous subsection, associated with wage differential OF is outmigration of OC and job creation OD, leaving $DB + AC$ Maritimers unemployed. One obvious solution would be for Maritime wage rates to fall relative to those in Ontario so that wage differential OE is reached. But suppose that there are sufficient rigidities in the system (minimum wage laws, nationwide wage bargaining, uniform scale of federal wages across the country, union strength, and the like) such that the wage differential remains at OF. Under those circumstances, what is the optimal (or probably more correctly, the least costly) policy? One answer is that which duplicates the separate currency area solution.

To arrive at this answer, assume that the government has full information with respect to the outmigration and job-creation functions and, further, that it can act as a perfect discriminator (that is, it will pay only what is needed to require the additional migrant to move and to have the additional worker employed). Under those assumptions, the government will offer subsidies to both outmigration and job creation such that, at the margin, the effective wage differential again becomes OE. Thus, the cost of having the marginal person migrate (GL) is equal to the marginal cost of employing an additional worker (HK), where these costs are measured horizontally (and, ideally, those costs should be expressed in present value terms). The total cost of the subsidy program is the sum of the two triangles NHK and LGM.

The assumptions underlying this result are very restrictive. If firms and people are able to conceal their preferences, it is possible that all new jobs and all outmigrants will receive a subsidy. In that case, the marginal subsidy cost of employing the last person will be BK, not HK (assuming that the job-creation function goes through the origin). David Springate (1973) found, using interview techniques, that many recipients of regional development grants would have invested in the Maritimes without the grant. Hence, subsidies are often given even to people who would not need such subsidies to motivate their actions. The present analysis, however, maintains the assumption that governments have full information with respect to these reaction functions.

Therefore, under the assumption that the federal government is committed to a policy of full employment and that it takes the existing relative regional wage rates as given, an optimal subsidy scheme would involve both outmigration (bringing people to jobs) and job-creation (bringing jobs to people) subsidies. What should be clear, however, is that the cost of achieving this goal will be increased substantially if the provinces mount development policies of their own.

Provincial strategies

Suppose now that the Maritime provinces know that the federal government is committed to absorbing any and all new labor force entrants. This scenario sets the stage for the provinces to take advantage of Ottawa's commitment or to demand "ransom" from the federal government, as it were. An obvious strategy for these provinces is to attempt to shift the outmigration function downward (for example, from OM to OM' in figure 1.2). One way in which this strategy might be accomplished is to allow the provinces the right to select the training or retraining programs for their citizens. If these programs are designed to train people for within-region skills rather than skills that would equip them better for employment in other regions, the result will be to tilt the outmigration curve downward. Similarly, these provinces can lobby the federal government to incorporate regionally differentiated benefits within unemployment insurance (as is now the case, because beneficiaries can collect unemployment insurance for longer periods if they reside in high-unemployment regions), which will also move the OM curve in the direction of OM'.

What happens if the outmigration curve shifts from OM to OM' in figure 1.2? The new equilibrium is at X (that is, the effective equilibrium wage differential now becomes OX). Outmigration equals OU, and job creation equals OV, where by construction UV (that is, $OU + OV$) is equal to AB or RS is equal to LK. The marginal cost of employing or moving the last labor force participant is now equal to QS (which equals PR) compared with the previous marginal cost of HK. The net result is that the federal government is enticed to devote more resources to the regional problem and, in the process, to shift its policy mix in the direction of bringing jobs to the Maritimes rather than sending people to jobs in other regions.

Obviously, the policies of the other provinces can also influence the cost to the federal government of achieving this regional goal. Were the richer provinces to mount barriers to internal migration (through provincial licensing of skill accreditations, for example), this policy would be equivalent to the previous example (that is, a downward shift in the outmigration function in figure 1.2). Were the richer provinces to counter the federal initiative by offering competing job-creation subsidies, this policy would shift the job-creation function upward in figure 1.2. Not only would this action result in larger overall costs (as in the previous case), but now more of the adjustment arising from the imposition of an optimal set of subsidies would be thrown on outmigration from the Maritimes and less on job creation in the region.

With a bit of creativity, it is not difficult to envision scenarios in which the effective wage rate in the Maritimes falls relative to Ontario (that is, the equilibrium exchange rate vis-à-vis Ontario falls) but the actual wage rate rises relative to Ontario. In terms of figure 1.2, such scenarios imply that the separate currency area solution moves left from E, but the actual wage differential moves right from F. This situation is, of course, the classic case of transfer dependency, in which regional wages are progressively patterned after national wages and in which the population is enticed to stay in the region through a comprehensive set of distortive transfers. (With perhaps some degree of misrepresentation, this case corresponds to what in European circles is referred to as *wage demonstration effects*.)

One example will suffice here. Because of the operations of Canada's unemployment insurance in have-not regions (that is, the number of weeks needed to qualify is lower and the number of benefit weeks for each week worked is enhanced), unemployment insurance in the Maritimes has become more of a work-sharing program. Specifically, for 11 or 12 weeks of work, a person can collect benefits for the rest of the year. Not surprisingly, the moral hazard element here is close to overwhelming. Working for 10 weeks' wages of Can$5,000 might trigger unemployment insurance benefits on the order of, say, Can$13,000 or Can$14,000. In effect, this situation represents a lottery ticket with a guaranteed payoff—the only lottery element here is to get the 10 weeks of work in the first place. Not surprisingly, stories are making the rounds of people actually borrowing from banks or credit unions in order to help "pay" for their 10-week jobs. Compounding this problem is that unemployment insurance is now becoming an important income-support system for communities. Immense pressure is frequently placed on workers to pass their jobs on to other community members after 10 weeks so that others, too, can be part of the lottery. The degree to which this practice has become a way of life is evident from the following comment by Frank McKenna, premier of New Brunswick: "I inherited the province in 1987 where we had 128 fish plants, every one of them geared to work 10 weeks, because that's all they needed" (McKenna 1993: 20–21). Although the focus in this section has been on the Maritime provinces (which include New Brunswick), it is important to recognize that these distortive incentives are evident throughout the country.

By way of final comment, it is instructive to devote a few sentences to Canada's equalization program. Indeed, were equalization not covered so extensively in the fiscal federalism literature, it would be an appropriate candidate for macro federalism, because the dynamic growth aspects of equalization are frequently short-changed in the fiscal federalism analyses. Nowhere is this truer than in Canada, where the equalization program brings all provinces' standardized revenues up to the revenue level of the five provinces that make up the standard (that is, all provinces except Alberta and the four Atlantic provinces). To see the implications of this equalization program, assume that New Brunswick manages to generate 20,000 jobs with a payroll of Can$50 million. Assume further that as a result New Brunswick's own-source revenues increase by Can$15 million. Because New Brunswick is not part of the "five-province standard," its overall revenues (own-source revenues plus equalization) will not increase by one cent as a result of this job growth (that is, equalization is in effect a confiscatory tax). New Brunswick's overall revenue situation would be identical had it lost 20,000 jobs. This situation is not much different for small provinces that are included in the five-province standard, because their weight in the standard is relatively low. The general point is that a system that ensures that there are no revenue implications for alternative provincial policies is wholly inappropriate and is part and parcel of the transfer dependency syndrome that afflicts Canada.[3]

More on Regional Adjustment: The Blanchard-Katz Analysis

An alternative way of focusing on regional disparities has been provided by Blanchard and Katz (1992). The motivation underlying their research on the economic prospects of the various U.S. states is as follows:

> The most striking feature is the range of employment growth rates across states. Over the last 40 years, some states have consistently grown at 2 percent above the national average, while some states have barely grown, with rates 2 percent below the national average. Rather than leading to fluctuations around trends, employment shocks typically have permanent effects. A state that experiences an acceleration or a slowdown in growth can expect to return to the same growth rate, but on a permanently different path of employment. The picture is very different when one looks at unemployment rates. Relative

unemployment rates have exhibited no trend; moreover, shocks to relative unemployment rates have lasted for only one-half decade or so. Thus unemployment patterns present an image of vacillating state fortunes as states move from above to below the national unemployment rate, and vice versa. Finally, the last 40 years have been characterized by a steady convergence of relative wages, a fact documented recently (1991) by Robert Barro and Xavier Sala-I-Martin (using personal income per capita rather than wages). As for unemployment, the effects of shocks to relative wages appear to be transitory, disappearing within a decade or so. (Blanchard and Katz 1992: 2)

Blanchard and Katz (1992) then develop a model consistent with these facts and submit the model to empirical verification, focusing on changes in employment, participation rates, and unemployment rates. They summarize their results as follows:

We find very similar results across states. A negative shock to employment leads initially to an increase in unemployment and a small decline in participation. Over time, the effect on employment increases, but the effect on unemployment and participation disappears after approximately five to seven years. Put another way, a state typically returns to normal after an adverse shock not because employment picks up, but because workers leave the state. These results raise an obvious set of questions: does employment fail to pick up because wages have not declined enough or because lower wages are not enough to boost employment? (Blanchard and Katz 1992: 3)

In terms of the question posed in the last sentence of this quotation, the Blanchard and Katz research suggests the following:

In response to an adverse shock in demand, relative nominal wages indeed decline, but they do not decline by a large enough amount to prevent increases in unemployment. What they trigger is mostly labor out-migration, rather than job in-migration or job creation. (Blanchard and Katz 1992: 56)

This work represents a most creative research effort, one that deserves to be carried over to other federations. In a sense, it dynamizes the comparative-static focus on the Canadian regional disparities highlighted in the previous subsection. On the surface, Blanchard and Katz's results for the United States appear much more consistent with Australian data (where disparities relate largely to income, not unemployment, differentials) than with Canadian data. Were one to present a time-series analysis for Canada, one would find that Canadian regional disparities have been stubbornly persistent, thanks no doubt to Canada's generous regional payments, which arguably have served to entrench, if not exacerbate, these regional disparities. This approach contrasts with the hands-off U.S. approach to regional shocks and regional disparities:

> New England is a prosperous region of the country because it got out of its old dying industries and into new growth industries. If Washington had protected New England's old dying industries, New England would still be depressed. It is correct to point out that New England went through 40 years of economic pain before it made the transition, but the correct answer to this is a national policy for aiding individuals and speeding up that transition. To prop up dying industries will only prolong the pain. (Thurow 1981: 30–31)

Canada has chosen to prolong the pain.

What is needed on the research front is to integrate the historical snap-shots of regional disparity with the dynamic adjustment profiles from the Blanchard-Katz analysis and then overlay these findings with the regional-intergovernmental transfer policies of the various federations.

Regional Stabilization

Up to this point in the analysis of regional policy, the emphasis has been on regional disparities and the adjustment process. However, a related issue—regional stabilization—has begun to attract attention. The motivation for the recent interest in regional stabilization arises from the potential impli-cations of the EMU. With exchange rates fixed and member states con-strained by the Maastricht Treaty's fiscal guidelines (deficits cannot exceed 3 percent of GDP and the debt-to-GDP ratio must not exceed 60 percent), what flexibility rests with member states if they are hit by an unexpected negative shock? Exchange rate changes are ruled out. So are protectionist measures under Europe 1992, as well as fiscal changes if the member country is running up against the Maastricht Treaty's guidelines. Moreover, the EU has not opted for much in the way of intergovernmental transfers, although the transfers under the Common Agriculture Policy remain large, as do the structural funds. But there is no equalization-type program of the sort that exists in Australia, Canada, and Germany. About all that remains is labor-market policy, including wages, fringe benefits, and migration. Is this program adequate in terms of flexibility, or is some alternative necessary?

This scenario is the backdrop for an article by Goodhart and Smith (1993). Their focus is on stabilization, not on redistribution. They define as inherently redistributive any grants or transfers that are functions of the level of economic activity. Thus, they would classify a system in which the level of federal expenditure depended on the level of regional or state income or employment as falling in the redistributive camp (Goodhart and Smith 1993: 419). In contrast, pure stabilization would involve variations in fiscal grants and transfers that were functions of the rate of change in economic activity.

This distinction is important because "a regional transfer system where the amount to be transferred was a function of the average level of income in each region over the previous five years would have a considerable redistributive, but a virtually zero stabilization, function" (Goodhart and Smith 1993: 419–20). The Canadian system illustrates this point. If a province suffers a negative revenue shock (that is, a negative divergence from trend), the equalization system will kick in. Presumably, this result would classify as a stabilization measure. However, if a province's revenue remains on trend but the province receives an increase in equalization because the revenues of some other provinces are rising, then this result would be more in the nature of a redistributive measure. Note that this discussion refers to changes in the level of equalization: the level of equalization itself would be a redistributive measure. However, under the Goodhart and Smith (1993) pure stabilization scheme, each member state would, in principle, stand an equal chance of being eligible for stabilization benefits, because these benefits do not relate to the relative prosperity of member states but, rather, to deviations of some indicator (such as income or employment) from the trend. Actually, there is a version of a pure stabilization scheme associated with the Canadian equalization system: any province whose revenues fall from one year to the next (at unchanged tax parameters) is eligible for compensation. Because of the turbulent economic times since the mid-1980s, more than half of the provinces have benefited from this program, including the three "rich" (or non-equalization-receiving) provinces.

Goodhart and Smith (1993) proceed to estimate the stabilization component of instruments such as the tax-transfer system in federal nations and then devise their own stabilization facility. Among the desirable features of a stabilization facility are that it be timely, be temporary, and not be subject to moral hazard. Intriguingly, a pure stabilization facility that provided as much stabilization as the personal income tax in federal systems could probably be implemented at the community level for less than 0.5 percent of European Communities' GDP (Commission of the European Communities 1993: 76).

As noted, the rationale for a stabilization facility in the EU is that in the absence of the exchange rate mechanism there may need to be an insurance mechanism against cyclical fluctuations. Presumably, this rationale would carry over to subnational governments in federal systems, because they, too, lack an exchange rate adjustment mechanism (although mobility of labor as an avenue of adjustment is more likely within federations than it is across the member states in the EU). However, this distinction between the redistributive versus the stabilization implications of regional transfers within federations has not as yet emerged as a critical policy issue.

Toward a Research Agenda

Much of the existing fiscal federalism literature, as it relates to transfers, puts primary emphasis on equity or static-efficiency concerns. Scholars in this area are familiar with concepts such as *fiscal residuums* and *fiscal-induced migration*. In this section, the focus has shifted to *dynamic efficiency* and to stabilization issues surrounding these transfers and, more generally, regional policy. Attention was directed initially to two macro formulations of regional policy—the federal gold-standard analogy and the geometry of regional trade. This discussion was then followed by a focus on the dynamics of regional adjustment across U.S. states, drawing from the research of Blanchard and Katz. The final substantive section shifted from the dynamic-efficiency perspective to a stabilization perspective, with reference to the EU and the study by Goodhart and Smith.

It would appear that this general area of regional policy is a fruitful area for further research, with potentially significant implications for macro federalism. Thus far, the area has been taken over by the convergence theorists. Their work is important research, but it represents more of an effort to provide background information than to detail the growth or convergence implications of alternative policy approaches to the regional and fiscal federalism challenges. What is required now is, first, to extend the Canadian analysis to other federations and, second, to extend the Blanchard-Katz approach to all mature federations so as to better understand the processes of adjustment within federal countries.

Given that the earlier proposition that the regional-international interface will become increasingly important as economic integration proceeds, this general area is likely to grow in importance. Indeed, as international trade agreements proliferate, subnational units of federal systems are likely to find themselves more and more in the position of EU member states, so that the importance of distinguishing between redistributive and stabilization aspects of regional policy may well come to the fore in federal systems. At one extreme, it could be argued that what is required here is a comprehensive reworking of the existing fiscal federalism literature to incorporate dynamic efficiency and stabilization. At the other extreme, it may well be that the preferred course is to approach this area afresh from the perspective of macro federalism.

Monetary Policy and Central Banking

The focus of the chapter now shifts to aspects of monetary and fiscal policy, with the following section focusing on aspects of fiscal policy while the current section addresses the structure of the monetary authority in federal systems.

If one defines *monetary policy* as the process whereby a central bank influences the economy through its control over the expansion of money and credit, then it is unlikely that there is a macro federalism issue with respect to monetary policy. With a few notable exceptions, all nation-states have central banks, and the range of monetary policy instruments is likewise similar across federal and unitary states alike.

However, if one looks beyond monetary policy, per se, and into central bank structure, then some federal issues do arise, both among federal systems and between federal and unitary states. In particular, central banks in federal states are more likely to be independent. To make this case, this section focuses on the policy and structural characteristics of the five mature federations (table 1.4), supplemented by some references to unitary states.

Column 1 of table 1.4 elaborates on the policy mandate of the central banks. Only the Bundesbank and the proposed Eurofed have a price stability mandate. The central bank of inflation-conscious Switzerland has a general mandate even though, as noted in the table, it interprets this mandate largely in terms of pursuing price stability. Since 1988, the Bank of Canada has been pursuing price stability, but it, too, has a general mandate. Among unitary states, the New Zealand Reserve Bank now has a mandate that focuses only on prices. This focus on the central bank mandates is largely informative in nature and is not particularly relevant to the independence issue (except that the presence of a mandate that is cast solely in terms of achieving price stability does imply a large measure of independence). However, more and more nations are thinking seriously about making the achievement of price stability the principal goal of central banks.

Columns 2 and 3 of table 1.4 address the independence issue. The details in the table are left to the reader. What is striking is that the British Commonwealth federations (Australia and Canada) are quite different from the other three. Not only do these federations allow for government directives, but also they are structured quite differently. Specifically, what enhances the independence of the U.S. Federal Reserve and the Bundesbank is that a large part of their board of directors comes from their reserve district banks

TABLE 1.4 Central Bank Structure

Federation	Policy mandate	Structure of board	Relation to government	Cukierman's (1992) independence ranking (out of 21 industrial countries)
Australia	General mandate.[a]	The Reserve Bank Board consists of the governor, the deputy governor, the secretary to the Department of Treasury, and 7 other members appointed by the government for 5-year terms (renewable).	The government (through the treasurer) can issue directives to the Reserve Bank. The Reserve Bank is probably the central bank most open to government influence among the mature federations (for example, the secretary to the Department of Treasury is a voting member of the Reserve Bank Board).	12
Canada	The formal mandate is very general.[b] Since 1988, however, the Bank of Canada has pursued price stability as a goal.	The Board of Directors of the Bank of Canada consists of 12 outside, part-time directors plus the governor, senior deputy governor, and deputy minister of finance (nonvoting). The outside directors are appointed by the government for 3-year terms (renewable). The role of the outside directors is to provide corporate oversight, but not policy oversight. Ontario and Quebec have 2 directors, with 1 from each of the remaining 8 provinces.	The government can issue directives to the Bank of Canada, although such a directive has never been issued.	6

(continued)

Germany	German law states that the "Deutsche Bundesbank regulates the quantity of money in circulation . . . with the aim of safeguarding the currency." The Bundesbank interprets this provision as referring to price stability.	The Central Bank Council (the policy-making branch of the Bundesbank) is made up of (a) the directorate and (b) and the presidents of the 11 central banks of the *Länder*. The directorate (consisting of the president, the vice president, and up to 8 other people) is nominated by the federal government. Thus, the Bundesbank Act prevents the federal government from appointing a majority of the Central Bank Council.c	The Bundesbank is independent of instruction from government and is not directly accountable to either the upper or lower chamber. [2]
Switzerland	In principle, the mandate is quite general (for example, it regulates money and credit in support of overall economic goals). In practice, "the Swiss National Bank interprets its mandate to be the pursuit of price stability as the principal objective of monetary policy" (Bank of Canada 1991: 3).	The principal body responsible for monetary policy, the Governing Board, consists of 3 members appointed by the federal government for 6-year terms. The majority of shares of the Swiss National Bank are held by the cantons and the cantonal banks.	This line of accountability is to the federal government, but the government may not issue directives to the Swiss central bank. [1]

TABLE 1.4 Central Bank Structure (*continued*)

Federation	Policy mandate	Structure of board	Relation to government	Cukierman's (1992) independence ranking (out of 21 industrial countries)
United States	The formal mandate is very general.[d] However, Chairman Alan Greenspan has indicated his support for proposals that would "direct monetary policy toward a single goal, price stability, that monetary policy is uniquely suited to pursue" (Bank of Canada 1991: 3).	The principal monetary policy committee, the Federal Open Market Committee, decides policy by a majority vote. The committee is composed of the 7 members of the Board of Governors, who are appointed by the president (subject to Senate ratification) for 14-year terms, and 5 presidents of the 12 district Reserve Banks. Reserve Bank presidents are appointed by the boards of directors of the Reserve Banks, subject to approval of the Board of Governors of the Federal Reserve System.	The Federal Reserve Board is accountable to Congress. The Board of Governors is required to report semiannually to Congress on monetary policy objectives. Nonetheless, the structure of the Federal Reserve has been designed to provide a significant degree of independence	4
European Union	The European Central Bank notes that the "primary objective of the System shall be to maintain price stability."	The Governing Council would comprise all members of the Executive Board and the governors of the national central banks. The Executive	The European Central Bank, the national banks or central banks, and any member of those banks' decision-making bodies are prohibited from seeking or	n.a.

Board would comprise the president, the vice president, and 4 other members, all full time. The board members would be appointed by common accord by the governments of the member states (after consulting the European Parliament and the Governing Council) from among people with recognized standing and professional experience on monetary or banking matters.	taking instructions from community institutions or bodies, from any government of a member state, or from any other body.

Source: Author's compilation.

Note: n.a. = not applicable.

a. According to the Reserve Bank Act, it is the duty of the Reserve Bank Board, within the limits of its powers, to ensure that the monetary and banking policy of the Reserve Bank is directed to the greatest advantage of the people of Australia and that the powers of the bank, under Banking Act 1959 and the regulations under that act, are exercised in a manner that, in the opinion of the board, will best contribute to (a) the stability of the currency in Australia, (b) the maintenance of full employment in Australia, and (c) the economic prosperity and welfare of the Australian people.

b. According to the preamble of the Bank of Canada Act, the Bank of Canada is "to regulate credit and currency in the best interests of the economic life of the nation, to control and protect the external value of the national monetary unit, and to mitigate by its influence fluctuations in the general level of production, trade, prices, and employment, so far as may be possible within the scope of monetary action, and generally to promote the economic and financial welfare of Canada."

c. Subsequent to German reunification, a modification of the Bundesbank Act was proposed. According to this proposal, there would be only 9 central banks of the *Länder*. The Central Bank Council would consist of the president, the vice president, and up to six other members of the directorate, plus the nine presidents of the central banks of the *Länder*. This arrangement would not alter the requirement that a majority of the Central Bank Council not be government appointees.

d. The Federal Reserve Act requires the Federal Reserve System to "maintain long-run growth of the monetary and credit aggregate commensurate with the economy's long-run potential to increase production, so as to promote effectively the goals of maximum employment, stable prices, and moderate long-term interest rates."

(United States) and their *Länd* central banks (Germany). The Swiss central bank is also tied to cantons and cantonal banks through share ownership. In the case of Australia and Canada, the outside directors are part time and, for the most part, are political appointments. In Australia's case, independence is further compromised by the presence of the secretary of the Department of Treasury as a voting member of the Federal Reserve Board.

It is important to note that this de jure approach to central bank independence need not be synonymous with de facto independence. The example par excellence here is Canada. Under Governor John Crow from 1988 to 1994, the Bank of Canada had arguably become the "Bundesbank of North America" by launching a dedicated commitment to price stability. To be sure, Governor Crow was not reappointed, but his successor, Gordon Thiessen, was the former senior deputy governor, and the policy (as of 1995) remains intact. In this case, independence resides in the power of the institution and the support it garners domestically and internationally.

The final column of table 1.4 presents an independence ranking of central banks compiled by Cukierman (1992). This index is a composite of 16 variables designed to assess the legal independence of central banks. Of the 21 industrial countries, the top four places in terms of independence go to federal nations: Switzerland, Germany, Austria, and the United States. Canada is sixth, after Denmark. Australia is in the middle of the pack.

Is this a lesson for macro federalism? The answer is probably yes. Central bank independence is emerging as an important feature of a mature economy in the new global economic order. More to the point, central bank independence appears to come more naturally to federations than to unitary states—partly because, in some of these countries, there is also a "federation of banks," and some members of the board of directors of the central bank come from this second tier of banks. As time passes, we will probably see more central banks gain independence (or become part of a larger currency area that focuses on central bank independence and price stability). The Eurofed proposal (see the last row of table 1.4) has heightened the importance of both independence and price stability as the principal mandate. Among unitary states, New Zealand has, as already noted, moved in this direction, and France appears ready to grant substantial independence to its central bank.

The relevance of this discussion for macro federalism is twofold. First, federal nations have led the way here. Second, among federal nations there are certain design features that seem to lead naturally to greater central bank independence. However, those federations that have emerged from the British parliamentary tradition do not possess these features, so they will have to find alternative ways to enhance central bank independence. Perhaps this observation is not surprising, because the British approach to central banking does not provide much in the way of a model:

> The United Kingdom is almost alone among the major industrial countries in not having a central bank with its main powers, functions, and responsibilities defined in law. Nowhere in legislation is the Bank of England described as the central bank of the United Kingdom, and its performances of central banking functions owes more to practice and precedent than to legislation. (Bank of Canada 1991: 3)

Fiscal Policy

Fiscal policy as a macro or stabilization instrument has, in principle, little in the way of federal implications in the sense that whatever challenges exist apply equally to federal and unitary states. Where the federal dimension enters is in terms of what is referred to as the *assignment problem*—namely, the allocation of taxes and expenditures between the federal and subnational governments. However, the literature on this issue is very extensive, both in analytical terms and in comparative terms, so little would be accomplished in the present context by reviewing this literature. Readers wishing to read an overview of the issues can consult Bird (1994). It is probably the case that globalization and the regional-international interface have altered the perspective one might take on the optimal tax assignment. The resulting decentralization would argue for tilting personal income taxation to the subnational level (to allow the provinces to integrate the education-training-welfare-work nexus) and to convert subnational sales taxes to value added taxes to be levied at the national level (which would provide for export-import neutrality and would allow countries to have different dimensions for government). But this option is one of many that are adequately covered in the existing literature.

Rather, the ensuing analysis will take its cue from the Maastricht Treaty and the debt-deficit guidelines for subnational governments. Under the Maastricht Treaty—or more correctly under the proposal for a single European currency—member states must ensure that their deficits are less than 3 percent of GDP and that their debt-to-GDP ratios do not exceed 60 percent. Part of the rationale for these guidelines is to ensure that member states' fiscal (debt-deficit) profligacy will not jeopardize the price stability–oriented monetary policy. This rationale has a direct carryover to federal nations: what flexibility do states, provinces, cantons, and *Länder* have with respect to running debts and deficits, and is there a potential for such activity to create problems for the monetary authority? The first part of the analysis will focus on whether these guidelines are adequate. To anticipate what follows, the argument will be that they are not. In particular, the fiscal behavior of the province of Ontario severely constrained the operations of the Bank of Canada, even though for the relevant period Ontario was well within the Maastricht Treaty's guidelines. The analysis then shifts to a discussion of the arrangements with respect to debts and borrowing for the Canadian provinces, with a lesser focus on the remaining mature federations. Some conclusions and implications complete the section.

Prior to this analysis, it is instructive to note that there are some associated requirements on member states in the EU. In particular, member states shall not seek to influence the proposed European Central Bank (ECB) nor the central banks of the member states. In other words, the central banks of member states cannot be used as a lender of last resort to their governments. Moreover, governments of member states cannot be bailed out by the ECB or by any other EU or member state body. Although these provisions may be far reaching in terms of the EU member states, they are rather straight-forward in terms of the operating environment of subnational governments of federal states. Certainly all these EU provisions apply to the subnational governments of the five mature federations.[4] However, as Bomfim and Shah (1991) point out, the arrangements in Brazil would appear to run afoul of these provisions. Similar problems may well apply to other emerging federations. To the extent that such problems exist, they are serious design defects that are almost sure to compromise the ability of the central bank to pursue an independent monetary policy. In effect, if subnational governments have access to either or both of (a) the guarantee of a bailout and (b) preferential loans from the banking sector, then they can essentially "print" money. This situation is a recipe for disaster on the inflation front.

An Evaluation of the Maastricht Guidelines

Given that much of what is occurring in the context of Europe 1992 and the Maastricht Treaty is having a dramatic influence on federal nations, it is important that some of the EU's provisions be subject to further analysis. At issue here are the Maastricht debt-deficit guidelines and whether they will ensure that the price stability mandate of the ECB will not be put in the balance. The thrust of the analysis that follows is that they are not adequate.

It is useful to note that under a single European currency, all member states would henceforth be borrowing in the new European currency, not in their own currency. The fear is that the removal of erstwhile currency risk from debt obligations of member states might encourage even more borrowing on the part of several member states. Phrased differently, debt-prone countries such as Greece might, without the Maastricht guidelines, be tempted to run up their debts or deficits even further. However, fiscal profligacy on the part of Greece within the EMU, much like, say, a profligate Prince Edward Island within Canada, is really too small to influence overall monetary stability, and in any event both Greece and Prince Edward Island would be brought into line by the credit rating agencies (focusing in both cases on country or province risk rather than on currency risk).

The challenges to overall stabilization policy will likely come from else-where. To see these challenges, one may find it convenient to focus on the fiscal policies of the province of Ontario during Canada's 1983 to 1989 boom. By the mid-1980s, inflation was clearly on the rebound in Canada, and it was equally clear that the pressure on wages and prices was most acute in booming Ontario. Given that roughly 40 percent of Canada's GDP originates in Ontario, the appropriate macro stance for Ontario would have been to temper its boom by saving some of its revenue dividend. However, Ontario went on a government spending spree. For example, between 1986 and 1989, welfare spending increased annually between 14 percent and 17 percent because Ontario chose that timeframe to enrich its social programs. In the event, the Ontario inflationary pressure spilled over to the rest of Canada in precisely the timeframe (1988) that the Bank of Canada opted for price stability. The result was a degree of monetary restraint far more brutal (at one point Canadian interest rates were 500 basis points above comparable U.S. rates) than would have been the case had there been some over-arching coordination of aggregate (federal and provincial) fiscal policy. What is critical in terms of this example is that throughout this period Ontario would not have been violating any EU-type deficit or debt guide-lines. In the early boom, its deficits, as a percentage of GDP, were slightly above 2 percent, falling to 1 percent in mid-boom and to roughly balance at the end. What was feeding the aggressive government spending was a combination of record revenue increases and hikes in tax rates.

The general point is that the Eurofed (or Bank of Canada) inflation targets are far more likely to be put in jeopardy when a superpower such as Germany (or Ontario), operating well within the Maastricht Treaty's guide-lines, strikes off on its own fiscal strategy than when a lesser member state such as Greece (or Prince Edward Island) runs up deficits. Admittedly, German unification is a unique event, but it should not obscure the essential point that overall fiscal coordination is necessary. This observation is not meant to downplay the importance of the Maastricht Treaty's guidelines for errant states. But the guidelines do little to discipline the errant fiscal behavior of powerful states that are operating well within the guidelines. More generally, it would appear that the EU should take a leaf out of the experience of federal nations and establish a European fiscal authority as a counterpart to the proposed Eurofed. For a more general discussion of the relationship between monetary and fiscal policy under the Eurofed, see, for example, Buiter, Corsetti, and Roubini (1993) and Eichengreen (1993) and the references therein.

By way of summary comment, one can come at all this from a quite different perspective—namely, that deficit and debt problems at the subnational level are likely to arise only in legislative federations (that is, those federations in which the subnational governments have considerable taxing flexibility). From this perspective, it is not surprising that Australia and Germany perform rather well in terms of fiscal coordination or deficit control. And their potential for indebtedness would likely be held in check by capital markets if this route were chosen, because capital markets would be very leery indeed of underwriting large deficits to states or *Länder* whose capacity for discretionary tax increases was limited or, in the German case, practically nil. One could go even further and suggest that the only way that these states or *Länder* could borrow substantial sums is by virtue of an agreement with the federal government, whether this agreement took the form of some Loan Council approval process or were related to the full integration of the states or *Länder* into the fiscal coordination process, as has occurred in Germany. Phrased differently, it is possible to argue that there is a federal guarantee of sorts backstopping subnational debt.

At the other end of the spectrum are the legislative federalisms. What keeps the U.S. states in check (apart from the presence of some state constitutional provisions and, as hinted earlier, a degree of Swiss-type innate fiscal conservatism) is that their jurisdictional powers are not particularly wide (at least in comparison with that of the Canadian provinces), nor do they have the Canadian- or Swiss-type flexibility on the tax side. As already mentioned, the limits on the borrowing proclivities of the Swiss appear to be rooted in their economic and cultural history and, as such, they represent a special case.

This leaves the Canadian federation. But even in Canada there is little tax flexibility for the smaller and poorer provinces, because the comprehensive Canadian system of equalization effectively confiscates any additional revenues arising from improvements in economic activity (although tax rate increases do increase overall revenues). Hence, it is only the *have* provinces—Alberta, British Columbia and Ontario—along with Quebec[5] that would mirror the situation of the EU member states under the proposed Eurofed. And of these provinces, Ontario is probably the only jurisdiction that is large enough (Ontario represents about 40 percent of Canadian GDP) to contemplate active fiscal policy, even if this policy has in the recent past largely been perverse. Thus arose the earlier recommendation for greater aggregate (federal and provincial) fiscal policy coordination in the Canadian federation. This recommendation also relates to the criticism of the Maastricht Treaty's guidelines in terms of isolating monetary policy from fiscal influence. The loss of the exchange rate mechanism, the severing of the link between EU member state governments and their former central banks, and the Europe 1992 directives relating to the unified economic space mean that countries such as Greece and Portugal will be held on a rather tight leash by the capital markets whether or not Maastricht-type guidelines are in place. Safeguarding the monetary stance must mean more in the way of overall fiscal coordination than quantitative attempts to straitjacket erstwhile fiscally profligate member states that under the Eurofed would neither be large enough nor be allowed capital-market flexibility to create problems in terms of the pursuit of price flexibility.

Miscellaneous Macro Federalism Issues

In this final substantive section, the analysis deals with a variety of other issues that can be deemed to fall within the purview of macro federalism: the environment, the influence of international agreements on the internal division of powers, and the emergence of democracy deficits. Attention is directed first to the role of the environment in the division of powers of federal systems.

The Environment and Macro Federalism

The lack of any earlier reference to the environment is probably a more serious omission than the scant attention devoted to the area of financial services. The rationale for this omission is straightforward: the area is so complex that it probably merits a full-length study on its own. What follows are a few observations that might inform such an analysis.

The obvious first comment is that concern about the environment is a recent issue, at least with respect to the timeframe in which most of the constitutions of the mature federations were penned. Therefore, the jurisdiction over the environment essentially remains unassigned in most of these constitutions. This situation should not pose serious problems for administrative federations such as Germany, where most legislation is federal and the role of the *Länder* is to implement and administer this federal legislation. Likewise, the interstate implications of the environment in the United States will presumably come under the sweep of the federal trade and commerce power. But the essential point is that most of the mature federations are probably scrambling to sort out the jurisdictional competencies in this area. Hence, the various federations will experiment with quite different approaches—approaches that may well be nation specific. Thus, it is not obvious that these differing arrangements will provide much of a model to emerging federal nations that have the flexibility to include environmental jurisdiction directly in the assignment of powers.

The second observation is related. The environmentalist slogan—"think globally, act locally"—emphasizes the global nature of environmentalism. Even if aspects of environmental regulation were assigned to the federal level, it is nonetheless the case that much of the activity that generates the potential for environmental degradation occurs at the subnational level. Mines, hydroelectric plants, irrigation, power generation, and so on are under the control of the states (in Australia and the United States) and the provinces (in Canada). There are exceptions—in Canada the federal government controls the nuclear industry—but the general point is that federal governments are typically not actively involved in the processes that generate concerns relating to habitat or to the environment. Once again, the issue is probably best cast within a principal-agent framework.

Third, the "think globally" aspect of the environment issue is increasingly formalized in terms of international (confederal) agreements or protocols. Thus, in terms of these international agreements, nation-states themselves are in a situation not unlike subnational governments in relation to their federal governments. In turn, this situation adds complications and uncertainty in terms of the powers of subnational governments. An obvious example is the Australian federal government's rolling back of the Tasmanian dam project on the basis that it ran afoul of the Australian Commonwealth's obligations under an international environmental agreement to which Australia was a signatory.

These observations are but a few relating to the many complexities that the environment has introduced into federal systems. It may well be that a thorough comparative analysis of the manner in which the mature federations are grappling with this issue will provide important insights regarding how best to enshrine the environment into the constitution. The traditional assignment issue may be less important here than the process dimension.

Given that there is an international (confederal) dimension to the ultimate resolution of environmental problems, this provides a convenient segue to (a) the interaction between subnational governments and the international sector and (b) the role of globalization in terms of extending federal principles to the supranational level.

Some Reflections on the International Dimension of Macro Federalism

It is a safe bet that the principles of federalism will progressively be applied at the supranational level, given that the spread of international agreements implies that most nation-states will find themselves in a "federal" or "confederal" relationship in terms of those agreements. Although these confederal arrangements have long existed, their nature is changing. The comment by Daniel Elazar (1994: 12), although quoted in an earlier section, merits repetition in the present context:

> the difference between earlier and contemporary confederations is that the primary purpose of earlier confederations was military security, while in postmodern society it is economic.

This remark provides a further rationale for extending the focus of macro federalism to selected issues at the supranational level.

Paradiplomacy: An extension of the regional-international interface

The conception of a regional-international interface vying with the traditional national-national interface was introduced at the beginning of the chapter. Courchene (1994a) extends this relationship in terms of the tendency for subnational entities to dispatch ambassadors or to engage in agreements with subnational entities in other nations. One example that is often referred to is the 1988 agreement among the so-called four motors of continental Europe (Baden-Württemberg, Catalonia, Lombardy, and Rhône-Alpes) designed to coordinate their various economic, industrial, and other cross-border interests. Barcelona, Montepelier, and Toulouse have also attempted to forge economic links that will take them out from under Madrid and Paris and into the larger EU framework.

This "domestication of international politics" (Ravenhill 1990: 112) is becoming quite pervasive. Ravenhill (1990: 98) offers the following rationale in the Australian context:

> The states have argued that the functions carried out by their offices [abroad] are simply too important to be left to the Commonwealth, which they do not trust to pursue their particular interests with the same vigor. There is also a

realization that, in seeking foreign markets and sources of investment, they are competing not only with foreign countries but also with other states.

Brown, Fry, and Groen (1993: 11) offer the following observations of the behavior of the U.S. states:

> U.S. states as direct international actors are a rather new phenomenon, for prior to the globally induced economic developments . . . the sheer size and domestic opportunities within the U.S. precluded the need for elaborate international strategies. In the 1960s, only three states had opened foreign offices. This number increased to over 25 in the 1970s. Today, 43 of the states have opened over 160 offices abroad to promote trade, investment, tourism, almost three times the level of the early 1980s.

Along similar lines, but more general, Soldatos (1993: 62) notes:

> The globalization of the economy and communications will increase the degree of geographical discontinuity in the interactions of federal units and will favour the constitution of more worldwide functional networks of subnational actors. Federated units are already very active in the world arena, and their paradiplomacy goes increasingly beyond their micro-regional environment (transborder or transregional), reaching out to macro-regional and global spheres of action.

In terms of this regional-international interface, the ongoing European situation is most intriguing. Will the increasing cross-border economic integration lead to a Europe of regions aligned to the EU infrastructure rather than to a Europe of nation-states? What is the nature of the evolutionary dynamic involved in the EU decision to integrate economically through a unified economic space and even a common currency but to defer the process of political deepening? Were political deepening to occur now, it would of necessity revolve around the role of the member nation-states. However, if the existing framework holds sway for a decade or so, the nature of the resulting economic integration (not only its cross-border aspect alluded to earlier but also the evolution of the associated special interests that will be brought to bear at the Brussels level) could well imply a radically different type of political deepening. Presumably, one important factor in terms of how this situation will eventually play out will relate to the manner in which enterprise is organized across the unified European economic space. National governments will be able to exert a greater role under a system of "national champions" in each area of commerce than will be the case if integration proceeds largely in terms of a "Europeanization of enterprise," where communitywide transnationals dominate the economic space, replete with intrafirm transfers of goods and people. In any event, that the regional-international interface in Europe will intensify is not in doubt. What may be in doubt is whether the ultimate political evolution of Europe can proceed independently of what is happening on this economic integration front.

A final point is that causation can also run the other way—from the international to the regional. Policy making is increasingly becoming international and, in many cases, is reverberating back as much on regional economies as on national economies. Much in the way of evidence could be brought to bear on this point, but this chapter will make just one, admittedly glib, comment—namely, that the good burghers of the U.S. northeast now have considerable control over Quebec Hydro, that British Columbia lumber policy must now answer to the citizens of Germany and the United Kingdom, and that Brigitte Bardot has long controlled the Atlantic sealing industry. This situation, too, is part of globalization and the regional-international interface.

International agreements and the division of powers in federal nations

Although the emergence of the regional-international interface points in the direction of greater decentralization in federal systems (and even in unitary states because, for example, two of the "four motors"—namely, Lombardy and Rhône-Alpes—are regions of unitary states), other forces in the integrating global economy work in the opposite direction. The one selected for highlight in this subsection relates to the effect of the proliferation of international agreements on the division of powers in federations.

University of Melbourne's Greg Craven (1993: 11) effectively zeros in on the core issue: "can the central [federal] government, simply through the exercise of its capacity in the field of foreign relations, significantly alter what would otherwise be the constitutional balance of powers?" Craven amplifies as follows:

> On the one hand, allowing a central government free rein to enter into and effectuate any international agreement which it chooses may place the federal units in grave danger of the progressive erosion of their constitutional powers. But to hedge the central power . . . with too many federalist restrictions may hamstring the federation as an international actor. This problem is greatly exacerbated at a time when the expanding scope of international agreements is such that central governments will be subject both to far greater temptations and [to] considerably increased imperatives to use their international capacities to the detriment of their respective federal units.

A full discussion of the manner in which these issues may play out in various federations is well beyond the scope of this chapter. But a few comments, by country, are probably in order:

■ In the United States, it is "manifestly clear that the executive government . . . has a substantially unrestrained power to enter into a full range of international agreements," although the requisite two-thirds concurrence of the Senate "may be understood as imposing some restraint in the interests of federalism upon the central government's use of its power over external affairs" (Craven 1993: 15).

■ In Australia, judicial interpretation of the external affairs power has led to the situation in which "the power is now one of treaty implementation" and to the concern in some quarters that "the federal balance achieved by the Constitution is now at the mercy of the treaty-making powers of the federal executive" (Craven 1993: 22).

■ In Switzerland, the constitution provides that it is "within the sole power of the federation to conclude treaties and alliances" (Craven 1993: 12).

■ In Canada, pursuant to the *Labour Conventions* case in 1937, "while the federal government can enter into any international obligations they wish, they can implement . . . those obligations only as far as they are matters of federal constitutional responsibility" (Wilkinson 1993: 208).

For each of these countries, numerous caveats apply. Moreover, many federations consult widely with subnational governments and other interests in the run-up to major international agreements. And even where the federal government has the constitutional right to use the external affairs–cum–executive power to override the competence of subnational governments, the domestic political climate may not permit it.

As Wilkinson (1993: 203–4) points out, the GATT regulations may be an exception to the earlier comments with respect to Canada:

> Article XXIV.12 of the GATT requires each contracting party to "take such reasonable measures as may be available to it to ensure observance of the provisions" of the GATT by the sub-national authorities within its territory. This is a reasonable and quite acceptable provision. However, in an interpretative note on this article in the draft Uruguay Round final text it adds that "each party is fully responsible" for the observance by sub-nationals of all provisions of the GATT. This is of great concern [to the provinces] because of the possibility of a misinterpretation of the respective authorities of federal and provincial governments in Canada for implementation. The federal government argues that "responsibility" only means "accountable," whereas the provinces are concerned that it may be interpreted as meaning "responsible for acting."

Presumably, these concerns are shared by subnational governments in other federal systems as well. Even decentralists do not get too worked up about certain aspects of the reach of GATT if what is at stake is the removal of discriminatory provincial barriers to the internal economic union. Admittedly, however, in some areas more than internal market issues are at stake.

In terms of creative institutional and constitutional responses to the potential impact of the federal treaty-making authority on the internal division of powers, the clear leader is Germany. As Leonardy (1992) notes, the scope of the resulting proposed amendments to the Basic Law encompasses (a) a clarification of the role of the *Länder* in foreign relations (article 32); (b) a revised federal-*Länder* power-sharing relationship with respect to treaty making with, and the transfer of sovereign functions to, international bodies other than the European Union (article 24); and (c) a new article 23 focusing the federal-*Länder* relationship with respect to the European Union. Although all of these aspects of proposed constitutional architecture are pertinent here, this chapter will focus only on the arrangements relating to the European Union.

In this context, three provisions appear especially important. The first is that "the Treaty on European Union and all its future alterations should, since they represent indirect amendments to the Basic Law, be subject to the same two-thirds majorities required in both Bundestag and Bundesrat for direct amendments to the constitution" (Leonardy 1992: 130). This provision is, of and by itself, a significant safeguard for the *Länder* since the Bundesrat is composed of *Länder* government delegations that vote on the instructions of their respective governments. Beyond this provision, however, there are two other novel features. Leonardy (1992: 131) writes:

> The main controversy in the discussion of the constitutional reforms necessitated by the Maastricht Treaty centered, however, on the aim of the *Länder* to enhance their rights of participation in European secondary legislation in two ways. Firstly and with regard to their influence on internal German policy-making prior to voting in the Council of Ministers, they insisted that Bundesrat comments should be "decisive" and thus binding on the federal government in all matters which have their legal "center of gravity in the legislative competence of the Länder, in the establishment of their administrative authorities, or in their administrative procedures." Secondly, and concerning negotiation and voting in the Council itself, the *Länder* demanded that "the exercise of rights vested in the Federal Republic of Germany as a Member State of the European Union shall be transferred to a representative of the *Länder* nominated by the Bundesrat if the center of gravity of the issue at stake concerns legislative competence of the Länder."

Leonardy hastens to add that these measures were not grounded in any hostility on the part of the *Länder* to the Maastricht Treaty. Rather, "the matter at stake was and remains a straightforward and even natural contest over power-sharing within a federal state which is itself growing into the fully accepted, new federal structure emerging above it" (Leonardy 1992: 132).

It may seem anomalous that such arrangements would arise in what arguably is the most centralized of the mature federations. Part of the explanation may be that because Germany finds itself a federation within a confederalizing superstructure, these issues are more pressing than they are to other federations. Part also may be traceable to the special nature of Germany's upper chamber, which has no counterpart in the other mature federations. Leonardy (1992: 133) hints at yet another explanation—namely, that some version and vision of subsidiarity has always been an integral influence on German federalism, as reflected in Otto von Bismarck's 1869 maxim: the center should not have more power "than is absolutely necessary for the cohesion of the whole and for the effect presented to the outside."

Presumably these German initiatives will receive careful scrutiny from other federations. Whether they are importable in some version into other constitutional systems is, for present purposes, not as important as the fact that the inevitable spread of international trade and integration agreements may play havoc with the existing internal constitutional balance in federal systems. This effect can come about (a) by way of the exercise of the central government's external affairs or executive power, (b) by way of an internal redesign à la Germany, or (c) by way of a combination of the two.

Democracy Deficits and the Process of Global Confederalizing

This section concludes with what is admittedly a highly speculative analysis and one that may relate only peripherally to macro federalism. What triggers the ensuing analysis is the final column under panel f of table 1.1. The thrust of panel f is that globalization can be viewed as the advent of consumer sovereignty (that is, the freer trade and information explosion aspects of globalization have enhanced individuals as consumers). What may be in considerable doubt is whether globalization empowers individuals as citizens. This issue arises because as powers (and sovereignty) travel upward and outward from the nation-state, citizens no longer have direct access to the new institutions that now control important aspects of their lives. And to the extent that "captive rider" circumstances prevail (captive rider in the sense that a country joining a trade bloc may have to sign on to all the existing provisions), citizens may not even have, through their governments, meaningful indirect or confederal access. This resulting lack of congruence between the citizen-voter domain and the domain of decision making has been a theme of the writings of David Held. For example:

> The structure of interlocking political decisions and outcomes, which leaves nation-states unable to control a large variety of resources and forces, and which places nation-states themselves in a position to infringe and impose on others, requires that the notion of a relevant constituency be expanded to incorporate the domains and groups of people significantly affected by such interconnectedness. Democratic autonomy requires, in principle, an expanding framework or federation of democratic states and agencies to embrace the ramifications of decisions and to render them accountable. There are two separate issues here: changing the territorial boundaries of systems of accountability so that those issues which escape control of a nation-state . . . can be brought under better control (a change that would imply, for instance, the shifting of some decisions from a nation-state to an enlarged regional or global framework). Second, it is necessary to articulate territorially delimited polities with the key agencies, associations, and organizations of the international system such that the latter become part of a democratic process—adopting, within their very *modus operandi*, a structure of rules and principles compatible with those of democratic autonomy. In the face of the global system, democracy requires recasting both the nature and scope of territorially delimited polities and the form and structure of the central forces and agencies of international civil society. What is at stake, in sum, is the democratisation of both the states system and the interlocking frameworks of the international civil order. (Held 1991: 165)

Without necessarily buying into this precise conception of the challenge, one recognizes that globalization has undoubtedly triggered *democracy deficits*, to use the European terminology. Moving from confederal to federal governance structures at the international level is obviously one approach to the issue. In EU terms, for example, this approach would imply a popularly elected assembly with decision-making powers related to the full range of EU activities. Although such an arrangement may or may not be in the cards, the general point is that federalizing all supranational arrangements is a most unlikely outcome. If federalizing is unlikely to be the full solution, what other forces can or will step into this breach?

What follows is an admittedly rudimentary and speculative attempt to argue that one answer could well be the harnessing, internationally, of information-empowered citizens. The starting point is the recognition that capital has become the hegemon in this new global economic order. This development is hardly surprising. Not only was mobile capital (or the international private sector as embodied in the transnational corporations) much more able to globalize (in comparison with national government structures, for example) and, therefore, much quicker off the mark in terms of taking advantage of the new institutional regime, but also much of the rationale for the new global order was to privilege capital in this regard. Although economists may well view this state of affairs as appropriate, the fact remains that power in this new order is now tilted sharply in capital's favor. Countervailing forces will arise. Table 1.1 hints that the ongoing process of nation-state confederalizing can in part be viewed as countervail to the internationalization of capital—but only in part because the business of GATT remains business and, in terms of the free trade arrangements, the role of nation-states is to deliver on the agreed-on commitments. Indeed, what complicates the issue in some respects is that citizens can now take their governments to court if the latter do not comply with the provisions of these international commitments or directives. In the United Kingdom, for example, the findings of the European Court of Justice (ECJ) have led to changes in U.K. law on issues as far reaching as sexual discrimination and equal pay. Indeed, appellate courts in the EU member states are now expected to enforce the interpretations of the ECJ. If anything, this situation magnifies the problem, because "national" institutions are, in this sense, now beyond the democratic control of their own citizens. This scenario enhances the need to bring more democracy to the level of these international decision-making or regulatory bodies.

One potential source of countervail comes from the new technoeconomic paradigm itself—namely, the information explosion (panel e of table 1.1). It is possible that concerted, transnational groupings of citizens coalescing around successive issues will emerge as a new policy and institutional force to challenge the property rights bestowed on capital. Initially at least, this process will probably work through influencing individual governments (that is, enhancing the processes of confederalism). But given the increasing returns of the information superhighway and the democratization of information under the new technoeconomic paradigm, the effect is likely to extend even further. As information increasingly flows, from citizen to citizen, over, around, and through political boundaries, the resulting potential for the concerted exercise, internationally, of collective citizen sovereignty may begin to have effects not unlike those associated with the environmental movement.

At one level, all of these points are rather obvious. International policy lobbies are already very powerful. As previously noted, one could argue that in Canada Brigitte Bardot controls the sealing industry, that the residents of northeast United States control the future construction activities of Quebec

Hydro, and that European citizen lobbies are redesigning British Columbia's forest policy. Those developments are only the beginning of the effect that the information explosion will have on policy and, more generally, on governance. The result is an intriguing juxtaposition of policy jurisdictions. The paradiplomacy subsection referred to the "domestication of international politics." The present message is the "internationalization of domestic policy." As an important aside, this latter development implies that some research must be devoted to understanding and assessing the emerging role in the policy formation process of the so-called information superhighway.

But the core of the argument relates to something more fundamental. Nearer to the mark is the fact that over a two-week period in the spring of 1994 Philip Morris appeared before legislative and parliamentary committees in Australia, Canada, and the United States (and perhaps elsewhere as well). The precise issues varied from country to country, but they all touched on the nature and scope of existing copyright and trademark rights. This case is fairly close to an example of international citizen countervail against the deemed international property rights of global capital.

Admittedly, it is not immediately apparent where these transnational citizen coalitions will or could focus their attention. Beyond that example, a list of candidates might include lobbying for some version of a global capital tax, creating pressure for a multination carbon tax, challenging the drug patent laws so as to provide earlier access to generics, and seeking out various avenues for ameliorating the impact on income distribution of the technoeconomic paradigm. However, in reiteration of the underlying point, globalization has so democratized information and, therefore, power that it is unrealistic to expect that citizens would not take up this challenge, particularly given the power disjuncture that has arisen because nation-states have transferred major chunks of sovereignty to international capital.

Note than none of this discussion is meant to be cast in a normative light. Rather, it falls in the realm of positive analysis. In particular, it recognizes as quite natural that capital would be quick off the mark in terms of benefiting from globalization, in part because global capital was a catalyst in aspects of the process. In turn, this has led to an overshooting of the long-term equilibrium in terms of capital hegemony. What does have normative overtones is the suggestion that one of the potentially equilibrating forces is the emergence of information-triggered empowerment of citizens. This suggestion assumes that sovereignty is being transferred upward and outward from nation-states. Perhaps this chapter should have focused on what might happen if some nation-states refuse to allow this transfer of sovereignty. U.S. citizens are finally coming to the recognition that the FTA and NAFTA have, indeed, impinged on their sovereignty, and they are beginning to make a major issue of this concern, with obvious implications for the emerging institutions like the World Trade Organization, let alone for the way in which NAFTA may evolve. The general point is that the supranational institutional-governance space will surely influence the manner and degree to which economic space will be integrated.

No doubt much or all of this discussion may be viewed as either foreign to economics (let alone macro federalism) or the legitimate concern of other disciplines. This view would be a mistake. If one sets aside the particular—perhaps peculiar—angle by which this chapter has arrived at this question, the larger issue must surely be relevant to economists: redesigning aspects of the national and international institutional order as it relates to the new paradigm as well as rethinking the citizen-state relationship. After all, the new paradigm is largely economics driven and economists' methodology, including principal-agent analysis, is clearly flexible enough to make a significant contribution. Indeed, economists are playing an important role on one side of this general area—GATT, free trade agreements, and the like. Should they not broaden themselves a bit to focus as well on some of the larger institutional and even "democracy" implications of the paradigm?

All of this discussion can be phrased differently. Macro federalism, as defined for purposes of the previous sections, relates to those configurations of tax, expenditure, and regulatory assignments on the one hand and to the set of complementary processes on the other hand that serve to promote and enhance the pursuit of various macro goals within federal nations. The message contained in the latter part of the present section is that the underlying principles of federalism—self-rule, shared rule—will, of necessity, be replicated at the supranational level with important implications for the functioning of both the resulting international federal-confederal structures and the existing federations. In effect, the challenge is to write the economic constitution of the integrating global order and to develop consistent political economy provisions or political provisions to complement the economic integration. Implicit in this analysis is the assumption that a macro federal framework can play an important, perhaps pivotal, role in this unfolding process.

Overall Conclusions

The purpose of this chapter was to engage in exploratory research relating to the manner in which federal nations address selected macro policy issues. The data set consisted of the constitutions, institutions, and processes of the five mature federations (Australia, Canada, Germany, Switzerland, and the United States), with occasional reference to the European Union. In terms of the potential output of this exercise, the challenge was essentially twofold: first, at the specific macro policy level, to ascertain whether there are analytical principles or best-practice patterns that merit highlight in terms of how emerging federations ought to address aspects of the assignment of competencies or the process dimension of their respective federations; second, at the more aggregate level, to ascertain whether there are some underlying principles capable of integrating the various parts of the analysis within a consistent macro federalism framework.

Most of this brief concluding section will be devoted to the second challenge: can one meaningfully speak of macro federalism as an integrating analytical concept capable of underpinning some or most of the existing macro policy areas in federal nations? The observations that follow are intended to address aspects of this challenge.

All Economics Is International

Peter Drucker (1993) has asserted that "all economics is now international." This assertion is also the dominant theme in this chapter, although it is couched largely in terms of globalization and the information-knowledge revolution. International trade in goods and capital has long been a key feature of the global economy. But the degree of integration over the recent past is without precedent, particularly as the result of the information-related services explosion, which, among other things, has dramatically reduced the effects of both time and distance on economic activity. Thus, to the extent that there is an integrating factor in this chapter, it surely is that policy areas have to be rethought from the perspective that all economics is international.

Several significant implications derive from this observation. One is that a good number of policy areas that have typically been viewed in the context of a national economy must now be revisited in an increasingly international context. Social policy is an obvious example.

A second implication is that while that generalization applies to all nations, it has a special message for federal nation-states. With some degree of misrepresentation, the division of powers in most federal systems tends to assign the obvious international areas to the federal government and matters of a more local level to subnational governments. The thrust of the focus on globalization is that some of these erstwhile local or regional issues are becoming internationalized. In part, at least, this conception was captured in the discussion about the regional-international interface, or what could be called the "glocalization" of economic activity. In other words, whereas subnational governments will still have to act or legislate locally, they will now have to do so in light of global considerations.

The third implication follows naturally from the second, and it relates to the fiscal federalism literature. One of the motivations for this chapter was to ascertain whether the area labeled *macro federalism* could ever mirror the systematic body of literature that has come to be referred to as *fiscal federalism*. What the focus on globalization reveals is that fiscal federalism itself probably has to be rethought as a result of the internationalization of economics. Fiscal federalism's focus on fiscal equity and (fiscal) efficiency—particularly the former—typically takes place within the confines of a closed economy. One can cast this idea in the context of the Canadian case. Are the lessons from applying a fiscal federalism framework to an east-west transfer system within an east-west trading system the same as the lessons from viewing an east-west transfer system within a north-south trading system? Probably not. It seems, therefore, that one has either to incorporate a macro or open-economy growth objective to accompany equity and efficiency in the fiscal federalism literature or to embark on a new field called macro federalism that over time will progressively encroach on the traditional domain of fiscal federalism.

In this sense, therefore, one can probably make a case that there is an integrating feature to macro federalism. However, analytically it may not be all that different from what might be referred to as open-economy macroeconomics applied to federal systems.

Federalism as Structure versus Federalism as Process

Much of the emphasis in the previous subsection was on the "macro" rather than on the "federalism" side of macro federalism. Analytically, "macro" is arguably the easier side of the equation. In terms of at least some of the issues discussed herein, what is appropriate for Quebec as a province may not differ that much from what would be appropriate were Quebec an independent country. In other words, there is a sort of macro determinism to many issues that is driven by the particular economic and cultural geography or milieu in which the particular jurisdiction finds itself.

However, the reality is that regional economies invariably find themselves embedded within political structures that may or may not allow them to capitalize on their potential comparative advantage. In a sense, therefore, what could result is a political disequilibrium. For example, would Scotland be better off severing its ties to the United Kingdom and pursuing a more independent future by attaching itself to the EU infrastructure? Although this question is intended to be rhetorical, the implicit assumptions underlying it are, nonetheless, very important—the effects of globalization and the information-knowledge revolution on the one hand and the emergence of supranational infrastructures on the other hand are likely to feed back to political configurations. Arguably, this is what the evolution of Europe, from the Treaty of Rome to the Treaty of Maastricht, is all about.

Returning to federalism, this analysis leads to at least two generalizations. The first is that federal systems are continually evolving in response to these macro challenges. The most obvious aspect of this process is that the assignment of competencies in four of the five mature federations occurred a long time ago. In turn, what this aspect means is that these federal structures had to evolve as external circumstances (such as globalization) altered the environment within which these constitutions operated. One solution would be to amend the constitution. A second accommodating route would be judicial interpretation. With respect to the court's role in preserving and promoting the internal economic union, one cannot but be impressed with the broad powers that the U.S. Supreme Court has attached to the interstate commerce clause. It was not always so. Relatedly, now that Canada is part of NAFTA, almost surely the Canadian Supreme Court will also begin to expand the sweep of the federal trade and commerce power. Although both of these routes—particularly the latter—have played a role in the evolution of powers in federations, there is overwhelming evidence in this chapter that most of the accommodation over time has come about through the political rather than the formal constitutional route. As the title of this subsection indicates, this route is "federalism as process." Given that the provinces still wield all the power in terms of the operations of the Canadian securities industry, it is clear that "federalism as process" has generated an effective national securities market. Carl Friedrich's important observation is worth recalling in this context:

> [F]ederalism should not be seen only as a static pattern or design, characterized by a particular and precisely fixed division of powers between government levels. Federalism is also and perhaps primarily the process . . . of adopting joint policies and making joint decisions on joint problems (cited in Bastien 1981: 48).

Although there are probably a large number of factors that will trigger this process dimension of federalism, it is probably fair to claim that over the recent past and no doubt for the foreseeable future, the principal catalyst will be globalization and the information-knowledge revolution (that is, macro factors).

In terms of emerging federations, the obvious way to accommodate the challenges of macro federalism is through the assignment of competencies. In other words, new federations have the ability to design their constitutions in a way that makes them consistent with the challenges of the 21st century. But if the past is any guide, this ability is not enough. The constitutions must be capable of evolving in response to future challenges. An iron-clad assignment of taxing, expenditure, and regulatory powers designed to capture the reality of 1995 will almost surely be outmoded by, say, 2010. In this sense, "federalism as process" will always be an integral component of a modern federal nation-state.

In turn, however, this problem complicates any attempt to generate principles or best-practice approaches to macro federalism, because at any given point in time the achievement of an appropriate macro policy in a specific area can come from either structure or process.

Thus far, the theme in this subsection has been that constitutions are to an important degree endogenous. In other words, they will evolve in response to the dictates of macro federalism. For example, had Canada and the United States adopted each other's constitutions in 1789 and 1867, respectively, almost surely Canada would still be the more decentralized federation. In this sense, the constitution is indeed endogenous. But this definition of *constitution* or *structure* is probably too narrow. Suppose that the United States had only 10 states and that Canada had 50 provinces. In that case, surely the United States would be the more decentralized federation. At this deeper level, structure clearly does matter.

Thus, the second generalization is that the principles of macro federalism have to be filtered through what, for lack of a better term, may be called the *institutional configuration* of federal systems, where institutional configuration incorporates both the elements of constitutional-institutional design and the characteristics (cultural, economic, geographic, and so forth) of the subnational governments. Essentially, this approach highlights the subject matter of the section titled "Globalization, Confederalism, and the Information Revolution"—namely, variations on the federal principle. Thus, we can categorize federal systems in terms of the degree of decentralization; in terms of the manner in which the subnational governments are represented in the central government (that is, interstate or intrastate federalism and varieties thereof); in terms of the operational relationship between the two levels of government (that is, administrative federalism versus legislative federalism); and so on. When some combination of these characteristics is overlain on a set of subnational entities, the end result is, as noted, an institutional configuration. Consider Germany. One of the preeminent features of German federalism is the pursuit of "uniformity of living conditions," as outlined in article 72(2) of the Basic Law. Given this provision, one could argue that the institutional configuration of German federalism is optimally designed (at least before unification). However, it would be inconceivable to overlay such a constitution on the Canadian provinces, which are so culturally, economically, and geographically distinct. In other words, though administrative federalism may be appropriate for Germans, legislative federalism is probably essential for Canadians.

These configurations clearly matter a great deal in terms of implementing the precepts of macro federalism. As seen in the section titled "Internal Economic Integration," promoting an internal economic union is relatively easy in Germany, given that most legislation is federal. In other words, the German constitutional structure is adequate to the task of securing an internal economic union. This is not true in legislative federalisms such as Canada, where creative processes must accompany the constitutional architecture in order to secure the internal economic union.

But administrative federations do not always make things easier. For example, the exercise of competitive federalism, as well as the pursuit of subnational comparative advantage by following aspects of the regional-international interface, comes much more naturally to legislative federations.

One can take this analysis further by questioning whether the institutional configurations of federal nations are likely to remain stable in the face of the emerging dictates of globalization and the information-knowledge revolution. Passing reference has already been made to the situations of Belgium, Quebec, and Scotland. Australia poses an intriguing case. The subnational units are, geographically at least, sufficiently distinct that one would have thought that a decentralized legislative federalism would have been appropriate. Yet the Australian federation is, in key aspects, highly centralized and is underpinned by a sense of egalitarianism that corresponds to the "uniformity of living conditions" that underpins the German federation. Not surprisingly, constitutional issues loom large in Australia as the country approaches its 100th anniversary as a federation, and in this context Macphee (1993), for example, argues that Australia should become a unitary state. Courchene (1995b) takes the other view—namely, that globalization will push Australia in the opposite direction, toward a more decentralized federation. The argument is simply that the manner in which Perth and West Australia are likely to integrate into the West Pacific will be quite different than the manner in which Sydney and New South Wales will integrate with their principal trading partners.

Although this argument suggests that the forces of globalization may have an effect on the institutional configuration of federal states, it is nonetheless the case that at any point in time macro federalism has to take these institutional configurations as given. As already noted, this situation complicates the manner in which the principles of macro federalism will be applied across federations. However, it is not evident that this test differs from the existing challenges to fiscal federalism, given that the institutional configurations relative to fiscal federalism also differ markedly across federations.

All Nations Are Now Federal

In the penultimate section, the analysis broadened substantially to reflect the fact that the federal principle is now becoming a dominant institutional principle at the supranational level. Just as all economics is now international, so too all economic relations between governments are increasingly federal (or confederal). Because this territory has adequately, albeit speculatively, been covered, only two observations are necessary. The first is fairly obvious: most macro federalism issues addressed in this chapter have a counterpart at the international level. The second is potentially the more important for the present analysis: many of these macro federalism issues are emanating from—or at least given higher profile by—the principles and practices at the supranational level (such as the European Union). For example, issues relating to central bank structure, the promotion of the internal economic union, and the borrowing power of subnational governments can now draw on an extensive literature at the supranational level. Likewise, the relevant experiences of federal nations with respect to these issues are now informing the analysis at the supranational level. To a degree at least, one of the objectives of this chapter was to attempt to integrate these two bodies of literature.

Notes

1. These subsections are adopted, verbatim in places, from Courchene (1994b).
2. Actually, the trade-account deficit for the Atlantic region vis-à-vis the rest of Canada was in excess of Can$6 billion in 1984, for example, so the assumption is entirely realistic.
3. For further details on this issue, as well as on ways in which Canada's equalization system could be changed to embody more appropriate incentives, see Courchene (1994b).
4. Australia may have been an exception during the period in which the Australian Commonwealth borrowed on behalf of the states.
5. Although Quebec is an equalization-receiving province, it is also large (it represents more than 20 percent of Canada's population) and well diversified. Moreover, with its own separate personal income tax and its expanded set of expenditure functions (relative to the rest of the provinces), Quebec surely qualifies as the most independent subnational jurisdiction in any federal system in terms of revenue and expenditure powers. Finally, until recently, the strength of Quebec Hydro had a lot to do with maintaining the province's credit rating.

References

Bank of Canada. 1991. "Opening Statement by John Crow, Governor of the Bank of Canada, before the House Standing Committee on Finance." Bank of Canada, Ottawa, November 19.

Barro, Robert J., and Xavier Sala-I-Martin. 1991. "Convergence across States and Regions." *Brookings Papers on Economic Activity* 1: 107–58.

Bastien, Richard. 1981. *Federalism and Decentralization: Where Do We Stand?* Ottawa: Ministry of Supply and Services.

Bell, Daniel. 1987. "The World and the United States in 2013." *Daedalus* 116 (3): 1–31.

Bird, Richard. 1994. "A Comparative Perspective on Federal Finance." In *The Future of Fiscal Federalism*, ed. Keith Banting, Douglas Brown, and Thomas Courchene, 293–322. Queen's University, School of Policy Studies, Kingston, Canada.

Blanchard, Olivier Jean, and Lawrence F. Katz. 1992. "Regional Evolutions." *Brookings Papers on Economic Activity* 1: 1–62.

Bomfim, Antulio, and Anwar Shah. 1991. "Macroeconomic Management and the Division of Powers in Brazil." Policy Research Working Paper 567, World Bank, Washington, DC.

Breton, Albert. 1985. "Supplementary Statement." In *Report of the Royal Commission on the Economic Union and Development Prospects for Canada*, vol. 3, 486–526. Ottawa: Ministry of Supply and Services.

Brown, Douglas, Earl Fry, and James Groen. 1993. "States and Provinces in the International Economy Project." In *States and Provinces in the International Economy*, ed. Douglas Brown and Earl Fry, 1–22. Kingston, Canada: Queen's University, Institute of Intergovernmental Relations.

Buiter, Willem, Giancarlo Corsetti, and Nouriel Roubini. 1993. "Maastricht's Fiscal Rules." *Economic Policy* 16 (April): 57–100.

Commission of the European Communities. 1993. "Stable Money—Sound Finances." European Economy 53, Commission of the European Communities, Brussels.

Courchene, Thomas J. 1992. *Rearrangements: The Courchene Papers*. Oakville, ON: Mosaic Press.

———. 1994a. "Globalization: The Regional/International Interface." Luncheon address to the 41st North American Meetings of the Regional Science Association International, Niagara Falls, ON, November 17–20.

———. 1994b. *Social Canada in the Millennium*. Toronto, ON: C. D. Howe Institute.

———. 1995a. "Macrofederalism: Some Exploratory Research Relating to Theory and Practice." Monograph prepared for the Policy Research Department, World Bank, Washington, DC.

———. 1995b. "Two Cheers for Australian Federalism." Centre for Comparative Constitutional Studies, Melbourne.

Craven, Greg. 1993. "Federal Constitutions and External Relations." In *Foreign Relations and Federal States*, ed. Brian Hocking, 7–26. London and New York: Leicester University Press.

Cukierman, Alex. 1992. *Central Bank Strategy, Credibility, and Independence: Theory and Evidence*. London: MIT Press.

Drucker, Peter. 1993. *Post-Capitalist Society*. New York: Harper Business.

Eichengreen, Barry. 1993. "European Monetary Unification." *Journal of Economic Literature* 31 (3): 1321–57.

Elazar, Daniel. 1994. "Is This the Age for the Revival of Confederation?" Centre for the Study of Federalism, Temple University, Philadelphia, PA.

Freeman, Christopher, and Carlota Perez. 1988. "Structural Crisis of Adjustment: Business Cycles." In *Technical Change and Economic Theory*, ed. Giovanni Dosi, Christopher Freeman, Richard Nelson, and Luc Soete, 38–66. London: Pinter.

Goodhart, Charles P. E., and Stephen Smith. 1993. "Stabilization." In *European Economy* 5: 417–55.

Hayes, John. 1982. *Economic Mobility in Canada: A Comparative Analysis*. Ottawa: Ministry of Supply and Services.

Held, David. 1991. "Democracy, the Nation State, and the Global System." *Economy and Society* 20 (2): 138–72.

Leonardy, Uwe. 1992. "Federation and Länder in German Foreign Relations: Power-Sharing in Treaty Making and European Affairs." *German Politics* 1 (3): 119–35.

Leslie, Peter. 1991. *The European Community: A Model for Canada?* Ottawa: Ministry of Supply and Services.

Lipsey, Richard G. 1994. "Markets, Technological Change, and Economic Growth." *Pakistan Development Review* 33 (4): 327–52.

Macphee, Ian. 1993. "Politics, Economics, and Constitutional Reform." Opening address to the conference on Challenges to Australia's Second Century of Federalism, Griffith University, Queensland, Australia.

McKenna, Frank. 1993. "Lifelong Learning at Work." Keynote address to the 62nd Annual Couchiching Conference, Orillia, ON, August 5–8.

Musgrave, Richard. 1959. *The Theory of Public Finance*. New York: McGraw-Hill.

Ohmae, Kenichi. 1990. *The Borderless World: Power and Strategy in the Interlinked Economy*. New York: Harper Business.

Paquet, Gilles. 1995. "Institutional Evolution in an Information Age." *Technology, Information, and Public Policy*, ed. Thomas J. Courchene, 197–220. Kingston, ON: John Deutsch Institute for the Study of Economic Policy, Queen's University.

Ravenhill, John. 1990. "Australia." In *Federalism and International Relations: The Role of Subnational Units*, ed. Hans J. Michelmann and Panayotis Soldatos, 76–123. Oxford, U.K.: Clarendon Press.

Reich, Robert. 1991. *The Work of Nations*. New York: Alfred A. Knopf.

Soldatos, Panayotis. 1993. "Cascading Subnational Paradiplomacy in an Interdependent and Transnational World." In *States and Provinces in the International Economy*, ed. Douglas Brown and Earl Fry, 45–64. Berkeley: University of California, Institute of Governmental Studies Press.

Springate, David. 1973. *Regional Incentives and Private Investment*. Montreal: C. D. Howe Institute.

Thurow, Lester. 1981. "The Productivity Problem." In *Policies for Stagflation: Focus on Supply*, vol. 2, ed. Ontario Economic Council, 11–34. Toronto: Ontario Economic Council.

Wilkinson, Derrick. 1993. "International Trade Policy and the Role of Non-central Governments: The Recent Canadian Experiences." In *Foreign Relations and Federal States*, ed. Brian Hocking, 202–10. London and New York: Leicester University Press.

Globalization, the Information Revolution, and Emerging Imperatives for Rethinking Fiscal Federalism

ANWAR SHAH

Globalization and the information revolution are profoundly influencing economic governance in both the industrial and the industrializing world. Globalization has lifted millions of people out of poverty, and the information revolution has brought about a degree of citizen empowerment and activism in state affairs that is unparalleled in history. They have also acted as catalysts for reshuffling government functions within and beyond nation-states (Castells 1998; Courchene 2001; Friedman 1999). Because of globalization, it is increasingly apparent that "nation-states are too small to tackle large things in life and too large to address small things" (Bell 1987: 13–14). In other words, nation-states are gradually losing control of some of their customary areas of authority and regulation, including macroeconomic policy, corporate taxation, external trade, environment policy, telecommunications, and financial transactions. Globalization is also making small open economies vulnerable to the whims of large hedge funds and polarizing the distribution of income in favor of skilled workers and regions with lower skills and access to information, thus widening income disparities within nations while improving the levels of incomes. Because of the information revolution, governments have less ability to control the flow of goods and services, ideas, and cultural products. The twin forces of globalization and the information revolution are also strengthening localization. They are empowering local governments and "beyond-government" service providers, such as neighborhood associations; nongovernmental, nonprofit, and for-profit organizations; self-help groups; and networks, to exercise a broader role in improving economic and social outcomes at the local level through greater connectivity to markets and resources elsewhere. Localization is leading to citizen empowerment in some areas while simultaneously strengthening local elites in others. Courchene (1993, 2001; see also chapter 1 of this volume) has termed the overall effect of these changes *glocalization*, which implies the growing roles of global regimes, local governments, and beyond-government entities and the changing roles of national and state governments in an interconnected world.

This chapter analyzes the potentials and perils associated with the effect of these mega changes on governance structure in the 21st century. The chapter reflects on the governance implications of globalization and the information revolution and draws inferences for the divisions of power in multicentered governance. It highlights emerging challenges and local responses to those challenges. A discussion of policy options to deal with this regional economic divide within nations follows the analysis. The final section presents a new vision of multicentered governance in which governmental and intergovernmental institutions are restructured to reassert the role of citizens as governors.

Governance Implications of Globalization and the Information Revolution

Globalization represents the transformation of the world into a shared space through global links in economics, politics, technology, communications, and law.[1] This global interconnectedness means that events in one part of the world can profoundly influence the rest of the world. Such new links introduce growing decoupling of production in manufacturing and services from location, thereby increasing the permeability of borders and diminishing the influence of national policy instruments. Increasing internationalization of production has decoupled firms from the resource endowments of any single nation. Drucker (1986: 21) noted three fundamental decouplings of the global economy (see also Courchene 1995b, 2001):

■ The primary sector has become uncoupled from the industrial economy.
■ In the industrial sector itself, production has become uncoupled from employment.
■ Capital movements rather than trade in goods and services have become the engine and the driving force of the world economy.

   As globalization marches on, it is introducing a mega change that exposes the fragility of existing systems of global governance. It is adversely affecting national welfare states that link incentives to national production. The sheer magnitude of this social and economic change gives governments and individuals difficulty in coping with its consequences, especially those nations and individuals who suffer a reversal of fortune as a result of this change. The following sections discuss the implications of this mega change for national governance.

Reorientation of the Nation-State, Emergence of Supranational Regimes, and Strengthening of Localization

Globalization of economic activity poses special challenges to constitutional assignment within nations. Strange (1996: 4) argues that "the impersonal forces of world markets . . . are now more powerful than the states to whom ultimate political authority over society and economy is supposed to belong. . . . [T]he declining authority of states is reflected in growing diffusion of authority to other institutions and associations, and to local and regional bodies." More simply, nation-states are fast losing control of some of their traditional areas of authority and regulation, such as macroeconomic policy, external trade, competition policy, telecommunications, and financial transactions. National governments are experiencing diminished ability to regulate or control the flow of goods and services, ideas, and cultural products. For example, the East Asian financial crisis manifested behavior on the part of financial institutions and hedge funds that would have been subject to regulatory checks within nation-states. The loans made in the precrisis period by banking institutions in industrial countries to Indonesian financial institutions with insufficient collateral and the role of large hedge funds in destabilizing national currencies serve as striking examples of practices that would not have been permitted within a nation-state (see Whalley 1999).

Similarly, enhanced mobility of capital limits governments' ability to tax capital incomes, especially given the fierce tax competition to attract foreign direct investment that exists in most developing countries. Taxation of capital income is also increasingly constrained by governments' inability to trace cross-border transactions. For example, the government of Japan would have difficulty taxing the income of a stockbroker who trades U.K. securities on the Brussels stock exchange. Opportunities are also expanding for multinational corporations to indulge in transfer pricing to limit their tax liabilities. Although Internet commerce has exploded, bringing those activities within tax reach is a difficult task even for industrial countries. Thus, the ability of governments to finance public goods—especially those of a redistributive nature—may be impaired because governmental access to progressive income taxes (that is, corporate and personal income taxes) is reduced while access to general consumption taxes (valued added taxes, or VATs) is improved with economic liberalization and global integration. Possible erosion of the taxing capacity of governments through globalization and tax competition might be considered a welcome change by citizens of countries with a poor record of public sector performance in providing public services, as is the case in most developing countries.

Globalization implies that not much is "overseas" any longer and that "homeless" transnational corporations can circumvent traditional host- or home-country regulatory regimes. These difficulties are paving the way for the emergence of specialized institutions of global governance, such as the World Trade Organization and the Global Environmental Facility, with many more to follow—especially institutions to regulate information technology, satellite communications, and international financial transactions. For countries facing economic crises and seeking international assistance, even in areas of traditional economic policy, the power of international development finance institutions to influence local decision making is on the rise. Globalization is therefore gradually unbundling the relationship between sovereignty, territoriality, and state power (see Castells 1997; Ruggie 1993). This transformation implies that governance and authority will be diffused to multiple centers within and beyond nation-states. Thus, nation-states will be confederalizing in coming years and relinquishing responsibilities in those areas to supranational institutions.

The Information Revolution and Citizen Empowerment

With the information revolution, "the ability to collect, analyse, and transmit data, and to coordinate activities worldwide has increased massively, while the costs of doing so have fallen dramatically" (Lipsey 1997: 76). Firms now have the ability to "slice up the value added chain" (Krugman 1995: 333) to gain international competitiveness. The information revolution empowers citizens to access, transmit, and transform information in ways that governments find themselves powerless to block, and in the process, it undermines authoritative controls. It also constrains the ability of governments to withhold information from their citizens. Globalization of information—satellite television, Internet, phone, and fax—serves also to enhance citizens' awareness of their rights, obligations, options, and alternatives and strengthens demands both for devolution (power to the people) and localization of decision making. Consumer sovereignty and citizen empowerment through international coalitions on specific issues work as a counterweight to global capital. The influence of such coalitions is especially remarkable on environmental issues such as building large dams and discouraging the sealing industry (Courchene 2001).

Consumer Sovereignty and Democracy Deficit

In the emerging borderless world economy, the interests of residents as citizens are often at odds with their interests as consumers. Internationalization of production empowers them as consumers because performance standards are set by the market rather than by bureaucrats. However, it disenfranchises them as citizen-voters because their access to decision making is further curtailed as decision centers in both public and private sectors move beyond the nation-state, thereby creating a democracy deficit. For example, a citizen in a globalized economy has no direct input into vital decisions affecting his or her well-being. Such decisions are made at the headquarters of supranational agencies and regimes such as the International Monetary Fund, the World Bank, and the World Trade Organization or at transnational corporations such as Coca-Cola and McDonald's. Similarly, as noted by Courchene (2001), the European Union Council of Ministers issues hundreds of directives binding on nation-states and their citizens. Friedman (1999: 161) writes, "When all politics is local, your vote matters. But when power shifts to . . . transnational spheres, there are no elections and there is no one to vote for." In securing their interests as consumers in the world economy, individuals are, therefore, increasingly seeking localization and regionalization of public decision making to better safeguard their interests. To respond to these developments, Castells (1997: 303–5) has argued that national governments will shed some sovereignty to become part of the global order or network of governance and that "the central functions of the nation-state will become those of providing legitimacy for and ensuring the accountability of supranational and national governance mechanisms."

Internationalization of Cities and Regions

With greater mobility of capital and loosening of the regulatory environment for foreign direct investment, local governments, as providers of infrastructure-related services, may be more appropriate channels for attracting such investment than are national governments. As borders become more porous, cities are expected to replace countries in transnational economic alliances in the same way that people across Europe are already discovering that national governments have diminishing relevance in their lives. People are increasingly more inclined to link their identities and allegiances to cities and regions. For example, the Alpine Diamond alliance, which links Lyon with Geneva and Turin, has become a symbol for one of Europe's most ambitious efforts to break the confines of the nation-state and to shape a new political and economic destiny (Courchene 1995b, 2001).

Knowledge and International Competitiveness

With mobility of capital and other inputs, skills rather than resource endowments increasingly determine international competitiveness. Skilled labor, especially in "symbolic-analytic" services,[2] qualifies to be treated as capital rather than as labor. Courchene (1995b) argues that for resources to remain important, they must embody knowledge or high-value-added techniques. These developments imply that even resource-rich economies must make a transformation to an economy based on human capital (the so-called knowledge-based economy) and that social policy is no longer distinguishable from economic policy. However, education and training are typically a subnational government responsibility. Therefore, this responsibility needs to be realigned by giving the national government a greater role in skills enhancement. The new economic environment also polarizes the distribution of income in favor of skilled workers, thereby accentuating income inequalities and possibly wiping out the lower-middle-income classes. Because national governments may not have the means to deal with this social policy fallout, subnational governments working in tandem with national governments may have to devise strategies to deal with the emerging crises in social policy.

A Potential Source of Conflict within Nations

International trade agreements typically embody social and environmental policy provisions, but these policies are usually the responsibility of subnational governments. These agreements represent an emerging area of conflict among different levels of government as national decisions in foreign relations affect the balance of power within nations. To avoid these conflicts, these agreements must, to the extent that they embody social and local environmental policy provisions, be subject to ratification by subnational governments, as is currently the practice in Canada.

Reorienting the State as a Counterweight to Globalization

The progress of globalization has created a void in the regulatory environment and has weakened the ability of small open economies to deal with external shocks (Rodrik 1997a, 1997b). Such external shocks typically lead to major disruptive influences on social safety nets, income distribution, and the incidence of poverty, as witnessed recently in the East Asian crisis. This social and economic disruption leads to enhanced demand for public spending, especially for social protection and redistribution. Globalization also empowers skilled workers to command a greater premium. Courchene (1993, 2001) has argued that the premium on skilled workers will result in the wages of unskilled workers falling to a "global maximum" wage rate as such workers are replaced by cheaper workers elsewhere. Firms may resort to "social dumping" (that is, to reducing income security and social safety net benefits to retain international competitiveness). Rodrik's (1998) empirical work involving countries of the Organisation for Economic Co-operation and Development provides some support for this view. Rodrik finds that economic liberalization is positively associated with public social security and welfare expenditures. With increased globalization, greater social security and welfare expenditures must be made by the public sector to maintain social cohesion (see Rodrik 1997a, 1997b). The widening gap between the incomes of skilled employees and those of unskilled workers has the potential to create bipolarized incomes and to make the lower-middle-income class disappear. Thus, Rodrik (1997a) has warned that the resulting social disintegration will ultimately erode the domestic consensus in favor of open markets to a point where one might see a global resurgence of protectionism. Some reversals on economic liberalization were observed in response to recent financial crises in several countries. Some governments of developing countries have attempted to dampen these shocks by introducing capital controls (for example, Malaysia) or by attempting to strengthen social safety nets with international assistance (for example, Indonesia and Thailand). The role of supranational agencies in dealing with competition policy, regulating short-term capital movements, and overseeing the activities of hedge funds is currently under debate.

The information revolution may allow national governments to be more responsive to the needs of their citizens and to limit demands for decentralization. The information revolution is leading to a decrease in transaction costs and is therefore lowering the costs of correcting for information asymmetries and of writing and enforcing better contracts (see Eid 1996). Hart (1995) has argued that in such a world, organizational form is of lesser consequence and that therefore the need for decentralized institutions is diminished.

In conclusion, globalization by no means implies a demise of the nation-state; rather, globalization implies a reorientation of the nation-state to deal with the more complex governance structure of an interconnected world. Leaders in some countries might even visualize a more activist state role in smoothing the wheels of global capital markets to deal with social and economic policy fallouts, as experienced in East Asia.

Localization

A large and growing number of countries are reexamining the roles of various levels of government and their partnership with the private sector and civil society to create governments that work and serve their people.[3] The overall thrust of these changes manifests a trend toward either devolution (empowering people) or localization (decentralization).

Localization of authority has proved to be a controversial proposition. It is perceived both (a) as a solution to problems such as a dysfunctional public sector, a lack of voice, and exit by people and (b) as a source of new problems, such as capture by local elites, aggravation of macroeconomic management caused by lack of fiscal discipline, and perverse fiscal behavior by subnational units. Conceptual difficulties arise in choosing the right balance of power among various orders of government, as discussed in Shah (1994) and Boadway, Roberts, and Shah (1994). Beyond these conceptual issues, a number of practical considerations bear on the quest for balance within a nation. They include the level of popular participation in general elections, feudal politics, civil service culture and incentives, governance and accountability structure, and capacities of local governments.

Emerging Jurisdictional Realignments: Glocalization

The debate on globalization and localization and the growing level of dissatisfaction with public sector performance are forcing a rethinking of assignment issues and forcing a jurisdictional realignment in many countries. Box 2.1 presents a newer federalism perspective on the assignment of responsibilities by taking into account the considerations noted previously. Functions such as regulation of financial transactions, international trade, the global environment, and international migration have gradually passed upward (centralized) beyond nation-states; some subnational functions, such as training, are coming under greater central government inputs (centralization); and local functions are being decentralized to local governments and "beyond-government" local entities through enhanced participation by the civil society and the private sector. In developing countries, rethinking these arrangements has led to gradual and piecemeal decentralization of responsibilities for local public services to lower levels in a small but growing number of countries. The development and strengthening of institutional arrangements for the success of decentralized policies have significantly lagged. Strengthening of local capacity to purchase or deliver local services has received only limited attention. Even strengthening of the central- and intermediate-level functions required for the success of this realignment has not always materialized. In fact, in some countries, decentralization is motivated largely by

---

BOX 2.1   Emerging Rearrangements of Government Assignments: Glocalization

Beyond nation-states: Regulation of financial transactions, corporate taxation, international trade, the global environment, telecommunications, international standards, international migration, surveillance of governance conditions, global security and risk management, transnational production, investment and technology transfer, combating of money laundering, corruption, pandemics, and terrorism.

   Centralization: Social and environmental policy through international agreements, skills enhancement for international competitiveness, social safety nets, oversight, and technical assistance to subnational governments.

   Regionalization, localization, and privatization: All regional and local functions.

Source: Shah 1998a.

a desire to shift the budget deficit and associated debt burdens to subnational governments.

Emerging Governance Structure in the 21st Century

Rearrangements taking place in the world today embody diverse features of supranationalization, centralization, provincialization, and localization. Nevertheless, the vision of a governance structure that is slowly taking hold indicates a shift from unitary constitutional structures in a majority of countries to federal or confederal constitutions. This shift implies that the world is gradually moving from a centralized structure to a globalized and localized (glocalized) one. In such a world, the role of the central government would change from that of a managerial authority to a leadership role in a multicentered government environment. The culture of governance is also slowly changing from a bureaucratic to a participatory mode of operation, from a command-and-control model to one of accountability for results, from being internally dependent to being competitive and innovative, from being closed and slow to being open and quick, and from being intolerant of risk to allowing freedom to fail or succeed. Past global financial crises have hampered this change, but with improved macro stability, the new vision of governance is gradually taking hold in the 21st century (see table 2.1). Nevertheless, in many developing countries, this vision may take a long time to materialize because of political and institutional difficulties.[4]

Emerging Imperatives for Rethinking Fiscal Federalism

Fiscal federalism is concerned with economic decision making in a federal system of government where public sector decisions are made at various government levels.[5] Federal countries differ a great deal in their choices about the character of fiscal federalism—specifically, about how fiscal powers are allocated among various tiers and what the associated fiscal arrangements are. For example, Brazil, Canada, and Switzerland are highly decentralized federations, whereas Australia, Germany, Malaysia, and Spain are relatively centralized. Allocation of fiscal powers among federal members may also be asymmetric. For example, some members may be less equal (enjoy less autonomy because of special circumstances) than others, as in the case of Jammu and Kashmir in India and Chechnya in the Russian Federation. Alternatively, some members may be treated as more equal than others, as in the case of Sabah and Sarawak in Malaysia and Quebec in

TABLE 2.1 Governance Structure: 20th versus 21st Century

20th century	21st century
Unitary	Federal or confederal
Centralized	Globalized and localized
Center that manages	Center that leads
Citizens as agents, subjects, clients, and consumers	Citizens as governors and principals
Bureaucratic	Participatory
Command and control	Responsive and accountable
Internally dependent	Competitive
Closed and slow	Open and quick
Intolerance of risk	Freedom to fail or succeed
Focus on government	Focus on governance with interactive direct democracy
Competitive edge for resource-based economies	Competitive edge for human capital–based economies
Federalism as a tool for coming together or holding together	Global collaborative federalism with a focus on network governance and reaching out
Residuality principle, ultra vires, "Dillon's rule"	Community governance principle, subsidiarity principle, home- or self-rule and shared rule
Limited but expanding role of global regimes with democracy deficits	Wider role of global regimes and networks with improved governance and accountability
Emerging federal prominence in shared rule	Leaner but caring federal government with an enhanced role in education, training, and social protection
Strong state (province) role	Ever-diminishing economic relevance of states (provinces) and tugs-of-war to retain relevance
Diminishing role of local government	Pivotal role of local government as the engine of economic growth, primary agent of citizens, gatekeeper of shared rule, facilitator of network governance; wider role of "beyond government" entities
Tax and expenditure centralization with conditional grants (with input conditionality) to finance subnational expenditures	Tax and expenditure decentralization with fiscal capacity equalization and output-based national minimum standards grants

Sources: Author's representation, based on Courchene 2001; Shah 1998a, 2002, 2003, 2007a, 2007b, 2007c.

Canada. Or a federal system may give members a choice to be unequal or more equal, such as the Canadian opting-in and opting-out alternatives, Spanish agreements with breakaway regions, and European Union treaty exceptions for Denmark and the United Kingdom. Further fiscal arrangements resulting from these choices are usually subject to periodic review and redefinition to adapt to changing circumstances within and beyond nations. In Canada, the law mandates such a periodic review (the sunset clause), whereas in other federal countries, changes may occur simply as a result of how courts interpret various constitutional provisions and laws (as in Australia and the United States) or through various government orders (as in the majority of federal countries). As noted earlier, in recent years, these choices have come under significant additional strain from the great changes arising from the information revolution and the emergence of a new borderless world economy. The following paragraphs highlight a few important common challenges resulting from division of fiscal powers and emerging local responses in federal countries.

Division of Fiscal Powers

The information revolution and globalization are posing special challenges to constitutional assignment within nations. The information revolution, by letting the sun shine on government operations, empowers citizens to demand greater accountability from their governments. Globalization and the information revolution represent a gradual shift to supranational regimes and local governance. In adapting to this world, various orders of governments in federal systems are feeling growing tension to reposition their roles to retain relevance.

   One continuing source of tension among various orders of government is vertical fiscal gaps, or the mismatch between revenue means and expenditure needs at lower orders of government. Vertical fiscal gaps and revenue autonomy at subnational orders remain an area of concern in those federal countries where the centralization of taxing powers is greater than necessary to meet federal expenditures inclusive of federal spending power. Such centralization results in undue central influence and political control over subnational policies and may even undermine bottom-up accountability. This scenario is a concern at the state level in Australia, Germany, India, Malaysia, Mexico, Nigeria, Russia, South Africa, and Spain. In Nigeria, a special concern exists regarding the central assignment of resource revenues. In Germany, these concerns are prompting a wider review of the assignment problem and a rethinking of the division of powers among federal, *Länder* (state), and local governments. A consensus has yet to be formed on a new vision of fiscal federalism in Germany.

The two emerging trends in the shifting balance of powers within nations are (a) a steady erosion in the economic relevance of the role of the states and provinces—the second (intermediate) tier—and (b) an enhanced but redefined role of local government in multiorder governance.

Diminishing economic relevance of the intermediate order of government, or toward an hourglass model of federalism

The federal governments in Brazil, Canada, Germany, India, Malaysia, Russia, and the United States have carved out a large role in areas of federal-state shared rule. In Brazil, entitlements and earmarked revenues are the restraining influences on budgetary flexibility at the state level. In South Africa, the national government has taken over the responsibility for social security financing. In the United States, the federal government is assuming an ever-widening role in policy-making areas of shared rule while devolving responsibilities for implementation to state and local governments. This shift frequently occurs through unfunded mandates or with inadequate financing. In both Canada and the United States, federal governments are partly financing their debts through reduced fiscal transfers to provinces or states.

Another dimension of emerging federal-state conflict is that in countries with dual federalism—as in Australia, Canada, and the United States, where local governments are the creatures of state governments—federal governments are attempting to build direct relationship with local governments and, in the process, are bypassing state governments. In Brazil, Canada, and the United States, state governments have increasingly diminished economic relevance in people's lives, although their constitutional and political roles remain strong. This realignment makes vertical coordination more difficult and affects a state's ability to deal with fiscal inequities within its boundaries. In India, the federal government retains a strong role in state affairs through appointment of federal officials to key state executive decision-making positions. Overall, the economic role of the intermediate order of government in federal systems is on the wane, except in Switzerland, where the cantons have a stronger constitutional role as well as stronger support from local residents. Cantons in Switzerland are similar to local governments in large federations such as Canada, India, and the United States. The political role of states, however, remains strong in all federal nations and is even on the rise in some, such as Germany and Pakistan. In Germany, the *Länder* have assumed a central role in implementing European Union directives and policies for regional planning and development. In Pakistan, the newly elected government in 2008 ran on the platform of restoring greater powers and the autonomy for the provinces.

New vision of local governance but growing resistance from state governments

Globalization and the information revolution are strengthening localization and broadening the role of local governments through network governance at the local level. This realignment requires local governments to operate as purchasers of local services and facilitators of networks of government and beyond-government providers, gatekeepers, and overseers of state and national governments in areas of shared rule. Nevertheless, local governments are facing some resistance from their state governments in social policy areas. In Brazil, India, and Nigeria, local governments have constitutional status and, consequently, a greater ability to defend their roles. In Switzerland, direct democracy ensures a strong role for local governments, and in both Brazil and Switzerland, local governments have an expansive and autonomous role in local governance. In most other federal countries, local governments are the wards of the state; they are supplicants of federal and state governments that have little autonomy. Their ability to fend for themselves depends on the citizen empowerment engendered by the information revolution. Russia stands out; in recent years, centralization has proceeded without resistance from oblasts and local governments or from the people at large. In Canada, some of the provinces have centralized school finance. In South Africa, primary health care has been reallocated to the provincial order of government. In most countries, local governments lack fiscal autonomy and have limited or no access to dynamic productive tax bases, whereas demand for their services is growing fast. In Canada and the United States, existing local tax bases (especially property taxes) are overtaxed with no room to grow. In the United States, this problem is compounded by limits on raising local revenues and by unfunded mandates in environmental and social spending.

Bridging the Fiscal Divide within Nations

The fiscal divide within nations represents an important element of the economic divide within nations. Reasonably comparable levels of public services at reasonably comparable levels of taxation across the nation foster mobility of goods and factors of production (labor and capital) and help secure a common economic union.

Most mature federations, with the important exception of the United States, attempt to address regional fiscal disparities through a program of fiscal equalization. The United States has no federal program, but state education finance uses equalization principles. In Canada, such a program is enshrined in the Canadian constitution and is often referred to as "the glue that holds the federation together." Most equalization programs are federally financed, except for those of Germany and Switzerland. In Germany, wealthy states make progressive contributions to the equalization pool, and poor states receive allocations from this pool. In Switzerland, the new equalization program effective in 2008 has a mixed pool of contributions from the federal government and wealthier cantons.

Institutional arrangements across federal countries to design, develop, and administer such programs are diverse. Brazil, India, Nigeria, South Africa, and Spain take into account a multitude of fiscal capacity and need factors in determining equitable state shares in a revenue-sharing program. Malaysia uses capitation grants. Russia uses a hybrid fiscal-capacity equalization program. Fiscal equalization programs in Canada and Germany equalize fiscal capacity to a specified standard. The Australian program is more comprehensive and equalizes both the fiscal capacity and the fiscal needs of Australian states, constrained by a total pool of revenues from the goods and services tax.

The equity and efficiency implications of exiting equalization programs are a source of continuing debate in most federal countries. In Australia, the complexity introduced by expenditure needs compensation is an important source of discontent with the existing formula. In Canada, provincial ownership of natural resources is a major source of provincial fiscal disparities, and the treatment of natural resource revenues in the equalization program remains contentious. In Germany and Spain, the application of overly progressive equalization formulas results in a reversal of fortunes for some rich jurisdictions. Some rich *Länder* in Germany have in the past taken this matter to the Constitutional Court to limit their contributions to the equalization pool. In Brazil, India, Malaysia, Nigeria, Russia, and South Africa, equity and efficiency effects of existing programs generate much controversy and debate.

Fiscal Prudence and Fiscal Discipline under "Fend-for-Yourself" Federalism

Significant subnational autonomy combined with an opportunity for a federal bailout makes fiscal indiscipline at subnational levels a matter of concern in federal countries. In mature federations, fiscal policy coordination to sustain fiscal discipline is exercised both through executive and legislative federalism and through formal and informal fiscal rules. In recent years, legislated fiscal rules have come to command greater attention. These rules take the form of budgetary balance controls, debt restrictions, tax or expenditure controls, and referendums for new taxing and spending initiatives. Most mature federations also specify "no bailout" provisions in setting up central banks. In the presence of an explicit or even an implicit bailout guarantee and preferential loans from the banking sector, hard budget constraints at subnational levels could not be enforced. Recent experiences with fiscal adjustment programs suggest that although legislated fiscal rules are neither necessary nor sufficient for successful fiscal adjustment, they can help in forging sustained political commitment to achieve better fiscal outcomes, especially in countries with divisive political institutions or coalition regimes. For example, such rules can be helpful in sustaining political commitment to reform in countries with proportional representation (Brazil), in countries with multiparty coalition governments (India), or in countries with a separation of legislative and executive functions (Brazil and the United States). Fiscal rules in such countries can help restrain pork-barrel politics and thereby improve fiscal discipline, as has been demonstrated by the experiences in Brazil, India, Russia, and South Africa. Australia and Canada achieved the same results without legislated fiscal rules, whereas fiscal discipline continues to be a problem even though Germany has legislated fiscal rules. The Swiss experience is the most instructive in demonstrating sustained fiscal discipline. Two important instruments create incentives for cantons to maintain fiscal discipline. First, fiscal referendums allow citizens the opportunity to veto any government program. Second, some cantons have legislated the set-aside of a fraction of fiscal surpluses, which puts a brake on debt on rainy days.

Fragmentation of the Internal Common Market

Although preserving the internal common market is a primary goal of all federal systems as well as a critical determinant of their economic performance, removing impediments to such an economic union remains an unmet challenge in federal countries in the developing world. "Beggar-thy-neighbor" or "race-to-the-bottom" fiscal policies and barriers to goods and factor mobility have the potential to undermine the gains from decentralized decision making, as recent experiences in Brazil, India, Mexico, and Spain indicate. In contrast, the Canadian and U.S. federal systems have successfully met this challenge by securing a common economic union.

Failure of the Fiscal System to Provide Incentives for Responsive and Accountable Governance

In most federal countries, especially in the developing world, intergovernmental transfers focus on dividing the pie without any regard to creating incentives for responsive and accountable service delivery. Revenue-sharing arrangements often discourage local tax efforts and introduce perverse fiscal incentives through gap-filling approaches. Conditional transfers in most federal countries focus on input controls and micromanagement, thereby undermining local autonomy. In a few countries, such as the United States, they serve as a tool for pork-barrel politics. The practice of basing output transfers on national minimum standards to create incentives for results-based accountability is virtually nonexistent.

Federalism and Regional Equity: Reflections on Alternative Approaches to Reducing Regional Disparities

Constituent units of a nation-state encompassing a large geographic area usually differ considerably in population size, resource base, economic and demographic composition of the population, and topography. These differences contribute to divergent income levels and growth rates across subnational units. Most nations, federal and unitary alike, undertake policies to reduce regional disparities to ensure political and economic stability for the political union. In unitary countries, the national government is relatively unconstrained to pursue policies to induce convergence in regional incomes. In federal countries, constituent units can undertake actions to mitigate the effects of federal policies. The task of reducing regional disparities is a daunting one that has no assurance of success even in the long term. Despite active policies, these disparities persist in both federal and unitary countries alike. Experience shows that in some cases the very policies adopted to overcome such disparities ironically ensure the long-term deprivation of the disadvantaged regions.

As noted in earlier sections, globalization introduces further complexities in meeting this challenge. Under globalization, skill mix and knowledge capital rather than a country's resource base determine its international competitiveness. Regions with less education and training and with a higher relative concentration of unskilled workers lose out to regions with skilled workers. Thus, globalization compounds the problems of regional convergence within nations.

This section discusses the responses to this challenge in federal systems. First, commonly pursued policies in support of regional development are outlined and their downside risks are briefly highlighted. An elaboration of policies that create a level playing field and support market-led development follows. The main thrust of these policies is creating an enabling environment for free mobility, competition, and technological diffusion. Finally, the section draws policy implications from earlier discussions.

Paternalism and Regional Equity: Building Transfer Dependencies?

A paternalistic view of regional equity calls for an aggressive fiscal and regulatory stance by the central government to mitigate regional disparities by discouraging outmigration of labor and capital and protection of local industry against competition from the rest of the country. Examples of such policies include regional tax holidays and credits, regionally differentiated social benefits, protection for regional industries, central financing of regional expenditures, and direct central government expenditures. Overall, these policies emphasize creating protective barriers to nourish "infant" regions and to slow down, if not to impede, the natural adjustment mechanism. Unfortunately, such a policy environment may create an incentive structure that could undermine a region's long-term growth potential.

This dysfunctional result is called *transfer dependency* (see Courchene 1995b and chapter 1 of this volume). Transfer dependency does not refer to the overwhelming dependence of constituent units on central government handouts of revenues without accountability—although such a situation may be a contributing factor. Instead, according to Courchene (see chapter 1), the term refers to a situation in which the central government's regional policies create incentives for individuals and subnational governments to act inconsistently with their long-term interests absent such policies. Transfer dependency also creates incentives for residents to stay in the region because of the regionally differentiated income-transfer policies. For example, recipient states or provinces can provide public sector wages that are above their productivity levels. They can run persistent trade deficits with other states with little impact on internal wages and prices because typically the central government's redistributive policies finance these deficits. As a result, these policies impede market adjustment responses; they lead to maintaining or even to worsening existing income and employment disparities. Transfer dependency is said to exist (a) when regional unemployment rates are observed to be persistently higher than the national average; (b) when wages in the depressed regions are higher than what labor productivity would indicate; and, in extreme cases, when (c) regional personal incomes are higher than the gross domestic product. Thus, the overwhelming generosity of the regional policies works to the disadvantage of recipient states and undermines their long-term growth potential. Alternative policies that do not suffer from these downside risks focus instead on creating an internal common market so that poorer regions are able to integrate into the national economy. Atlantic Canada, north and northeast Brazil, Balochistan province of Pakistan, and southern Italy suffer to varying degrees from the ill effects of such transfer dependency.

Partnership Approach to Regional Equity: Securing an Economic Union

Although most policies for regional convergence remain controversial, an area of emerging consensus is that free mobility of labor, capital, goods, and services and technological diffusion are the most important factors for regional convergence. For this reason, regional convergence has not worked well in China and Russia. In both countries, state policies have actively discouraged migration and technical diffusion. In mature federations, such as Australia, Canada, and the United States, securing an economic union remains high on the policy agenda and is pursued through a variety of instruments, as discussed in the following sections.

Preservation of the internal common market

Preservation of an internal common market remains an important area of concern to most nations undertaking decentralization. In their pursuit of labor and capital, subnational governments may indulge in beggar-thy-neighbor policies and in the process erect barriers to goods and factor mobility. Thus, decentralization of government regulatory functions creates a potential for disharmonious economic relations among subnational units. Accordingly, regulation of economic activity such as trade and investment is generally best left to the federal or central government. Nevertheless, central governments themselves might pursue policies detrimental to the internal common market. Therefore, as suggested by Boadway (1992), constitutional guarantees of a free domestic flow of goods and services may be the best alternative to assigning regulatory responsibilities solely to the center.

The constitutions of mature federations typically have a free trade clause (as in Australia, Canada, and Switzerland); federal regulatory power over interstate commerce (as in Australia, Canada, Germany, Switzerland, and the United States); and individual mobility rights (as in most federations).

The U.S. constitution imposes two constraints on state powers (see Rafuse 1991: 3):

- The commerce clause (article I, section 8): "The Congress shall have power . . . To regulate commerce with foreign nations, and among the several states, and with the Indian tribes."
- The due process clause (amendment XIV, section 1): "No state shall . . . deprive any person of life, liberty, or property, without due process of law."

The Indonesian constitution contains a free trade and mobility clause. But in a large majority of developing countries, the internal common market is impeded both by subnational government policies that are supported by the center and by formal and informal impediments to labor and capital mobility. For example, in India, local governments rely on a tax on inter-municipal trade (*octroi*) as the predominant source of revenues. In China, mobility rights of individuals are severely constrained by the operation of the *hukou* system of household registration, which is used to determine eligibility for grain rations, employment, housing, and health care.

Tax harmonization and coordination

Tax competition among jurisdictions can be beneficial by encouraging cost-effectiveness and fiscal accountability in state governments. By itself, it can lead to a certain amount of tax harmonization. At the same time, decentralized tax policies can cause certain inefficiencies and inequities in a federation as well as lead to excessive administrative costs. Tax harmonization is intended to preserve the best features of tax decentralization while avoiding its disadvantages.

Inefficiencies from decentralized decision making can occur in various ways. For one, states may implement policies that discriminate in favor of their own residents and businesses relative to those of other states. They may engage in beggar-thy-neighbor policies intended to attract economic activity from other states. Inefficiency may also occur simply because distortions will arise from different tax structures chosen independently by state governments with no strategic objective in mind. Inefficiencies can also occur if state tax systems adopt different conventions for dealing with businesses (and residents) that operate in more than one jurisdiction at the same time. These policies can lead to double taxation of some forms of income and nontaxation of others. State tax systems may also introduce inequities as mobility of persons encourages them to abandon progressivity. Administration costs are also likely to be excessive in an uncoordinated tax system (see Boadway, Roberts, and Shah 1994). Thus, tax harmonization and coordination contribute to efficiency of the internal common market, reduce collection and compliance costs, and help achieve national standards of equity.

The European Union has placed a strong emphasis on tax coordination issues. Canada has used tax collection agreements, tax abatement, and tax base sharing to harmonize the tax system. The German federation emphasizes uniformity of tax bases by assigning tax legislation to the federal government. In developing countries, because of tax centralization, tax coordination issues are relevant only for larger federations such as Brazil and India. In Brazil, use of the (origin-based) ICMS (*imposto sobre circulação de mercadorias e prestação de serviços*, or tax on the circulation of goods and services) as a tool for attracting capital inflow from other regions has become an area of emerging conflict among states. Even though the Council of States sought to harmonize the ICMS base and rates, some of the tax concessions rejected by the council are evidently practiced by many states anyway. The states can also resort to tax base reductions or grant unindexed payment deferrals. For example, some northeastern states have offered 15 years' ICMS tax deferral to industry. In an inflationary environment, such a measure can serve as an important inducement for attracting capital from elsewhere in the country (Shah 1991).

Intergovernmental fiscal transfers

Federal-state transfers in a federal system serve important objectives: alleviating structural imbalances, correcting for fiscal inefficiencies and inequities, providing compensation for benefit spillouts, and achieving fiscal harmonization. The most critical consideration is that the grant design be consistent with the grant's objectives.[6]

In industrial countries, two types of transfers dominate: transfers to achieve national standards and equalization transfers to deal with regional equity. A third type of transfer that would be desirable would foster regional stabilization. Such a temporary transfer would be linked to the rate of change rather than the level of economic activity.

In developing countries, with a handful of exceptions, conditional transfers are of the pork-barrel variety, and equalization transfers with an explicit standard of equalization are not practiced. Instead, pass-the-buck transfers in the form of taxing through tax sharing and revenue sharing with multiple factors are used. With limited or no tax decentralization, pass-the-buck transfers in the developing world finance the majority of subnational expenditures. In the process, they build transfer dependencies and discourage development of responsive and accountable governance (see Shah 1998a, 1998c). Ehdaie (1994) provides empirical support for this proposition. He concludes that simultaneous decentralization of the national government's taxing and spending powers, by directly linking the costs and benefits of public provision, tends to reduce the size of the public sector. Expenditure decentralization accompanied by revenue sharing delinks responsibility and accountability and thereby fails to achieve this result.

In general, pass-the-buck transfers create incentives for subnational governments to make decisions that are contrary to their long-run economic interests in the absence of such transfers. Thus, they impede natural adjustment responses, leading to a vicious cycle of perpetual deprivation for less developed regions (see Courchene, chapter 1 in this volume, for further discussion).

Experience in industrial countries shows that successful decentralization cannot be achieved in the absence of a well-designed fiscal transfer program. The design of these transfers must be simple, transparent, and consistent with their objectives. Properly structured transfers can enhance competition for the supply of public services, accountability of the fiscal system, and fiscal coordination—just as general revenue sharing has the potential to undermine it. The Indonesian experience in striving to achieve minimum standards in access to education offers important insights into grant design. For example, Indonesia's education grants have used simple and objectively quantifiable indicators in allocating funds, and the conditions of continued eligibility for these grants emphasized objective standards in accessing these services. This grant program (now defunct) helped Indonesia make great strides toward its education policy objectives in the 1990s.

Policy makers should not overlook the role of fiscal transfers in enhancing competition for the supply of public goods. For example, transfers for basic health and primary education could be made available to both the public and the not-for-profit private sectors on an equal basis, using as criteria factors such as the demographics of the population served, the school-age population, and student enrollments. These transfers would promote competition and innovation because both public and private institutions would compete for public funding. Chile permits Catholic schools access to public education financing. The Canadian provinces allow individual residents to choose between public and private schools as recipients of their property tax dollars. Such an option has introduced strong incentives for public and private schools to improve their performance and to be competitive. Such financing options are especially attractive for providing greater access to public services in rural areas (see Shah 2007b).

Fiscal equalization

As noted earlier, regional inequity is an area of concern for decentralized fiscal systems, and most systems attempt to deal with it through the spending powers of the national government or through fraternal programs. Mature federations, such as Australia, Canada, and Germany, have formal equalization programs. This important feature of decentralization has only recently been recognized in a handful of developing countries—for example, Indonesia and Russia. Despite serious horizontal fiscal imbalances in a large number of developing countries, explicit equalization programs are untried in most, although equalization objectives are implicitly attempted in the general revenue-sharing mechanisms used in countries such as Brazil, Colombia, India, Mexico, Nigeria, and Pakistan. These mechanisms typically combine diverse and conflicting objectives in the same formula and fall significantly short on individual objectives. Because these formulas lack explicit equalization standards, they fail to address regional equity objectives satisfactorily.

Facilitating local access to credit

Local access to credit requires well-functioning financial markets and creditworthy local governments. Although these prerequisites are easily met in industrial countries, traditions of higher-level governments assisting local governments are well established in these countries. An interest subsidy for state and local borrowing is available in the United States because the interest income of such bonds is exempt from federal taxation. Such a subsidy has many distortionary effects: it favors richer jurisdictions and higher-income individuals; it discriminates against nondebt sources of finance, such as reserves and equity; it favors investments by local governments over investments by autonomous bodies; and it discourages private sector participation in the form of concessions and build-operate-transfer alternatives. Various U.S. states assist borrowing by small local governments through municipal bond banks (MBBs). MBBs are established as autonomous state agencies that issue tax-exempt securities to investors and apply the proceeds to purchase the collective bond issue of several local governments. By pooling a number of smaller issues and by using the superior credit rating of the state, MBBs reduce the cost of borrowing to smaller communities (see El Daher 1996).

In Canada, most provinces assist local governments with the engineering, financial, and economic analysis of projects. Local governments in Alberta, British Columbia, and Nova Scotia are assisted in their borrowing by provincial finance corporations that use the higher credit ratings of the province to lower the costs of funds for local governments. Some provinces, notably Manitoba and Quebec, assist in preparing and marketing local debt.

Canadian provincial governments on occasion have also provided debt relief to their local governments. Autonomous agencies run on commercial principles assist local borrowing in Western Europe and Japan. In Denmark, local governments have collectively established a cooperative municipal bank. In the United Kingdom, the Public Works Loan Board channels central financing to local public works.

An important lesson arising from industrial countries' experience is that municipal finance corporations operate well when they are run on commercial principles and compete for capital and borrowers. In such an environment, such agencies allow pooling of risk, better use of economies of scale, and application of knowledge of local governments and their financing potentials to provide access to commercial credit on more favorable terms (see McMillan 1995 and chapter 8 in this volume). In developing countries, undeveloped markets for long-term credit and weak municipal creditworthiness limit municipal access to credit. Nevertheless, the predominant central government policy emphasizes central controls; consequently, less attention has been paid to assistance for borrowing. In a few countries, such assistance is available through specialized institutions and central guarantees to jump-start municipal access to credit. Ecuador, Indonesia, Jordan, Morocco, the Philippines, and Tunisia have established municipal development banks, funds, or facilities for local borrowing. These institutions are quite fragile, unlikely to be sustainable, and open to political influences. Interest rate subsidies provided through these institutions impede emerging capital-market alternatives. Colombia and the Czech Republic provide a rediscount facility to facilitate local access to commercial credit. Thailand has established a guarantee fund to assist local governments and the private sector in financing infrastructure investments (see Gouarne 1996).

In conclusion, because macroeconomic instability and lack of fiscal discipline and appropriate regulatory regimes have impeded the development of financial and capital markets, the menu of choices available to local governments for financing capital projects is quite limited, and available alternatives are not conducive to developing a sustainable institutional environment for such finance. In addition, revenue capacity at the local level is limited because of centralized taxation. A first transitional step in providing limited credit-market access to local governments may be to establish municipal finance corporations run on commercial principles and to encourage the development of municipal rating agencies to assist in such borrowing. Tax decentralization is also important to encourage private sector confidence in lending to local governments and in sharing the risks and rewards of such lending.

Social risk management through transfer payments and social insurance

Along with providing public goods and services, transfer payments to persons and businesses constitute most government expenditures (especially in industrial countries). Some of these transfers are for redistributive purposes in the ordinary sense, and some are for industrial policy or regional development purposes. Some are also for redistribution in the social insurance sense, such as unemployment insurance, health insurance, and public pensions. Several factors bear on the assignment of responsibility for transfers. In the case of transfers to business, many economists would argue that they should not be used in the first place. Given that such transfers are used, however, they are likely to be more distortionary if used at the provincial level than at the federal level because the objective of subsidies is typically to increase capital investments by firms, which are mobile across provinces. As for transfers to individuals, because most of them are for redistributive purposes, their assignment revolves around the extent to which the federal level of government assumes primary responsibility for equity. From an economic point of view, transfers are just negative direct taxes. One can argue that transfers should be controlled by the same level of government that controls direct taxes so that they can be integrated for equity purposes and harmonized across the nation for efficiency purposes. The case for integration at the central level is enhanced when one recognizes the several types of transfers that may exist to address different dimensions of equity or social insurance. Coordinating unemployment insurance with the income tax system or pensions with payments to the poor is advantageous. Decentralizing transfers to individuals to state or provincial levels will likely lead to inefficiencies in the internal common market, to fiscal inequities, and to interjurisdictional beggar-thy-neighbor policies.

Mitigating adverse consequences of globalization

Globalization of economic activity poses special challenges to fiscal federalism. As noted earlier, in the emerging borderless world economy, interests of residents as citizens are often at odds with their interests as consumers. In securing their interests as consumers in the world economy, individuals are increasingly seeking localization and regionalization of public decision making to better safeguard their interests. With greater mobility of capital and loosening of the regulatory environment for foreign direct investment, local governments as providers of infrastructure-related services may serve as more appropriate channels for attracting such investment than do national governments. As borders become more porous, cities are expected to replace countries in transnational economic alliances (as people across Europe are already discovering that national governments have diminishing relevance in their lives). People are increasingly more inclined to link their identities and allegiances to cities and regions (see Courchene 1995b and chapter 1 in this volume for further discussion).

With mobility of capital and other inputs, skills rather than resource endowments will determine international competitiveness. This point also has implications for regional inequalities, because regions with lower skills may lag in economic development. Lester Thurow (1999: 5) has expressed this view succinctly: "If capital is borrowable, raw materials are buyable, and technology is copyable, what are you left with if you want to run a high-wage economy? Only skills, there isn't anything else." This situation calls for a greater role of national government in enhancing skills, overcoming problems with access to information and skills in lagging regions, and dealing with social policy fallouts.

Concluding Remarks on Policies for Regional Development

If one examines the country experiences with regional convergence, an obvious conclusion can be drawn that whereas the partnership approach has yielded some degree of success, the paternalistic approach has not worked. In this context, examples from the U.S. experience are quite instructive. For example, Blanchard and Katz (1992) find that states that experience an adverse shock in demand experience outmigration. The partnership approach to regional disparities undertaken in the United States is highlighted by Lester Thurow (1981) in reflecting on the New England case. Thurow argues that New England is prosperous today because it went through a painful transition from old dying industries to new growth industries. According to him, if Washington had protected New England's old dying industries, the region might still be in a depressed and sick state.

Dealing with regional inequalities is a daunting task for development economists. There is no consensus about what works and what does not. Yet if one adopts a policy of doing no harm when the level of ignorance is so high, then a clear policy lesson emerges from a review of past experiences. A partnership approach that facilitates an economic union through (a) free mobility of factors by ensuring common minimum standards of public services and by dismantling barriers to trade and (b) wider information and technological access offers the best policy alternative in regional integration.

Conclusions: The New Vision of Multicentered Governance

During the past two decades, globalization and the information revolution have brought about profound changes in the governance structures within and across nations. A few trends discerned from this mega change in division of powers within nations are (a) the growing importance of global regimes in some traditional functions of central and federal governments, such as macroeconomic and trade policies and regulation; (b) a wider federal role in social and environmental policies, which are the traditional domain of provinces and states in federal countries; (c) the diminished economic relevance yet strong and growing political role of the intermediate order (provincial or state) government; (d) the growing importance of local government and "beyond-government" entities for improving economic and social outcomes for citizens; and (e) most important, the growing activism by citizens to reassert their role as governors and principals and to reign in global regimes and governments rather than be treated as subjects and consumers or clients.

The growing importance of global regimes has accentuated democracy deficits because the governance structures of these regimes are at present neither responsive nor accountable to citizens at large. Over the coming decades, citizen activism is expected to force these institutions to reform their governance structures to be more responsive to the citizens' voice. Within nations, increasing pressures to realign governance structures are likely to encourage greater bottom-up accountability of government for integrity and service delivery and to reduce transaction costs for citizens in dealing with governments.

This trend will mean revamping current inwardly focused government structures and replacing them with structures that are amenable to direct citizen control. It implies an enhanced role of local governments to serve as the primary agent of its citizens. In this role, a local government would serve as (a) a purchaser of local services, (b) a facilitator of a network of government providers and entities beyond government, and (c) a gatekeeper and overseer of state and national governments in the shared rule (see Shah and F. Shah 2007; Shah and S. Shah 2006). This role represents a fundamental shift in the division of powers from higher to local governments and "beyond-government" entities and networks. It has important constitutional implications. Residual functions would reside with local governments. State governments would perform intermunicipal services and finance social services. The national government would deal with redistributive, security, foreign relations, and interstate functions, such as harmonization and consensus on a common framework. Supranational regimes would deal with global public goods and would have transparent, responsive, and accountable democratic governance structures. Such rearrangements would reassert the power of citizens as governors and would foster competition and innovation for improving local economies and their connectedness with national and global markets. Globalization and the information revolution support such realignments for citizen empowerment, whereas existing political and economic institutions, as well as security and terrorism concerns, undermine such a paradigm shift. The world's social and economic well-being critically depends on how soon the latter obstacles are overcome.

Notes

1. This section is inspired by Courchene (1993, 1995a, 2001) and chapter 1 of this volume and draws heavily on his works and Shah (1998a, 1998c, 2002).
2. Reich (1991) identifies these services as problem-solving, problem-identifying, and strategic brokerage services.
3. See Shah (1998a) for motivations for such a change and Shah (2007c) for new visions of local governance.
4. See Shah (2007a) for a view on rearrangements in division of powers in decentralized fiscal systems.
5. This section is based on Shah (2006, 2007c).
6. See Shah (2007b) for principles of grant design and practices.

References

Bell, Daniel. 1987. "The World and the United States in 2013." *Daedalus* 116 (3): 1–31.

Blanchard, Olivier Jean, and Lawrence F. Katz. 1992. "Regional Evolutions." *Brookings Papers on Economic Activity* 1: 1–62.

Boadway, Robin. 1992. *The Constitutional Division of Powers: An Economic Perspective.* Ottawa: Economic Council of Canada.

Boadway, Robin, Sandra Roberts, and Anwar Shah. 1994. "The Reform of Fiscal Systems in Developing and Emerging Market Economies: A Federalism Perspective." Policy Research Working Paper 1259, World Bank, Washington, DC.

Castells, Manuel. 1997. *The Power of Identity.* Oxford, U.K.: Blackwell.

———. 1998. *End of Millennium.* Oxford, U.K.: Blackwell.

Courchene, Thomas J. 1993. "Glocalization, Institutional Evolution, and the Australian Federation." In *Federalism and the Economy: International, National, and State Issues,* ed. Brian Galligan, 64–117. Canberra: Federalism Research Centre, Australian National University.

———. 1995a. "Glocalization: The Regional/International Interface." *Canadian Journal of Regional Science* 18 (1):1–20.

————. 1995b. "Macrofederalism: Some Exploratory Research Relating to Theory and Practice." Monograph prepared for the Policy Research Department, World Bank, Washington, DC.

————. 2001. *A State of Minds: Towards a Human Capital Future for Canadians.* Montreal: Institute for Research on Public Policy.

Drucker, Peter. 1986. "The Changed World Economy." *Foreign Affairs* 64 (4): 3–17.

Ehdaie, Jaber. 1994. "Fiscal Decentralization and the Size of Government." Policy Research Working Paper 1387, World Bank, Washington, DC.

Eid, Florence. 1996. "Agency Theory, Property Rights, and Innovation in the Decentralized Public Sector." Department of Urban Studies and Planning, Massachusetts Institute of Technology, Cambridge, MA.

El Daher, Samir. 1996. "Municipal Finance/Municipal Bond Markets." World Bank, Washington, DC.

Friedman, Thomas. 1999. *The Lexus and the Olive Tree: Understanding Globalization.* New York: Farrar, Straus and Giroux.

Gouarne, Vincent. 1996. "Investing in Urban Infrastructure: Roles and Instruments." World Bank, Washington, DC.

Hart, Oliver. 1995. *Firms, Contracts, and Financial Structure.* Oxford, U.K.: Clarendon Press.

Krugman, Paul. 1995. "Growing World Trade: Causes and Consequences." *Brookings Papers on Economic Activity* 1: 327–62.

Lipsey, Richard G. 1997. "Globalization and National Government Policies: An Economist's View." In *Governments, Globalization, and International Business,* ed. John H. Dunning, 73–113. Oxford, U.K.: Oxford University Press.

McMillan, Melville L. 1995. "Local Perspectives on Fiscal Federalism." World Bank, Washington, DC. http://www.worldbank.org/wbi/publicfinance.

Rafuse, Robert W. 1991. "Revenue Raising Powers, Practice, and Policy Coordination in the Federal System of the United States." Photocopy.

Reich, Robert. 1991. *The Work of Nations.* New York: Alfred A. Knopf.

Rodrik, Dani. 1997a. *Has Globalization Gone Too Far?* Washington, DC: Peterson Institute for International Economics.

————. 1997b. "Trade, Social Insurance, and the Limits to Globalization." NBER Working Paper 5905, National Bureau of Educational Research, Cambridge, MA.

————. 1998. "Why Do More Open Economies Have Bigger Governments?" *Journal of Political Economy* 106 (5): 997–1032.

Ruggie, J. G. 1993. "Territoriality and Beyond: Problematizing Modernity in International Relations." *International Organization* 47 (1): 139–74.

Shah, Anwar. 1991. *The New Fiscal Federalism in Brazil.* Washington, DC: World Bank.

————. 1994. *The Reform of Intergovernmental Fiscal Relations in Developing and Emerging Market Economies.* Washington, DC: World Bank.

————. 1998a. "Balance, Accountability, and Responsiveness: Lessons about Decentralization." Policy Research Working Paper 2021, World Bank, Washington, DC.

————. 1998b. "Fiscal Federalism and Macroeconomic Governance: For Better or for Worse?" Policy Research Working Paper 2005, World Bank, Washington, DC.

————. 1998c. "Fostering Fiscally Responsive and Accountable Governance: Lessons from Decentralization." In *Evaluation and Development: The Institutional Dimension,* ed. Robert Picciotto and Eduardo Wiesner, 83–96. London: Transaction.

————. 2002. "Globalization and Economic Management." In *Public Policy in Asia: Implications for Business and Government*, ed. Mukul Asher, David Newman, and Thomas Snyder, 145–73. London: Quorum Books.

————. 2003. "Fiscal Decentralization in Transition Economies and Developing Countries." In *Federalism in a Changing World: Learning from Each Other*, ed. Raoul Blindenbacher and Arnold Koller, 432–60. Montreal: McGill-Queen's University Press.

————. 2006. "Comparative Reflections on Emerging Challenges in Fiscal Federalism." In *Dialogues on the Practice of Fiscal Federalism*, ed. Raoul Blindenbacher and Abigail Ostien Karos, 40–46. Montreal: McGill-Queen's University Press.

————, ed. 2007a. *The Practice of Fiscal Federalism: Comparative Perspectives.* Montreal: McGill-Queen's University Press.

————. 2007b. "A Practitioner's Guide to Intergovernmental Fiscal Transfers." In *Intergovernmental Fiscal Transfers*, ed. Robin Boadway and Anwar Shah, 1–53. Washington, DC: World Bank.

————. 2007c. "Rethinking Fiscal Federalism." *Federations* 6 (1): 9–11, 25.

Shah, Anwar, and Furhawn Shah. 2007. "Citizen-Centered Local Governance: Strategies to Combat Democratic Deficits." *Development* 50 (1): 70–80.

Shah, Anwar, and Sana Shah. 2006. "The New Vision of Local Governance and the Evolving Roles of Local Governments." In *Local Governance in Developing Countries*, ed. Anwar Shah, 1–46. Washington, DC: World Bank.

Strange, Susan. 1996. *The Retreat of the State: The Diffusion of Power in the World.* London and New York: Cambridge University Press.

Thurow, Lester. 1981. "The Productivity Problem." In *Policies for Stagflation: Focus on Supply*, vol. 2, ed. Ontario Economic Council, 11–34. Toronto: Ontario Economic Council.

————. 1999. *Building Wealth: The New Rules for Individuals, Companies, and Nations.* New York: Harper Business.

Whalley, John. 1999. "Globalization and the Decline of the Nation State." Paper presented at the First International Conference on Federalism, Forum of Federations, Mont Tremblanc, Quebec, October 6–7.

Federalism and Macroeconomic Performance

ANWAR SHAH

A large and growing number of countries around the globe are reexamining the roles of various orders of government and their partnerships with the private sector and civil society to create governments that work and serve their people (see Shah 2004 for motivations for change). This rethinking has led to a resurgence of interest in fiscal federalism principles and practices because federal systems provide safeguards against the threat of both centralized exploitation and decentralized opportunistic behavior while bringing decision making closer to the people. Federalism represents either the "coming together" or the "holding together" of constituent geographic units to take advantage of the benefits of being both a large and a small state. In a flat (globalized) world, nation-states are both too large to address the small things in life and too small to address large tasks. According to some influential writers, however, federal fiscal systems to accommodate "coming together" or "holding together" pose a threat to macro stability. Those writers argue that a decentralized governance structure is incompatible with prudent fiscal management (see, for example, Prud'homme 1995; Tanzi, 1996). This chapter investigates the conceptual and empirical bases of such arguments. More specifically, the chapter addresses the following questions:

- Are risks of macroeconomic mismanagement and instability greater within decentralized fiscal systems (federal versus unitary countries)?
- What has been the experience to date in macroeconomic management in federal countries compared with that in unitary countries? What has been the effect of decentralization on fiscal discipline and macro stability?

To address these questions, the chapter takes a simple institutional cum econometric analysis perspective. The institutional perspective uses as a benchmark fiscal institutions in federal countries compared with those in unitary countries. This perspective is useful because the federal constitutions place a greater premium on vertical and horizontal coordination. Nevertheless, the practice of fiscal federalism in various federal countries may lead to a significant degree of centralization in decision making, as in Australia, India, and Mexico. As a corollary, some unitary countries in practice may be quite decentralized, such as Colombia. Thus, no one-to-one mapping is possible between federalism and decentralized decision making, although as a group federal countries are more decentralized than unitary countries. The econometric perspective overcomes this deficiency by considering measures of the degree of fiscal decentralization, but it is weaker in capturing the institutional details. In view of these limitations of the individual approaches, the chapter uses a combination of both approaches to understand better the underpinnings of the relationship between fiscal decentralization and economic performance.

The strengths and weaknesses of fiscal and monetary policy institutions under alternative fiscal regimes are examined, drawing on neoinstitutional economics perspectives on fiscal institutions (see von Hagen 2002, 2005; von Hagen, Hallet, and Strauch 2002). A neoinstitutional economics perspective aims to reduce transaction costs for citizens (principals) to induce compliance with mandates by various orders of governments (agents). A fiscal system that creates countervailing institutions to limit the opportunistic behavior of various agents and that empowers principals to take corrective action is expected to result in superior fiscal outcomes. In the context of this chapter, the relevant question is what type of fiscal system (centralized or decentralized) offers greater potential for contract enforcement or rules or restraints that discourage imprudent fiscal management. The chapter undertakes a qualitative review of institutional arrangements for monetary and fiscal policy in federal and unitary countries. Two country case studies and a broader cross-country econometric analysis supplement this review to examine fiscal outcomes under alternative fiscal systems. These results are used to draw some general lessons of public policy interest.

The chapter concludes that, contrary to a common misconception, decentralized fiscal systems offer a greater potential for improved macroeconomic governance than do centralized fiscal systems. Although empirical evidence on these questions is quite weak, it nevertheless further supports the conclusion that fiscal decentralization is associated with improved fiscal and economic performance. This result is to be expected because decentralized fiscal systems require greater clarity in the roles of various players (centers of decision making), greater transparency in the rules, and greater care in design of institutions that govern their interactions to ensure fair play and to limit opportunities for rent-seeking. The rest of the chapter is organized as follows. The next section discusses the institutional environment for macroeconomic management. Monetary and fiscal policies are discussed separately, and in each subsection, a literature review is supplemented by econometric analysis and country case studies from Brazil and China. The final section draws some general conclusions.

Institutional Environment for Macroeconomic Management

Using Musgrave's trilogy of public functions—namely, allocation, redistribution, and stabilization—the fiscal federalism literature has traditionally reached a broad consensus that while the first function can be assigned to lower levels of government, the latter two functions are more appropriate for assignment to the national government. Thus, macroeconomic management—especially stabilization policy—was seen as clearly a central function (see, for example, Musgrave 1983: 516; Oates 1972). The stabilization function was considered inappropriate for subnational assignment for several reasons:

- Raising debt at the local level would entail higher regional costs, but benefits for such stabilization would spill beyond regional borders and, as a result, too little stabilization would be provided.
- Monetization of local debt would create inflationary pressures and pose a threat to price stability.
- Currency stability requires that the center alone carry out both monetary and fiscal policy functions.
- Cyclical shocks are usually national in scope (symmetric across all regions) and therefore require a national response.

These views have been challenged by numerous writers (see, for example, Biehl 1994; Dafflon 1977; Gramlich 1987; Mihaljek 1995; Shah 1994; Sheikh and Winer 1977; Walsh 1992) on theoretical and empirical grounds, yet they continue to command a considerable following. An implication that is often drawn is that decentralization of the public sector, especially in developing countries, poses significant risks for the "aggravation of macroeconomic problems" (Tanzi 1996: 305).

To form a perspective on this issue, the chapter reviews the theoretical and empirical underpinnings of the institutional framework required for monetary and fiscal policies.

Institutional Setting for Monetary Policy

Monetary policy is concerned with control over the level and rate of change of nominal variables, such as price levels, monetary aggregates, exchange rates, and nominal gross domestic product (GDP). Commentators commonly agree that control over these nominal variables to provide for a stable macro environment is a central function, and monetary policy is centralized in all nation-states, federal and unitary alike. Nevertheless, occasional arguments favor adding a regional dimension to the design and implementation of monetary policies. For example, Mundell (1968) argues that an optimal currency area may be smaller than the nation-state in some federations, such as Canada and the United States, and in such circumstances, the differential effect of exchange rate policies may be inconsistent with the constitutional requirement of fair treatment of regions. Further complications arise when the federal government raises debt domestically, but provincial governments borrow from abroad. This situation occurs in Canada because federal exchange rate policies affect provincial debt servicing. Similarly, Buchanan (1997) argues against the establishment of a confederal central bank such as the European Union Central Bank because it negates the spirit of competitive federalism.

In a centralized monetary policy environment, Barro (1996) has cautioned that a stable macro environment may not be achievable without a strong commitment to price stability by the monetary authority. If people anticipate growth in money supply to counteract a recession, the lack of such a response will deepen the recession. A strong commitment to price stability gains credibility when formal rules, such as a fixed exchange rate, or monetary rules are strictly adhered to. Argentina's 1991 Convertibility Law, establishing parity in the value of the peso in terms of the U.S. dollar, and Brazil's 1994 Real Plan helped achieve this level of credibility.

Argentina's central bank strengthened the credibility of this commitment by enduring a severe contraction in the monetary base from December 1994 to March 1995, when speculative reactions to the Mexican crisis resulted in a decline in the bank's foreign exchange reserves. Alternatively, for a central bank whose principal mission is price stability, guaranteeing independence from all levels of government could establish the credibility of such a commitment (Barro 1996; Shah 1994: 11). Barro considers the focus on price stability so vital that he regards an ideal central banker as one who is not necessarily a good macroeconomist but one whose commitment to price stability is unshakable. He writes, "The ideal central banker should always appear somber in public, never tell any jokes, and complain continually about the dangers of inflation" (Barro 1996: 58). Empirical studies show that from 1955 to 1988, the three most independent central banks (the Bundesbank of Germany, the Swiss National Bank, and the U.S. Federal Reserve Board) had average inflation rates of 4.4 percent compared with 7.8 percent for the three least independent banks (the banks of Italy, New Zealand until 1989, and Spain). Moreover, the inflation rate in the former countries showed lower volatility. The same studies show that the degree of central bank independence is unrelated to the average rate of growth and average rate of unemployment. Thus, Barro (1996: 57) argues that a "more independent central bank appears to be all gain and no pain." The European Union (EU) has recognized this principle by establishing an independent European Central Bank.

The critical question, then, is whether independence of the central bank is compromised under a decentralized fiscal system. One would expect, a priori, that the central bank would have greater stakes and independence under a decentralized system because such a system would require clarification of the rules under which a central bank operates, its functions, and its relationships with various governments. For example, when Brazil in 1988 introduced a decentralized federal constitution, it significantly enhanced the independence of the central bank (Bomfim and Shah 1994; Shah 1991). Yet independence of the central bank in Brazil remains relatively weak compared with the case in other federal countries (see Huther and Shah 1998). In contrast, in centralized countries, the Ministry of Finance typically shapes and influences the role of the central bank. In one extreme case, the functions of the Bank of England, the central bank of the United Kingdom (a unitary state), are not defined by law but have developed over time by a tradition fostered by the U.K. Treasury. Only in May 1997 did the newly elected Labour Party government of Prime Minister Tony Blair assure the Bank of England a free hand in its pursuit of price stability. On occasion, such independence may still be compromised because the chancellor of the exchequer retains a presence on the board of directors as a voting member. France and New Zealand (unitary states) have lately recognized the importance of central bank independence for price stability and have granted independence to their central banks. The 1989 Reserve Bank Act of New Zealand mandates price stability as the only function of the central bank and expressly prohibits the government from involvement in monetary policy. The People's Bank of China, in contrast, does not enjoy such independence and often works as a development bank or as an agency for central government "policy lending," in the process undermining its role of ensuring price stability (see Ma 1995). For monetary policy, it has only the authority to implement the policies authorized by the State Council. The Law of the People's Bank of China 1995, article 7, states that the bank's role is simply to "implement monetary policies under the leadership of the State Council" (see Chung and Tongzon 2004).

For a systematic examination of this question, Huther and Shah (1998) relate the evidence presented in Cukierman, Webb, and Neyapti (1992) on central bank independence for 80 countries to indexes of fiscal decentralization for the same countries. Cukierman and others assess the independence of a central bank by examining 16 statutory aspects of central bank operations, including the term of office for the chief executive officer, the formal structure of policy formulation, the bank's objectives as stated in its charter, and the limitations on lending to the government. Huther and Shah (1998) find a weak but positive association between fiscal decentralization and central bank independence, confirming this chapter's a priori judgment that central bank independence is strengthened under decentralized systems. Table 3.1, column 1, using a cross-section of 40 countries for the period 1995–2000, provides an econometric analysis that confirms the positive effect of expenditure decentralization on central bank independence.

Increases in the monetary base caused by the central bank's bailout of failing state and nonstate banks occasionally represent an important source of monetary instability and a significant obstacle to macroeconomic management. In Pakistan, a centralized federation, both the central and provincial governments have, in the past, raided nationalized banks. In Brazil, a decentralized federation, state banks have made loans to their own governments without due regard for their profitability and risks, causing the so-called R$100 billion state debt crisis in 1995. Brazil, nevertheless, later dealt with this issue head-on with successful privatization of state-owned banks in the late 1990s and through prohibition of government borrowing from state banks or from the central bank (Levy 2005). Thus, a central bank role in ensuring arm's-length transactions between governments and the banking sector would enhance monetary stability regardless of the degree of decentralization of the fiscal system.

Available empirical evidence suggests that such arm's-length transactions are more difficult to achieve in countries with a centralized structure of governance than those that have a decentralized structure and a larger set of players, because a decentralized structure requires greater clarity in the roles of various public players, including the central bank. No wonder one finds that the four central banks most widely acknowledged to be independent—the Bundesbank, Österreichische Nationalbank (the central bank of Austria), Swiss National Bank, and U.S. Federal Reserve Board—have all been the products of highly decentralized federal fiscal structures. Interestingly, the German constitution does not ensure the independence of the Bundesbank. The Bundesbank Law, which provides such independence, also stipulates that the central bank has an obligation to support the economic policy of the federal government. In practice, the Bundesbank has primarily sought to establish its independence by focusing on price stability issues. That role was demonstrated in the 1990s by the bank's decision to raise interest rates to finance German unification despite the adverse impacts on federal debt obligations (see also Biehl 1994).

The Swiss federal constitution (article 39) assigns monetary policy to the federal government. The federal government has, however, delegated the conduct of monetary policy to the Swiss National Bank, a private limited company regulated by a special law. The National Bank Act of 1953 granted independence in the conduct of monetary policy to the Swiss National Bank, although the bank is required to conduct its policy in the general interests of the country. The Swiss National Bank allocates a portion of its profits to the cantons to encourage a sense of regional ownership and participation in the conduct of monetary policy (Gygi 1991).

This chapter examines empirically some additional questions regarding the effect of fiscal decentralization on monetary stability. They include the effect of fiscal decentralization on growth of money supply, on control of inflation, and on inflation and macroeconomic balances. Regression results reported in table 3.1, column 2, show that growth of money supply is primarily determined by central bank independence, and fiscal decentralization has an insignificant positive effect. Similarly, fiscal decentralization has a negative but insignificant effect on price inflation (table 3.1, column 3). Finally, the effect of fiscal decentralization on inflation and macroeconomic balances is insignificant (table 3.1, column 4).

TABLE 3.1 Fiscal Decentralization and Fiscal Performance: Selected Regressions

Dependent variables

Independent variables	Central bank independence (Cukierman index) (1)	Money supply (M2 growth) (2)	Inflation (growth in GDP deflator) (3)	Management of inflation and macroeconomic imbalances (4)	Management of public debt (external and domestic) (5)	Overall fiscal policy quality ratings (6)	Efficiency in revenue mobilization (7)	Tax effectiveness (8)	Consolidated public expenditure as a % of GDP (9)	Budget balance as a % of expenditures (10)	Ratio of total debt to GDP (11)	Public sector management and institutions (12)	Growth rate of GDP (13)
Expenditure decen. (fraction subnational expenditures)	0.46* (2.11)	26.18 (1.90)											
Fiscal decen. qualitative index (principal components)			−67.80 (−1.25)	0.02 (0.22)	0.08 (0.47)		−0.03 (−0.29)		−1.51 (−1.21)				
Fiscal decen. qualitative composite score index						0.36* (2.24)		0.15* (2.28)		−0.77 (−1.03)	0.03 (0.56)	0.17 (1.45)	0.77 (1.01)
GDP growth average 1990–2000										0.27* (2.08)			
Log GDP per capita	−0.06** (−3.39)	−11.86** (−5.51)		0.26 (1.07)	0.55* (2.39)	0.27 (1.26)	0.67** (3.61)	0.49** (6.27)					
GDP per capita													
Log initial GDP per capita											0.16** (3.5)	$0.1e^{-3}$ (1.1)	
Initial GDP per capita									2.71 (1.46)				−0.16** (−3.11)
Political stability index	−0.04** (−6.82)				$0.53e^{-2}$ (0.27)					−0.51** (−4.34)	0.71** (3.65)		
Exchange rate regime	−0.13** (−3.63)		48.65 (1.90)										
Inflation (consumer price index change)	$0.32e^{-2}$ (1.32)				−0.09* (−2.62)						0.01 (.58)		−0.20 (−1.96)

	(1)	(2)	(3)	(4)	(5)	(6)	(7)	(8)	(9)	(10)	(11)	(12)	(13)
Central budget balance	1.59 (1.68)	8.58 (0.39)											
Central bank independence		−25.82* (−2.24)											
Growth income per capita			−98.16 (−2.23)										
Population				1.15e-2** (2.30)									
Percentage of population over 65									0.50** (3.02)				
Log population									−1.7* (−2.43)				
Urbanization									0.16 (1.17)				
Fiscal transfers as a % of subnational revenues									15.63* (2.24)				
Openness to trade				0.59e-2 (1.06)	0.01 (1.36)		−0.17e-2 (−0.38)	0.43 (1.37)				0.6e-2 (1.39)	0.74e-2 (0.44)
Freedom index					−0.11 (−0.63)		−0.09 (−0.53)	0.12 (1.08)				−0.01 (−0.09)	
Ethnicity					0.63 (1.0)		0.80 (1.38)	−0.14 (−0.46)				−0.22 (−0.61)	
Origin of law (English)					0.33 (0.68)		0.29 (0.84)	0.53* (2.87)				0.26 (0.94)	
Religious fraction Catholic					−0.36e-2 (−0.67)		0.36e-2 (1.13)	0.16e-2 (0.64)				0.33e-2 (1.25)	
Development dummy											−1.63* (−2.54)		
LAC dummy					−0.33 (−0.54)	0.02 (0.04)	−1.0* (−2.49)	−0.77* (−2.85)		−0.15 (−0.76)		−0.34 (−1.26)	−3.13** (−3.29)
African dummy					0.52 (0.84)		−0.60 (−1.28)	−0.12 (−0.47)		−0.08 (−0.46)			−1.04 (−0.93)
EECA dummy					−0.56 (−1.06)	−0.59 (−1.66)	−0.24 (−0.92)	−0.04 (−0.28)		0.021 (0.13)		−0.36 (−1.98)	
Constant	1.18** (6.70)	126.65** (5.67)	474.93* (2.69)	1.90 (1.34)	1.05 (0.70)	0.02 (0.02)	−1.15 (−0.89)	−1.70** (−4.02)	14.83 (1.00)	−3.81 (−1.94)	−0.83* (−2.40)	2.39** (6.52)	2.84* (1.16)
Number observed	40	27	27	27	24	27	27	33	24	24	23	27	33
R-square	0.43	0.63	0.50	0.21	0.46	0.50	0.54	0.90	0.60	0.30	0.44	0.48	0.55

Source: Shah 2006.

Note: EECA = Eastern Europe and Central Asia; LAC = Latin America and the Caribbean. White-corrected *t*-statistics are in parentheses. * denotes significance at the 5 percent level; ** denotes significance at the 1 percent level. Detailed explanations of variables and data sources are available from the author upon request.

Monetary management in Brazil: A decade of successful reforms

Brazil has a long history of state ownership of the banking system and imprudent borrowing by governments from their own banks and subsequent bailouts. This tradition has undermined fiscal discipline and macro stability. Of late, the federal system has been able to come to grips with those issues. To this end, Brazil has given substantial independence to its central bank and has adopted a variety of policies to promote arm's-length transactions between governments and financial sector institutions. In August 1996, the federal government launched the Programa de Incentivo á Redução do Setor Público Estadual na Atividade Bancária (Program to Reduce State Involvement with Banking Activities), which offered state governments support in financing the costs of preparing state banks for privatization, liquidation, or restructuring (some state banks were converted to development agencies). In addition, the program offered a voluntary alternative to delegate control of the overall process of reform to the federal government (Beck, Crivelli, and Summerhill 2003). Government efforts have successfully led to reducing the number of state-owned banks.[1]

More recently, the Lei de Responsibilidade Fiscal (Law of Fiscal Responsibility, or LRF), enacted in 2000, prohibits a government from borrowing from its own bank or from the central bank. The law requires that all new government borrowing receive the technical approval of the central bank and the approval of the Senate. Borrowing operations are prohibited altogether during the 180 days before the end of the incumbent's government mandate (Afonso and de Mello 2002). For capital markets, the LRF declares that financing operations in violation of debt ceilings are not legally valid, and amounts borrowed should be repaid fully without interest. The nullification of unpaid interest due constitutes a loss to the lender. Overall, Brazil has achieved monetary discipline since 1997 and sustained price stability since 1995.

Monetary management in China: Still muddling through

China is a unitary country whose one-party system strongly reinforces its unitary character. Until the early 1980s, China had an unsophisticated banking system comprising the People's Bank of China (PBC) and a few specialized banks, such as the People's Construction Bank, an arm of the Ministry of Finance. The central budget and the banking system provided the working capital needed by enterprises and provided cash used principally to cover labor costs and purchases of agricultural products. The role of the banking system was limited because direct transfers or grants from the government budget financed most investments in fixed assets in enterprises. In 1983, in a major reform, interest-bearing loans to production enterprises replaced direct grants. Consequently, the banking system gradually became the primary channel through which investments were financed, and the central authority exercised macroeconomic control. In 1984, the PBC was transformed into the central bank of China under the State Council, and its commercial banking operations were transferred to the Industrial and Commercial Bank of China. A network of provincial branches came to serve as the relays for the central bank's monetary operations. At the same time, other specialized banks and nonbank financial institutions and numerous local branches also emerged. The banks and the central bank established municipal, county, and sometimes township branches. The pressure on the central bank to lend originated in investment demand from state-owned enterprises (SOEs).

These developments have made possible a decentralization of enterprise financing, but they have also created a wider financial arena for the scramble after resources and have greatly complicated the management of monetary policy from the center. Under the deconcentrated system, provincial and local authorities have substantial powers in investment decision making and exert great influence on local bank branches' credit expansion. Although the provinces are given certain credit ceilings at the beginning of the year, the central bank is often forced to revise the annual credit plans under pressure from localities. Local branches of the central bank were given discretionary authority over 30 percent of the central bank's annual lending to the financial sector. Provincial and local governments used this discretionary authority of central bank branches to their advantage by borrowing at will, thereby endangering price stability. According to Qian and Wu (2003), 70 percent of central bank loans to state banks were channeled through central bank regional branches. Consequently, double-digit inflation occurred in 1988 and 1989, followed by a credit squeeze. Monetary (inflation) cycles appeared to be more frequent than during the prereform era and caused significant resource waste. Because 1992's credit ceilings were again exceeded by a surprisingly high margin, double-digit inflation recurred in 1993, 1994, and 1995. Given those effects, some studies have identified monetary deconcentration during this period as a mistake (Qian 2000a, 2000b).[2]

As a response, the Central Bank Law of 1995 recentralized monetary policy by reassigning the supervisory power of the central bank's regional branches solely to headquarters of the central bank. The Chinese monetary authorities have taken several steps to promote arm's-length transactions in the government-owned banking sector, albeit with limited success. To reduce provincial government influence on the PBC's regional branches, they first reorganized the PBC into nine regions from its earlier configuration of

31 provincial jurisdictions. Then, they limited subnational influences on state-owned banks. This effort was met with little success because the SOEs borrowing from these banks could not be restrained, and the nonperforming portfolio of these banks grew. Finally, the Chinese monetary authorities instituted interest rate liberalization to bring market discipline.

These policies have not been very successful because although state commercial banks are not controlled by local governments and have the authority to decide how to allocate their loans, the central government nevertheless strongly pressured state banks either to directly fund SOEs that could not cover wage payments (Cull and Xu 2003) or to purchase bonds issued by policy banks (Yusuf 1997). State banks are willing to comply with these demands on the expectation of a central government bailout in case of default. In this vein, Cull and Xu (2003) present empirical evidence that the link between bank loans and profitability weakened in the 1990s, whereas Shirai (2001) finds empirically that commercial bank investments in government bonds are associated with lower levels of profitability. Results from both of these studies buttress the notion that Chinese reforms have not been successful in promoting arm's-length transactions in the banking system, which is riddled with lending operations of a bailout nature. The central government's use of the banking system to finance subnational governments and SOEs deleteriously affected price stability governance of the financial sector.

Monetary policy and fiscal decentralization: Some conclusions

Empirical evidence presented in this chapter and elsewhere supports the view that an independent central bank with a singular focus on price stability is essential for keeping inflation in check, both in centralized and decentralized fiscal systems. In practice, evidence confirms that such independence is more likely to be granted under decentralized fiscal systems because of the presence of multiple orders of government with diverse and conflicting interests. The politics of federalism dictate such independence. No such political imperatives exist in a centralized and unitary fiscal system unless an unstable coalition regime is in power. Thus, although central bank behavior governs monetary policy issues, central bank governance itself is influenced by the country's fiscal structure. Decentralized fiscal structure appears to exert positive influences in this regard.

Institutional Setting for Fiscal Policy

In a unitary country, the central government assumes exclusive responsibility for fiscal policy. In federal countries, fiscal policy becomes a responsibility shared by all levels of government, and the federal government in such a country uses its spending power—the power of the purse (fiscal transfers)—and moral suasion through joint meetings to induce a coordinated approach to fiscal policy. The allocation of responsibilities under a federal system also pays some attention to the conduct of stabilization policies, often by assigning stable and cyclically less sensitive revenue sources and expenditure responsibilities to subnational governments. Such an assignment attempts to insulate local governments from economic cycles, thus leaving the national government to conduct stabilization policy. In large federal countries, such insulation is usually possible only for the lowest tier of government because the intermediate tier (states and provinces) shares responsibilities with the federal government in providing cyclically sensitive services, such as social assistance. These intermediate-tier governments are allowed access to cyclically sensitive revenue bases that act as built-in (automatic) stabilizers.

Fiscal federalism as a bane of fiscal prudence

Several writers have argued, without empirical corroboration, that the financing of subnational governments is likely to be a source of concern within open federal systems because subnational governments may circumvent federal fiscal policy objectives. A few of these writers (for example, Tanzi 1996) are also concerned with deficit creation and debt management policies of junior governments. A number of recent studies highlight institutional weaknesses in federal constitutions that may work against coordination of fiscal policies in a federal economy (Iaryczower, Saiegh, and Tommasi 2000; Saiegh and Tommasi 1998, 1999; Seabright 1996; Weingast 1995). These studies note that the institutional framework defining a federal governance structure is usually composed of a body of incomplete contracts.[3] In the presence of undefined or vague property rights over taxing and spending jurisdictions among layers of government, suboptimal policies would emerge that represented the outcome of the intergovernmental bargaining process rather than evolution from sound economic principles. These studies argue that the federal bargaining process is subject to the common property resource problem (that is, the zero-sum game of dividing the fiscal pie) as well as the "norm of universalism" or "pork-barrel politics," both of which lead to overgrazing. For example, Jones, Sanguinetti, and Tommasi (1998) assert that the problem of universalism manifests in Argentina at two levels: first, among provinces lobbying for federal resources, and second, among local governments looking for greater stakes from each provincial pool of resources.

Fiscal federalism as a boon to fiscal prudence

Available theoretical and empirical work does not support the validity of those concerns. On the first point, at the theoretical level, Sheikh and Winer (1977) demonstrate that relatively extreme and unrealistic assumptions about discretionary noncooperation by junior jurisdictions are needed to conclude that stabilization by the central authorities would not work at all simply because of a lack of cooperation. These untenable assumptions include regionally symmetric shocks, a closed economy, segmented capital markets, a lack of supply-side effects of local fiscal policy, the unavailability of built-in stabilizers in the tax-transfer systems of subnational governments and in interregional trade, constraints on the use of federal spending power (such as conditional grants intended to influence subnational behavior), unconstrained and undisciplined local borrowing, and extremely uncooperative collusive behavior by subnational governments (see also Gramlich 1987; Mundell 1963; Spahn 1997). The empirical simulations of Sheikh and Winer (1977) for Canada further suggest that failure of federal fiscal policy in most instances cannot be attributed to uncooperative behavior by junior governments. Saknini, James, and Sheikh (1996) further demonstrate that in a decentralized federation that has markedly differentiated subnational economies with incomplete markets and nontraded goods, federal fiscal policy acts as insurance against region-specific risks, and therefore decentralized fiscal structures do not compromise any of the goals sought under a centralized fiscal policy (see also CEPR 1993).

Gramlich (1987) points out that in open economies, exposure to international competition would benefit some regions at the expense of others. The resulting asymmetric shocks, he argues, can be more effectively dealt with by regional stabilization policies in view of the better information and instruments that are available at the regional and local levels. The effect of oil price shocks on oil-producing regions is an example supporting Gramlich's view. For example, the province of Alberta in Canada dealt with such a shock effectively by siphoning off 30 percent of oil revenues received during boom years to the Alberta Heritage Trust Fund, a "rainy day" umbrella or stabilization fund. This fund was later used for stabilization purposes—that is, it was spent when the price of oil fell. The Colombia Oil Revenue Stabilization Fund follows the same tradition.

The preceding conclusion, however, must be qualified by the fact that errant fiscal behavior by powerful members of a federation can have an important constraining influence on the conduct of federal macro policies. For example, the inflationary pressures arising from the province of Ontario's increases in social spending during the boom years of the late 1980s made achievement of the Bank of Canada's goal of price stability more difficult. Such difficulties stress the need for fiscal policy coordination under a decentralized federal system.

Interjurisdictional competition in decentralized fiscal systems, by providing high-quality public services at lower tax prices, may be more efficient in controlling the "Leviathan," as argued by Brennan and Buchanan (1980). Empirical evidence on this question is nevertheless inconclusive (see Oates 1985; Stein 1999; and table 3.1, column 9, in this chapter).

On the potential for fiscal mismanagement with decentralization, as noted by Tanzi (1996), empirical evidence from a number of countries suggests that while national, central, and federal fiscal policies typically do not adhere to the EU guidelines that deficits should not exceed 3 percent of GDP and debt should not exceed 60 percent of GDP, junior governments' policies typically do. This result obtains both in decentralized federal countries, such as Brazil and Canada, and in centralized federal countries, such as Australia and India. Centralized unitary countries do even worse on the basis of these indicators. For example, Greece, Portugal, and Turkey, as well as a large number of developing countries, do not satisfy the EU guidelines. National governments also typically do not adhere to EU requirements that central banks should not act as a lender of last resort.

The failure of collective action in forcing fiscal discipline at the national level arises from the tragedy of commons, norm of universalism, or pork-barrel politics. But these problems are not unique to a federal system. In their attempt to avoid deadlock, legislators in both federal and unitary countries trade votes and support one other's projects, implicitly agreeing, "I'll favor your best project, if you favor mine" (Inman and Rubinfeld 1991: 13). Such behavior leads to overspending and higher debt overhang at the national level. It also leads to regionally differentiated bases for federal corporate income taxation and thereby loss of federal revenues through these tax expenditures. Such tax expenditures accentuate fiscal deficits at the national level.

In the first 140 years of U.S. history, the negative impact of universalism was kept to a minimum by two fiscal rules: the constitution formally constrained federal spending power to narrowly defined areas, and an informal rule was followed allowing the federal government to borrow only to fight recession or wars (Niskanen 1992). The Great Depression and the New Deal led to an abandonment of these fiscal rules. Inman and Fitts (1990) provide empirical evidence supporting the working of universalism in the United States after the New Deal.

Various solutions are proposed to overcome previously noted difficulties with national fiscal policy, including the following: instituting "gatekeeper" committees (Eichengreen, Hausmann, and von Hagen 1996; Weingast and Marshall 1988); imposing party discipline within legislatures (Crémer 1986); using constitutionally imposed or legislated fiscal rules (Kennedy and Robins 2001; Kopits 2004; Niskanen 1992; Poterba and von Hagen 1999); setting an executive agenda (Ingberman and Yao 1991); imposing market discipline (Lane 1993); and decentralizing when potential inefficiencies of national government democratic choice outweigh economic gains with centralization. Observing a similar situation in Latin American countries prompted Eichengreen, Hausmann, and von Hagen (1996) to propose establishing an independent gatekeeper in the form of a national fiscal council to periodically set maximum allowable increases in general government debt. Although federal and unitary countries alike face these problems, federal countries have demonstrated greater adaptability in limiting the discretionary and unwelcome outcomes of political markets by trying the solutions proposed. Interestingly, fiscal stabilization failed under a centralized structure in Brazil but achieved major successes in this arena later under a decentralized fiscal system. The results in table 3.1, column 4, provide further confirmation of these observations. Showing the results of regression analysis, the table indicates that debt management discipline (country ratings by the World Bank staff) had a positive but insignificant association with the degree of fiscal decentralization for a sample of 24 countries.

Because the potential exists for errant fiscal behavior of national and subnational governments to complicate the conduct of fiscal policy, what institutional arrangements are necessary to safeguard against such an eventuality? As discussed in the next subsection, mature federations place a great deal of emphasis on intergovernmental coordination through executive or legislative federalism, as well as on fiscal rules to achieve synergy among policies at different levels. In unitary countries, in contrast, the emphasis traditionally has been on use of centralization or direct central controls. These controls typically have failed to achieve a coordinated response because of intergovernmental gaming. Moreover, the national government completely escapes any scrutiny except when it seeks international help from external sources such as the International Monetary Fund. But external help creates a moral hazard problem in that it generates bureaucratic incentives on both sides to ensure that such assistance is always in demand and used.

Fiscal policy coordination in mature federations

In mature federations, fiscal policy coordination is exercised through executive and legislative federalism as well as through formal and informal fiscal rules. In recent years, legislated fiscal rules have come to command greater attention in both federal countries and unitary countries (see table 3.2 and box 3.1). These rules take the form of budgetary balance controls, debt restrictions, tax or expenditure controls, and referendums for new tax and spending initiatives. For example, the EU, in its goal of creating a monetary union through the provisions of the Maastricht Treaty, established ceilings on national deficits and debts and supporting provisions prohibiting bailout of any government by member central banks or by the European Central Bank. The EU is also prohibited from providing an unconditional guarantee of the public debt of a member state. These provisions were subsequently strengthened by the Growth and Stability Pact provisions (legislated fiscal rules adopted by the European Parliament).

TABLE 3.2 Fiscal Rules at a Glance

Country or subnational division	Budgetary balance controls	Debt restrictions	Tax or expenditure controls and establishment of stabilization funds	Referendum for new taxes and expenditures	Penalties for noncompliance
EU, the Growth and Stabilization Pact	Yes	Yes	No	No	Yes, but ineffective for large states
U.S. states (50 total)	48	41	30	3	Yes
Canadian provinces (10 total)	8	3	2	4	Yes
Germany	Yes	No	No	No	No
New Zealand	Yes	No	No	No	No
Sweden	No	No	Yes	No	No
Switzerland	Yes	Yes	Yes	Yes	
Brazil, 2000–	Yes	Yes	Yes	No	Yes, including prison terms
Argentina, 2004–	Yes	Yes	Yes	No	No
Argentinian provinces (23 total)	Yes (17)	Yes (17)	Yes (17)	No	No
India, 2003–	Yes	Yes	No	No	No
Indian states	Yes	Yes	No	No	No

Sources: Adapted from Finance Canada 2004.

BOX 3.1   Legislated Fiscal Rules: Do They Matter for Fiscal Outcomes?

During the past decade, fiscal rules defined as legislated controls on budgetary balance, debt restrictions, tax and expenditure controls, and referendums for new initiatives on taxation and spending have assumed center stage in policy discussions in attempts to restore fiscal prudence in countries facing fiscal stress. The central question in these discussions is the link between legislated rules and fiscal performance. A growing body of literature on this subject fails to reach any definitive conclusions regarding the causal links (see Kopits 2004 for a review of experiences with fiscal rules in emerging markets). The literature suggests that some countries with legislated fiscal rules, such as Italy and Sweden, had a remarkable turnaround in fiscal performance over the period from 1995 to 2003, as did Brazil since 2001. India has also shown some progress since 2003. Other countries with legislated fiscal rules, such as France, Germany, New Zealand, and the United States, did not do so well over the same period. Some countries without legislated fiscal rules also succeeded in achieving fiscal adjustment, such as Australia, Canada, and the United Kingdom, whereas Japan was less than successful (see Finance Canada 2004: 74). Noncompliance of France and Germany with the Growth and Stability Pact provisions (EU legislated fiscal rules) further illustrates the difficulty in binding large constituent units in a federation to fiscal rules.

   A closer look at these experiences suggests that successful fiscal adjustment requires sustained political commitment. Such commitment is easier to obtain under single-party majority rule, as in Australia, Canada, and the United Kingdom in recent years. Such a commitment, however, may not be forthcoming in countries with proportional representation (Brazil), with multiparty coalition governments (India), or with separation of legislative and executive functions (Brazil and the United States). Fiscal rules in such countries can help restrain pork-barrel politics and thereby improve fiscal discipline. A remarkable example of this achievement is the experience in Brazil. Brazil is a large, highly decentralized federation of 26 states and a federal district with a population of 182 million (as of 2005). By the mid-1990s, price stabilization policies and associated decline in GDP growth contributed to growing fiscal imbalances at federal, state, and local levels. A majority of states faced fiscal crisis as the state debt service–to–GDP ratio reached 3 percent of GDP, and growing personnel expenditures (in some states and local governments reaching 90 percent of operating expenditures) limited their abilities to meet ever-increasing demands for social services.

   Against this backdrop, federal and state treasury secretaries undertook a study tour of Australia and New Zealand to reflect on options for arresting the impending fiscal crisis. At a retreat in Auckland, New Zealand, in 1997, they reached a consensus that to avert the crisis, Brazil must enact fiscal rules that were binding at all levels. While initiating a campaign to build consensus for

(Box continues on the following page.)

such future legislation, the federal government commenced a program of state fiscal strengthening that offered states incentives to enter into formal contracts on a bilateral basis with the federal government to close down or sell state-owned banks and to undertake expenditure restraints. By 2000, a political consensus was forged to enact stringent fiscal rules binding on all governments. This legislation, the Fiscal Responsibility Law of 2000, prohibited intergovernmental debt financing; placed stringent limits on debt and personnel expenditure; imposed verifiable fiscal targets, transparency rules, and adjustment rules; and mandated institutional and personal sanctions, including fines and jail terms for political and bureaucratic officials of all orders of governments. The legislation had a positive effect on fiscal performance. By 2004, all states had achieved primary surplus, all had restrained personnel expenditures to 50 percent of current revenues, and all states and municipalities had reduced debt burdens.

India is a much larger country, but compared with Brazil, it is a relatively less decentralized federation of 28 states, 7 union territories, and 1 billion people (as of 2001). India's fiscal situation paralleled that of Brazil in the 1990s, and the country has essentially followed Brazil's lead in dealing with fiscal imbalances at federal and state levels. The state of Karnatka took the lead in enacting fiscal responsibility legislation in August 2002 and established specific targets for reducing revenue and fiscal deficits and introducing fiscal transparency. The federal government followed this action with its own legislation enacted exactly one year later in August 2003. Subsequently, seven more states have followed suit. In April 2005, the 12th Finance Commission, in a report to the government of India, recommended federal assistance to encourage enactment of state fiscal responsibility legislation and added incentives when states complied with their legislation. This inducement proved attractive, and by December 2007, most states had enacted fiscal responsibility legislation. Unlike the Brazilian law, the Indian legislation does not specify institutional and personal sanctions in the event of noncompliance, and it lacks stringent fiscal rules for spending and debt restraints. Instead, it includes long-run goals and timetables for eliminating revenue deficits and restraining fiscal deficits. Although it is too early to judge the effects of this legislation, initial results appear promising, and several states have been successful in reducing operating deficits (see Howes 2005 for details). More important, however, this legislation is creating new political dynamics. For example, the chief minister of the state of Orissa has used the legislated fiscal rules to restrain spending demands by his cabinet colleagues and by state legislators.

In conclusion, although legislated fiscal rules are neither necessary nor sufficient for successful fiscal adjustment, they can help forge sustained political commitment to achieve better fiscal outcomes, especially in countries with divisive political institutions or coalition regimes.

Source: Boadway and Shah forthcoming.

Most mature federations specify no bailout provisions in setting up central banks, with the notable exceptions of Australia until 1992 and Brazil until 1996. In the presence of an explicit or even an implicit bailout guarantee and preferential loans from the banking sector, subnational governments are not subject to hard budget constraints and instead may go on a spending binge using borrowed funds, thereby fueling inflation. EU guidelines provide a useful framework for macro coordination in federal systems, but such guidelines may not ensure macro stability because they may restrain smaller countries with little influence on macro stability, such as Greece, but may not restrain superpowers like France and Germany, as demonstrated by recent history. Thus, proper enforcement of guidelines may require a fiscal coordinating council. Recent experiences with fiscal adjustment programs suggest that although legislated fiscal rules are neither necessary nor sufficient for successful fiscal adjustment, they can help in forging sustained political commitment to achieve better fiscal outcomes, especially in countries with divisive political institutions or coalition regimes. For example, such rules can be helpful in sustaining political commitment to reform in countries with proportional representation (Brazil), in countries with multiparty coalition governments (India), or in countries with separation of legislative and executive functions (Brazil and the United States). Fiscal rules in such countries can help restrain pork-barrel politics and thereby improve fiscal discipline. Based on a review of EU experiences with fiscal rules, von Hagen (2005) concludes that budgetary institutions matter more than fiscal rules. The EU fiscal rules may have encouraged European countries to strengthen budgetary institutions, which in turn had welcome effects on fiscal discipline and fiscal outcomes.

Mature federations vary a great deal in terms of mechanisms to coordinate fiscal policy. In the United States, no overall federal-state coordination of fiscal policy takes place, and no constitutional prohibitions restrain state borrowing, but the states' own constitutional provisions may prohibit operating deficits. Intergovernmental coordination often comes through fiscal rules established through acts of Congress, such as the Gramm-Rudman Act. Fiscal discipline primarily arises from three distinct incentives offered by the political and market cultures. First, the electorates are conservative and elect candidates with a commitment to keep public spending in check. Second, the pursuit of fiscal policies that are perceived as imprudent lowers property values, thereby lowering public revenues. Third, capital markets discipline governments that live beyond their means (see Inman and Rubinfeld 1991).

In Canada, there are elaborate mechanisms for federal-provincial fiscal coordination. They take the form of intergovernmental conferences (periodic first ministers' conferences and finance ministers' or treasurers' conferences) and the Council of the Federation (an interprovincial consultative body). The majority of direct program expenditures in Canada are at the subnational level, but Ottawa (that is, the Canadian federal government) retains flexibility and achieves fiscal harmonization through conditional transfers and tax collection agreements. In addition, Ottawa has established a well-knit system of institutional arrangements for intergovernmental consultation and coordination. Much of the discipline on public sector borrowing comes from the private banking sector, however, which monitors deficits and debt at all levels of government. Overall, financial markets and electorates impose a strong fiscal discipline at the subnational level.

In Switzerland, societal conservatism, fiscal rules, and intergovernmental relations play an important part in fiscal coordination. Borrowing by cantons and communes is restricted to capital projects that can be financed on a pay-as-you-go basis and requires a popular referendum for approval. In addition, cantons and communes must balance current budgets, including interest payments and debt amortization. Intergovernmental coordination is also fostered by common budget directives applicable to all levels of government. These directives embody the following general principles: (a) the growth rates of public expenditures should not exceed the expected growth of nominal gross national product (GNP); (b) the budget deficit should not be higher than that of the previous year; (c) the number of civil servants should stay the same or increase only very slightly; and (d) the volume of public sector building should remain constant, and an inflation indexation clause should be avoided (Gygi 1991: 10).

The German constitution specifies that *Bund* (federal) and *Länder* (state-level governments) have budgetary independence (article 109(1) of the Basic Law) but must take into account the requirements of overall economic equilibrium (article 109(2) of the Basic Law). The 1969 Law of Stability and Growth established the Financial Planning Council and the Cyclical Planning Council as coordinating bodies for the two levels of government. It stipulates uniform budgetary principles to facilitate coordination. Annual budgets are required to be consistent with medium-term financial plans. The law further empowered the federal government to vary tax rates and expenditures on short notice and even to restrict borrowing and equalization transfers. *Länder* parliaments no longer have tax legislation authority, and the German constitution restricts *Bund* and *Länder* borrowing to projected outlays for capital projects (the "golden rule"). However, federal borrowing to pursue economic stabilization is exempt from the application of this rule. The federal government follows a five-year budget plan so that its fiscal policy stance is available to subnational governments. The 1969 law created two major instruments to forge cooperative federalism: (a) joint tasks authorized by the upper house of parliament, the Bundesrat, and (b) federal grants for state and local spending mandated by federal legislation or federal-*Länder* agreements. An additional helpful matter in intergovernmental coordination is that the Bundesbank is independent of all levels of government and focuses on price stability as its objective. Most important, full and effective federal-*Länder* fiscal coordination is achieved through the Bundesrat, where *Länder* governments are directly represented. The Bundesrat represents the most noteworthy institution for formal intergovernmental coordination. Such formal institutions for intergovernmental coordination are especially useful in countries with legislative federalism. The South African Constitution Act 1996 has established such an institution for intergovernmental coordination; it is called the National Council of the Provinces.

Commonwealth-state fiscal coordination in Australia offers important lessons for federal countries. Australia established a loan council in 1927 as an instrument of credit allocation because it restricted state governments to borrowing only from the Commonwealth. An important exception to this rule was that states could use borrowing by autonomous agencies and local government for their own purposes. This exception proved to be the Achilles' heel for the Commonwealth Loan Council, because states used this exception extensively in their attempt to bypass the cumbersome procedures and council control over their capital spending plans. The Commonwealth government ultimately recognized in 1993 that its central credit allocation policy was a flawed and ineffective instrument. It lifted restrictions on state borrowing and reconstituted the Loan Council so that the council could serve as a coordinating agency for information exchange to ensure greater market accountability. The new council attempts to provide greater flexibility to states to determine their own borrowing requirements and to coordinate borrowing with fiscal needs and overall macro strategy. It further instills a greater understanding of the budgetary process and provides timely and valuable information to the financial markets on public sector borrowing plans. The process seems to be working well so far.

For the European Union, Wierts (2005) concludes that subnational governments' contributions to consolidated public sector deficits and debts were relatively small compared with those of the central governments in most EU countries—federal and unitary countries alike.

The impact of fiscal decentralization on fiscal management: Econometric evidence

Econometric analysis carried out for this chapter and presented in table 3.1 (columns 6–13) examines the effect of fiscal decentralization on various dimensions of the quality of fiscal management. Econometric evidence presented here supports the hypothesis that fiscal decentralization has a significant positive effect on the quality of fiscal management (column 6). The effect of fiscal decentralization on the efficiency of revenue collection is negative but insignificant (column 7). Fiscal decentralization leads to prudent use of public resources (column 8). Growth in public spending is negatively associated with fiscal decentralization but insignificantly so with the composite (principal component) index of fiscal decentralization (column 9). Fiscal decentralization is negatively but insignificantly associated with the control of deficits (column 10). Fiscal decentralization has a positive but insignificant effect on growth of public debt (column 11). Fiscal decentralization contributes to enhanced transparency and accountability in public management (column 12). Finally, fiscal decentralization has a positive yet insignificant association with growth of GDP (column 13).

Fiscal policy coordination in Brazil: From fiscal distress to fiscal discipline—a giant leap forward

Tax assignments mandated by the 1988 constitution in Brazil reduced federal flexibility in the conduct of fiscal policies. The new constitution transferred some productive federal taxes to lower-level jurisdictions and increased subnational governments' participation in federal revenue-sharing schemes. One of the most productive taxes, the value added tax on sales, was assigned to states, and the Council of State Finance Ministers was set up to play a coordinating role. Federal flexibility in the income tax area, however, remained intact. This arrangement gives the federal government some possibility of not only affecting aggregate disposable income—and therefore aggregate demand—but also exerting direct influence over the revenues and fiscal behavior of the lower levels of government, which end up receiving nearly half of the proceeds of this tax. The effectiveness of such a policy tool is an open question and critically depends on the goodwill of subnational governments. Consider the case in which the federal government decides to implement a discretionary income tax cut. The measure could have a potentially significant effect on the revenues of state and local governments, given their large share in the proceeds of this tax. To offset this substantial loss in revenues from federal sources, lower levels of government might choose either (a) to increase the rates or the bases of taxes within their jurisdiction (or both) or (b) to increase their taxing effort. Such state and local government responses could potentially undermine the effectiveness of income taxes as a fiscal policy instrument. Thus, a greater degree of intergovernmental consultation, cooperation, and coordination would be needed for the success of stabilization policies.

An overall effect of the new fiscal arrangements was to limit federal control over public sector expenditures in the federation. The success of federal expenditures as a stabilization tool again depends on subnational governments' cooperation in harmonizing their expenditure policies with the federal government. Once again, the constitution has put a premium on intergovernmental coordination of fiscal policies. Such a degree of coordination may not be attainable in times of fiscal distress.

A reduction in revenues at the federal government's disposal and an incomplete transfer of expenditure responsibilities have further constrained the federal government. The primary source of federal revenues is income taxes. These taxes are relatively easy for taxpayers to evade; therefore, they are declining in relative importance as a source of revenues. Value added sales taxes, which are considered a more dynamic source of revenues, have been assigned to the state level. Thus, federal authorities lack access to more productive tax bases to alleviate the public debt problem and to gain more flexibility in implementing fiscally based macroeconomic stabilization policies.

According to Shah (1991, 1998) and Bomfim and Shah (1994), this situation could be remedied if a joint federal-state value added tax to be administered by a federal-state council were instituted as a replacement for the federal tax on industrial products (*imposto sobre produtos industrializados*, or IPI); the state tax on the circulation of goods and services (*imposto sobre circulação de mercadorias e prestação de serviços*, or ICMS); and the municipal services tax, whose bases partially overlap. Such a joint tax would help alleviate the current federal fiscal crisis as well as streamline sales tax administration. Bomfim and Shah argued that federal expenditure requirements could be curtailed with federal disengagement from purely local functions and with the elimination of federal tax transfers to municipalities. Transfers to the municipalities would be better administered at the state level because states have better access to data on municipal fiscal capacities and tax efforts in their jurisdictions. Some rethinking is in order on the role of negotiated transfers, which have traditionally served to advance pork-barrel politics rather than to address national objectives. If these transfers were replaced by performance-oriented conditional block (per capita) federal transfers to achieve national (minimum) standards, both accountability and coordination in the federation would be enhanced. These rearrangements would provide the federal government with greater flexibility to pursue its macroeconomic policy objectives. Finally, Bomfim and Shah advocated the development of fiscal rules binding on all levels of government and a federal-state coordinating council to ensure that these rules were enforced.

Significant progress has occurred on most of these issues in recent years. For example, negotiated transfers have become insignificant because of the fiscal squeeze experienced by the federal government. The Senate of Brazil has prescribed guidelines (Senate Resolution 69, 1995) for state debt: maximum debt service is not to exceed 16 percent of net revenue or 100 percent of current revenue surplus, whichever is less, and the maximum growth in stock of debt (new borrowing) within a 12-month period must not exceed the level of existing debt service or 27 percent of net revenues, whichever is greater (Dillinger 1997). More recently, in 1998, pension and civil service entitlements reforms have introduced greater budgetary flexibility for all levels of government. Likewise, after the suboptimal results achieved from letting capital markets discipline subnational borrowings, the Brazilian federal government opted to establish a fairly constraining set of fiscal responsibility institutions. First, Law 9696 of September 1997 set up the framework for a series of debt restructuring contracts between December 1997 and June 1998, whereby a portion of debt (20 percent) would be paid with the proceeds of privatization of state assets, while the remaining portion of state and local debt was restructured with maturities up to 30 years at a subsidized interest rate (6 percent annual real rate). Debt restructuring contracts became comprehensive in scope because 25 of 27 states and more than 180 municipalities signed debt restructuring agreements (Goldfajn and Refinetti Guardia 2003; IMF 2001). In exchange, the contracts required the subnational governments' commitments to engage in adjustment programs aimed at reducing the ratio of debt to net revenue to less than 1 over a period negotiated case by case. The contracts have established sanctions for violations to adjustment program agreements, such as increased debt service caps (annual debt service–to–net revenue ratio of 13 to 15 percent, above which service debt is capitalized) and substitutions of the market interest rate for the subsidized interest rate. Debt restructuring contracts also have imposed stringent penalties for noncompliant states and, in the event of a default, have authorized the federal government to withhold fiscal transfers or, if further steps are needed, to withdraw the amount due to the states from their bank accounts (Goldfajn and Refinetti Guardia 2003: 18). Debt restructuring agreements have prohibited further credit or restructuring operations involving other levels of government. This provision helps avoid moral hazard incentives from the possibility of intergovernmental bailouts (IMF 2001).

Building on Law 6996 of 1997 and complementary regulations, the Brazilian federal government adopted the LRF in May 2000 and a companion law (Law 10028 of 2000) binding for federal, state, and municipal or local governments. The LRF is likely the most significant reform after the 1988 constitution in terms of its effect on the dynamics of federalism in Brazil: subsequent compromises between states and the federal government have continuously increased the negotiation leverage of the latter, increasing also its effectiveness in macroeconomic management. The LRF imposes requirements in areas such as a threshold state debt and deficit and personnel spending ceilings. According to the LRF, states and municipalities must maintain debt stock levels below ceilings determined by the federal regulations. If a subnational government exceeds this debt ceiling, the excessive amount must be reduced within a one-year period, during which the state or municipality is prohibited from incurring any new debt and becomes ineligible for receiving discretionary transfers (World Bank 2002). The LRF also requires all new borrowing to have the technical approval of the central bank and the approval of the Senate. Borrowing operations are prohibited altogether during the 180 days before the end of an incumbent's government mandate (Afonso and de Mello 2002). In terms of personnel management, the LRF provisions define ceilings on payroll spending, which should not exceed 50 percent of the federal government's net revenues or 60 percent of the state and local governments' net revenues. The LRF also instituted various provisions to enforce its regulations. For governments, violations of the personnel or debt ceiling can lead to fines up to 30 percent of the annual salary of the responsible party, impeachment of mayors or governors, and even prison terms in case of violation of mandates regarding election years. For capital markets, the LRF declares that financing operations in violation of debt ceilings is not legally valid and amounts borrowed will be repaid fully without interest. This provision is aimed at discouraging such lending behavior by financial institutions.

The Brazilian federation was remarkably successful in ensuring fiscal policy coordination and fiscal discipline at all levels in recent years. By June 2005, the LRF had significant positive effects on fiscal performance in Brazil. All states and the federal government have complied with the ceiling on personnel expenditures. On debt, only 5 of 27 states (including the federal district) are still above the ceiling of 200 percent of revenues, owing to the 2002 currency devaluation. Of municipalities, 92 percent have reduced debt below 1.2 times revenue levels, and only a handful of large municipalities have unsustainable debt levels. Primary surplus was achieved by all states by 2004 (Levy 2005).

Fiscal management in China: An unmet challenge

Before 1980, decentralized revenue collection followed by central transfers characterized China's fiscal system—that is, all taxes and profits were remitted to the central government and then transferred back to the provinces according to expenditure needs approved by the center through bilateral negotiations. Under that system, the localities had little managerial autonomy in local economic development. In 1980, the system was changed to a contracting system. Under the new arrangements, each level of government makes a contract with the next level up to meet certain revenue and expenditure targets. A typical contract defines a method of revenue sharing, which could be a percentage share that goes to the center or a fixed fee plus a percentage share. This contracting system clearly identifies the economic interests of each level of government.

Under the fiscal contract system introduced in the early 1980s, the localities have controlled the effective tax rates and tax bases in the following two ways. First, they have controlled tax collection efforts by offering varying degrees of tax concessions. Second, they have found ways to convert budgetary funds into extrabudgetary funds, thus avoiding tax sharing with the center. As a result, the center has had to resort to various ad hoc instruments to influence revenue remittance from the localities, and these instruments have led to perverse reactions from the localities. On the expenditure side, the center has failed to achieve corresponding reductions in expenditure when revenue collection has been decentralized. The lack of centrally controlled financial resources and the heavy burden of "capital constructions" have seriously undermined the center's flexibility in using expenditure policy. Between 1978 and 1992, the ratio of government revenue to GNP dropped from 31 percent to 17 percent. Increasing deficits became a problem, and the lack of funds for infrastructure investment exacerbated bottlenecks in the economy.

Because of the lack of fiscal resources and policy instruments, the central government has had increasing difficulty in achieving the goals of macroeconomic stabilization, regional equalization, and public goods provision. In early 1994, the central government initiated reform of the tax assignment system in an attempt to address these difficulties. Under the new system, the center will recentralize the administration and collection of central and shared taxes and will obtain a larger share of fiscal resources because of the new revenue-sharing formula. Initially, among the major taxes, only the value added tax was centralized. Later in 2002, the administration of personal income tax and enterprise income tax was also centralized. The value added tax is shared 75:25 (center:local), and all extra central revenues above the 1993 levels are then shared 60:40. Revenues are returned to provinces on a derivation or point-of-collection basis. The central government expected to improve significantly its ability to use tax and expenditure policies in macroeconomic management as a result of those steps. Nevertheless, the new system fails to address a number of flaws in the old system: (a) the division of tax bases according to ownership will continue to motivate the center to reclaim enterprise ownership whenever necessary; (b) the division of expenditure responsibility is not yet clearly defined; (c) the new system impedes local autonomy because the localities are not allowed to determine the bases or rates for local taxes; and (d) the design of intergovernmental transfers is not fully settled. In 1994 and 1995, the central government also imposed administrative restrictions on investments by provincial and local governments and their enterprises (see Ma 1995 for further details) to deal with inflationary pressures. The introduction of State Council Document No. 29 in 1996 and other measures in 1997 to consolidate budgetary management of extrabudgetary funds sharply restricted the authority of local governments—especially rural local governments—to impose fees and levies to finance their own expenditures.

The 1994 Budget Law prohibits the central government from borrowing from the People's Central Bank of China. The Budget Law also requires local governments to have balanced budgets and restricts subnational governments from borrowing in financial markets and issuing bonds (Qian 2000b). Legal restraints on subnational borrowing and unfunded central mandates have encouraged provincial and local governments to assume hidden debts. Such borrowing is channeled through state-owned entities, such as urban construction and investment companies, that borrow from banks or issue bonds on behalf of the local government (World Bank 2005). Such hidden debts pose significant risks for macro stability.

A combination of unfunded mandates and extremely constrained taxing powers generates incentives for local governments to develop informal channels of taxation. This trend is evidenced by the high levels of extrabudgetary funds (self-raised funds) at the subprovincial levels, comprising surcharges, fees, and utility and user charges that while technically legal are not formally approved by the central government. A pilot experiment in Anhui province identified collection of per capita fees from peasants for local education, health, militia training, road construction and maintenance, welfare for veterans, and birth control (Yep 2004). This type of quasi-fiscal income accounted for as much as 56 percent of total tax revenues in 1996 (Eckaus 2003) or 8 to 10 percent of GDP in 1995 (World Bank 2000). This nontax type of revenue extraction has often imposed excessive burdens on local constituents, generating continual confrontations between peasants and local officials (Bernstein and Lü 2000; Lin and Lou 2000; Yep 2004). As noted by Krug, Zhu, and Hendrischke (2005: 11), subprovincial government agencies' de facto control of the property rights of revenues not covered by the tax-sharing system enables "subprovincial governments at all levels to maintain their residual tax rights over the informal tax system." In fact, institutions controlling subprovincial taxation are shaped as a complex and asymmetric system of contracts between the provincial government and lower layers of government. More recently, in 2002, the central government abolished the agricultural income tax and rural fees and charges through the Tax-for-Fee Program. These prohibitions have had deleterious consequences for county finances because compensating transfers do not fully cover these growing sources of revenue.

Promoting greater fiscal discipline at the subnational level in China remains an impossible task as long as local governments retain ownership of enterprises providing private goods, lack clarity in their spending and taxing responsibilities, and obtain a disproportionate amount of local revenues from ad hoc central transfers. Thus, fiscal policy coordination and fiscal discipline remain an unfinished challenge in China.

Fiscal policy coordination: Some conclusions

Fiscal policy coordination represents an important challenge for federal systems. In this context, fiscal rules and institutions provide a useful framework but not necessarily a solution to this challenge. Fiscal rules binding on all levels can help sustain political commitment in countries having coalitions or fragmented regimes in power. Coordinating institutions help in the use of moral suasion to encourage a coordinated response. Industrial countries' experiences show that unilaterally imposed federal controls and constraints on subnational governments typically do not work. Instead, societal norms based on fiscal conservatism, such as the Swiss referendum, and political activism of the electorate play important roles. Ultimately, capital markets and bond rating agencies provide more effective discipline on fiscal policy. In this context, it is important not to backstop state and local debt and not to allow ownership of the banks by any level of government. Transparency of the budgetary process and institutions, accountability to the electorate, and general availability of comparative data encourage fiscal discipline.

TABLE 3.3 Fiscal Decentralization and Fiscal Performance:
A Summary of Empirical Results

Fiscal performance indicator	Effect of fiscal decentralization
Central bank independence	Positive and significant
Growth of money supply	Positive but insignificant
Inflation	Negative but insignificant
Management of inflation and macroeconomic imbalances	Positive but insignificant
Quality of debt management	Positive but insignificant
Quality of fiscal policies and institutions	Positive and significant
Efficiency in revenue collection	Mixed but insignificant
Prudent use of tax monies	Positive and significant
Growth of government spending	Negative and significant
Control of fiscal deficits	Negative but insignificant
Growth of public debt	Positive but insignificant
Public sector management: transparency and accountability	Positive and significant
GDP growth	Positive but insignificant

Source: Shah 2006.

Fiscal Decentralization and Fiscal Performance: Some Conclusions

Fiscal decentralization poses significant challenges for macroeconomic management. These challenges require careful design of monetary and fiscal institutions to overcome adverse incentives associated with "common property" resource management problems or with rent-seeking behaviors. These fiscal institutions determine the success of macroeconomic management policies. Experiences of federal countries indicate significant learning and adaptation of fiscal systems are needed to create incentives compatible with fair play and to overcome incomplete contracts. In unitary countries, especially under single-party majority rule, political imperatives to create fiscal institutions of restraint, including fiscal rules, are less pressing and simply depend on the commitment of the leadership to bind itself to some discipline, as occurred in Chile. This finding explains why, paradoxically, the decentralized fiscal systems appear to do better than centralized fiscal systems on most aspects of monetary and fiscal policy management and transparent and accountable governance (see table 3.3).

Notes

This chapter is a revised version of the Shah (2006), "Fiscal Decentralization and Macro-economic Management," which was published in *International Tax and Public Finance* 13 (4): 437–62. It is reprinted here with the permission of the journal. The author is grateful to Professor Jürgen von Hagen and an anonymous referee of the *International Tax and Public Finance* journal for helpful comments and to Javier Arze and Sarwat Jahan for research assistance.

1. Among some of the privatized institutions are former state banks of Rio de Janeiro (Banco do Estado do Rio de Janeiro, or BANERJ) in June 1997; Minas Gerais (Banco do Estado de Minas Gerais, or BEMGE) in September 1998; Pernambuco (Banco do Estado de Pernambuco, or BANDEPE) in November 1998; Bahia (Banco do Estado da Bahia, or BANEB) in June 1999; Paraná (Banco do Estado do Paraná, or BANES-TADO) in October 2000; São Paulo (Banco do Estado de São Paulo, or BANESPA) in November 2000; Paraíba (Banco do Estado da Paraíba, or PARAIBAN) in November 2001; Goiás (Banco do Estado de Goiás, BEG) in December 2001; and Amazonas (Banco do Estado do Amazonas, or BEA) in January 2002.
2. According to Ma (1995), because of current monetary and fiscal institutions, local government incentives are not aligned with those of the central level. Therefore, significant decentralization reforms in 1989 and 1993 were immediately followed by inflation, forcing the central government back to centralization.
3. Incompleteness of these contracts arises as unforeseen issues come to the policy agenda. Several of these issues could not possibly have been contemplated at the original contract—constitution—or, if covered, could not have been fully addressed in it because of the ever-increasing complexity in public management over time or because of the prohibitively high costs that designing policy for an immensely large number of future possible scenarios would entail.

References

Afonso, José Roberto Rodrigues, and Luiz de Mello. 2002. "Brazil: An Evolving Federation." In *Managing Fiscal Decentralization*, ed. Ehtisham Ahmad and Vito Tanzi, 265–85. London: Routledge.

Barro, Robert J. 1996. *Getting It Right: Markets and Choices in a Free Society.* Cambridge, MA: MIT Press.

Beck, Thorsten, Juan Miguel Crivelli, and William Summerhill. 2003. "State Bank Transformation in Brazil: Choices and Consequences." Paper presented at the World Bank Conference on Bank Privatization and International Society for New Institutional Economics, Washington, DC, November 23.

Bernstein, Thomas P., and Xiaobo Lü. 2000. "Taxation without Representation: Peasants, the Central and the Local States in Reform China." *China Quarterly* 163 (September): 742–63.

Biehl, Dieter. 1994. "Intergovernmental Fiscal Relations and Macroeconomic Management—Possible Lessons from a Federal Case: Germany." In *Intergovernmental Fiscal Relations and Macroeconomic Management in Large Countries*, ed. S. P. Gupta, Peter Knight, and Yin-Kann Wen, 69–121. Washington, DC: World Bank.

Boadway, Robin, and Anwar Shah. Forthcoming. *Fiscal Federalism: A Textbook on the Principles and the Practice of Decentralized Public Governance.* New York: Cambridge University Press.

Bomfim, Antulio, and Anwar Shah. 1994. "Macroeconomic Management and the Division of Powers in Brazil: Perspectives for the 1990s." *World Development* 22 (4): 535–42.

Brennan, Geoffrey, and James M. Buchanan. 1980. *The Power to Tax: Analytical Foundations of a Fiscal Constitution.* New York: Cambridge University Press.

Buchanan, James M. 1997. *Post-Socialist Political Economy: Selected Essays.* Cheltenham, U.K.: Edward Elgar.

CEPR (Centre for Economic Policy Research). 1993. *Making Sense of Subsidiarity: How Much Centralization for Europe.* London: CEPR.

Chung, Connie Wee-Wee, and José L. Tongzon. 2004. "A Paradigm Shift for China's Central Banking System." *Journal of Post Keynesian Economics* 27 (1): 87–103.

Crémer, Jacques. 1986. "Cooperation in Ongoing Organizations." *Quarterly Journal of Economics* 101 (1): 33–49.

Cukierman, Alex, Steven B. Webb, and Bilin Neyapti. 1992. "Measuring the Independence of Central Banks and Its Effect on Policy Outcomes." *World Bank Economic Review* 6 (3): 353–98.

Cull, Robert, and Lixin-Colin Xu. 2003. "Who Gets Credit? The Behavior of Bureaucrats and State Banks in Allocating Credit to Chinese State-Owned Enterprises." *Journal of Development Economics* 71 (2): 533–59.

Dafflon, Bernard. 1977. *Federal Finance in Theory and Practice: With Special Reference to Switzerland.* Bern, Switzerland: Paul Haupt.

Dillinger, William. 1997. "Brazil's State Debt Crisis: Lessons Learned." Economic Note 14, World Bank, Washington, DC.

Eckaus, Richard S. 2003. "Some Consequences of Fiscal Reliance on Extrabudgetary Revenues in China." *China Economic Review* 14 (1): 72–88.

Eichengreen, Barry J., Ricardo Hausmann, and Jürgen von Hagen. 1996. "Reforming Budgetary Institutions in Latin America: The Case for a National Fiscal Council." Paper prepared for the Seminar on Fiscal Institutions to Overcome Volatility in Latin America. Inter-American Development Bank, Washington, DC, March 24.

Finance Canada, Fiscal Policy Division. 2004. "The Role of Fiscal Rules in Determining Fiscal Performance: The Canadian Case." *International Journal of Public Budget* 32 (56): 51–100.

Goldfajn, Ilan, and Eduardo Refinetti Guardia. 2003. "Fiscal Rules and Debt Sustainability in Brazil." Technical Note 39, Banco Central do Brasil, Brasília.

Gramlich, Edward M. 1987. "Federalism and Federal Deficit Reduction." *National Tax Journal* 40 (3): 299–313.

Gygi, Ulrich. 1991. "Maintaining a Coherent Macroeconomic Policy in a Highly Decentralized Federal State: The Experience of Switzerland." Organisation for Economic Co-operation and Development, Paris.

Howes, Stephen. 2005. "The Experiences of the Indian States with Fiscal Responsibility Legislation." World Bank, New Delhi.

Huther, Jeff, and Anwar Shah. 1998. "Applying a Simple Measure of Good Governance to the Debate on Fiscal Decentralization." Policy Research Working Paper 1894, World Bank, Washington, DC.

Iaryczower, Matías, Sebastián Saiegh, and Mariano Tommasi. 2000. "Coming Together: The Industrial Organization of Federalism." Paper presented at the Meeting of the Latin American Studies Association, Miami, Florida, March 16–18.

IMF (International Monetary Fund). 2001. "Brazil: Report on Observance Standards and Codes (ROSC)—Fiscal Transparency." IMF Country Report 01/217, International Monetary Fund, Washington, DC.

Ingberman, Daniel E., and Dennis A. Yao. 1991. "Presidential Commitment and the Veto." *American Journal of Political Science* 35 (2): 357–89.

Inman, Robert, and Michael Fitts. 1990. "Political Institutions and Fiscal Policy: Evidence from the U.S. Historical Record." *Journal of Law, Economics, and Organizations* 6 (special issue): 79–100.

Inman, Robert P., and Daniel L. Rubinfeld. 1991. "Fiscal Federalism in Europe: Lessons from the United States Experience." NBER Working Paper Series 3941, National Bureau of Educational Research, Cambridge, MA.

Jones, Mark, Pablo Sanguinetti, and Mariano Tommasi. 1998. "Politics, Institutions, and Fiscal Performance in Federal System: An Analysis of the Argentine Provinces." Universidad de San Andrés, Buenos Aires, Argentina.

Kennedy, Suzanne, and Janine Robins. 2001. "The Role of Fiscal Rules in Determining Fiscal Performance." Working Paper 2001-16, Canadian Department of Finance, Ottawa.

Kopits, George, ed. 2004. *Rules-Based Fiscal Policy in Emerging Markets.* New York: Palgrave.

Krug, Barbara, Ze Zhu, and Hans Hendrischke. 2005. "China's Emerging Tax Regime: Devolution, Fiscal Federalism, or Tax Farming?" Paper presented at the Annual Meeting of the European Public Choice Society, Durham, U.K., March 31–April 3.

Lane, Timothy D. 1993. "Market Discipline." *International Monetary Fund Staff Papers* 40 (1): 53–88.

Levy, Joaquim Vieira. 2005. "Fiscal Rules and Fiscal Performance." Presentation at the International Workshop on Intergovernmental Finance System, World Bank, Urmuqi, China, July 18–22.

Lin, Justin Yifu, and Zhiqiang Lou. 2000. "Fiscal Decentralization and Economic Growth in China." *Economic Development and Cultural Exchange* 49 (1): 1–21.

Ma, Jun. 1995. "Macroeconomic Management and Intergovernmental Relations in China." Policy Research Working Paper 1408, World Bank, Washington, DC.

Mihaljek, Dubravko. 1995. "Hong Kong's Economy Two Years before 1997: Steady Sailing, Prosperous Voyage." *International Monetary Fund Survey* 25: 109–12.

Mundell, Robert A. 1963. "Capital Mobility and Stabilization Policy under Fixed and Flexible Exchange Rates." *Canadian Journal of Economics and Political Science* 29 (4): 475–85.

———. 1968. *International Economics.* New York: Macmillan.

Musgrave, Richard. 1983. "Public Finance, Now and Then." *Finanzarchiv (Neue Folge)* 41 (1): 1–13.

Niskanen, William A. 1992. "The Case for a New Fiscal Constitution." *Journal of Economic Perspectives* 6 (2): 13–24.

Oates, Wallace. 1972. *Fiscal Federalism.* New York: Harcourt Brace Jovanovich.

———. 1985. "Searching for the Leviathan: An Empirical Study." *American Economic Review* 75 (4): 748–53.

Poterba, James, and Jürgen von Hagen, eds. 1999. *Fiscal Institutions and Fiscal Performance.* Chicago, IL: University of Chicago Press.

Prud'homme, Remy. 1995. "The Dangers of Decentralization." *World Bank Research Observer* 10 (2): 201–20.

Qian, Yingyi. 2000a. "The Institutional Foundations of Market Transition in the People's Republic of China." ADB Institute Working Paper 9, Asian Development Bank, Tokyo.

———. 2000b. "The Process of China's Market Transition (1978–1998): The Evolutionary, Historical, and Comparative Perspectives." *Journal of Institutional and Theoretical Economics* 156 (1): 151–79.

Qian, Yingyi, and Jinglian Wu. 2003. "China's Transition to a Market Economy: How Far across the River? In *How Far across the River?*, ed. Nicholas C. Hope, Dennis Tao Yang, and Mu Yang Li, 31–64. Stanford, CA: Stanford University Press.

Saiegh, Sebastián, and Mariano Tommasi. 1998. "Argentina's Federal Fiscal Institutions: A Case Study in the Transaction-Cost Theory of Politics." Paper presented at the conference on Modernization and Institutional Development in Argentina, Programa de Naciones Unidas para el Desarrollo, Buenos Aires, Argentina, May 20–21.

———. 1999. "Why Is Argentina's Fiscal Federalism So Inefficient? Entering the Labyrinth." *Journal of Applied Economics* 2 (1): 169–209.

Saknini, Humam, Steven James, and Munir A. Sheikh. 1996. "Stabilization, Insurance, and Risk Sharing in Federal Fiscal Policy." Department of Finance, Ottawa.

Seabright, Paul. 1996. "Accountability and Decentralization in Government: An Incomplete Contract Model." *European Economic Review* 40 (1): 61–89.

Shah, Anwar. 1991. *The New Fiscal Federalism in Brazil.* Washington, DC: World Bank.

———. 1994. *The Reform of Intergovernmental Fiscal Relations in Developing and Emerging Market Economies.* Washington, DC: World Bank.

———. 1998. "Fostering Fiscally Responsive and Accountable Governance: Lessons from Decentralization." In *Evaluation and Development: The Institutional Dimension,* ed. Roberto Picciotto and Eduardo Wiesner, 83–96. London: Transaction.

———. 2004. "Fiscal Decentralization in Developing and Transition Economies: Progress, Problems, and the Promise." Policy Research Working Paper 3282, World Bank, Washington, DC.

———. 2006. "Fiscal Decentralization and Macroeconomic Management." *International Tax and Public Finance* 13 (4): 437–62.

Sheikh, Munir A., and Stanley L. Winer. 1977. "Stabilization and Nonfederal Behaviour in an Open Federal State: An Econometric Study of the Fixed Exchange Rate, Canadian Case." *Empirical Economics* 2 (3): 195–211.

Shirai, Sayuri. 2001. "Banking Sector Reforms in the People's Republic of China: Progress and Constraints." ADB Institute Research Papers Series 43, Asian Development Bank Institute, Tokyo.

Spahn, Heinz-Peter. 1997. "Schulden, Defizite und die Maastricht-Kriterien." *Konjunkturpolitik* 43 (1): 1–15.

Stein, Ernesto. 1999. "Fiscal Decentralization and Government Size in Latin America." *Journal of Applied Economics* 2 (2): 357–91.

Tanzi, Vito. 1996. "Fiscal Federalism and Decentralization: A Review of Some Efficiency and Macroeconomic Aspects." In *Proceedings of the Annual World Bank Conference on Development Economics, 1995,* ed. Michael Bruno and Boris Pleskovic, 295–316. Washington, DC: World Bank.

von Hagen, Jürgen. 2002. "Fiscal Rules, Fiscal Institutions, and Fiscal Performance." *Economic and Social Review* 33 (3): 263–84.

———. 2005. "Fiscal Rules and Fiscal Institutions: European Experiences." Paper presented at the 61st Congress of the International Institute of Public Finance on Macrofiscal Policies: New Perspectives and Challenges, Jeju Islands, Republic of Korea, August 22–25.

von Hagen, Jürgen, Andrew Hughes Hallet, and Rolf Strauch. 2002. "Budgetary Institutions for Sustainable Public Finances." In *The Behaviour of Fiscal Authorities: Stabilisation, Growth, and Institutions,* ed. Marco Buti, Jürgen von Hagen, and Carlos Martinez-Mongay, 94–114. Basingstoke, U.K.: Palgrave.

Walsh, Cliff. 1992. "Infrastructure Funding and Federal-State Financial Relations." Discussion Paper 21, Federalism Research Centre, Australian National University, Canberra.

Weingast, Barry R. 1995. "The Economic Role of Political Institutions: Market Preserving Federalism and Economic Growth." *Journal of Law, Economics, and Organization* 11 (1): 1–31.

Weingast, Barry R., and W. Marshall. 1988. "The Industrial Organization of Congress; or, Why Legislatures, Like Firms, Are Not Organized as Markets." *Journal of Political Economy* 96 (1): 132–63.

Wierts, Peter. 2005. "Federalism and the EU: Fiscal Policy Coordination within and between EU Member States." Paper presented at the International Conference on Federalism, Brussels, March 1–5.

World Bank. 2000. "China: Managing Public Expenditures for Better Results." Report 20342-CHA, World Bank, Washington, DC.

———. 2002. "Brazil: Issues in Fiscal Federalism." Report 22523-BR, World Bank, Washington, DC.

———. 2005. "China Quarterly Update." World Bank, Beijing, February.

Yep, Ray. 2004. "Can 'Tax-for-Fee' Reform Reduce Rural Tension in China? The Process, Progress, and Limitations." *China Quarterly* 177 (March): 42–71.

Yusuf, Shahid. 1997. "China's State Enterprise Sector: Problems and Reform Prospects." Working Paper. World Bank, Washington, DC.

Regional Income Disparities and Convergence: Measurement and Policy Impact Evaluation

RAJA SHANKAR AND ANWAR SHAH

Regional inequalities represent an ever-present development challenge in most countries, especially those with large geographic areas under their jurisdiction. Globalization heightens these challenges because it places a premium on skills. With globalization, skills rather than the resource base of regions determine their competitiveness. Skilled workers gain at the expense of unskilled ones. Because rich regions typically also have better-educated and better-skilled labor, the gulf between rich and poor regions widens. Large regional disparities represent serious threats in federal states because the inability of the state to deal with such inequities creates potential for disunity and, in extreme cases, for disintegration. Although the policy challenges in reducing regional disparities are large, the division of powers in a federation curtails federal flexibility in the choice of instruments. In contrast, central governments in unitary states are relatively unconstrained in their choice of appropriate policies and instruments. Under these circumstances, there is a presumption in development economics that a decentralized fiscal constitution would lead to ever-widening regional inequalities. This chapter attempts to provide an empirical test of that hypothesis.

The chapter is organized as follows. The next section provides an introductory overview of various measures of regional inequality that are available from the literature. Then the chapter estimates inequality measures for a sample of 8 industrial[1] and 18 developing countries. These countries are further subgrouped into federal and unitary countries for analytical purposes. For a smaller subset of 14 countries, the chapter presents evidence on historical trends in regional disparities in per capita income. The final section provides a summary scorecard on national policies for regional development.

Measures of Regional Inequality

Income inequality can be measured in several ways. Two types of measures are of interest in this chapter: static and dynamic. Static measures provide a snapshot of these inequalities at a point of time, whereas dynamic measures capture historical trends. These two measures are described in the following subsections.

Static Measures of Regional Inequality

The measurement of regional disparities is an arduous task, and no single statistical measure is able to capture its myriad dimensions. Recognizing these difficulties, this chapter has applied a variety of measures to highlight various dimensions of these inequalities. The selected measures are briefly described in the following paragraphs.

Maximum-to-minimum ratio

A comparison of the per capita gross regional domestic product (GRDP) of the region with the highest income (maximum per capita GRDP) to that of the region with the lowest income (minimum per capita GRDP) provides a measure of the range of these disparities. If this measure is small (close to 1), the different regions have relatively equal incomes. If this measure is large, the interpretation is more problematic. The high ratio could be attributable to substantial variation in the distribution of per capita GRDPs, or it could indicate the presence of outliers. Nevertheless, maximum-to-minimum ratio (MMR) provides a quick, easy to comprehend, and politically powerful measure of regional income inequality.

Coefficient of variation

The coefficient of variation (CV) is one of the most widely used measures of regional inequality in the literature (see, for example, Akita and Lukman 1995; Decressin 1999; Dev 2000; Lyons 1991; Nagaraj, Varoudakis, and

Véganzonés 2000; Raiser 1998; Sacks 1999; Tsui 1996; Williamson 1965). The CV is a measure of dispersion around the mean. This dispersion can be calculated in a few different ways. Several authors have used the standard deviation of the logarithm of real per capita GRDP (Bajpai and Sachs 1996; Cashin and Sahay 1996; Garcia and Soelistianingsih 1998; Jian, Sachs, and Warner 1996). In this study, however, the CV attempts to capture the dispersion of per capita GRDP. This measure is standardized and can be used to make comparisons between countries and over time (especially if GRDP data are available only in current prices). In the following analysis, the CV is calculated in two ways: the simple coefficient of variation and the weighted coefficient of variation. The *simple coefficient of variation* is an unweighted measure as given in equation 4.1:

$$CV_U = \frac{\sqrt{\sum_i \frac{(y_i - \bar{y}_U)^2}{N}}}{\bar{y}_U}, \tag{4.1}$$

where y_i is the income per capita of region i, N is the number of regions, and $\bar{y}_U$ is the mean per capita GRDP. The expression $\bar{y}_U$ is computed as the mean of the regional incomes per capita without weighting them by population as follows:

$$\bar{y}_U = \frac{1}{N} \sum_i y_i. \tag{4.2}$$

Equation 4.2 is slightly different from Williamson's (1965: 11) formula for the unweighted CV, where the mean income, $\bar{y}$, is taken as the national mean per capita GRDP. The Williamson measure is not appropriate in this application because it uses a weighted measure for the denominator and an unweighted one for the numerator. The measure CV_U varies from 0 for perfect inequality—equal per capita GRDP for the different regions—to $\sqrt{N-1}$ for perfect inequality—only one region has all the gross domestic product (GDP). Although this measure can be used for comparisons of regional disparities in countries across time, it is problematic for comparisons between countries because the inequality value is sensitive to the number of regions.

This problem is somewhat overcome by the weighted coefficient of variation (CV_W), where each regional deviation is weighted by its share in the national population. This measure is calculated as given in equation (4.3):

$$CV_W = \frac{\sqrt{\sum_i (y_i - \bar{y})^2 \frac{P_i}{P}}}{\bar{y}}, \tag{4.3}$$

where y_i is the income per capita of region i, and $\bar{y}$ is the national mean per capita GDP. P is the national population, and p_i is the population of region i. The measure CV_W varies from 0 for perfect equality to $\sqrt{(P - p_i)/p_i}$ for perfect inequality where region i has all the GDP. This measure is better than CV_U for cross-country comparison because the measure of inequality depends not on the number of regions but on the population proportion of the regions.

Relative mean deviation

As in Williamson (1965: 16) and Kakwani (1980: 79), the relative mean deviation (R_w) of per capita GRDP is computed as follows:

$$R_w = \frac{\sum_i |y_i - \bar{y}| \dfrac{p_i}{P}}{\bar{y}}, \tag{4.4}$$

where y_i is the income per capita of region i, and $\bar{y}$ is the national mean income per capita. P is the national population, and p_i is the population of region i. The measure R_w is weighted by population proportions of the regions. Because CV is computed by squaring differences, it could be unnecessarily sensitive to outliers. The measure R_w, which avoids this problem, can thus be used to check the CV results. The measure R_w varies from 0 for perfect equality to 2 for perfect inequality. Kakwani (1980) divides R_w by 2 to get his measure of relative mean deviation, because this approach gives the desirable property of the measure becoming equal to 1 for perfect inequality. However, because R_w is used only to check the CV results for outlier effects, the chapter does not follow Kakwani (1980) in this regard.

Gini index

The Gini index, like the CV, is widely used in the inequality literature (Kakwani and Son 2005; Tsui 1996; Yao and Liu 1998). Following Kakwani (1980), the unweighted Gini index (G_U) is computed as follows:

$$G_U = \left(\frac{1}{2\bar{y}_U}\right) \frac{1}{n(n-1)} \sum_i^n \sum_j^n |y_i - y_j|, \tag{4.5}$$

where y_i and y_j are the incomes per capita of region i and region j, respectively. The expression n is the number of regions, and $\bar{y}_U$ is the unweighted mean of the per capita GRDPs. The measure G_U varies from 0 for perfect equality to 1 for perfect inequality. The Gini index thus measured is the arithmetic average of $n(n-1)$ differences of per capita GRDPs, taken as absolute values divided by the maximum possible value of this average, $2\,\bar{y}_U$.

The weighted Gini index (G_W), which weights each difference of per capita GRDPs by respective population proportions, is calculated as shown in equation (4.6):

$$G_W = \left(\frac{1}{2\bar{y}}\right)\sum_i^n \sum_j^n |y_i - y_j|\frac{p_i p_j}{P^2}, \tag{4.6}$$

where $\bar{y}$ is the national mean per capita GDP. The expressions p_i and p_j are the populations of regions i and j, respectively. P is the national population, and n is the number of regions. The measure G_W varies from 0 for perfect equality to $1-(p_i/p)$ for perfect inequality. If p_i is small compared to P—that is, if the region with a small proportion of the population produced all the GDP—then the value for perfect inequality would approach 1.

Theil index

The Theil index (T) is a final measure of inequality used in this chapter. It is an information or entropy measure of inequality. In accordance with Theil (1967), it is computed as follows:

$$T = \sum_i x_i \log\left(\frac{x_i}{q_i}\right) \tag{4.7}$$

The expression x_i is the GDP share of region i, and q_i is the population share of region i. For equal per capita GRDPs—that is, with GRDPs proportional to regional populations—T takes a value of 0. In a case where region i gets all the income, T becomes $\log(p/p_i)$, where p is total population of the country and p_i is the population of region i. Note here that as the population share of region i goes down, T rises if region i gets all the income.

Dynamic Concepts of Regional Inequality

Although a snapshot view of regional income disparities is illuminating, a longer-term perspective is more helpful in ascertaining the effect of public policies. Achieving this perspective requires developing a time profile of static measures and discerning whether these inequalities appear to diminish (the *convergence hypothesis*) or accentuate (the *divergence hypothesis*) over time. A strong convergence hypothesis suggests that equality in factor productivity and income levels will be achieved regardless of initial conditions, provided diffusion and adoption of technological change are unrestrained. A weak convergence hypothesis, in contrast, requires competitive market structures to send the right signals for allocation of productive factors (see Boldrin and Canova 2001). Under the weak convergence hypothesis, differences in technology alone do not explain the differences in factor productivity. Lack of competitive price signals, such as those observed with regional incentives and subsidies; infant industry protection; and barriers to trade may perpetuate regional differences in factor productivity and income.

At the conceptual level, regional convergence is ensured under perfect competition, constant returns to scale with no external effects, and free and costless mobility of factors across relatively homogeneous (with respect to resource endowment, topography, composition of population, human capital, political and legal environment, informal culture, and the like) regions within the nation-state. This regional convergence requires that political units are commensurate with reasonably large geographic areas that have reasonably diverse endowments, so that regional income differentials are attributable to policy and institutional considerations rather than simply to irreversible acts of nature. For example, one should not expect to have convergence among three completely heterogeneous regions comprising solely desert, mountainous, and arable lands.

Regional convergence becomes more difficult to achieve under increasing returns to scale and with externalities of investment and growth. Strong nonconvergence (divergence) hypothesis places a greater emphasis on path dependency (initial conditions matter), increasing returns to scale, and externalities of investment as sources of differences in factor productivity and growth (see Krugman 1991; Romer 1990). Realization of increasing returns to scale, agglomeration economies under perfect mobility in one of the regions and not others, or both would accentuate regional divergence. Divergence would also happen if factors are either unable (because of impediments) or unwilling (for example, because of age and ethnicity considerations) to move. Under a strong divergence hypothesis, inequality in levels of income and resource endowments will prevent convergence in regional growth rates. Under a weak divergence hypothesis, attainment of a minimum threshold of physical and knowledge capital in the leading regions is necessary for persistence in the divergence of growth paths. Thus, some regions that attain the minimum thresholds in these factors may form clubs or growth poles and may grow faster than others and achieve club convergence. Public policies to break this regional concentration of powers may have tradeoffs between national growth and overcoming regional inequalities (for a discussion of this issue in the European Union context, see Boldrin and Canova 2001). In federal countries, regional inequalities are likely to be given significant importance in evaluating any tradeoffs that may be observed. The section titled "Regional Income Disparities and Convergence" provides empirical evidence on the outcome of the choices on these tradeoffs that are made in various countries.

Two statistical concepts are helpful in looking at the dynamics of regional inequalities. First, a reduction in the dispersion of regional income over time is termed *sigma convergence*. Second, any catching up in incomes by relatively poorer regions through faster growth is called *beta convergence* (see Barro and Sala-i-Martin 1995: 383). The section titled "Regional Income Disparities and Convergence" provides empirical estimates on sigma convergence for 16 countries and on beta convergence for 8 countries.

Regional Disparities: A Cross-Country Snapshot

Data on regional incomes are available for only a surprisingly small number of developing countries. Such data were available for 8 industrial and 17 developing countries. In the following discussion, measures of regional income inequality are presented separately for industrial and nonindustrial countries. The experiences of federal and unitary countries are also compared.

Industrial Countries

Table 4.1 presents the authors' calculations of the different measures of regional inequality of per capita GRDP in seven industrial countries—four federal and three unitary. For Germany, the inequality measures are presented for the unified Germany as well as for the states that were part of the Federal Republic of Germany (FRG) prior to unification. As expected, the FRG is less unequal than unified Germany.

By most measures of inequality, the federal countries have lower levels of regional disparity than the unitary countries in the sample. This result is especially true for the population-weighted measures, which are more appropriate for cross-country comparisons. Figure 4.1 shows the weighted measures of regional inequality for industrial countries. The figure is in descending order of the weighted CV. Except for the United Kingdom, the federal countries in the sample have lower values for all the inequality measures.

Canada and the United States have the lowest levels of inequality on almost all measures, as shown in table 4.1. Furthermore, the weighted values are smaller than the unweighted ones, showing that the provinces or states with extreme per capita GRDPs are generally those with smaller populations. Canada and the United States are followed by the United Kingdom,

TABLE 4.1 Regional Disparities in Industrial Countries

Country	Year	Maximum-to-minimum ratio	Simple coefficient of variation	Weighted coefficient of variation	Relative mean deviation	Unweighted Gini index	Weighted Gini index	Theil index
Federal								
Canada	1997	1.838	0.201	0.137	0.123	0.118	0.067	0.008
	1998	1.718	0.195	0.137	0.127	0.113	0.068	0.006
Federal Republic								
of Germany[a]	1995–97	2.033	0.241	0.207	0.140	0.128	0.076	0.010
Spain	1995–97	1.866	0.189	0.210	0.189	0.111	0.118	0.022
United States	1997	1.927	0.162	0.122	0.097	0.090	0.039	0.007
	1995–97	3.048	0.341	0.262	0.197	0.191	0.122	0.027
Unitary								
France	1995–97	2.039	0.178	0.267	0.206	0.096	0.126	0.032
Italy	1995–97	2.228	0.262	0.264	0.243	0.152	0.145	0.037
United Kingdom	1995–97	1.794	0.177	0.178	0.123	0.085	0.083	0.015

Source: Authors' calculations based on sources listed in annex 4B.
a. States that were part of the Federal Republic of Germany prior to unification.

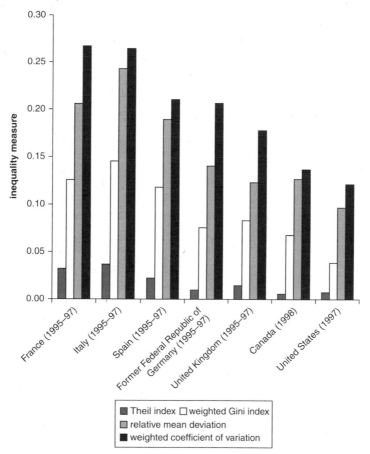

Source: Authors' calculations based on sources listed in annex 4B.

FIGURE 4.1 Regional Disparities in Industrial Countries

and then the FRG and Spain. France and Italy have the highest regional disparities. The weighted and unweighted values of inequality for the United Kingdom and Italy are similar, showing that regions at different points of the income distribution have similar populations. As expected, unified Germany is more unequal than just the states of the former FRG. The weighted values are lower as in the case of Canada and the United States. Spain's and France's weighted inequality measures are higher than the unweighted ones, which means that regions with extreme per capita GRDPs have larger populations in these countries. The relative mean deviation, which is used to check for a few extreme deviations, is significantly different only for the United Kingdom and the FRG.

Nonindustrial Countries

Table 4.2 presents the authors' calculations of the different measures of regional inequality in 18 developing countries—5 federal and 13 unitary. In general, on all the measures of inequality, the developing countries are much more unequal than the industrial countries. Except for Pakistan and Romania, all the developing countries are more unequal than the most unequal industrial country in the sample, Italy. On average, if one takes the weighted CV, developing countries are two to six times more unequal than the industrial countries.

As in the case of industrial countries, unitary developing countries are, in general, more unequal than federal developing countries. Figure 4.2 presents the weighted measures of inequality for developing countries for 1997 or the latest available year before 1997. The countries are presented in descending order of the weighted CV. The countries with the highest measures of inequality are large unitary countries: Vietnam, Thailand, China, and Indonesia. Inequalities in federal and smaller unitary countries are considerably lower.

Pakistan, Romania, Chile, Brazil, and Indonesia have lower values for the weighted measures than the unweighted ones, signifying that regions with extreme values of per capita GRDPs have smaller populations. In contrast, the higher values for the weighted measures signify that India, Sri Lanka, Mexico, China, and Thailand have regions with larger populations at the extremes of the per capita GRDP distribution. Uzbekistan, the Philippines, the Russian Federation, South Africa, and Vietnam have relatively more equal distribution of the populations in the regions at different points of the per capita GRDP distribution. The relative mean deviation, which is used to check for a few extreme deviations, is significantly different for Pakistan, Russia, Indonesia, the Philippines, Uzbekistan, and Vietnam.

Federal versus Unitary Countries

In general, federal countries are less unequal in terms of per capita GRDP than are unitary countries. In this subsection, the chapter looks at this relationship between decentralization and regional inequality. The study regressed three weighted measures of inequality on a dummy variable representing whether a country is unitary or federal.[2] The value of the dummy is 1 if the country is unitary and 0 if the country is federal. For each measure of inequality, two regressions were carried out: the first just on the unitary dummy and the second with the natural logarithm of population as the control variable. The

TABLE 4.2 Regional Disparities in Nonindustrial Countries

Country	Year	Maximum-to-minimum ratio	Simple coefficient of variation	Weighted coefficient of variation	Relative mean deviation	Unweighted Gini index	Weighted Gini index	Theil index
Federal								
Brazil	1997	7.567	0.563	0.468	0.409	0.334	0.267	0.116
India	1997	3.811	0.387	0.414	0.334	0.226	0.227	0.082
Mexico	1997	5.793	0.473	0.571	0.422	0.253	0.301	0.136
	1998	5.874	0.469	0.566	0.421	0.251	0.300	0.134
Pakistan	1997	1.514	0.186	0.150	0.094	0.113	0.072	0.009
	1998	1.516	0.183	0.141	0.095	0.114	0.069	0.008
Russian Federation	1997	21.307	0.625	0.645	0.387	0.283	0.280	0.153
Unitary								
Chile	1994	5.696	0.486	0.334	0.243	0.267	0.165	0.052
China	1997	11.625	0.692	0.924	0.666	0.351	0.250	0.111
	1998	12.183	0.709	0.952	0.679	0.357	0.254	0.115
	1999	12.507	0.730	0.987	0.694	0.365	0.264	0.125
Indonesia	1997	11.048	0.827	0.716	0.401	0.378	0.274	0.176
	1998	11.436	0.832	0.722	0.416	0.381	0.277	0.178
Nepal	1996	1.440	0.157					
Philippines	1997	6.653	0.530	0.532	0.367	0.307	0.261	0.123
	1998	6.760	0.536	0.537	0.369	0.311	0.262	0.125
Poland	1996	2.031	0.206					
Romania	1996	1.783	0.189	0.174	0.132	0.106	0.090	0.012

(continued)

TABLE 4.2 Regional Disparities in Nonindustrial Countries *(continued)*

Country	Year	Maximum-to-minimum ratio	Simple coefficient of variation	Weighted coefficient of variation	Relative mean deviation	Unweighted Gini index	Weighted Gini index	Theil index
South Africa	1994	7.038	0.621	0.639	0.558	0.352	0.341	0.195
Sri Lanka	1995	3.362	0.394	0.452	0.397	0.230	0.249	0.101
Thailand	1997	8.273	0.797	0.925	0.745	0.438	0.442	0.351
Uganda	1997–98	1.760	0.274					
Uzbekistan	1997	3.047	0.353	0.355	0.238	0.155	0.170	0.054
	1998	2.991	0.321	0.320	0.218	0.147	0.159	0.046
	1999	2.779	0.304	0.301	0.206	0.142	0.152	0.041
Vietnam	1997	24.746	1.067	0.996	0.596	0.372	0.410	0.306

Source: Authors' calculations based on sources listed in annex 4B.

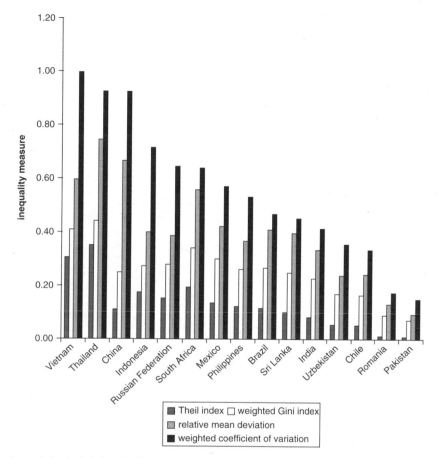

Source: Authors' calculations based on sources listed in annex 4B.

FIGURE 4.2 Regional Disparities in Nonindustrial Countries

measures of inequality used in the regression were from 1997 or the latest year available before 1997.

Positive coefficients on the unitary dummy were obtained in all the regressions, signifying that unitary countries tend to be more unequal. However, except in the case of weighted CV as the dependent variable, the R-square value was too small or the coefficients were not statistically significant. Table 4.3 shows the results of the regression with weighted CV as the dependent variable and the natural logarithm of the country population as a control variable. The coefficient on the unitary dummy is positive and statistically significant at the 5 percent level with the two-tailed test. This finding provides some evidence for the proposition that centralization leads to greater regional

TABLE 4.3 Regression Results

	Dependent variable: weighted coefficient of variation	
Independent variable	Regression 1	Regression 2
Intercept	−1.86	−1.54
	0.048**	0.054*
Unitary dummy	0.28	0.2
	0.016**	0.044**
Log (population)	0.12	0.09
	0.022**	0.036**
Developing dummy		0.28
		0.008***
Number of observations	22	22
R-square	0.344	0.567

Source: Authors' econometric analysis.
Note: p-values in italics; * = significant at the 10 percent level; ** = significant at the 5 percent level;
*** = significant at the 1 percent level (all two-tailed tests).

disparities. The coefficient on the log of population also has a positive sign and is statistically significant at the 5 percent level with the two-tailed test. This finding is not surprising because, other things being equal, countries with larger populations would be expected to have greater regional inequalities.

Spearman rank correlations of the weighted inequality measures with the unitary dummy were also computed in two different ways. First, an average rank of 5.5 was assigned to all 9 federal countries and of 15.5 to all 12 unitary countries. In the second case, the countries were ranked within each group (federal or unitary) according to the level of decentralization. The level of decentralization was measured as the proportion of subnational government expenditures to that of total expenditures. Government expenditure data were taken from the International Monetary Fund's Government Finance Statistics data set.

Table 4.4 presents the results of the calculations. The first row presents the rank correlations of the 22 countries in the sample, according only to whether a country is federal or unitary. The second row shows the results when the ranking takes into account the level of decentralization in each country. In this case, the sample contains only 15 countries[3] because government expenditure data were not available for the others. All the correlation values are positive. These values may not be large, but they do question the conventional wisdom from the literature (Musgrave 1959; Oates 1972) that a centralized form of government is better for the reduction of inequalities between jurisdictions.

TABLE 4.4 Spearman Rank Correlation

Indicator	Weighted coefficient of variation	Weighted Gini index	Theil index
Federal/unitary	0.458	0.423	0.458
Federal/unitary and decentralization	0.382	0.371	0.411

Source: Authors' calculation.

In conclusion, significant regional inequalities persist in many developing countries. By most measures of regional inequality, developing countries are two to six times more unequal than industrial countries. Similarly, the unitary countries are more unequal than federal countries. This finding challenges the widespread assumption that centralized countries are better at equalizing economic differences among regions. On the contrary, the federal countries have a better record at ensuring regional equity.

Regional Income Disparities and Convergence

In this section, the time trends of inequality for 16 different countries are presented to discern the degree of convergence. Canada and the United States are industrial countries, and the rest are developing countries. Of the developing countries, five are federal countries and nine are unitary countries.

Regional Disparity Trends in Federal Countries

Figure 4.3 shows regional inequality trends in the federal countries over the period 1980 to 1999. Panel a plots the trends in the weighted CV, panel b the weighted Gini index, and panel c the Theil index. Trends for different countries are plotted over different subperiods, depending on data availability. Table 4.5 presents evidence on beta convergence in the federal countries. This table contains the results of basic regressions of the growth rate of per capita GRDP on the logarithm of initial GRDP. The United States, Canada, and Pakistan have the lowest levels of regional inequality, followed by India, Brazil, Mexico, and Russia.

The United States saw a decline in regional inequality from 1990 to 1994, after which it stabilized. Canada's inequality remained more or less constant from 1994 to 1998. Pakistan saw a decline in inequality from 1990 to 1998, with a relatively sharp drop in 1994. Its level of inequality is comparable to that of Canada and the United States. The low levels of regional inequality in industrial countries are expected because they are at an advanced stage of economic development[4] and because they have few barriers to interregional trade and factor mobility. Pakistan's low level

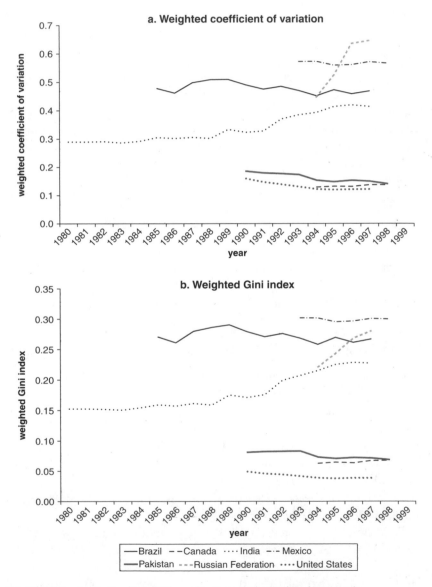

FIGURE 4.3 Regional Disparity Trends in Federal Countries

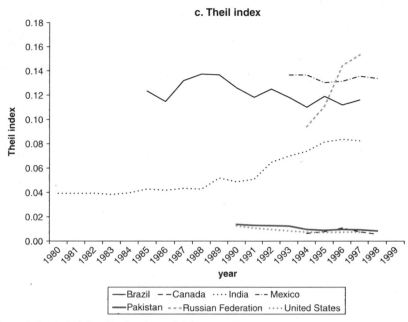

c. Theil index

Source: Authors' calculations based on sources listed in annex 4B.

FIGURE 4.3 Regional Disparity Trends in Federal Countries (*continued*)

TABLE 4.5 Beta Convergence Results in Federal Countries

Country	Time period	Independent variable	Beta	p-value	R-square	Number of regions
Brazil	1994–97	Log (1994 per capita GRDP)	−0.020	0.566	0.013	27
Canada	1994–98	Log (1994 per capita GRDP)	−0.019	0.751	0.012	11
India**	1980–97	Log (1980 per capita GRDP)	0.283	0.040	0.307	14
Mexico	1993–98	Log (1993 per capita GRDP)	−0.010	0.730	0.004	32
Pakistan[a]	—	—	—	—	—	—
Russian Federation	1994–97	Log (1994 per capita GRDP)	0.010	0.824	0.001	79
United States***	1990–97	Log (1990 per capita GRDP)	−0.297	0.000	0.462	50

Source: Authors' calculations based on sources listed in annex 4B.
Note: ** = significant at the 5 percent level; *** = significant at the 1 percent level; — = not available.
a. Too few data points.

of regional inequality, uncharacteristic of developing countries, may be surprising. It could be explained, however, by the fact that Pakistan has a small number of provinces and the two richest provinces have over 80 percent of the country's population; moreover, interprovincial migration of labor and capital is significant.

India has seen a constant rise in regional disparity from 1980 to 1996, followed by a slight fall in 1997. Regional inequality dramatically increased in 1992 after the liberalization reforms started. Its level of inequality has risen from about twice that of the United States in 1990 to more than three times in 1997. This chapter's findings, which show that India has not witnessed sigma convergence, are consistent with those of other authors who have looked at regional inequalities in India. Bajpai and Sachs (1996) find evidence of divergence of state domestic products in the period 1971 to 1993. Cashin and Sahay (1996) also find a widening in the dispersion of the net domestic products of Indian states from 1971 to 1991. Das and Barua (1996); Nagaraj, Varoudakis, and Vèganzonès (2000); Rao, Shand, and Kalirajan (1999); and Yagci (1999) also find similar evidence of divergence in India. Some of these authors have also found evidence against beta convergence in India. Rao, Shand, and Kalirajan (1999) find that the growth of state domestic product per capita is positively related to initial levels for various subperiods beginning in 1965 and ending in 1994 and 1995. Yagci (1999) reports that higher-income states have grown faster since 1980 than have lower-income states. Bajpai and Sachs (1996) also find evidence of a weak positive relationship between initial state domestic product and the economic growth rate in the period 1971 to 1993. Cashin and Sahay (1996), however, report evidence of weak beta convergence. But they also point out that the speed of convergence, 1.5 percent per year, is slower than that of regional convergence in industrial economies (Australia, Canada, Japan, and the United States), whose rate of convergence has been 2 percent. In fact, the speed of convergence is slower than between countries of the Organisation for Economic Co-operation and Development, which is a surprising result because one would expect faster convergence within national borders.

There could be several reasons for increasing regional inequality in India. One explanation could be that India is in an early stage of development and therefore is on the wrong side of the inverted U pattern of regional inequalities (Williamson 1965). Another reason could be the relatively high barriers to interstate trade in India. A third reason could be the perverse nature of the central government's regional development policies and the intergovernmental transfer system (Shankar and Shah forthcoming).

Brazil saw a rise in inequality in the 1980s, a slight fall in the early 1990s, and then a slight rise from 1995 to 1997. Its inequality has been about three to four times that of the United States. The level of regional inequality has remained stable within a relatively narrow band. The weighted CV has fluctuated between a high of 0.51 and a low of 0.45 during this period. The weighted Gini index has varied between 0.29 and 0.26, while the Theil index has stayed between 0.14 and 0.11 (see annex 4A).

Mexico's regional inequality is about five times that of the United States and has remained more or less stable in the 1990s. A slight dip occurred in 1995, which was the year when the Mexican economy contracted 6.2 percent, the worst recession since the Great Depression. Mexico is the most centralized of the federal countries in the sample. The state governments depend largely on central transfers for their revenues. Transfers to states from revenue sharing were almost six times as large as states' own revenues in 1996 (Giugale and others 2000: 19). This highly centralized nature of the Mexican federation may be one of the reasons for its high level of regional inequality (Shah and Shankar forthcoming).

Russia had a dramatic rise in inequality from 1994 to 1997, with its 1997 weighted CV being 50 percent more than its 1994 value. During this period, the Russian economy has undergone a major structural transformation. It underwent a long period of recession from 1990 until 1997, when it had a positive growth rate of 0.9 percent. The increasing regional inequality may be caused by the complex political and economic changes taking place in Russia, especially with economic power being concentrated in Moscow and a few other regions.

Regional Disparity Trends in Unitary Countries

Figure 4.4 shows regional inequality trends in the unitary countries from 1978 to 1999. Panel a plots the trends in the weighted CV, panel b the weighted Gini index, and panel c the Theil index. Trends for different countries are plotted over different subperiods depending on data availability. Table 4.6 presents evidence on beta convergence in the unitary countries. The table contains the results of basic regressions of the growth rate of per capita GRDP on the logarithm of initial GRDP.

The smaller unitary countries in the sample have relatively lower levels of regional inequality, with the major exception of Vietnam. Romania, Sri Lanka, Uzbekistan, and Chile have relatively low levels of inequality, whereas the Philippines, China, Indonesia, Thailand, and Vietnam have high levels of inequality. In general, except for the smaller countries other than Vietnam, the levels of inequality in these countries are significantly higher than in the federal countries.

Romania, which has the lowest level of regional inequality, experienced a rise in regional inequality from 1993 to 1996. Its inequality, measured by the weighted CV, is around a third more than that of the United States. Another transition country, Uzbekistan, has experienced a decline in its

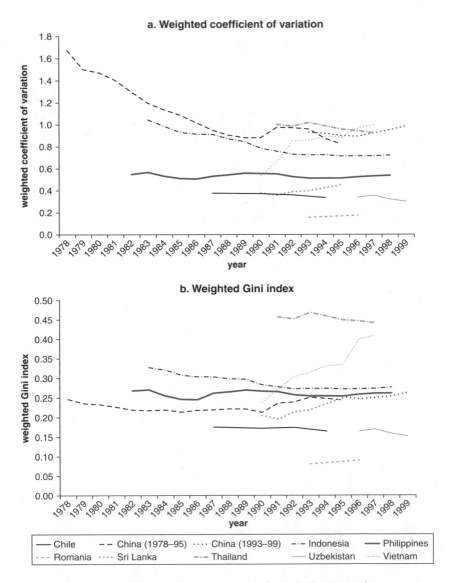

FIGURE 4.4 Regional Disparity Trends in Unitary Countries

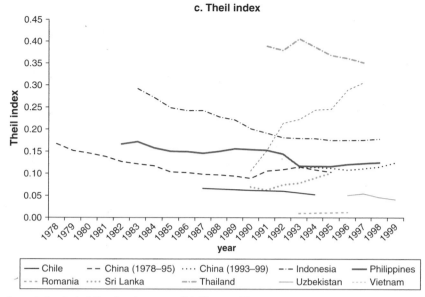

c. Theil index

Legend:
— Chile   – – China (1978–95)   ···· China (1993–99)   –·– Indonesia   — Philippines
--- Romania   ···· Sri Lanka   —·— Thailand   — Uzbekistan   ···· Vietnam

Source: Authors' calculations based on sources listed in annex 4B.

FIGURE 4.4 Regional Disparity Trends in Unitary Countries (*continued*)

regional inequality during 1996 to 1999. Its weighted CV is around two and a half times more than that of Canada and the United States. Uzbekistan is a highly centralized country with 14 regions whose leaders can be sacked by the country's president. The most important activity happens in a sparsely populated region, Navoi, where most gold and uranium are mined. Because gold is one of the country's major exports, this factor could account for some of Uzbekistan's regional inequality.

Chile has seen a decline in its level of regional inequality from 1987 to 1994. Its weighted CV has been about three times that of the United States. The decline may be because Chile's development stage is on the right side of the inverted U. Moreover, market liberalization in Chile may be causing convergence. Economic activity is heavily concentrated in the central region. Centralizing trends appear to have stopped, however, as a result of the mining boom in the north and the economic dynamism achieved in the extreme south by salmon breeding, tourism, and large-scale methanol production. Tourism and export agriculture are strong engines of growth in the center-north, while forestry, tourism, fruit production, and traditional agriculture are important to the center-south regions. Furthermore, the traditionally strong centralist bias is being reversed through a gradual

TABLE 4.6 Beta Convergence Results in Unitary Countries

Country	Time period	Independent variable	Beta	p-value	R-square	Number of regions
Chile*	1987–94	Log (1987 per capita GRDP)	−0.155	0.068	0.271	13
China***	1978–90	Log (1978 per capita GRDP)	−0.229	0.000	0.393	28
	1990–95	Log (1990 per capita GRDP)	0.011	0.882	0.000	29
	1993–99	Log (1993 per capita GRDP)	0.052	0.273	0.044	29
Indonesia***	1983–92	Log (1983 per capita GRDP)	−0.164	0.000	0.505	27
	1993–98	Log (1993 per capita GRDP)	−0.030	0.356	0.034	27
Philippines	1982–86	Log (1982 per capita GRDP)	−0.103	0.023	0.388	13
	1986–90	Log (1986 per capita GRDP)	0.063	0.499	0.040	13
	1990–94	Log (1990 per capita GRDP)	−0.048	0.439	0.051	14
	1994–98	Log (1994 per capita GRDP)	0.002	0.959	0.000	15
Romania	1993–96	Log (1993 per capita GRDP)	−0.014	0.936	0.001	0
Sri Lanka	1990–95	Log (1990 per capita GRDP)	0.0950	0.619	0.053	7
Uzbekistan	1996–99	Log (1996 per capita GRDP)	−0.058	0.373	0.067	14
Thailand	1991–97	Log (1991 per capita GRDP)	−0.014	0.821	0.011	7
Vietnam	1990–97	Log (1990 per capita GRDP)	−0.068	0.652	0.004	52

Source: Authors' calculations based on sources listed in annex 4B.
Note: * = significant at the 10 percent level; ** = significant at the 5 percent level; *** = significant at the 1 percent level.

devolution of power to the municipalities, regional offices of ministries and public agencies, and other regional organizations.[5]

Although Sri Lanka has a lower level of inequality among the unitary countries, it is more unequal than India. Its weighted CV is almost four times that of the United States. Sri Lanka saw a fall in regional inequality in 1991, after which it has steadily increased. Inadequate infrastructure development in rural areas, the concentration of industry close to the main ports and the airport, and the poor performance of the agricultural sector have led to an unequal distribution of the benefits of economic growth between regions. Because of its proximity to the port and airport, Western province is home to 85 percent of industry and generates over 40 percent of GDP, while predominantly agricultural areas such as North Western and Uva provinces remain backward because of the stagnation in coconut and domestic agriculture.[6]

Vietnam has seen a dramatic rise in regional inequality in the 1990s. The weighted CV has almost doubled during this period. A big spurt in inequality occurred from 1990 to 1992, after which it increased at a slower pace until 1995. The period 1995 to 1997 has seen another big increase. In 1990, Vietnam's weighted CV was more than three times that of the United States. In 1997, the weighted CV became more than eight times that of the United States. Vietnam's economy has grown strongly during the 1990s after the country started a policy of economic liberalization in the late 1980s. Its performance since 1989 was close to that of China. Since economic reform began in 1986, Ho Chi Minh City and the nearby provinces (especially Dong Nai and Binh Duong) have consolidated their position as the country's industrial heartland, although the Hanoi-Haiphong area has grown equally quickly over the past few years. Left behind are the mountainous areas of the north and most of the north-central coastal provinces, which have traditionally been the poorest parts of the country. The widening regional inequality is counterbalanced to a limited extent by the budget, which raises revenue mainly in the wealthier areas but spreads the expenditure (on infrastructure, health, and education) more widely.

There is no major discernible trend in regional inequality in the Philippines according to the weighted measures for 1982 to 1998. Inequality increased in 1983 and then declined until about 1986, after which it increased until 1989. After 1989, inequality declined until about 1995 and increased from 1995 to 1998. The weighted CV of the Philippines has varied from about three and a half times that of the United States in 1990 to about four and a half times in 1997. Table and figure 4A.11 in the annex show that the weighted measures, which were higher than the unweighted ones in the 1980s, have fallen below the unweighted measures in the 1990s. This finding might mean that most of the bigger population regions have tended to converge nearer the mean per capita GRDP, while the smaller population regions have moved to the extremes. Furthermore, the relative mean deviation is significantly different from the weighted CV, which would mean that there are a few extreme outliers.

The figures for overall GDP of P = 2.42 trillion (US$85.7 billion) and for per capita GDP of P = 32,961 (US$1,166) in 1997 conceal a wide disparity in wealth between different regions of the country. The National Capital Region, the region centered on Manila, accounts for 14 percent of the population and produces one-third of GDP. Its per capita GRDP is well over double the national average. Only two other regions—South Tagalog and Cordillera Administrative Region—have income per capita that is above the national average, while four register about half that figure, and the four autonomous provinces in Mindanao only one-third. This finding reflects the concentration of manufacturing activities in the Manila area. However, growth points have been developing in other regions, where industrial parks have been the focus for much investment, both domestic and foreign, in recent years.[7]

Indonesia has seen a constant drop in regional inequality since 1983. The drop was more pronounced until about 1992, after which the decline slowed. With the 1997 economic crisis, regional inequality increased slightly in 1997 and 1998. In 1983, Indonesia was almost four times as unequal as India; in 1985, its weighted CV was almost twice as unequal as Brazil's; and in 1990, it was five times as unequal as the United States. In 1997, Indonesia's weighted CV was three-fourths more than that of India, about 55 percent more than that of Brazil, and six times that of the United States. In other words, Indonesia has improved its position relative to India and Brazil, but in the 1990s its rate of convergence has been slower than that of the United States.

Akita and Lukman (1995) also find a constant decline in the weighted CV from 1975 to 1992. When they exclude the mining sector, however, no trend is discernible in regional inequality. They conclude that the decreasing weighted CV could be attributed to the decline of the mining sector's share in GDP. Akita and Lukman also find that the contribution of the tertiary sector to regional inequality has declined during this period, while that of the secondary sector has increased. Indonesia has averaged an annual growth rate of 6 percent from 1970 to 1996.

Asra (1989) estimates the Gini index for regional inequality for expenditure for the period 1969 to 1981. He finds that if one adjusts the standard inequality measures for the differential impact of inflation on different expenditure groups, regional inequality in Indonesia has increased from 1969 to 1976 and then declined from 1976 to 1981.

Garcia and Soelistianingsih (1998) find evidence for both sigma convergence and beta convergence for per capita GRDP during 1975 to 1993. But they also find that regions at the top and bottom of the distribution in 1983 remained at the top and bottom of the distribution in 1993. This chapter's data set also shows the same result during 1983 to 1998: the top and bottom regions remained the same.

Regional inequality in China fell from 1978 to 1990, after which it increased until 1993. Inequality fell again from 1993 to 1996 and then increased until 1999. The weighted CV for China has varied from about five times that of the United States in 1990 to about eight times in 1999. Its weighted CV has been higher than that of almost all other countries in the sample. Only Thailand in the early to mid-1990s and Vietnam in the late 1990s have had a higher value for the weighted CV.

However, on other weighted measures of inequality—the weighted Gini index and the Theil index—China has performed better than Indonesia, the Philippines, Thailand, and Vietnam. This finding is intriguing, especially because the weighted CV for China is higher than the unweighted CV, while the weighted Gini index is lower than the unweighted Gini index (see figure 4A.9, panels a and b). This result could be attributable to the presence of provinces with larger populations at the lower end of the distribution. In fact, almost 70 percent of the population is in provinces with per capita GRDP below the national average. The median per capita GRDP is signifi-cantly lower than the mean per capita GRDP. For example, the national mean GRDPs per capita in current prices for 1978 and 1999 are Y 357 (US$210) and Y 7,242 (US$826), respectively. The corresponding population-weighted medians are Y 313 (US$184) and Y 5,400 (US$621), respectively. This result would skew the estimates of weighted CV, which is also evident from the fact that the relative mean deviation is significantly lower than the weighted CV.

Several authors have looked at regional inequality in China. Jian, Sachs, and Warner (1996) have found that the economies of Chinese provinces converged somewhat during 1952 to 1965 and then diverged during the Cul-tural Revolution years of 1966 to 1977. After 1977 until about 1990, during the reform period, they find statistically significant evidence for beta con-vergence. Raiser (1998) also finds evidence of beta convergence after 1978 until about 1990. Both studies find that the economies of the Chinese provinces diverge after 1990. A look at sigma convergence yields a similar picture. Jian, Sachs, and Warner (1996) find that the standard deviation of log of real per capita GRDP fell slightly from 1952 to 1965, increased from 1966 to 1977, and fell significantly from 1977 to 1990. The period after 1990 has seen an increase in the dispersion of per capita GRDP. Raiser finds similar results in the period 1978 to 1992 using the coefficient of variation.

Jian, Sachs, and Warner (1996) suggest that two forces were at work during 1952 to 1965: (a) a government-induced bias against agricultural regions, causing divergence, and (b) unidentified forces pushing toward convergence, leading to slight overall convergence. During 1966 to 1977, the autarkic years of the Cultural Revolution led to divergence, while the market reforms after 1978 led to convergence. However, Jian, Sachs, and Warner (1996) point out that almost all of the convergence is attributable to a narrowing of income inequality among the coastal provinces, rather than to a narrowing of inequality between the coastal and interior provinces or a narrowing of inequality in the interior provinces. Raiser (1998) finds similar results. The divergence between the coast and the interior is in large part caused by the special economic privileges (in tax policy and trade policy) granted to the coastal regions as part of the economic reforms. These reforms have exacerbated the contradiction between the poor, inaccessible, and inhospitable terrain of most of the interior and the more fertile coastal deltas and plains. The coastal areas have been far more able to achieve rapid growth, while the interior provinces have been left behind.

In the sample, Thailand has the highest level of regional inequality. Its level of inequality has slightly declined from 1991 to 1997. The weighted CV has varied from seven times that of the United States in 1991 to a little more than seven and a half times in 1997. The weighted measures have been greater than the unweighted measures throughout this period (see figure 4A.14), signifying that large population regions are at the extreme ends of the distribution. Although rapid growth rates have led to a steady rise in real per capita income levels over the past 30 years, alarming disparities exist in national wealth distribution. Income per capita in the northeast is only 52 percent of the national average and just over 20 percent of that in the Bangkok metropolitan area. Recent governments have responded by pushing economic decentralization, generally with disappointing results. These results could be attributable to the strong role of the center in regional development. Since 1993, about 65 percent of promoted investment has gone outside Bangkok, but most reached only the Eastern Seaboard Industrial Zone, an hour or so from the city. The Board of Investment responded in 1997 by setting up the country's first special economic zones in 13 of the poorest provinces, but by early 1999, the response had been little because of a perception of poor infrastructure in these areas. Tax incentives will be targeted at 21 industries located in the zones. Specialist free trade zones are also being established for more technologically advanced industries. The Eighth Five-Year Development Plan incorporates plans for decentralization, and the old zones system seems likely to be replaced by more localized incentives.[8]

Regional Inequalities and Convergence: A Scorecard on National Policies for Regional Development

The empirical analysis presented in the earlier sections is summarized in table 4.7. The following conclusions emerge from this analysis.

Regional development policies have failed in almost all countries— federal and unitary alike. Of the 10 countries listed in table 4.7 with a high or substantial degree of regional income inequalities, only 1 country (Thailand) has experienced convergence in regional incomes. Federal countries, how- ever, do better in restraining regional inequalities. This result is because widening regional disparities pose a greater political risk in federal countries. In such countries, inequalities beyond a threshold may lead to calls for sepa- ration by both the richest and the poorest regions. Whereas the poorest regions may consider such inequalities as manifestations of regional injustice, the richest regions may view a union with the poorest regions as possibly holding them back in their drive to prosperity in the long run.

The table further provides the following classification of countries by the degree of convergence:

■ *Countries experiencing regional income divergence*—Vietnam, China, Indonesia, Russia, Philippines, Brazil, Sri Lanka, India, and Romania
■ *Countries experiencing no significant change in regional income variations*— Mexico and Canada
■ *Countries experiencing regional income convergence*—Thailand, Uzbekistan, Chile, Pakistan, and the United States.

Regional development outcomes observed here provide a revealing look at the effect of regional development policies. For example, countries expe- riencing divergence largely focus on interventionist policies for regional development. In contrast, countries experiencing convergence have had a hands-off approach to regional development policies and instead focused on policies to promote a common economic union by removing barriers to factor mobility and ensuring minimum standards of basic services across the nation. For example, regional income convergence in Chile is largely attributable to economic liberalization and removal of distortions in the economy so that regions could discover their own comparative advantage in the economic union. In Pakistan and the United States, such conver- gence is attributable to greater factor mobility rather than region-specific policies. These findings lead to the conclusion that, paradoxically, creation of a level playing field is more helpful to disadvantaged regions than following paternalistic protectionist policies.

TABLE 4.7 Regional Inequalities and Convergence: A Summary View

Country	Federal or unitary?	Degree of regional inequality[a]	Trends: sigma convergence (C), divergence(D), or stable (S)	Trends: beta convergence (C), divergence (D), or stable (S)[b]
Vietnam	Unitary	High	D (1990–97)	S– (1990–97)
Thailand	Unitary	High	C (1991–97)	S– (1991–97)
China	Unitary	High	C (1978–90)	C (1978–80)
			D (1990–93)	S+ (1990–95)
			C (1993–96)	S+ (1993–99)
			D (1996–99)	
Indonesia	Unitary	High	C (1983–95)	C (1983–92)
			D (1995–98)	S– (1993–98)
Russian Federation	Federal	High	D (1994–97)	S+ (1994–97)
Mexico	Federal	Substantial	S (1993–98)	S– (1993–98)
Philippines	Unitary	Substantial	C (1982–86)	C (1982–86)
			D (1986–89)	S+ (1986–90)
			C (1989–95)	S– (1990–94)
			D (1995–98)	S+ (1994–98)
Brazil	Federal	Substantial	D (1985–89)	S– (1994–97)
			C (1989–94)	
			D (1994–97)	
Sri Lanka	Unitary	Substantial	D (1990–95)	S+ (1990–95)
India	Federal	Moderate to substantial	D (1980–97)	D (1980–97)
Uzbekistan	Unitary	Moderate	C (1996–99)	S– (1996–99)
Chile	Unitary	Moderate	C (1987–94)	C (1987–94)
France	Unitary	Moderate	—	—
Italy	Unitary	Moderate	—	—
Spain	Unitary	Low	—	—
Federal Republic of Germany[c]	Federal	Low	—	—
United Kingdom	Unitary	Low	—	—
Romania	Unitary	Low	D (1993–96)	S– (1993–96)
Pakistan	Federal	Low	C (1990–98)	
Canada	Federal	Low	S (1994–98)	S– (1994–98)
United States	Federal	Low	C (1990–97)	C (1990–97)

Source: Authors' calculations based on sources listed in annex 4B.

Note: — = not available; at the time of the study, no trend data were available.

a. "High" signifies countries included in our analysis with weighted CVs greater than 0.6 during all or most of the years. "Substantial" signifies countries with weighted CVs from 0.4 to 0.6. "Moderate" signifies countries with weighted CVs from 0.25 to 0.4. ""Low" signifies countries with weighted CVs less than 0.25.

b. In the beta convergence column, a + (–) sign after S denotes a positive (negative) coefficient on the log of initial GDP, but this coefficient is not statistically significant at the 10 percent level.

c. States that were part of the Federal Republic of Germany prior to unification.

Annex 4A: Regional Disparity Trends

Federal Countries: Industrial

TABLE 4A.1   Regional Disparity Trends in Canada

Year	Maximum-to-minimum ratio	Simple coefficient of variation	Weighted coefficient of variation	Relative mean deviation	Unweighted Gini index	Weighted Gini index	Theil index
1994	1.781	0.193	0.129	0.112	0.114	0.063	0.006
1995	1.785	0.205	0.132	0.118	0.119	0.065	0.008
1996	1.949	0.221	0.131	0.116	0.128	0.064	0.011
1997	1.838	0.201	0.137	0.123	0.118	0.067	0.008
1998	1.718	0.195	0.137	0.127	0.113	0.068	0.006

Source: Authors' calculations based on sources listed in annex 4B.

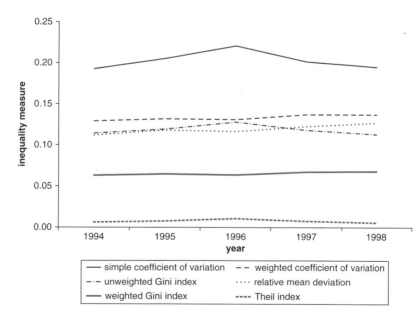

Source: Authors' calculations based on sources listed in annex 4B.

FIGURE 4A.1 Regional Disparity Trends in Canada

TABLE 4A.2 Regional Disparity Trends in the United States

Year	Maximum-to-minimum ratio	Simple coefficient of variation	Weighted coefficient of variation	Relative mean deviation	Unweighted Gini index	Weighted Gini index	Theil index
1990	2.871	0.229	0.159	0.132	0.118	0.049	0.013
1991	2.522	0.207	0.147	0.122	0.109	0.046	0.011
1992	2.281	0.189	0.139	0.114	0.102	0.044	0.010
1993	2.157	0.180	0.130	0.105	0.097	0.042	0.008
1994	1.966	0.167	0.122	0.096	0.092	0.039	0.007
1995	1.976	0.166	0.120	0.095	0.091	0.038	0.007
1996	1.943	0.163	0.121	0.096	0.090	0.039	0.007
1997	1.927	0.162	0.122	0.097	0.090	0.039	0.007

Source: Authors' calculations based on sources listed in annex 4B.

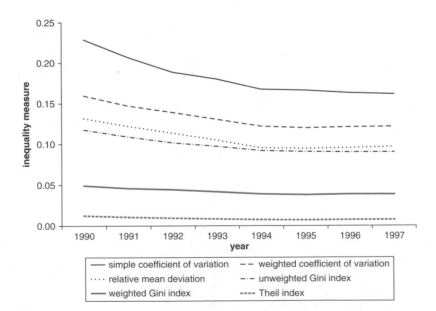

Source: Authors' calculations based on sources listed in annex 4B.

FIGURE 4A.2 Regional Disparity Trends in the United States

Federal Countries: Developing

TABLE 4A.3 Regional Disparity Trends in Brazil

Year	Maximum-to-minimum ratio	Simple coefficient of variation	Weighted coefficient of variation	Relative mean deviation	Unweighted Gini index	Weighted Gini index	Theil index
1985	7.679	0.491	0.478	0.411	0.281	0.270	0.123
1986	6.995	0.479	0.462	0.399	0.275	0.261	0.115
1987	8.287	0.510	0.498	0.423	0.287	0.280	0.132
1988	8.457	0.525	0.509	0.434	0.296	0.286	0.137
1989	8.314	0.550	0.510	0.441	0.340	0.290	0.137
1990	7.254	0.525	0.490	0.432	0.322	0.279	0.126
1991	8.775	0.571	0.475	0.416	0.334	0.271	0.118
1992	7.771	0.567	0.485	0.432	0.340	0.276	0.125
1993	7.409	0.551	0.470	0.421	0.335	0.268	0.118
1994	6.968	0.532	0.452	0.399	0.326	0.258	0.110
1995	7.576	0.551	0.473	0.419	0.333	0.269	0.119
1996	6.881	0.550	0.458	0.405	0.330	0.261	0.112
1997	7.567	0.563	0.468	0.409	0.334	0.267	0.116

Source: Authors' calculations based on sources listed in annex 4B.

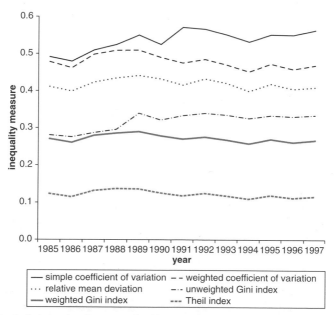

Source: Authors' calculations based on sources listed in annex 4B.

FIGURE 4A.3 Regional Disparity Trends in Brazil

TABLE 4A.4 Regional Disparity Trends in India

Year	Maximum-to-minimum ratio	Simple coefficient of variation	Weighted coefficient of variation	Relative mean deviation	Unweighted Gini index	Weighted Gini index	Theil index
1980	2.848	0.312	0.290	0.221	0.175	0.152	0.039
1981	2.903	0.318	0.289	0.216	0.178	0.152	0.039
1982	2.867	0.327	0.291	0.211	0.182	0.152	0.039
1983	2.808	0.308	0.286	0.219	0.172	0.151	0.038
1984	2.702	0.323	0.292	0.235	0.182	0.154	0.040
1985	2.804	0.345	0.305	0.239	0.191	0.159	0.043
1986	2.712	0.342	0.302	0.239	0.190	0.157	0.042
1987	2.945	0.343	0.306	0.238	0.191	0.161	0.043
1988	2.825	0.333	0.302	0.227	0.186	0.159	0.043
1989	3.196	0.350	0.333	0.248	0.196	0.175	0.052
1990	3.034	0.345	0.323	0.240	0.195	0.171	0.049
1991	3.271	0.349	0.328	0.255	0.198	0.176	0.051
1992	3.464	0.369	0.370	0.286	0.212	0.199	0.065
1993	3.521	0.373	0.385	0.296	0.215	0.207	0.070
1994	3.576	0.375	0.393	0.312	0.219	0.215	0.074
1995	4.051	0.386	0.414	0.323	0.224	0.225	0.081
1996	3.838	0.398	0.419	0.327	0.232	0.228	0.084
1997	3.811	0.387	0.414	0.334	0.226	0.227	0.082

Source: Authors' calculations based on sources listed in annex 4B.

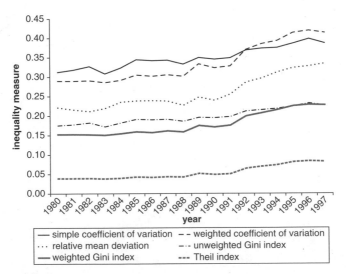

Source: Authors' calculations based on sources listed in annex 4B.

FIGURE 4A.4 Regional Disparity Trends in India

TABLE 4A.5 Regional Disparity Trends in Mexico

Year	Maximum-to-minimum ratio	Simple coefficient of variation	Weighted coefficient of variation	Relative mean deviation	Unweighted Gini index	Weighted Gini index	Theil index
1993	5.591	0.473	0.572	0.414	0.251	0.302	0.137
1994	5.583	0.471	0.573	0.417	0.250	0.301	0.137
1995	5.479	0.461	0.559	0.413	0.246	0.295	0.130
1996	5.618	0.464	0.561	0.415	0.249	0.297	0.131
1997	5.793	0.473	0.571	0.422	0.253	0.301	0.136
1998	5.874	0.469	0.566	0.421	0.251	0.300	0.134

Source: Authors' calculations based on sources listed in annex 4B.

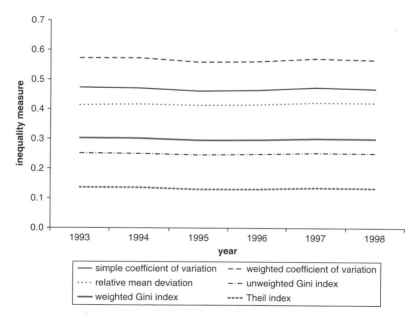

Source: Authors' calculations based on sources listed in annex 4B.

FIGURE 4A.5 Regional Disparity Trends in Mexico

TABLE 4A.6 Regional Disparity Trends in Pakistan

Year	Maximum-to-minimum ratio	Simple coefficient of variation	Weighted coefficient of variation	Relative mean deviation	Unweighted Gini index	Weighted Gini index	Theil index
1990	1.512	0.215	0.186	0.125	0.116	0.081	0.014
1991	1.562	0.213	0.179	0.118	0.122	0.082	0.013
1992	1.577	0.214	0.177	0.115	0.125	0.083	0.013
1993	1.613	0.216	0.174	0.109	0.131	0.083	0.012
1994	1.525	0.191	0.153	0.096	0.116	0.073	0.010
1995	1.507	0.186	0.148	0.094	0.113	0.071	0.009
1996	1.511	0.188	0.153	0.096	0.112	0.073	0.010
1997	1.514	0.186	0.150	0.094	0.113	0.072	0.009
1998	1.516	0.183	0.141	0.095	0.114	0.069	0.008

Source: Authors' calculations based on sources listed in annex 4B.

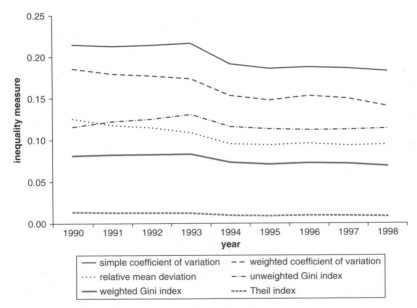

Source: Authors' calculations based on sources listed in annex 4B.

FIGURE 4A.6 Regional Disparity Trends in Pakistan

TABLE 4A.7 Regional Disparity Trends in the Russian Federation

Year	Maximum-to-minimum ratio	Simple coefficient of variation	Weighted coefficient of variation	Relative mean deviation	Unweighted Gini index	Weighted Gini index	Theil index
1994	14.065	0.479	0.447	0.313	0.247	0.221	0.094
1995	17.739	0.539	0.524	0.345	0.263	0.243	0.111
1996	20.778	0.629	0.635	0.377	0.278	0.268	0.144
1997	21.307	0.625	0.645	0.387	0.283	0.280	0.153

Source: Authors' calculations based on sources listed in annex 4B.

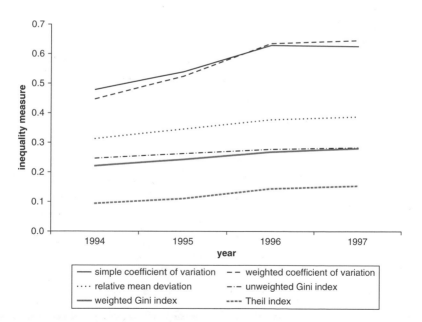

Source: Authors' calculations based on sources listed in annex 4B.

FIGURE 4A.7 Regional Disparity Trends in the Russian Federation

Unitary Countries

TABLE 4A.8 Regional Disparity Trends in Chile

Year	Maximum-to-minimum ratio	Simple coefficient of variation	Weighted coefficient of variation	Relative mean deviation	Unweighted Gini index	Weighted Gini index	Theil index
1987	6.841	0.599	0.377	0.250	0.313	0.176	0.066
1990	6.173	0.580	0.372	0.245	0.298	0.172	0.062
1992	5.959	0.528	0.359	0.258	0.282	0.174	0.060
1994	5.696	0.486	0.334	0.243	0.267	0.165	0.052

Source: Authors' calculations based on sources listed in annex 4B.

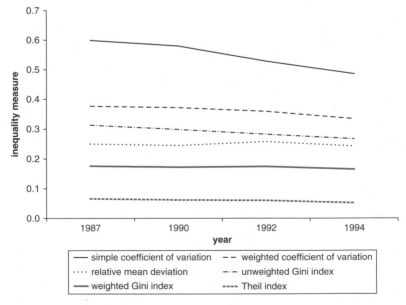

Source: Authors' calculations based on sources listed in annex 4B.

FIGURE 4A.8 Regional Disparity Trends in Chile

TABLE 4A.9   Regional Disparity Trends in China

Year	Maximum-to-minimum ratio	Simple coefficient of variation	Weighted coefficient of variation	Relative mean deviation	Unweighted Gini index	Weighted Gini index	Theil index
a. 1978–95							
1978	14.311	0.994	1.673	0.814	0.412	0.246	0.167
1979	12.499	0.938	1.501	0.765	0.375	0.235	0.152
1980	12.432	0.923	1.471	0.759	0.394	0.233	0.146
1981	12.442	0.891	1.403	0.741	0.362	0.226	0.138
1982	10.254	0.844	1.298	0.710	0.350	0.219	0.127
1983	9.739	0.809	1.197	0.667	0.346	0.218	0.121
1984	8.739	0.778	1.135	0.677	0.342	0.219	0.117
1985	9.131	0.757	1.086	0.606	0.337	0.214	0.104
1986	8.527	0.729	1.018	0.586	0.334	0.218	0.102
1987	7.991	0.698	0.950	0.566	0.329	0.219	0.098
1988	7.630	0.675	0.905	0.570	0.324	0.222	0.097
1989	7.321	0.652	0.882	0.580	0.317	0.222	0.094
1990	7.309	0.644	0.882	0.581	0.311	0.213	0.089
1991	7.483	0.683	0.976	0.662	0.334	0.236	0.106
1992	8.563	0.699	0.972	0.653	0.339	0.239	0.109
1993	9.352	0.682	0.960	0.681	0.342	0.251	0.115
1994	9.648	0.635	0.874	0.663	0.332	0.248	0.108
1995	9.690	0.618	0.822	0.626	0.326	0.244	0.103
b. 1993–99							
1993	9.323	0.664	0.931	0.680	0.339	0.252	0.113
1994	9.790	0.662	0.920	0.687	0.343	0.255	0.114
1995	10.223	0.669	0.900	0.664	0.345	0.253	0.112
1996	11.022	0.672	0.894	0.653	0.343	0.247	0.108
1997	11.625	0.692	0.924	0.666	0.351	0.250	0.111
1998	12.183	0.709	0.952	0.679	0.357	0.254	0.115
1999	12.507	0.730	0.987	0.694	0.365	0.264	0.125

Source: Authors' calculations based on sources listed in annex 4B.
Note: China adopted a new statistical series in 1993 with noncomparability of classifications with earlier years; hence, two panels are shown.

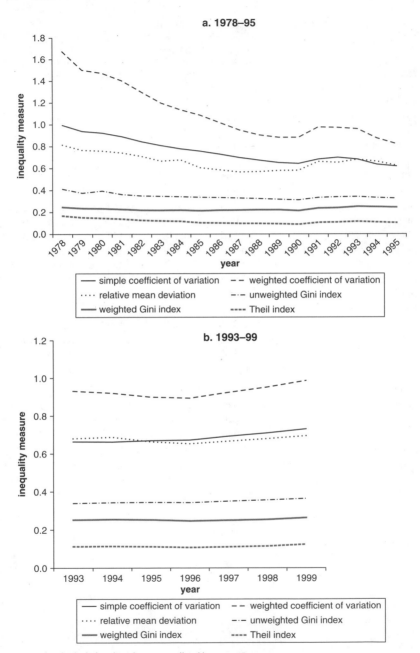

Source: Authors' calculations based on sources listed in annex 4B.
Note: China adopted a new statistical series in 1993 with noncomparability of classifications with earlier years; hence, two panels are shown.

FIGURE 4A.9 Regional Disparity Trends in China

TABLE 4A.10 Regional Disparity Trends in Indonesia

Year	Maximum-to-minimum ratio	Simple coefficient of variation	Weighted coefficient of variation	Relative mean deviation	Unweighted Gini index	Weighted Gini index	Theil index
1983	22.585	1.279	1.045	0.525	0.498	0.328	0.292
1984	23.515	1.260	0.987	0.510	0.496	0.321	0.272
1985	23.456	1.225	0.930	0.487	0.485	0.308	0.248
1986	22.142	1.198	0.915	0.478	0.477	0.304	0.242
1987	20.262	1.178	0.913	0.476	0.472	0.304	0.242
1988	18.337	1.121	0.871	0.461	0.459	0.299	0.228
1989	17.685	1.088	0.846	0.457	0.452	0.298	0.221
1990	16.514	1.004	0.786	0.440	0.426	0.283	0.201
1991	15.647	0.969	0.759	0.429	0.417	0.278	0.191
1992	14.691	0.936	0.731	0.419	0.407	0.273	0.181
1993	12.084	0.854	0.724	0.409	0.386	0.274	0.179
1994	12.069	0.856	0.725	0.406	0.385	0.274	0.179
1995	11.320	0.832	0.714	0.402	0.379	0.272	0.175
1996	11.259	0.830	0.715	0.401	0.379	0.273	0.175
1997	11.048	0.827	0.716	0.401	0.378	0.274	0.176
1998	11.436	0.832	0.722	0.416	0.381	0.277	0.178

Source: Authors' calculations based on sources listed in annex 4B.

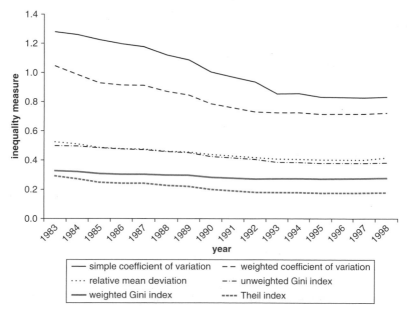

Source: Authors' calculations based on sources listed in annex 4B.

FIGURE 4A.10 Regional Disparity Trends in Indonesia

TABLE 4A.11   Regional Disparity Trends in the Philippines

Year	Maximum-to-minimum ratio	Simple coefficient of variation	Weighted coefficient of variation	Relative mean deviation	Unweighted Gini index	Weighted Gini index	Theil index
1982	5.366	0.506	0.550	0.365	0.216	0.268	0.166
1983	5.362	0.520	0.568	0.368	0.217	0.271	0.172
1984	4.803	0.485	0.533	0.352	0.203	0.255	0.158
1985	4.534	0.465	0.511	0.338	0.197	0.246	0.150
1986	4.669	0.463	0.507	0.337	0.198	0.246	0.149
1987	4.928	0.494	0.531	0.360	0.248	0.262	0.146
1988	4.976	0.504	0.544	0.362	0.287	0.265	0.150
1989	5.083	0.518	0.559	0.367	0.290	0.270	0.156
1990	5.005	0.515	0.556	0.365	0.285	0.267	0.154
1991	4.910	0.511	0.552	0.364	0.284	0.266	0.152
1992	4.689	0.494	0.526	0.348	0.280	0.258	0.144
1993	6.868	0.517	0.513	0.351	0.301	0.255	0.117
1994	6.627	0.515	0.513	0.352	0.302	0.255	0.116
1995	6.431	0.512	0.513	0.353	0.299	0.254	0.116
1996	6.516	0.525	0.524	0.362	0.305	0.259	0.120
1997	6.653	0.530	0.532	0.367	0.307	0.261	0.123
1998	6.760	0.536	0.537	0.369	0.311	0.262	0.125

Source: Authors' calculations based on sources listed in annex 4B.

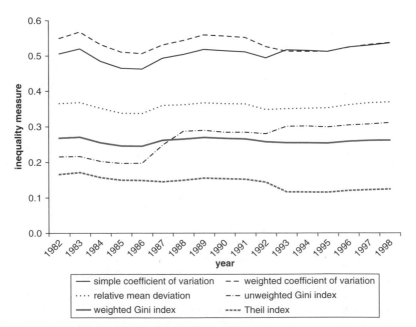

Source: Authors' calculations based on sources listed in annex 4B.

FIGURE 4A.11   Regional Disparity Trends in the Philippines

TABLE 4A.12 Regional Disparity Trends in Romania

Year	Maximum-to-minimum ratio	Simple coefficient of variation	Weighted coefficient of variation	Relative mean deviation	Unweighted Gini index	Weighted Gini index	Theil index
1993	1.693	0.171	0.156	0.111	0.095	0.081	0.010
1996	1.783	0.189	0.174	0.132	0.106	0.090	0.012

Source: Authors' calculations based on sources listed in annex 4B.

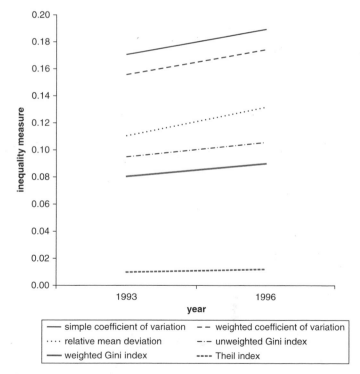

Source: Authors' calculations based on sources listed in annex 4B.

FIGURE 4A.12 Regional Disparity Trends in Romania

TABLE 4A.13 Regional Disparity Trends in Sri Lanka

Year	Maximum-to-minimum ratio	Simple coefficient of variation	Weighted coefficient of variation	Relative mean deviation	Unweighted Gini index	Weighted Gini index	Theil index
1990	2.506	0.354	0.376	0.340	0.209	0.205	0.069
1991	2.496	0.321	0.358	0.321	0.186	0.196	0.063
1992	2.769	0.345	0.390	0.344	0.200	0.214	0.074
1993	2.915	0.349	0.399	0.351	0.205	0.220	0.078
1994	3.121	0.374	0.426	0.375	0.219	0.235	0.090
1995	3.362	0.394	0.452	0.397	0.230	0.249	0.101

Source: Authors' calculations based on sources listed in annex 4B.

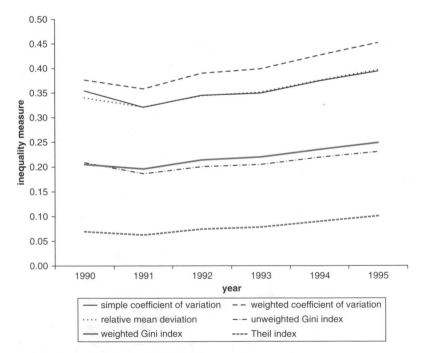

Source: Authors' calculations based on sources listed in annex 4B.

FIGURE 4A.13 Regional Disparity Trends in Sri Lanka

TABLE 4A.14 Regional Disparity Trends in Thailand

Year	Maximum-to-minimum ratio	Simple coefficient of variation	Weighted coefficient of variation	Relative mean deviation	Unweighted Gini index	Weighted Gini index	Theil index
1991	9.320	0.880	1.002	0.765	0.451	0.457	0.389
1992	9.077	0.865	0.986	0.756	0.446	0.452	0.379
1993	9.774	0.894	1.020	0.789	0.463	0.468	0.406
1994	9.262	0.861	0.989	0.772	0.454	0.459	0.387
1995	8.696	0.834	0.959	0.754	0.443	0.449	0.368
1996	8.529	0.816	0.944	0.751	0.442	0.447	0.361
1997	8.273	0.797	0.925	0.745	0.438	0.442	0.351

Source: Authors' calculations based on sources listed in annex 4B.

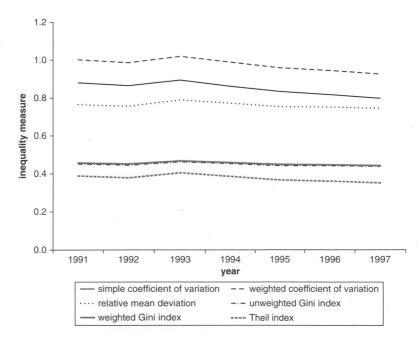

Source: Authors' calculations based on sources listed in annex 4B.

FIGURE 4A.14 Regional Disparity Trends in Thailand

TABLE 4A.15 Regional Disparity Trends in Uzbekistan

Year	Maximum-to-minimum ratio	Simple coefficient of variation	Weighted coefficient of variation	Relative mean deviation	Unweighted Gini index	Weighted Gini index	Theil index
1996	2.840	0.336	0.341	0.234	0.149	0.165	0.051
1997	3.047	0.353	0.355	0.238	0.155	0.170	0.054
1998	2.991	0.321	0.320	0.218	0.147	0.159	0.046
1999	2.779	0.304	0.301	0.206	0.142	0.152	0.041

Source: Authors' calculations based on sources listed in annex 4B.

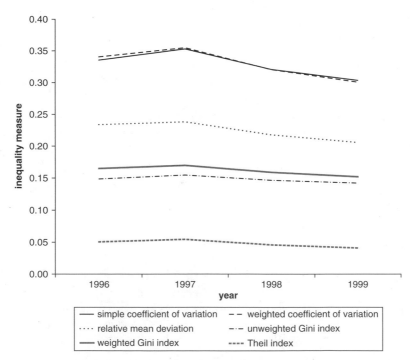

Source: Authors' calculations based on sources listed in annex 4B.

FIGURE 4A.15 Regional Disparity Trends in Uzbekistan

TABLE 4A.16   Regional Disparity Trends in Vietnam

Year	Maximum-to-minimum ratio	Simple coefficient of variation	Weighted coefficient of variation	Relative mean deviation	Unweighted Gini index	Weighted Gini index	Theil index
1990	11.625	0.668	0.537	0.346	0.257	0.239	0.106
1991	14.473	0.781	0.665	0.389	0.282	0.273	0.152
1992	21.881	1.062	0.854	0.448	0.318	0.304	0.214
1993	23.082	1.058	0.862	0.471	0.327	0.315	0.223
1994	24.079	1.053	0.890	0.502	0.336	0.332	0.244
1995	23.915	1.057	0.889	0.510	0.335	0.334	0.246
1996	27.723	1.047	0.967	0.580	0.366	0.400	0.290
1997	24.746	1.067	0.996	0.596	0.372	0.410	0.306

Source: Authors' calculations based on sources listed in annex 4B.

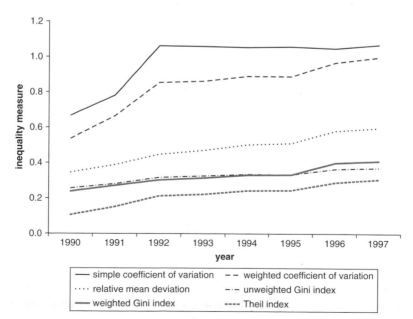

Source: Authors' calculations based on sources listed in annex 4B.

FIGURE 4A.16   Regional Disparity Trends in Vietnam

Annex 4B: Data Sources

Brazil: The source for the GRDP data is Instituto Brasileiro de Geografia e Estadística, Diretoria de Pesquisas, Departamento de Contas Nacionais, Contas Regionais do Brasil, 1985–1997, microdata. The population data are obtained from Instituto Brasileiro de Geografia e Estadística.

Canada: The data were obtained from Statistics Canada, CANSIM database, Matrices.

Chile: The source for the data is Encuesta de Caracterización Socioeconómica Nacional.

China: The data are from the National Bureau of Statistics' publications. The data from 1993 to 1998 are from National Bureau of Statistics (1999), and the data for 1999 are from National Bureau of Statistics (2000).

France, Germany, Italy, Spain, United Kingdom: The source for data on these countries is the EUROSTAT database.

India: Data are from an internal World Bank database.

Indonesia: Data are obtained from an internal World Bank database.

Mexico: The source for GRDP data is the Instituto Nacional de Estadística Geografía e Informática's Sistema de Cuentas Nacionales de México (System of National Accounts of Mexico). The sources for population data are the Instituto Nacional de Estadística Geografía e Informática's XI Censo General de Población y Vivienda, 1990; Encuesta Nacional de la Dinámica Demográfica, 1992; México, 1994; Encuesta Nacional de la Dinámica Demográfica, 1997; and Metodología y Tabulados México, 1999.

Nepal: The household income data by development region were obtained from the Nepal National Human Development Report 1998.

Pakistan: Population data are from census figures. Population for non-census years were interpolated from the actual census figures assuming constant growth rates between census years. The GRDP data are World Bank estimates.

Philippines: Data are from an internal World Bank database.

Poland: The source is Glówny Urzad Statystyczny w Warszawie, the country's central statistical office.

Romania: The data are from the National Commission for Statistics in Romania.

Russia: Data are from an internal World Bank database.

Sri Lanka: Data are from an internal World Bank database.

Thailand: Data are from an internal World Bank database and national government statistics.

Uganda: Regional household expenditure data were obtained from Appleton (1999).

United States: The population data are from the U.S. census.

Uzbekistan: GRDP and per capita GRDP data were obtained from the internal bulletins of the State Department of Statistics. The data were put together from these bulletins by Sayyora Umarova of the World Bank. The population data are from the annual bulletins of the State Department of Statistics.

Vietnam: Data are from an internal World Bank database.

Notes

This chapter is based on Shankar and Shah (2003) and is being reprinted with the permission of the journal. The authors are grateful to Homi Kharas, Peter Fallon, and members of the Decentralization and Subnational Thematic Groups at the World Bank for comments. They are also grateful to the following individuals for their valuable help in obtaining regional GDP data and other information used in this study: David Rosenblatt, Ritva Reinikka, Alberto Valdes, Viet Tuan Dinh, Hanid Mukhtar, Sayyora Umarova, Fahretin Yagci, Joachim von Amsberg, Magda Ariani, Princes Ventura, Xiofan Liu, Cornelia Giurescu, Timothy Heleniak, Marian Urbiola, Mariusz Safin, and Joven Balbosa.

1. This number includes both the former Federal Republic of Germany and unified Germany.
2. All the countries in the sample, except Nepal, Poland, and Uganda, were used in the regression analysis. Data could not be obtained to calculate the weighted measures of inequality for those countries.
3. The countries included are Brazil, Canada, Chile, France, the former Federal Republic of Germany, India, Indonesia, Italy, Mexico, Romania, Russia, Spain, Thailand, the United Kingdom, and the United States.
4. This finding is consistent with Williamson's (1965) inverted U thesis, which holds that inequalities widen in the early development stages, whereas mature development produces divergence.
5. Data and information are taken from the Economist Intelligence Unit's Country Profile data set for Chile.
6 Data and information are taken from the Economist Intelligence Unit's Country Profile data set for Sri Lanka.
7. Data and information are taken from the Economist Intelligence Unit's Country Profile data set for the Philippines.
8. Data and information are taken from the Economist Intelligence Unit's Country Profile data set for Thailand.

References

Akita, Takahiro, and Rizal Affandi Lukman. 1995. "Interregional Inequalities in Indonesia: A Sectoral Decomposition Analysis for 1975–92." *Bulletin of Indonesian Economic Studies* 31 (2): 61–81.

Appleton, Simon. 1999. "Changes in Poverty and Inequality in Uganda." University of Bath and Centre for the Study of African Economies, Oxford, U.K.

Asra, Abuzar. 1989. "Inequality Trends in Indonesia." *Bulletin of Indonesian Economic Studies* 25 (2): 100–10.

Bajpai, Nirupam, and Jeffrey D. Sachs. 1996. "Trends in Inter-State Inequalities of Income in India." Development Discussion Paper 528, Harvard Institute for International Development, Cambridge, MA.

Barro, Robert J., and Xavier Sala-i-Martin. 1995. *Economic Growth*. New York: McGraw-Hill.

Boldrin, Michelle, and Fabio Canova. 2001. "Inequality and Convergence in Europe's Regions: Reconsidering European Regional Policies." *Economic Policy* 16 (32): 205–53.

Cashin, Paul, and Ratna Sahay. 1996. "Regional Economic Growth and Convergence in India." *Finance and Development* 33 (1): 49–52.

Das, Sandwip Kumar, and Alokesh Barua. 1996. "Regional Inequalities, Economic Growth, and Liberalisation: A Study of the Indian Economy." *Journal of Development Studies* 32 (3): 364–90.

Decressin, Jörg. 1999. "Regional Income Redistribution and Risk Sharing: How Does Italy Compare in Europe?" IMF Working Paper 99/123, International Monetary Fund, Washington, DC.

Dev, S. Mahendra. 2000. "Economic Reforms, Poverty, Income Distribution, and Employment." *Economic and Political Weekly* 35 (10): 823–35.

Garcia, Jorge, and Lana Soelistianingsih. 1998. "Why Do Differences in Provincial Incomes Persist in Indonesia?" *Bulletin of Indonesian Economic Studies* 34 (1): 95–120.

Giugale, Marcelo M., Vinh Nguyen, Fernando Rojas, and Steven B. Webb. 2000. "Overview." In *Achievements and Challenges of Fiscal Decentralization: Lessons from Mexico*, eds. Marcelo M. Giugale and Steven B. Webb, 1–38. Washington, DC: World Bank.

Jian, Tianlun, Jeffrey Sachs, and Andrew M. Warner. 1996. "Trends in Regional Inequality in China." NBER Working Paper 5412, National Bureau of Economic Research, Cambridge, MA.

Kakwani, Nanak C. 1980. *Income Inequality and Poverty: Methods of Estimation and Policy Applications*. New York: Oxford University Press.

Kakwani, Nanak C., and Hyun Son. 2005. "On Measures of Inequality and Poverty with Welfare Implications." In *Public Expenditure Analysis*, ed. Anwar Shah, 33–48. Washington, DC: World Bank.

Krugman, Paul. 1991. "Increasing Returns and Economic Geography." *Journal of Political Economy* 99 (3): 483–99.

Lyons, Thomas P. 1991. "Interprovincial Disparities in China: Output and Consumption, 1952–87." *Economic Development and Cultural Change* 39 (3): 471–506.

Musgrave, Richard. 1959. *The Theory of Public Finance*. New York: McGraw-Hill.

Nagaraj, Rayaprolu, Aristomène Varoudakis, and Marie-Ange Véganzonès. 2000. "Long-Run Growth Trends and Convergence across Indian States." *Journal of International Development* 12 (1): 45–70.

National Bureau of Statistics. 1999. *Comprehensive Statistical Data and Materials on 50 Years of New China*. Beijing: China Statistics Press.

———. 2000. *China Statistical Abstract 2000*. Beijing: China Statistics Press.

Oates, Wallace. 1972. *Fiscal Federalism*. New York: Harcourt Brace Jovanovich.

Raiser, Martin. 1998. "Subsidizing Inequality: Economic Reforms, Fiscal Transfers, and Convergence across Chinese Provinces." *Journal of Development Studies* 34 (3): 1–26.

Rao, M. Govinda, Richard T. Shand, and Kaliappa P. Kalirajan. 1999. "Convergence of Income across Indian States: A Divergent View." *Economic and Political Weekly* 34 (13): 769–78.

Romer, Paul M. 1990. "Endogenous Technical Change." *Journal of Political Economy* 98 (5): S71–S102.

Sacks, Michael Paul. 1999. "Regional Inequality and Branch Employment in Russia between 1990 and 1995." *Post-Communist Economies* 11 (2): 149–59.

Shankar, Raja, and Anwar Shah. 2003. "Bridging the Economic Divide within Nations: A Scorecard on the Performance of Regional Development Policies in Reducing Regional Income Disparities." *World Development* 31 (8): 1421–41.

———. Forthcoming. "Regional Development Policies and Regional Inequality in India." In *Challenges of Fiscal Management of States and Regional Inequity in India*, eds. Govinda Rao and Anwar Shah. New Delhi: Oxford University Press.

Theil, Henri. 1967. *Economics and Information Theory*. Amsterdam: North-Holland.

Tsui, Kai-yuen. 1996. "Economic Reform and Interprovincial Inequalities in China." *Journal of Development Economics* 50 (2): 353–68.

Williamson, Jeffrey G. 1965. "Regional Inequality and Process of National Development: A Description of the Patterns." *Economic Development and Cultural Change* 13 (4, part 2): 2–84.

Yagci, Fahretin. 1999. "Narrowing Inter-State Disparities Agenda for Fiscal and Sector Reforms." World Bank, Washington, DC.

Yao, Shujie, and Jirui Liu. 1998. "Economic Reforms and Regional Segmentation in Rural China." *Regional Studies* 32 (8): 735–46.

5

Harmonizing Taxation of Interstate Trade under a Subnational VAT: Lessons from International Experience

MAHESH C. PUROHIT

A large number of countries have introduced value added tax (VAT). It is no coincidence, however, that none of the federations has been able to introduce a fully harmonized VAT. The key difference in introducing VAT in a unitary form of government and in a federal country lies in designing a destination-based subnational VAT. Therefore, in designing a subnational VAT, the important issue that needs to be addressed relates to treatment of interstate trade.

To understand the problems of introducing a harmonized VAT in a federation, this chapter presents case studies of the structure of VAT in a few select federal countries—Brazil, Canada, and India. It illustrates the case of the European Union (EU), drawing on the harmonized federal features of the member states of the union. Finally, the chapter derives lessons from these case studies about a suitable structure for a subnational VAT.

Brazil

Brazil is one of the oldest federations with a comprehensive division of tax powers between different tiers of government. The overall system of taxes on commodities and services is characterized by a variety of taxes. Besides taxes on income and property, it includes VAT at the federal level as well as at the state level. In addition, it has some cascade-type taxes at the municipal level.

Federal VAT

Brazil's system of VAT at the federal level is known as *imposto sobre produtos industrializados* (tax on industrial products, or IPI). IPI is confined to the manufacturing sector. It is levied on value added by the industrial manufacturing sector. That is, the tax is levied on raw materials, intermediary products, packaging materials, and finished goods, with a setoff for the tax paid on the earlier stage of transactions. Setoff is, however, not available on exempted goods. Agricultural and mineral products are also excluded from the purview of IPI. Capital goods, in general, are outside the creditable base, but the tax on machinery and equipment produced in Brazil forming part of fixed assets and used solely in the industrial process is eligible for credit.[1] As in most other countries, exports are zero-rated.

Imports are subjected to IPI, but products exempted from import duty are automatically exempt from IPI. Also, imports of specified machinery and equipment are exempt. Other exemptions under the IPI regime include (a) the output of firms installed in the Manaus Free Zone (Zona Franca de Manaus, or ZFM) and approved by proper authority; (b) a large number of notified products or projects; and (c) some specified inputs.

IPI has multiple rates, with considerable variations across commodities. In general, nine rate categories range from 4 percent to 333 percent.

More than half the revenue of IPI is generated from a few commodities. They include vehicles (16.2 percent), tobacco products (13.2 percent), beverages (10.1 percent), chemical products (8.1 percent), and products of the metal and mechanical industry (7.0 percent).

State VAT

The system of VAT at the state level, known as *imposto sobre circulação de mercadorias e prestação de serviços* (tax on the circulation of goods and services, or ICMS), replaced the sales and turnover taxes that prevailed in the

1960s. ICMS is levied on the sale of goods at all stages of the production-distribution process, including the retail trade, agriculture, and cattle-raising sectors (see Purohit 1997).

Unlike the multiplicity of rates under IPI, ICMS has only five rate categories: 7 percent on rice, beans, bread, salt, meat, and food items; 8.8 percent on capital goods; 12 percent on electricity consumption; 18 percent standard rate (applicable to most items); and 25 percent on sumptuary consumption items, such as liquor, cigarettes, tobacco, electronic goods, video games, sports, communications, gas, and alcohol.

ICMS does not cover services in its purview.[2] Also, it does not include a large number of capital goods produced in Brazil. In addition, many exemptions exist for notified inputs and intermediate goods, including fertilizers and pesticides, inputs for agricultural production, specified products such as intermediate imports, and sales of agricultural equipment in the northeastern states. Exports are zero-rated.

Harmonization of Interregional Transactions

Brazil is the only federal country other than India that has adopted the origin principle for taxation of interstate transactions. Accordingly, ICMS is levied on interregional transactions by the exporting state, but the tax levied by the exporting state varies according to destination. Whereas the general rate of tax on interregional transactions is 12 percent, the differential interregional rate is 7 percent for goods sent from southeast to northeast or to the central-west regions.[3]

To neutralize the tax's impact on these transactions, the importing state gives a setoff for the tax. Because a higher rate of 12 percent applies to exports from the southeast states and a lower rate of 7 percent applies to imports into that region and because a rebate of both of these taxes is allowed, ICMS revenue is effectively redistributed among the regions. The rate of tax on interregional transactions is prescribed by the National Public Finance Council (Conselho Nacional de Politica Fazendária, or CONFAZ).[4] In addition, the CONFAZ grants exemptions to some notified products, such as vegetables, eggs, and domestic fish.[5] Exemptions also include sale of agricultural equipment to the northeast and to Pará, Amapá, and Rondônia, and agricultural exports. Sales to the ZFM are zero-rated.

As indicated, a dual VAT system exists in Brazil: IPI (a federal VAT on the manufacturing sector) and ICMS (a state VAT on agriculture and industry). The federal VAT is primarily a tax on select commodities that is restricted to the manufacturing sector and offers many exemptions. It is also beset with several problems. The tax is not neutral, and entrepreneurs tend to undervalue their output to reduce their tax liability. Exemption from IPI is given to machinery produced in the country but not to imported machinery, thereby creating distortions in the system. No attempt has been made to harmonize IPI and ICMS; each operates independently of the other. Moreover, the separate tax on services is not integrated with IPI or ICMS but levied by municipal authorities on a gross sales basis.

Canada

Canada is an example of a federal country where better harmonization has been achieved between federal VAT and state sales tax or VAT (see Purohit 2001c).

Federal Level

At the federal level, a comprehensive VAT known as goods and services tax (GST) has been levied since 1991. It covers all sales of goods and services. The tax is levied at the rate of 6 percent.

Although it has comprehensive coverage, GST exempts specified goods and services. Sales made by small dealers with annual taxable turnover of less than Can$30,000 and occasional sales by private individuals (such as the private sale of a used car) are exempt. Residential rents (other than temporary accommodation), most health and dental services, financial services,[6] day care services, and educational services are also exempt. In addition, resale of old homes is exempt. Some individuals and agencies are exempt because of constitutional immunity granted to them. Purchases by aboriginal Indians living in reserve areas also are exempt.

Some purchases—including basic groceries (except for snack foods, nonfood beverages, prepared foods, and restaurant meals); prescription drugs; and medical devices—are zero-rated. All purchases made by provincial and territory governments are zero-rated either through mutual agreements or through treaties. Purchases by farmers are also generally zero-rated, including seeds and fertilizers bought in large quantities. Exports also fall into the category of zero-rated transactions. Individuals and organizations having diplomatic immunity are eligible to buy goods at the zero rate.

The GST legislation allows for a rebate of taxes paid on inputs to specified institutions: municipalities, academic institutions (such as universities and public colleges), schools, and hospitals.[7] These institutions are not exempt from tax, but special treatment is granted through a partial rebate of tax paid on their purchases. Municipalities receive a rebate of 57.14 percent of the tax paid, and universities and public colleges receive a rebate of 66 percent. The rebate is 68 percent for schools and 83 percent for public hospitals. Government-registered charities and nonprofit organizations are also entitled to a 50 percent rebate of all taxes paid on their purchases.

Provincial Level

In addition to the federal government's imposition of GST, all provinces except Alberta levy a provincial tax on sales of tangible personal property.[8] The structure of the tax varies depending on the province.

Five provinces—British Columbia, Manitoba, Ontario, Prince Edward Island, and Saskatchewan—levy a retail sales tax, known as *provincial sales tax* (PST). Of these, Prince Edward Island levies PST on the GST-inclusive base. The rest of the provinces impose PST on the price exclusive of GST. The PSTs levied by the five governments vary considerably in terms of coverage.

Quebec levies a VAT at the provincial level that is known as *Quebec sales tax* (QST). Quebec collects its own QST and the GST levied by the federal government. Quebec applies zero-rating of QST on interprovincial sales and exports. It remits the GST yield, net of cost of collection, to the federal government.

The federal government has made efforts to harmonize GST and the provincial sales taxes since the introduction of GST in 1991. After protracted negotiations, the federal government, in 1996, finally entered into an agreement with three provinces—New Brunswick, Newfoundland, and Nova Scotia—to introduce a harmonized sales tax (HST) to replace GST and the PST.

Effective April 1, 1997, HST is a VAT imposed by the federal government at 14 percent, consisting of two parts: the federal tax component at 6 percent and the provincial tax component at 8 percent. The federal government legislates and administers HST. The provinces receive their share from the federal government. The share is allocated primarily on the basis of consumption, although some other variables are considered in the distribution formula. Because under the old system provincial sales tax was levied at a higher rate, when the HST was first introduced the provinces also received adjustment assistance to compensate for the loss of revenue. The grant of Can$961 million was payable over a period of four years.

In the Canadian system, interprovincial transactions are not taxed. In provinces that have a retail sales tax, the tax is not imposed on interprovincial transactions. In other provinces, such transactions are zero-rated under the VAT system.

Thus, the Canadian federation has succeeded in fashioning a system that is essentially rational from the economic point of view. That is, there is no element of cascading, and interprovincial transactions are not taxed. However, there is no perfect or near-perfect harmonization. The Canadian system of VAT and sales tax offers three distinct, interesting situations:

■ Separate federal and provincial VATs administered provincially
■ Joint federal and provincial VATs administered federally
■ Provincial retail sales taxes administered separately.

European Union

The European Union's VAT structure could also be considered an illustration of VAT under a federal system, wherein VAT is levied by all the member states.

The European Union has ensured that the domestic trade taxes levied by the member states are rational by insisting that any country wishing to be part of the EU adopt a VAT and refrain from levying any tax on transactions between member states. The last has been achieved by abolishing fiscal frontiers and making VAT effectively destination based.

Coverage of the EU VAT includes both goods and services. The base and rates were substantially harmonized in 1977 through the adoption of the Sixth Directive. Furthermore, a degree of rate harmonization was achieved by stipulating a standard rate of VAT, with one or two reduced rates on a few specified items and a minimum rate of 5 percent following the removal of border controls. The standard rate of 15 percent was agreed to by the finance and economic ministers of the member states in 1992.

Thus, the European Union has succeeded in preserving the common market with a fully harmonized VAT. For doing so, it proposed two systems: a clearinghouse mechanism and a deferred payment system.

Clearinghouse Mechanism

Initially, harmonization of VAT in the European Union was proposed through the establishment of a clearinghouse mechanism. The Commission of the European Communities stipulated that out-of-state transactions would be taxed and that imports would be entitled to a tax credit for out-of-state VAT. To make the destination principle work, the exporting state would remit VAT collected on exports to the administration of the importing state. Only net balances would have to be settled, through the mechanism of a central clearinghouse. Each member was expected to calculate its total VAT sales and purchases for intra-EU trade for the month by aggregating all VAT charged and claimed by registered dealers on sales and purchases to EU members. The net position would be calculated with respect to the European Union as a whole and not against each state. So each country would create a monthly statement showing its total VAT input and output figures for intra-EU trade. The statement would establish a claim or payment. Under this system, clearing would be a perpetually ongoing process.

Although the benefits of the clearinghouse mechanism were evident, EU members anticipated problems related to the accuracy of likely claims involving large flows of money. The Commission of the European Communities proposed to tackle this issue through standardized audit trails and improved control and coordination of member states. Subsequently, the commission proposed that clearing occur on the basis of estimates of consumption in member states.

Because of enforcement asymmetry in the working of the clearinghouse, however, the member states were not ready politically or administratively to implement the clearinghouse mechanism system.

Deferred Payment System

The European Union subsequently adopted a transitional regime of deferred payment system to deal with the treatment of intra-EU supplies (exports) and acquisitions (imports). In conjunction with this transitional regime, a VAT information exchange system was set up to monitor VAT on supply and acquisition of goods (see Purohit 2001a). The transitional regime changed the taxable event in cross-border transactions from the country of origin to the country of destination. For example, consider the case of a manufacturing firm located in France that produces finished goods. The firm plans to import raw materials worth €500 from the United Kingdom, where such transactions are normally taxable at 10 percent. However, because the transaction occasions the movement of goods from the United Kingdom to France, the transaction is not taxed, provided that the sale is made by a registered dealer in the United Kingdom. To ensure that an unregistered dealer does not make the transaction, the registration number of the U.K. dealer must be printed on the invoice to the French dealer. Thus, for a sale to be free of tax, a supplier who sends goods to other EU countries must obtain the VAT registration number of his or her customers in other member states and include that number with his or her own VAT registration number on sales invoices.

In addition, when the U.K. supplier dispatches the raw materials, no paperwork need be presented to the customs officials at the frontier. Apart from spot checks for drugs, antiterrorism measures, and the like, no delays should occur at the frontier. Similarly, the French dealer is not required to clear the goods into France; neither is it required to pay or defer French VAT at the time the goods enter the country. When the raw materials arrive at the business premises of the French firm, the firm will account for French "acquisition" VAT on its VAT return.

Now, assume that the manufacturer in France uses the inputs received from the U.K. company to manufacture finished goods. When it later sells the goods, it will recover the acquisition VAT from the purchaser. The same procedure applies in reverse if the goods are moving from France to the United Kingdom (Buckett 1992). In this regime, the burden of tax effectively falls only in the consuming state.

This scheme was originally scheduled to apply only until 1993;[9] however, member states have reached no consensus about how to structure the new regime. Hence, the transitional regime continues to be in effect (Commission of the European Communities 1987: 7).

The Little Boat Model

The preceding examples relate to those existing in some federations, but some proposals that need serious consideration have been put forth in the literature of public finance. Varsano (2000) proposed a dual VAT called the *little boat model*. The model is a destination-based, consumption-type dual VAT without zero-rating of interstate exports.

Varsano's model suggests that tax levied by the province (or state) of origin from which goods are exported may not cross the border (or to use boat terminology, it may not cross the river, which in many cases borders happen to be). If it does, a tax credit must exist that will prevent double taxation in the next transaction. However, the province of origin cannot provide the credit to the importer, because the importer is a taxpayer in another jurisdiction.

To make the system destination based, the model assumes dual VAT: a federal VAT levied in all the provinces and a provincial VAT levied in each province. It further asserts that for the purposes of the federal VAT, provincial borders are irrelevant because the federal tax is levied all over the country. The tax jurisdiction of provincial VAT, however, ends when the commodity moves out of the province. Hence, the exporters and importers, who are federal taxpayers, transport the provincial tax across the border embodied in the federal tax. That is, the federal government collects both the provincial VAT and the federal VAT and provides the corresponding credit to the importer. The result is that subnational VAT reaches the other bank of the river free from previous tax collections and ready to follow its course as a tax of the province of destination.

This simple procedure is able to cover, automatically and practically at no cost, transactions between registered dealers subject to the normal tax regime, which form the bulk of interstate trade. If the importer is an identifiable household (distance selling), a nonregistered trader, or a small registered trader not assessed under the VAT regime, a different scheme must be used. The provincial tax is paid separately to the federal government so that total provincial tax collection can be determined. The proceeds of the tax are shared among the provinces in proportion to their respective VAT revenues.[10]

The little boat model requires that registered traders distinguish four components of their total sales:

- Intrastate sales, including those to unidentifiable residents of another jurisdiction (cross-border shopping), to which the federal and the state rates apply
- Interstate sales to registered taxpayers, except small traders subject to special simplified tax regimes, in which case the provincial tax is zero-rated and the federal tax is assessed at a rate equal to the sum of the federal and provincial rates
- Interstate sales to unregistered traders, small traders excepted from the previous case, and identifiable households domiciled in other jurisdictions (distance selling), to which the federal and provincial rates are applied, but the provincial tax is paid to the federal government (explicit compensating VAT, or CVAT)
- Exports to other countries, which are zero-rated.

At the end of the VAT assessment period, each registered trader is liable for three pieces of information on tax: (a) the net provincial tax liability (the difference between its provincial liabilities, except the explicit CVAT, and its provincial credits); (b) the net federal tax liability (the difference between its federal liabilities and its federal credits); and (c) the explicit CVAT paid to the federal government, which distributes the proceeds to provinces.[11]

The proposed procedure is superior to both of the EU approaches. First, its administrative costs are insignificant compared with those of other methods. For the taxpayer, accounting and administrative procedures would be less expensive and require less effort than existing tax arrangements. For the public sector, no new institution would be required to administer the procedure; even sharing of explicit CVAT among provinces could be managed automatically by the banks collecting the tax. All the banks would need to know is how to distribute provincial VAT revenue, a statistical requirement so that distribution can be based on the most contemporary information.

In contrast, the EU's clearinghouse method, though providing an accurate distribution of revenue among member states that is based on almost contemporary data, bears a very high cost of collecting and processing information contained in invoices. When the method is based on aggregates, information to process revenue sharing always lags. Moreover, a federation might not have reliable statistics on consumption. Because the value of trade flows from one province to another, information from the former ought to be the same as that obtained from the latter, and any differences that arise could create conflicts within the federation.

India

India's indirect tax system is unique in that under the Indian constitution the union government has the authority to impose a broad spectrum of union excise duties on the production or manufacture of goods, and the state governments are assigned the power to levy tax on sales of goods. Authority to tax services is not specifically assigned to either of the governments; it is enshrined in the residuary entry in the Union List.[12]

Under specific provisions of the constitution, however, states are empowered to levy tax on some services in the form of entertainment tax, electricity duty, motor vehicles tax, passengers and goods tax, entry tax, octroi, and so on. Because of this dichotomy of authority under the constitution, India has been rather slow in adopting a European-style VAT. Nevertheless, over the years, it has been able to adopt a dual VAT: a VAT at the federal level, known as *central VAT* (CenVAT), and a VAT at the state level, known as *state VAT*.

Central VAT

The union government levies CenVAT at the manufacturing level on almost all manufactured goods. CenVAT was initially an excise duty, known as *union excise duty* (UED), and was levied on about a dozen articles at very low rates. With the passage of time, the rates were raised, the base was enlarged, and more and more items were brought into the UED net. UED was then levied mainly on finished goods, but it also covered raw materials, intermediate goods, and capital goods.

In 1986, for the first time, UED reforms were initiated through the introduction of a modified value added tax (Modvat).[13] Modvat provided for setoff of taxes paid on inputs. The scheme was extended in 1987 to some additional commodities. Beginning in 1991 with the adoption of the policy of liberalization and globalization, Modvat was further extended to a large number of commodities.[14] Gradually, more and more items were brought under the purview of Modvat. It now covers almost all items except high-speed diesel, motor spirit (gasoline), and matchboxes. The procedures of Modvat have also been overhauled, resulting in the conversion of then-existing UED rates into a full CenVAT system.

CenVAT allows instant credit for all the taxes paid on inputs in the form of union excise duties (Modvat or CenVAT) or additional excise duties. Input credit is also given for an additional customs duty, known as *countervailing duty* (CVD),[15] collected at the time of importation. For capital goods, however, only 50 percent of the duty can be claimed as input credit in a financial year; the remaining credit can be claimed in the next financial year, provided the goods are still in use (except for spares and components). Manufacturers producing only exempt final products are not allowed to take this credit. However, a manufacturer that produces both dutiable and exempt final products in the same factory can take the credit.[16] The 2006–07 Union Budget moved the CenVAT toward a two-rate duty structure of 16 percent and 8 percent.

Along with CenVAT, the union government levies an additional excise duty in lieu of sales tax,[17] an additional excise duty on textiles and textile articles, and cess on specified commodities. The additional excise duty on textiles and cess on specified commodities are primarily meant to raise resources for the development of the concerned industries. The union revenue department administers these levies, with the help of other union departments.

Service Tax

Because the authority to levy tax on services was not specifically assigned to either level of government, using the powers given in the residuary entry in the Union List, the union government started levying this tax effective July 1, 1994. Initially, only three services—general insurance, stockbroker, and telephone services—were taxed. The coverage of the tax was gradually expanded, and currently it is levied on 100 services. The standard tax rate is 12 percent. Input tax credit is available for taxes paid on input of goods and services. In a sense, therefore, the service tax is integrated with CenVAT.

The union government has amended the constitution to include service tax in the Union List by inserting item 92(C) in the Seventh Schedule. This provision enables the union government to assign this tax to the states, solely or concurrently, if it so desires.

State VAT

In addition to the union government taxes (that is, CenVAT on all manu-factured goods and service tax, which is integrated with CenVAT), all the states levy a state VAT on goods sold within the state.

According to the Indian constitution, power to levy tax on interstate trade rests with the union government, but the union government has assigned this tax to the states. Accordingly, the tax is legislated by the union parliament, but it is administered by the states.

Developments before introduction of state VAT

Prior to the introduction of state VAT, the states had been levying a first-point cascade-type sales tax. In addition, many of the states levied other sales taxes, such as additional sales tax, turnover tax, or surcharge. Considerable varia-tions existed among the states in these levies.

The first-point sales tax suffered from many weaknesses, such as cascading and uncontrolled incidence of tax, multiplicity of rates, vertical integration of firms, and lack of neutrality and efficiency in the tax system (see Purohit 2001b). Because of the noted deficiencies in the then-prevailing structure of the tax, efforts were made to replace it with a system of subna-tional VATs.

The Committee of State Finance Ministers (in 1995 and 1998, respec-tively) and the Committee of the Chief Ministers (in 1999) had recommended replacing the sales tax with a subnational VAT. This recommendation was rat-ified by the conference of chief ministers and finance ministers on November 16, 1999.[18] Nevertheless, some preparations prior to the introduction of VAT were essential. To begin with, states attempted to rationalize their existing sales tax system by adopting two major reforms.

The first reform related to the adoption of a four-rate structure (0, 4, 8, and 12 percent) in the existing sales tax. These rates were in addition to two special rates of 1 percent and 20 percent for a few specified items. The rec-ommended rates were floors; the states were free to adopt higher rates on any commodities from the list. This possibility checked rate war and diversion of trade among the states.[19]

The second reform pertained to abolition of sales tax incentives. In the past, all the states granted such incentives to new industries. These incentives provided exemption from tax on the purchase of inputs as well as on the sale of finished goods. Incentives were also available in the form of sales tax loans and tax deferrals. Various studies and committee reports[20] had already argued against such incentives. In terms of loss of revenue, the states in aggregate sacrificed about 25 percent of their sales tax base. Moreover, incentives created tax competition or tax wars and other tax practices that are harmful in a federation.[21] All subnational governments have now stopped giving sales tax incentives to new industrial units. The concessions already granted to existing units still apply. Following the introduction of VAT, however, these incentives have been converted into a system of tax deferral or remission, which does not affect the chain of VAT transactions.

Introduction of state-level VAT

Following the implementation of reforms, VAT was introduced to replace the then-prevailing sales tax. Haryana was the first state to introduce VAT on April 1, 2003. A majority of the states (18 states) implemented VAT from April 1, 2005.[22] The rest eventually followed suit.[23]

All the states thus have a system of state VAT. Tax coverage includes sales of all goods except diesel oil, petrol (gasoline), aviation turbine fuel, natural gas, and liquor. State VAT has two basic rate categories—4 percent and 12.5 percent (the standard rate)—with some tax-exempt items. In addition, there are two special categories: 1 percent on gold, silver, and ornaments and 20 percent on petroleum products (Purohit 2006).

Harmonization of Interstate Tax

The Indian constitution, as stated earlier, empowers the states to levy tax on intrastate transactions only. Interstate transactions fall within the purview of the union government.

The union government enacted the Central Sales Tax Act 1956 to determine the principles that would govern taxation of such sales. Accordingly, the tax is levied at origin when goods are sold to another state. Although the authority to levy the tax remains under the jurisdiction of the union government, the tax has been assigned to the states. Thus, the power to administer, collect, and retain the revenue earned from the central sales tax (CST) lies with the exporting state on the basis of origin (table 5.1). The rate of tax on such transactions is now 3 percent when the goods are sold to a registered dealer and 10 percent when they are sold to an unregistered dealer or to a consumer.[24] The higher rate of tax on unregistered dealers is charged to prevent them from entering into interstate trade for any competitive advantage.

In addition, certain documentation procedures are required to ascertain that the goods have actually been sold to a dealer in another state. The officers of the sales tax department in the destination state manage this documentation through issuance of a C Form. The C Form must be submitted to the officer of the state of origin to enable a dealer to charge CST at the lower rate of 3 percent.

TABLE 5.1 Cascading Effects of Central Sales Tax in Consuming States

Indicator	Origin-based CST at 4% (Rs)	Destination-based CST at 0% (Rs)
State A producing raw materials		
Purchase price of raw materials	100.00	100.00
Value added	50.00	50.00
Value of output	150.00	150.00
CST collected	6.00	0.00
State B producing intermediate goods		
Purchase price from state A including CST	156.00	150.00
Value added	78.00	75.00
Value of output sold to state C	234.00	225.00
CST collected	9.36	0.00
Purchase price of intermediate goods in state C	243.36	225.00
Value added	121.80	112.50
Value of finished goods in state C when sold to state D	365.16	337.50
CST collected	14.60	0.00
Purchase price of goods in state D	379.76	337.50
Value added	189.88	168.75
Value of output	569.64	506.25
GST collected by consuming state D at 10%	56.96	50.62
Total CST collected by exporting states	29.96	0.00
Total tax burden on consumer	86.92	50.62

Source: Author's calculations.
Note: The calculations given above assume forward shifting of the tax. The rate of central sales tax was reduced from 4 percent to 3 percent effective April 1, 2007.

Phasing Out of CST

Because the CST is distortionary and breaks the chain of transactions in the Indian common market, the government has decided to phase it out by 1 percentage point each year to reduce it to zero by March 31, 2010.

The CST has, however, been an important source of revenue (yielding about 16 percent of sales tax revenue) for the exporting states (see table 5.2). Thus, reducing CST to zero will cause substantial revenue loss to these states. Therefore, these states did not agree to a reduction of CST for quite some time. Finally, the union government announced the following compensating measures:

- Withdrawing the benefit of the concessionary CST rate on interstate sales to government departments, against submission of D Form
- Enabling states to levy VAT on tobacco at a 12.5 percent rate

TABLE 5.2   Distribution of Revenue from CST among Indian States

State	1995–96 Amount (Rs 10 million)	1995–96 Share (%)	2001–02 Amount (Rs 10 million)	2001–02 Share (%)	2004–05 Amount (Rs 10 million)	2004–05 Share (%)	2005–06 Amount (Rs 10 million)	2005–06 Share (%)	2006–07 (revised estimates) Amount (Rs 10 million)	2006–07 (revised estimates) Share (%)	2007–08 (budget estimates) Amount (Rs 10 million)	2007–08 (budget estimates) Share (%)
Andhra Pradesh	520.54	10.64	646.07	5.88	1,051.96	7.36	1,017.37	6.52	1,691.06	8.92	1,791.06	9.00
Assam					6.79	0.05			506.61	2.67	557.26	2.80
Bihar			115.00	1.05	61.11	0.43	54.18	0.35	89.61	0.47	113.36	0.57
Chhattisgarh			376.19	3.42	326.69	2.29	415.19	2.66	700.00	3.69	850.00	4.27
Goa	15.84	0.32	36.10	0.33	64.49	0.45	71.48	0.46	75.00	0.40	89.00	0.45
Gujarat	555.26	11.35	1,015.71	9.25	1,607.40	11.25	1,915.21	12.27	2,050.00	10.82	3,069.05	15.42
Haryana	451.22	9.23	838.15	7.63	1,061.89	7.43	1,244.46	7.97	1,915.95	10.11	2,256.55	11.33
Himachal Pradesh	17.61	0.36	43.14	0.39	37.54	0.26	80.49	0.52	74.99	0.40	119.85	0.60
Jharkhand			259.93	2.37	527.52	3.69	650.79	4.17	650.79	3.43	738.65	3.71
Karnataka	240.65	4.92	679.35	6.18	1,164.07	8.15	1,255.23	8.04	1,858.68	9.81	2,035.67	10.23
Kerala	166.89	3.41	260.98	2.38	361.24	2.53	486.36	3.12	510.24	2.69	569.25	2.86
Madhya Pradesh	341.94	6.99	332.54	3.03	470.89	3.30	416.64	2.67	608.59	3.21	694.25	3.49
Maharashtra	1,154.13	23.60	2,036.99	18.54	2,417.10	16.92	2,318.18	14.85	2,514.00	13.27	2,055.00	10.32
Meghalaya	15.74	0.32	21.11	0.19	19.84	0.14	13.72	0.09	35.64	0.19	35.64	0.18
Orissa			51.82	0.47	410.16	2.87	487.55	3.12	546.64	2.89	443.57	2.23
Punjab	201.33	4.12	620.47	5.65	479.24	3.36	356.60	2.28	357.52	1.89	254.00	1.28
Rajasthan	81.90	1.67	199.80	1.82	296.76	2.08	348.23	2.23	378.52	2.00	436.92	2.19
Tamil Nadu	701.34	14.34	1,546.71	14.08	1,493.64	10.46	1,860.84	11.92	2,271.22	11.99	1,958.93	9.84
Uttaranchal			398.01	3.62	793.29	5.55	1,014.10	6.50	142.37	0.75	160.00	0.80
Uttar Pradesh	426.01	8.71	498.37	4.54			883.09	5.66	1,120.00	5.91	682.00	3.43
West Bengal			302.66	2.76	629.98	4.41	713.97	4.57	846.05	4.47	994.11	4.99
All states	4,890.40	100.00	10,985.68	100.00	14,284.10	100.00	15,610.97	100.00	18,947.48	100.00	19,908.12	100.00

Source: Reserve Bank of India, various years.

Note: Totals may not tally because some revenue of Union Territories may not be shown here. Cells with no data indicate that either the value of the item is insignificant or the details are not given in the budget.

■ Transferring to the states the revenue from 33 services currently subject to service tax and assigning 44 new services to them (as and when taxed)
■ Filling any revenue gap through budgetary support during 2007–08, 2008–09, and 2009–10, in case the first three measures do not fully cover the revenue loss.

While the CST is being phased out, a regulatory framework for effective tracking of interstate transactions has also been put in place, the tax information exchange system (TINXSYS). The process of setting up the TINXSYS is almost complete, and required data are being uploaded by the states.

The Recommended Options

Before looking for a suitable solution to the taxation of interstate transactions, one should consider which features would be desirable in a rational system of interstate taxation. Along with the other objectives of reforms, such as neutrality, efficiency, transparency, lack of vertical integration of firms, and autonomy of states, the aspects of administrative expediency for any recommended solution need to be considered. Taking into account the desirable features for a rational solution to the problem of taxation of interstate trade, one can draw some lessons from the different federal formulations discussed in this chapter.

First, as indicated by the international experience in Canada and the European Union, there should be no cascading and escalation of cost. Even in Brazil, which adopts an origin-based system for interstate taxation, the system ensures that no cascading takes place as a result of setoff in the consuming state.

Second, three alternative solutions emerge from the international experience: (a) the clearinghouse mechanism, (b) the little boat model, and (c) the zero-rating of interstate sales.

The advantage of the clearinghouse mechanism is that the rate of tax for a transaction will be the same for any given state. Thus, interstate and intrastate transactions need not be differentiated. The key problem with the clearinghouse mechanism, however, relates to transferring the tax collected to the central pool and redistributing the collected money by the central pool to the concerned states according to their respective imports. This task could be onerous for many countries and may not be feasible without proper computerization in tax administration. In fact, this mechanism has not been adopted in the European Union precisely for those reasons.

Nevertheless, the little boat model could be implemented, but only when federal VAT and state VAT have the same coverage.

For zero-rating of interstate sales, three alternative proposals for a federal country are given:

- *Zero-rating of state VAT.* Zero-rating of the state VAT with no separate tax on interstate transactions would convert the state VAT into a destination-based VAT. The tax would be levied in a state until the commodity was exported. When the commodity was exported, all the state tax already levied would be refunded, in effect meaning that all the taxes would be levied in the consuming state only.

- *Prepaid VAT.* In the case of a prepaid VAT (see NIPFP 1994; Poddar 2001; Purohit 2007), the dealers in the importing state would collect the VAT on imports into the state. The importing dealer would then provide proof of this payment to the dealer in the exporting state. On the submission of this proof (for example, in the form of a copy of the tax deposit receipt), the sale would be zero-rated in the state of origin. In this case, a registered dealer in the importing state would have a strong incentive to prepay the tax, which would then be creditable against its output in the state of destination. Unregistered dealers or consumers would have the choice of paying the local tax or the destination tax. This system would not place any additional burden of administration on dealers in exporting or importing states.

- *Destination-based central purchase tax.* The main features of a destination-based central purchase tax (DBCPT) would be as follows: First, the importer would pay the tax into the bank account of the destination state. That is, whereas tax on intrastate sales would be paid to the dealer, tax on interstate purchases would be paid to the bank account of the destination state. The importer would supply the receipt of payment of tax to the exporter.[25] The receipt would thus serve as a proof of export, and no tax would be charged by the exporter on the basis of origin. The dealer in the exporting state would refund the tax already borne by inputs in the exporting state on the basis of the proof of the tax paid on interstate purchases. The DBCPT paid by registered dealers would be eligible for input tax credit in the state of destination. If the proof of payment of DBCPT were missing, the VAT of the exporting state would be levied as if the commodity had been sold within the state. Such a system would not require any clearinghouse mechanism. Also, it would not require closely integrated interstate or national coordination, although states of origin and states of destination would have incentives to monitor the authenticity of payments made under the

DBCPT system. For the state of origin, monitoring would be important for refund of input tax, and for the importing state, it would be important for zero-rating under the local tax.

Conclusion

When attempting to introduce VAT, most federations face the problem of harmonizing tax on interstate trade. The examples of Canada and the European Union suggest that tax should not be imposed on the basis of origin. The case study of Brazil suggests that if tax is levied on the basis of origin, a setoff needs to be given in the importing state. This approach will both make the tax destination based and serve as an equalizing mechanism in the federal structure. The other models available in the literature suggest that the central and state VATs could support each other in carrying the tax of the origin state to the destination state. However, two other proposals, prepaid VAT and DBCPT, are also useful models.

Notes

1. Although the Ministry of Finance notifies the eligibility for the tax credit, the coordinator of the tax system approves additional items for the credit.
2. Services are taxed separately by the municipal authorities. The tax on services levied by these authorities is a cascade-type tax.
3. Nine states are in the northeast, four in the central-west, and seven in the north. These states are regarded as less developed states. In all, six states are considered developed states.
4. The CONFAZ consists of all states' representatives and 27 councilors. Unanimity is required for any resolution to go through. The 1988 constitution strengthened the legislative role of the CONFAZ. It now promotes treaties on tax benefits and harmonizes rates.
5. Although the CONFAZ harmonizes interstate trade, some of the states try to grant concessions (such as granting payment deferrals to attract industries) that are not permissible.
6. These items include interest on loans, charges for accounts, credit card fees, and commissions on transactions in stocks or other securities.
7. This group is known as the MASH (municipalities, academic institutions, schools, and hospitals) sector.
8. Alberta has considerable revenue from gasoline.
9. The European Commission was supposed to report to the Economic and Financial Affairs Council of the European Union before December 31, 1994, on the workings of the regime and submit a proposal for a final system. However, as of 2008, the same transitional system is in place.
10. McLure (2000) called the tax corresponding to the proposed scheme a *compensating VAT* (CVAT), which is an adequate technical name. Two different CVATs are collected,

however, the CVAT embodied in the federal tax and the explicit CVAT, as described in this example. Embodied, but not explicit, CVAT gives rise to a tax credit against the federal tax.

11. Regarding the net federal tax liability, both federal tax liabilities and federal tax credits include the value of the embodied CVAT. Concerning the explicit CVAT, no credit for previously paid taxes corresponds to explicit CVAT liabilities; credits are netted out against provincial tax liabilities.

12. Entry 97 of the Union List, known as the *residuary entry*, authorizes the union government to take recourse to "[a]ny other matter not enumerated in List II or List III, including any tax not mentioned in either of those Lists."

13. These reforms were based on the Report of the Jha Committee (Government of India 1978).

14. These reforms were based on the Report of the Chelliah Committee (Government of India 1991–93).

15. This duty is levied under the provisions of the Customs Act, which refers to it as the "Additional Duty of Customs"; however, it is popularly known as countervailing duty. The CVD rate on imported goods is equivalent to the CenVAT rate levied on indigenously manufactured goods.

16. This ability is subject to certain conditions, such as maintenance of separate records for inputs used to manufacture exempt products; payment of 8 percent of the total price (excluding taxes) of the exempt final products; or, in the case of a few specified items, payment of 8 percent of the total price on reversal of the credit.

17. This duty has been levied since 1956 on tobacco, textiles, and sugar under a tax-rental arrangement between the union and the states. Under the original arrangement, the union government levied the duty on the items, and the states refrained from levying sales tax on those same items. Until recently, the net proceeds of the duty were distributed among the states on the basis of consumption. With India's efforts to move toward VAT, the proceeds of this tax are now included in a shared pool, and the states are now allowed to levy VAT on the items.

18. See Government of India (1995, 1998, 1999) for the background of this recommendation.

19. When the states started implementing the four-rate categories, many of them found it difficult to follow the floor rates for some commodities. Either the classification had some problem or they had administrative difficulties in implementing the floor rates. Hence, a few changes were made in the items falling under the exempt list. Some changes were made in the items falling in other categories as well because the *Report of the Committee of State Finance Ministers on Sales Tax Reform* (Government of India 1995: 8) had suggested that "fine tuning of this classification would have to be done by a special group." Because it was not done before adoption of floor rates, the regime has now been revised. However, under the VAT regime, the states would have three rate categories, such as 0, 4.0, and 12.5 percent (or some rate category that could be revenue neutral for the state concerned).

20. See especially Government of India (1998, 1999).

21. Empirical studies undertaken for the National Capital Region indicate that sales tax concessions do not affect the location of industry. If relevant at all, such incentives have an effect only when given by one state alone. Similar results are seen from the other studies. When all the states give such concessions, they result in a zero-sum game in which no state benefits (see Purohit and others 1992).

22. These states were Andhra Pradesh, Arunachal Pradesh, Bihar, Dadra and Nagar Haveli, Daman and Diu, Delhi, Goa, Himachal Pradesh, Karnataka, Kerala, Maharashtra, Mizoram, Nagaland, Orissa, Punjab, Sikkim, Tripura, and West Bengal.

23. The order of adoption of VAT by other states was as follows: Jammu and Kashmir from April 4, 2005; Assam and Meghalaya from May 1, 2005; Manipur from July 1, 2007; Uttaranchal (now known as Uttarakhand) from October 1, 2005; Gujarat, Rajasthan, Jharkhand, Madhya Pradesh, and Chhattisgarh from April 1, 2006; Tamil Nadu from January 1, 2007; and Uttar Pradesh from January 1, 2008.

24. The rate of central sales tax was reduced from 4 percent to 3 percent effective April 1, 2007.

25. Such provisions exist today when dealers in India export commodities to countries such as Bhutan or Nepal. According to the treaties between India and those countries, the exporters get refunds of taxes paid in India when they pay tax in those countries. Generally, the dealers pay their tax in those countries and submit the proof for refund of tax paid in India on the strength of the receipt provided by the respective countries.

References

Buckett, Alan. 1992. *VAT in the European Community.* London: Butterworths.

Commission of the European Communities. 1987. *Completing the Internal Market: The Introduction of a VAT Clearing Mechanism for Intra-Community Sales.* Milan, Italy: Commission of the European Communities.

Government of India. 1978. *Report of the Indirect Taxation Enquiry Committee.* New Delhi: Ministry of Finance.

———. 1991–93. *Report of the Tax Reforms Committee, Vol. I to III.* New Delhi: Ministry of Finance.

———. 1995. *Report of the Committee of State Finance Ministers on Sales Tax Reform.* New Delhi: Ministry of Finance.

———. 1998. *Report of the Committee of State Finance Ministers for Charting a Time Path for Introduction of VAT.* New Delhi: Ministry of Finance.

———. 1999. *Report of the Committee of Chief Ministers on Value Added Tax and Incentives to Backward Areas.* New Delhi: Ministry of Finance.

McLure, Charles E. 2000. "Implementing Sub-national Value Added Taxes on Internal Trade: The Compensating VAT (CVAT)." *International Tax and Public Finance* 7 (6):732–40.

NIPFP (National Institute of Public Finance and Policy). 1994. *Reform of Domestic Trade Taxes in India: Issues and Options.* New Delhi: NIPFP.

Poddar, Satya. 2001. "Zero-Rating of Inter-state Sales under a Sub-national VAT: A New Approval." Paper presented at the 94th Annual Conference of National Tax Association, Baltimore, Maryland, November 8–10.

Purohit, Mahesh C. 1997. "Value Added Tax in a Federal Structure: A Case Study of Brazil." *Economic and Political Weekly* 32 (2): 357–62.

———. 2001a. "National and Sub-national VATs: A Road Map for India." *Economic and Political Weekly* 36 (9): 757–72.

———. 2001b. *Sales Tax and Value Added Tax in India.* New Delhi: Gayatri.

———. 2001c. "Structure and Administration of VAT in Canada: Lessons for India." *International VAT Monitor* 12 (6): 311–23.

———. 2006. *State-VAT in India: An Analysis of Revenue Implications.* New Delhi: Gayatri.

———. 2007. *Value Added Tax: Experiences of India and Other Countries.* New Delhi: Gayatri.

Purohit, Mahesh C., C. Sai Kumar, Gopinath Pradhan, and O. P. Bohra. 1992. *Fiscal Policy for the National Capital Region.* New Delhi: Vikas.

Reserve Bank of India. Various years. *Study of State Finances.* Mumbai: Reserve Bank of India.

Varsano, Ricardo. 2000. "Subnational Taxation and the Treatment of Interstate Trade in Brazil: Problems and Proposed Solutions." *In Decentralization and Accountability of the Public Sector,* eds. Shahid Javed Burki and Guillermo E. Peary, 339–56. Washington, DC: World Bank.

6

Subnational Borrowing, Insolvency, and Regulation

LILI LIU AND MICHAEL WAIBEL

Subnational borrowing has become an important source of subnational finance in developing countries, owing to widespread decentralization of spending responsibilities, taxation power, and borrowing capacity to subnational governments.[1] In particular, subnational governments have borrowed from the financial market to finance infrastructure,[2] matching the maturity of debt with the economic life of the assets that the debt is financing. Furthermore, subnational revenue coming from taxation and fiscal transfers is small relative to the large infrastructure demands created by rapidly accelerating urbanization, which also necessitates subnational borrowing.

The subnational debt market in developing countries is also going through a notable transformation. Private capital has emerged to play an important role in subnational finance in countries such as Hungary, Mexico, Poland, Romania, and the Russian Federation.[3] Subnational bonds increasingly compete with traditional bank financing. Both changes are facilitated by highly mobile international capital- and financial-market reforms in developing countries. Nonetheless, in many countries, only the most creditworthy subnational entities borrow. By the standards of industrial countries, subnational bond markets remain small. In the United States,

US$400 billion subnational bonds are issued per year on average.[4] In contrast, for example, 19 Mexican subnationals issued US$1.44 billion bonds from 2001 to 2005. The growth of the subnational bond market has been uneven, with wide swings since the 1990s.[5]

With borrowing comes the risk of insolvency.[6] The 1990s saw widespread subnational debt crises. To many observers, runaway provincial debt in Mendoza and Buenos Aires was a major factor behind Argentina's sovereign debt default in 2001. Brazil experienced two subnational debt crises following the early one in the 1980s. The 1995 Tequila crisis in Mexico exposed the vulnerability of subnational debt to the peso devaluation and led many Mexican subnationals into debt crises. In Russia, at least 57 of 89 regional governments defaulted from 1998 to 2001.[7]

Even without explicit defaults or debt crises, fiscal stress and implicit liabilities from borrowing are a real concern. In India, many states experienced fiscal stress in the late 1990s to the early 2000s, with a rapid increase in fiscal deficits, debt, and contingent liabilities. Subnational governments in Colombia, Hungary, and South Africa experienced fiscal stress in the 1990s. Although subnational governments in China cannot borrow directly from the financial market, they do borrow indirectly off budget to finance infrastructure through public utility companies, special-purpose vehicles, and urban development investment corporations. The implicit subnational debt is a real concern to the central government.[8]

The perils of subnational insolvency are serious. At a minimum, provision of local public goods and services may be severely impaired. When New York City was in a fiscal crisis in 1975, essential services such as fire protection, police patrols, garbage collection, and schools were cut back. Maintenance on bridges and roads was postponed. Many capital projects were delayed or canceled (Bailey 1984). Beyond local service delivery, subnational insolvency may impede the growth of subnational credit markets and curtail fiscal space for infrastructure financing. In developing a unifying legal framework for subnational finance after the fall of apartheid, the South African government viewed a lack of insolvency procedures as an impediment to the development of a competitive and diversified credit market for municipal finance (South Africa National Treasury 2001: 192–93). In Romania, the capital market is reluctant to extend maturity and lower spreads to subnational borrowers because of the absence of a collective framework for insolvency (Liu and Waibel 2008). Systemic subnational fiscal stress and insolvency also threaten macroeconomic and financial stability.[9]

The resolution to the threat of subnational insolvency should not lie in prohibiting subnational borrowing altogether. The benefits from subnationals' access to the financial market are numerous. Yet subnational borrowing, left unregulated, entails the risk of insolvency, which threatens local service delivery as well as macroeconomic and financial system stability. The way forward is to develop a regulatory framework that can help expand subnational borrowing, strengthen subnational fiscal discipline, and manage potential risks while at the same time supporting reforms in the intergovernmental fiscal system and financial markets for more efficient use of capital. The primary focus of this chapter is on the regulatory framework for subnational borrowing; the reforms of intergovernmental fiscal systems and the structure of financial markets are beyond the scope of the chapter.

The rest of the chapter is organized as follows. The next section analyzes the benefits and risks of subnational borrowing. The following section presents the motivation and rationales for regulating subnational borrowing. The chapter then summarizes regulatory frameworks for subnational borrowing based on cross-country experiences. First, it focuses on ex ante regulation, specifying purpose, types, and procedures of borrowing. Then, it examines ex post insolvency mechanisms that enforce and complement the preventive rules and discipline borrowers and creditors. The final section concludes.

Benefits and Risks of Subnational Borrowing

Allowing subnational governments to access the financial market brings about several principal benefits. First, it enables subnational governments to expand fiscal space for infrastructure. Pressing demands for infrastructure—particularly urban infrastructure—will continue to rise as cities strive to be successful conduits for innovation and growth while absorbing a massive influx of rural population. The unprecedented scale of urbanization in developing countries requires large-scale infrastructure financing much beyond fiscal transfers and subnational own-tax revenues.[10]

Second, subnational borrowing finances infrastructure more efficiently and equitably. Infrastructure investment benefits future generations, who should therefore also bear the cost. Maturity of debt should match the economic life of the assets that the debt is financing. Amortization of the liabilities should be matched by depreciation of the assets being financed. Matching asset life to maturity is sound public policy because these infrastructure services can be paid for by the beneficiaries of the services.[11]

Third, allowing subnational governments to access the financial market exposes subnationals to market disciplines and reporting requirements, hence strengthening fiscal transparency, sound budget and financial management, and good governance. Rigorous creditworthiness assessment by independent credit rating agencies is a precondition for accessing the capital market.[12] It requires disclosure of independently audited public financial accounts, thereby strengthening the role of markets in fiscal monitoring and surveillance. The promotion of credit ratings is an important step in the development of a broad-based subnational credit market. Credit ratings will also have a strong bearing on the dynamics of fiscal and financial risks at the subnational level. They help national and subnational governments manage debt rollover risks associated with interest and exchange rates and maturity structure,[13] as well as contingent liabilities such as locally managed infrastructure contracts and off-budget activities.

Fourth, expanding subnational borrowing facilitates the deepening of financial markets. A competitive subnational credit market with numerous buyers and sellers and financing options, such as bond financing competing with bank lending, can help diversify subnational credit markets and lower borrowing cost.[14] In several advanced countries, the subnational bond market represents a significant portion of the debt market. The United States has the largest subnational bond market. Individual investors are the largest holders of U.S. subnational bonds, followed by mutual funds, bank trust accounts, banks, insurance companies, and corporations (Maco 2001). Greater mobility of international capital and diversification of financial instruments have contributed to the rise of subnational bond markets in emerging markets.

Notwithstanding the benefits, risks to subnational borrowing exist in the absence of an effective regulatory framework, as manifested by recent subnational fiscal stress and debt crises in countries such as Brazil, India, Mexico, and Russia.[15] Understanding the root causes of these fiscal and debt crises helps develop an effective subnational regulatory framework that can minimize the occurrences of systemic crises. Although China and India, for instance, have not yet experienced explicit and systemic subnational insolvency,[16] the reported fiscal stresses by many lower levels of subnational governments and implicit liabilities share similarities with other emerging economies.[17]

Although expenditure-revenue imbalances may cause the development of subnational fiscal stress, the regulatory framework for borrowing profoundly affects the fiscal sustainability of a subnational government, because accumulation of fiscal deficits is feasible only when they have been financed.[18] Unregulated subnational borrowing grew rapidly in countries such as Hungary and Russia in the 1990s, contributing to subnational fiscal stress. Borrowing by subnational governments in Hungary and Russia was also facilitated by decentralization, which granted substantial autonomy in debt financing to subnational governments but failed to impose hard budget constraints.

Unregulated borrowing is particularly risky in an uncertain macroeconomic environment, as illustrated by the subnational debt crisis in Russia. Unfettered market access by subnational borrowers, especially in newly minted, speculative, and unregulated security markets, can outpace the development of sound revenue streams and a regulatory framework. In particular, foreign borrowing in an uncertain macroeconomic environment with the risk of currency speculation can be costly (Alam, Titov, and Petersen 2004). Because of the effect of macroeconomic policies, including interest rates and exchange rates on subnational fiscal profiles, the rating of the sovereign typically puts a ceiling on the ratings of its subnational entities.[19]

The fiscal deficit itself may not be a problem if borrowing finances capital investment and economic growth.[20] However, subnational governments borrowed heavily to finance substantial operating deficits in countries such as Hungary, India, and Russia, leading to unsustainable debt paths.[21] Borrowing for operating deficit violates the golden rule of public finance. In India, much of the growth in fiscal deficits of states in the late 1990s was driven by borrowing to finance revenue deficits; for example, at the height of the crisis, in some states more than 70 percent of new borrowing was merely to refinance existing debt.[22]

Furthermore, debt profiles of subnational governments can have inherent rollover risks, which would be exacerbated by macroeconomic and financial shocks. Before the macroeconomic crisis in Mexico in the mid-1990s and in Russia in the late 1990s, subnational governments there had risky debt profiles—short maturities, high debt service ratios, and variable interest rates. The macroeconomic crisis exposed the vulnerability of fiscal positions of subnational governments and triggered widespread subnational debt crises.[23]

Last but not least, contingent liabilities were a major source of fiscal deterioration in many developing countries, quietly eroding the financial health of subnational governments, thereby leading to the sudden onset of fiscal crises without warnings. Among Indian states in the late 1990s, special-purpose vehicles became a convenient way of circumventing tight budgets. Guarantees by states to support market borrowing of loss-making public sector undertakings, a contingent liability, grew rapidly. Early episodes of subnational debt development in the United States and developing countries today share striking similarities. Before the financial crisis in the early 1840s, many U.S. states aggressively sought debt financing of their large infrastructure projects. Several states owned public banks that participated in financing of infrastructure projects. Some infrastructure projects were developed by public enterprises created and owned by states; others were financed by states but owned and operated by private entities. States experimented with a variety of ways of financing investments. Some used taxless finance, which did not require raising tax immediately but resulted in taxpayers assuming contingent liabilities.[24]

In addition to off-budget liabilities of special-purpose vehicles and opaque transactions between subnational governments and their enterprises, there are other sources of hidden or contingent liabilities that are not captured by published fiscal accounts. Growing subnational civil-servant pension liabilities under the pay-as-you-go system have been a serious and growing threat to subnational financial health in Brazil and India. Nonperforming assets of banks owned by subnational governments in Argentina and Brazil partly explained subnational debt crises in the 1990s. Furthermore, the cash-reporting system systematically underestimates the financial liabilities of subnational governments in many developing countries. The cash-accounting system does not capture arrears to suppliers, contractors, or central government agencies or delayed payments of civil-servant wages and pensions.[25]

Subnational borrowing behavior is strongly influenced by the design of the intergovernmental fiscal system and the structure of financial markets. Market participants may tolerate unsustainable fiscal policy of a subnational government if the history backs their perception that the central government implicitly guarantees the debt service of the subnational government (Ianchovichina, Liu, and Nagarajan 2007). Imprudent lending based on anticipated or implicit guarantees from the central government contributed to the subnational fiscal crises in Hungary, Mexico, and Russia. Furthermore, lending to subnational governments was dominated by public banks in countries such as Brazil,[26] Hungary, and India, which have weak incentives to price returns and risks.

Soft budget constraints, a key aspect of fiscal incentives, allow subnational governments to live beyond their means, negating competitive incentives and fostering corruption and rent-seeking.[27] According to Webb (2004), subnational debt markets have three important agency problems:

- Subnational borrowers as agents have an incentive not to repay their lenders as principals if they anticipate bailouts.
- Subnational borrowers as agents have an incentive not to reveal certain characteristics about themselves to lenders as principals, resulting in adverse selection.[28]

■ Banks are implicit agents of the nation, entrusted to maintain the nation's payment system and creditworthiness, and they often abuse this trust by lending to uncreditworthy subnational governments with the expectation of bailouts by the national government in case of trouble.

The incidence of these agency problems varies considerably depending on the structure of each country's subnational debt market.

Rationales for Regulating Subnational Borrowing

The development since the late 1990s of regulatory frameworks for subnational borrowing in developing countries is the direct result of, and response to, subnational fiscal stress and debt crises. Regulatory frameworks for subnational borrowing should contain two parts: first, ex ante control, regulation of borrowing, and monitoring of the subnational fiscal position; second, ex post debt restructuring in the event that subnational governments become insolvent. The regulatory frameworks in many countries are still evolving, and the pace of putting together a full range of regulatory elements varies.[29] Furthermore, regulatory frameworks are inseparable from the reform of intergovernmental fiscal systems and financial markets because they profoundly shape incentives for subnational governments to pursue sustainable fiscal and debt policies and for creditors to price returns and risks appropriately.

Ex ante borrowing regulation and ex post insolvency mechanisms complement each other. Insolvency mechanisms increase the pain of circumventing ex ante regulation for lenders and subnational borrowers, thereby enhancing the effectiveness of preventive rules. Without an ex post insolvency mechanism, ex ante regulation can easily turn to excessive administrative control and game playing between the central and subnational governments.[30] Overreliance on ex ante regulations, including central government approval of individual loans, limits the role of markets in monitoring subnational borrowing and debt. In Canada and the United States, markets play a vital role in the surveillance of subnational borrowing. Although, realistically, developing countries cannot yet rely heavily on markets for monitoring subnational borrowing, developing countries should aim at carefully fostering the role of the market in the design of regulatory frameworks.[31]

Subnational borrowing legislation functions as a commitment device to allow subnational governments to access the financial market within a common framework. An individual subnational government may adopt unsustainable fiscal policies for a variety of reasons. Inherent incentives exist for a subnational government to free-ride—it bears only part of the cost of unsustainable fiscal policies, but it alone receives all the benefits. Realizing these benefits depends on good fiscal behavior by most of the other subnational governments. So collectively governments benefit from a system of rules to discourage such defection and free-riding. The commitment device controls and coordinates subnational governments across space in various localities and across time to commit future governments to a common borrowing framework (Webb 2004).

Ex ante regulations are unlikely to foster commitment in the absence of an ex post insolvency mechanism. A well-designed insolvency mechanism helps enforce the commitment device and hard budget constraints on subnational governments.[32] Equally important, insolvency procedures help an insolvent subnational government to maintain essential services while restructuring its debts. Because subnational governments perform public functions, they cannot be liquidated and dissolved like private corporations. Reorganization is the essence of the insolvency mechanism for public entities. Ultimately, subnational governments need to reenter the financial market.

But the insolvency proceeding must be fair to creditors; it ought to protect creditor rights, which are crucial to developing diversified subnational credit markets, to lowering borrowing cost, and to extending debt maturity. To balance the interests of creditors and the debtor, insolvency mechanisms establish a set of predetermined rules to allocate default risk. These rules anchor the expectations of both borrowers and lenders that both sides share the pain of insolvency.[33] Pressures for political ad hoc intervention decrease as restructurings become more institutionalized. Enhanced credibility for the no-bailout promise better aligns incentives. Effective insolvency and creditor rights systems allow better management of financial risks.[34]

The need for a collective framework for resolving debt claims is even greater in the context of subnational insolvency. Conflicts exist not only between creditors and debtor, but also among creditors. For instance, individual creditors often demand preferential treatment and threaten to derail debt restructurings voluntarily negotiated between a majority of creditors and the subnational debtor (the so-called holdout problem).[35] Creditors' remedies under contract law (instead of insolvency mechanisms) are effective to enforce discrete unpaid obligations, but they fail if there is a general inability to pay. Individual ad hoc negotiations are costly, impracticable, and harmful to the interests of a majority of creditors. The holdout problem is not as serious if debts are concentrated in a few banks. However, a collective framework for insolvency restructuring takes on more importance as the subnational bond markets develop—with thousands of creditors.

The motivations for developing regulatory frameworks differ significantly across countries, reflecting a country's political, economic, and legal and historical context, which in combination with triggering events results in country-specific motivations. These differences affect the entry point for reform, the framework's design, and its relation to subnational borrowing legislation.

For example, although the U.S. municipal bankruptcy framework offers a valuable reference for other countries,[36] the framework itself cannot be copied without care. Chapter 9 of the U.S. Bankruptcy Code was conceived with the narrow objective of resolving the holdout problem, against the background of a mature intergovernmental fiscal system and a market-oriented financial system. In countries where the intergovernmental systems are still evolving or where lending to subnational governments is dominated by a few public institutions, the development of a subnational insolvency mechanism must be sequenced with other reforms. The unique federal structure of the United States also profoundly influences the specific design of Chapter 9—for example, with respect to the role of federal courts in the debt adjustment plan of insolvent municipalities. Because the insolvency mechanism needs to define the respective role of different branches and tiers of the government, a country's political and economic history plays a key role in shaping the design of the insolvency mechanism.

Frameworks for Subnational Borrowing: Ex ante Regulation

Ex ante regulation deals with ex ante control of borrowing and with monitoring of the subnational fiscal position. Widespread subnational debt crises in the 1990s in countries such as Brazil and Mexico and prevalent subnational fiscal stress in countries such as Colombia and India have motivated these countries to develop or strengthen ex ante regulation to help prevent future systemic stress and crises. In countries such as Peru, where decentralization has recently started, the government has emphasized the importance of fiscal sustainability and the need to minimize the risks of decentralization.

Brazil has substantially strengthened ex ante regulations in response to repeated waves of subnational debt crises.[37] The federal government bailed out subnational debtors in earlier crises, but the resolution of the third debt crisis was conditioned on states undertaking difficult fiscal and structural reforms. The avoidance of unconditional bailouts in 1997 was to resolve moral hazard. The strengthened ex ante borrowing regulations were embedded in the debt restructuring agreements between 25 states and the federal government in 1997, sanctioned by legislation. The Fiscal Responsibility Law in 2000 consolidated various pieces of legislation into one unifying framework.[38] In Mexico, a new borrowing framework was developed in 2000 to address the subnational debt crisis triggered by the financial crisis in 1994 and 1995. Compared with the situation in Brazil and Mexico, subnational debt stress in Colombia was much less severe. But the country developed a borrowing framework, as defined by various pieces of legislation, including Law 358 in 1997, Law 617 in 2000, and the Fiscal Transparency and Responsibility Law in 2003. To avoid a subnational debt crisis as experienced by other countries in the region, Peru, while embarking on decentralization in 2002, developed subnational borrowing rules: the Fiscal Responsibility and Transparency Law in 2003 and the General Debt Law in 2005. In India, after the state fiscal crises in the late 1990s, the 12th Finance Commission put forward recommendations on fiscal rules and targets, as well as incentives for states to comply with the rules and targets.[39]

Several key elements in ex ante borrowing regulation across several countries can be surmised on the basis of Liu and Waibel (2006). First, borrowing is allowed only for long-term public capital investments. Some European countries, such as Germany and the United Kingdom, have enacted fiscal rules of a balanced budget net of public investment (the "golden rule").[40] This element links back to the earlier idea that only such borrowing is beneficial (and may be in the interest of future generations). A number of middle-income countries, such as Brazil, Colombia, India, Peru, Russia, and South Africa, have recently adopted the golden rule.[41]

Second, the frameworks specify limits on key fiscal variables, such as fiscal deficit, primary deficit, debt service ratios, and ceilings on guarantees issued. In India, a state with a debt service ratio exceeding 20 percent is classified as having a debt stress status, triggering the central government's close monitoring of additional borrowing by the state.[42] As recommended by the 12th Finance Commission, fiscal responsibility legislation is mandatory for all states, with the revenue deficit to be eliminated and the fiscal deficit to be reduced to 3 percent of gross state domestic product by fiscal year 2009.[43] Colombia sought to limit subnational debt to payment capacity (Law 358 in 1997 and the Fiscal Transparency and Responsibility Law in 2003). A traffic-light system was established to regulate subnational borrowing. Subnational governments rated in the red-light zone are prohibited from borrowing, and those in the green-light zone are permitted to borrow. The *red-light zone* is defined as the ratio of interest to operational savings greater than 40 percent and the ratio of debt stock over current revenues greater than 80 percent.[44] In Brazil, the debt restructuring agreements between the federal government and the states established a comprehensive list of fiscal targets— debt-to-revenue ratio, primary balance, personnel spending as share of total spending, own-source revenue growth, and investment ceilings—as well as a list of state-owned enterprises or banks to be privatized or concessioned. In the United States, the rules governing subnational borrowing depend on the type of debt issued, the revenue used to service the debt, and the type or form of government issuing it. These rules vary from state to state. Markets play a vital role in fiscal surveillance (Liu and Wallis 2008).

Third, several legal frameworks, such as those in Brazil, Colombia, and Peru, include procedural requirements that subnational governments establish a medium-term fiscal framework and a transparent budgetary process. This requirement is intended to ensure that fiscal accounts move within a sustainable debt path and that fiscal adjustment takes a medium-term approach to better respond to shocks and differing trajectories for key macroeconomic variables that affect subnational finance. The transparent budgetary process affords debates by executive and legislative branches on spending priorities, funding sources, and required fiscal adjustments. According to Peru's Fiscal Decentralization Law (2004), regional and local governments are required to prepare detailed multiyear budgetary frameworks that are consistent with the national government's multiyear budget framework.

Furthermore, fiscal transparency is increasingly becoming an integrated part of fiscal frameworks. Transparency includes having an independent audit of subnational financial accounts, making periodic public disclosures of key fiscal data, exposing hidden liabilities, and moving off-budget liabilities on budget. In India, several reforming states have started to move the off-budget liabilities onto the budget and have established the measure of consolidated fiscal deficit beyond the conventional cash deficit; the reported fiscal deficit does not capture the financing deficit of large public sector undertakings, which implicitly are states' liabilities.

In Brazil, the accrual accounting method for all levels of the government eliminates an important source of hidden liabilities: arrears. Moreover, article 48 of Brazil's Fiscal Responsibility Law (2000) enshrines fiscal transparency as a key component of the new framework. Proposals, laws, and accounts are to be widely distributed, including through the use of electronic media (all reports are made available on the Web site of the Ministry of the Treasury). Article 54 requires that all levels of government publish a quarterly fiscal management report that contains the major fiscal variables and indicates compliance with fiscal targets. Pursuant to article 57, this report is to be certified by the audit courts.

Ex ante regulation may not be purely on the borrower side. To improve fiscal transparency, Mexico introduced a credit rating system for subnational governments. Although subnational participation in the credit rating is voluntary, the requirements of the capital-risk weighting of bank loans introduced in 2000 and of loss provisions introduced in 2004 aim at imposing subnational fiscal discipline through market pricing of subnational credit. In Colombia, the Fiscal Transparency and Responsibility Law (2003) also tightened the regulations on the supply side. Lending to subnationals by financial institutions and territorial development institutions must meet the conditions and limits of various regulations, such as Law 617 and Law 817. Otherwise, the credit contract is invalid and borrowed funds must be restituted promptly without interest or any other charges.

Regulatory Frameworks for Subnational Borrowing: Insolvency Mechanisms

The ex post regulatory framework—that is, the subnational insolvency mechanism—deals with insolvent subnational governments.[45] Although ex ante regulation helps minimize the risk of defaults, it cannot prevent all defaults. Defaults may simply arise because of a subnational's own fiscal mismanagement, because of macroeconomic or exogenous shocks, or because of both. Several key design considerations arise concerning insolvency procedures—namely, the fundamental differences between public and private insolvency, the choices between judicial or administrative approaches, and the operation of the insolvency procedure itself. The central question is the resolution of the differing interests between creditors and the insolvent subnational borrower.

The public nature of the services provided by governments explains the fundamental difference between public insolvency and the bankruptcy of a private corporation. This factor leads to the basic tension between protecting creditors' rights and maintaining essential public services. Creditors' remedies against defaulting subnationals, as opposed to corporations, are narrower, leading to greater moral hazard (strategic defaults). Whereas a corporation is able to self-dissolve, this route is barred for subnational governments. When a private corporation goes bankrupt, all assets of the corporation are potentially subject to attachment. By contrast, the ability of creditors to attach assets of subnational governments is greatly restrained in many countries. In the case of subnational insolvency, the insolvency mechanism is generally a reorganization type, not liquidation of all assets.

There are two alternative approaches to subnational insolvency: the judicial and the administrative. Various hybrids also exist. Judicial procedures place courts in the driver's seat. Courts make key decisions to guide the restructuring process, including when and how a municipal insolvency is triggered, and to apply a priority structure for allocating assets among competing claims. The judicial approach has the advantage of neutralizing political pressures with regard to the debt discharge to be provided. However, because mandates for budgetary matters lie with the executive and legislature in many countries, the courts' ability to influence fiscal adjustment of subnational entities is extremely limited. Administrative interventions, by contrast, usually allow a higher level of government to intervene in the entity concerned, temporarily taking direct political responsibility for many aspects of financial management.

The choice of approach varies across countries, depending on the history, political and economic structure, and motivation for establishing an insolvency mechanism. In Hungary, a desire to neutralize political pressure for bailing out insolvent subnational governments favored the judicial approach. South Africa's legal framework for municipal bankruptcy is a hybrid, blending administrative intervention with the role of courts in deciding debt restructuring and discharge.[46] It uses sequential administrative interventions in the event of municipal financial distress: an early-warning system consisting of various indicators, intervention by provincial governments, and then intervention by the central government. Meanwhile, municipalities in South Africa can appeal to courts for staying, restructuring, or discharging debt. In Brazil, after having bailed out insolvent subnational entities in the two earlier debt crises, the federal government chose an administrative approach in dealing with the third debt crisis. The federal government intervened directly in fiscal and debt adjustment, imposing difficult structural reforms to tackle the root causes of fiscal insolvency, instilled fiscal transparency, and essentially imposed a fiscal and debt adjustment package that was based on reform conditions.[47]

The United States has both judicial and administrative approaches. In response to widespread municipal defaults during the Great Depression, the U.S. Congress adopted a municipal insolvency law in 1937,[48] known today as Chapter 9 of the U.S. Bankruptcy Code. The primary aim of this legislation was to deal with the holdout problem. The writ of mandamus was recognized as useful for enforcing unpaid discrete obligations; it is ineffective if the subnational is generally unable to pay.[49]

Chapter 9 is a debt restructuring mechanism for political subdivisions and agencies of U.S. states.[50] It provides the procedural machinery whereby a debt restructuring plan acceptable to a majority of creditors can become binding on a dissenting minority. Only debtors may file for Chapter 9. Many states have adopted their own frameworks for dealing with municipal financial distress, for two reasons. First, municipalities are political subdivisions of the states. Second, state consent is a precondition for municipalities to file for Chapter 9 in federal court. That requirement is one instance of how the U.S. constitution reserves control over municipalities to states. Moreover, federal courts may not exercise jurisdiction over policy choices and budget priorities of the debtor. No uniform approach exists across states: 21 of the 50 states give blanket consent, 3 states attach important conditions, and 27 states grant permission on a case-by-case basis (see Laughlin 2005).[51] New York City's bankruptcy in 1975 and Ohio's early-warning system monitoring of the financial health of municipalities are two prominent examples of direct state involvement in resolving financial distress.

Judicial or administrative, any insolvency mechanism contains three central elements: definition of the insolvency trigger for the procedure, fiscal adjustment by the debtor to bring spending in line with revenues and borrowing in line with the capacity to service debt, and negotiations between debtor and creditors to restructure debt obligations and potential relief.

Specific legal definitions serve as procedural triggers for initiating insolvency proceedings. While the United States and Hungary define *insolvency* as inability to pay, South Africa chooses one set of triggers for serious financial problems and another for a persistent material breach of financial commitments.[52] In all three countries, the bankruptcy code empowers the bankruptcy court to dismiss petitions not filed in good faith. Because bankruptcy procedures have the power to discharge debt, a subnational entity may file purely for the purpose of evading debt obligations. The U.S. Bankruptcy Code erects obstacles to municipal filing beyond those faced by private debtors, thereby discouraging strategic municipal bankruptcy filings.[53]

Who can file for bankruptcy? The class of eligible filers differs across countries. In the United States, under section 109(c)(2) of Chapter 9, only the municipality can file for bankruptcy, conditional on being insolvent, having worked out or attempted to work out a plan to deal with its debts, and having been authorized by the state to file for bankruptcy. The more stringent requirement for filing under Chapter 9, as compared with filing under Chapter 11, is due to the constraint set by the U.S. constitution. A creditor cannot bring a municipality into a federal court against its will, based on the constitution's 11th amendment. Like Chapter 9, Schwarcz's (2002) model law for subnational insolvency allows only municipalities to file. In South Africa, under chapter 13, section 151(a), of the 2003 Municipal Financial Management Act, any creditor can trigger the insolvency procedure. Similarly, in Hungary, a creditor can petition the court if a municipality is in arrears for more than 60 days.[54]

Fiscal adjustment and consolidation are preconditions for financial workouts. Often a subnational government's own fiscal mismanagement is the root cause of insolvency. Even when subnational insolvency is triggered by macroeconomic shocks, such as a sharp rise in real interest rates through a currency crisis, fiscal adjustment is inherent to any insolvency procedures. Ianchovichina, Liu, and Nagarajan (2007) present a framework for analyzing subnational fiscal adjustment. Similar to fiscal adjustment by central governments, real interest rates, economic growth (of the subnational economy), and the primary balance (of the subnational government) determine subnational debt sustainability.

They argue, however, that subnational fiscal adjustment qualitatively differs from national fiscal adjustment. The former is complicated by the respective legislative mandates of central vis-à-vis subnational governments and the intergovernmental fiscal system. Unable to issue their own currency, subnational governments cannot use seigniorage finance. They cannot freely adjust their primary balance because of legal constraints on raising their own revenue, dependence on central government transfers, and central government influences on key expenditure items such as wages and pensions. If public sector banks dominate lending, lending rates could be subsidized and credit risk concerns could be compromised. Many policies that affect economic growth and fiscal health of the subnational economy are designed largely or exclusively by the central government.

Even in a decentralized system such as that in the United States, where subnational governments have broad freedom to control expenditures, raise revenues, influence their local economic growth, and affect the interest rate spread (which links to the creditworthiness of each subnational entity) in a competitive capital market, fiscal adjustment often requires difficult political choices of cutting expenditure and raising revenues.

Debt restructuring lies at the heart of any insolvency framework. In administrative interventions, the higher level of government often restructures subnational debt obligations into longer-term debt instruments. The 1997 debt agreements between the Brazilian federal government and the 25 states, though strengthening ex ante regulations, might at the same time be seen as an ex post intervention, because the agreements were imposed on a case-by-case basis as a condition of debt restructuring.

The debt discharge, however, is a major departure from the principle that contracts ought to be fulfilled.[55] Discharges are typically limited to judicial mechanisms. A mature and independent judicial mechanism is viewed as well placed to ensure the fairness of discharges. Ex post modification of contracts needs to be tightly circumscribed. If creditors feel that they are treated unfairly, there is a substantial risk that they will stop lending. Perceptions of what is equitable are likely to differ across countries because distributional judgments are involved.

Debt restructuring and debt discharge are complex. But one basic question is who holds the cram-down power when both sides fail to reach an agreement.[56] Under Chapter 9 of the U.S. Bankruptcy Code, municipal debtors propose the debt adjustment plan, which may modify the terms of existing debt instruments. Such adjustment plans may be adopted over the objection of holdout creditors. Chapter 9 incorporates basic Chapter 11 requirements: at least one impaired class of claims approves the plan, and secured creditors must receive at least the value of the secured property. Unsecured creditors thus often lose out.[57]

In Hungary, the Debt Committee is chaired by a court-appointed independent financial trustee. Under the Law on Municipal Debt Adjustment (Law XXV, 1996), the committee prepares a reorganization plan and debt settlement proposal.[58] The plan and proposal are adopted by majority vote of the committee and are presented to creditors. A debt settlement is reached if at least half of the creditors whose claims account for at least two-thirds of the total undisputed claims agree to the proposal. Creditors within the same group must be treated equally (see Chapter III, section 23, of the Law on Municipal Debt Adjustment). The law also stipulates the priority of asset distributions. If disagreements arise on distribution, the court makes the final decision, which cannot be appealed (see Chapter IV, section 31).[59]

South Africa's legislation stipulates that debt discharge and settlement of claims must be approved by the court. The settlement of claims takes the following order: (a) secured creditor, provided that the security was given in good faith and at least six months before the mandatory intervention; (b) preferred claims, as provided by the 1936 Insolvency Act; and (c) non-preferential claims (see Chapter 13, section 155(4) of the Municipal Finance and Management Act, 2003).

The rescaling of debt obligations is a major intervention in contract rights. Insolvency law reconciles this clash of creditor rights and inability to pay. It formalizes the relationship between creditors and the subnational debtor in financial distress. Insolvency law preserves the legal order by superseding contractual violations with a new legal act.[60] A procedure for subnational insolvency recognizes that resolving financial distress through mechanisms guided by law is preferable to muddling through repeated, costly, and often unsuccessful negotiations.

The maturity of the legal system influences the choices of procedure. Implementation of insolvency procedures—in the corporate and the subnational contexts—rests on the shoulders of insolvency experts and on institutions (courts) resisting political influence and corruption. In many emerging economies, limited judicial and administrative capacity may be a binding constraint. The first focus should be on developing institutional ingredients and on training bankruptcy professionals. In countries where the judicial system is embryonic, formal procedural guidelines might be a stepping-stone to a fully developed mechanism. This interim solution can be used to build up institutional and professional capacity, buttressing concerns about the lack of substantive restructuring expertise (Gitlin and Watkins 1999).

Conclusions

Many developing countries will continue the decentralization process and reform their intergovernmental fiscal system. At the same time, large infrastructure demand at the subnational level will continue. As a result of these two trends, subnational borrowing legislation is likely to figure high on the policy agenda. In developing subnational borrowing legislation, experience in other countries offers valuable lessons. While indicating workable solutions, other countries' experience also highlights potential pitfalls in the design of ex ante and ex post subnational borrowing frameworks.

A subnational borrowing framework has several complementary components. First, access to financial markets depends on fiscal transparency. Timely availability of comprehensive fiscal information requires disclosure and independent audits of the subnational entity's accounts, including of all special-purpose vehicles. Second, ex ante rules specify the type and purpose of borrowing, the procedural steps for contracting debt, and any limitations on borrowing. Third, ex post insolvency mechanisms are essential to the borrowing framework. Even if rarely invoked, they shape expectations about defaults and allow and encourage the stakeholders to resolve subnational financial distress efficiently.

Subnational borrowing behavior is strongly influenced by the design of the intergovernmental fiscal system and the structure of financial markets. Market participants may tolerate the unsustainable fiscal policy of a subnational government if history backs their perception that the central government implicitly guarantees the debt service of the subnational government. The soft budget constraint embedded in the intergovernmental fiscal transfers system can undermine the effectiveness of borrowing regulations.[61] The principal-agent problem is particularly potent for subnational borrowing, and the threat of the soft budget constraint negates competitive incentives and fosters corruption and rent-seeking. The threat can be exacerbated by banks acting as implicit agents of the nation if they abuse this trust by lending to uncreditworthy subnational governments with the expectation of bailouts in case of trouble.

Introducing transparency into the subnational fiscal management system and subnational borrowing ought to be a policy priority. Off-budget liabilities, despite their potential to finance urgently needed infrastructure, present tremendous fiscal risks. Despite different local conditions, a clear and transparent subnational borrowing framework could substantially lessen those risks in a range of middle-income countries while opening access to financial markets. Such orderly borrowing helps expand fiscal space for infrastructure investment in a world of accelerating urbanization. Financial markets then play a greater role in intermediating savings and investments.

Even in countries with a general ban on subnational borrowing, subnational governments often resort to off-budget borrowing to accumulate implicit debt. The inefficacy of outright bans on subnational borrowing, coupled with lax enforcement and little monitoring, is now clear. A related macroeconomic concern is the level of implicit liabilities at the subnational level. Together with a lack of transparency and opaque accounting frameworks, this situation is a recipe for subnational financial distress.

Like ex ante regulation, subnational insolvency procedures invariably need to be adapted to country-specific circumstances. Although Chapter 9 of the U.S. Bankruptcy Code may serve as a starting point, it will rarely be a model to be copied one for one. First, Chapter 9's focus is the holdout problem; middle-income countries considering the introduction of subnational insolvency mechanisms might have different policy priorities in ex post resolution of subnational financial distress. Second, peculiarities of each country's intergovernmental fiscal system warrant special attention. Third, not only does introduction of an insolvency mechanism require sequencing with other reforms, but it also requires bankruptcy expertise and independent courts if a judicial approach is preferred. The entry point for reform, including the maturity of the legal system, influences the choices of procedure.

Insolvency mechanisms encourage voluntary bargaining in the shadow of bankruptcy; they anchor expectations about the risks and rewards of subnational borrowing. Insolvency is above all a distributional struggle for a fixed pool of assets. In such circumstances, clear and predictable rules on priority of repayment ease the struggle and allow faster resolution of financial distress. They increase the pain of circumventing ex ante rules and thereby enhance the effectiveness of preventive rules. Without ex post insolvency mechanisms, ex ante regulation can all too easily turn into excessive administrative control.

A comprehensive subnational borrowing framework also accomplishes several macroeconomic objectives. Together, ex ante regulation and ex post regulation, in conjunction with fiscal transparency, minimize the systemic risk of subnational borrowing. They lessen the incentives for individual subnational borrowers to free-ride on shared national creditworthiness and to incur unsustainable debt levels. If well designed, they also allow for more efficient access to credit and resource allocation.

Cross-country experience points to a number of central design considerations in such ex post mechanisms. First, balancing the tension between creditors' rights and the necessity of continued delivery of basic public services in financial distress requires some form of burden sharing between the subnational debtor and creditors. Second, well-designed mechanisms underpin hard budget constraints and render the central government's no-bailout policy credible. When restructurings become institutionalized, pressure for political ad hoc interventions will decrease. Third, the institutional setup differs across countries. Some mechanisms give a central role to courts, others opt for an administrative procedure, and still others combine both into a hybrid mechanism. The chosen design in large part depends on country-specific circumstances.

Subnational borrowing regulations alone are not sufficient for sustainable subnational finance and the emergence of competitive subnational credit markets. Broader institutional reforms need to proceed in tandem. Foremost is the maintenance of macroeconomic stability and improved country credit ratings, because the sovereign rating puts a ceiling on the rating of subnational governments,[62] thus affecting the cost and maturity of subnational borrowing. Moreover, the intergovernmental fiscal system underpins the fundamentals of the subnational fiscal path. Without increased fiscal autonomy and greater own-source revenues, subnational governments will rarely be in a position to borrow sustainably on their own. The hard budget constraint embedded in the insolvency proceeding can be offset by soft grant transfers. Furthermore, the development of competitive financial markets, by broadening the investor base, will increase the availability of capital. Competition among lending instruments such as bank lending and bond finance is also likely to lower borrowing costs. Introducing competition is particularly relevant for countries where a small number of public institutions dominate subnational lending. To maintain investor confidence, securities law and antifraud enforcement need to reach international standards.

Notes

This chapter draws on work as reflected in Liu and Waibel (2006, 2008) and Liu (2008). The findings and conclusions expressed herein are those of the authors. They do not necessarily reflect the views of the World Bank, its affiliated organizations, or those of the executive directors of the World Bank or the governments they represent.

1. For analysis on decentralization in developing countries, see Shah (2004). The term subnational refers to all tiers of government and public entities below the federal or central government. Subnational entities include states or provinces, counties, cities, towns, public utility companies, school districts, and other special-purpose government entities that have the capacity to incur debt.
2. The term *financial market* refers to both the banking system and the bond market.
3. Public institutions continue to dominate subnational lending in a number of countries, such as Brazil and India.
4. On January 1, 2006, subnational bonds outstanding reached US$2.26 trillion. This figure represents close to 10 percent of the U.S. domestic bond market and 26 percent of all U.S. public sector bonds (authors' calculation based on World Bank 2006). The figure of US$400 billion issues is from Petersen (2005).
5. The 1990s saw huge positive, but also strongly negative, growth rates. Subnational bonds issued outside Canada, Europe, and the United States were US$5.7 billion in 1992, US$9.4 billion in 1993, US$12.0 billion in 1994, US$22.2 billion in 1995, US$12.7 billion in 1996, US$4.3 billion in 1997, US$4.4 billion in 1998, US$1.5 billion in 1999, US$6.4 billion in 2000, and US$3.5 billion in 2001 (Thomson Financial Securities Database, available at http://www.thomson.com/solutions/financial/). Since 2001, growth in subnational bond markets has picked up in emerging markets such as Mexico, Poland, Romania, and Russia (Liu and Waibel 2008). The Russian subsovereign bond market has become the largest emerging subsovereign market, with US$5.6 billion bonds outstanding as of June 2006 (Noel and others 2006: xi).
6. A subnational entity unable to pay its debts as they fall due is insolvent. Over and above default (failure to pay according to the terms of the debt instrument), insolvency is characterized by a genuine, and not merely temporary, shortfall of resources to service the entire subnational debt stock.
7. For the case of Argentina, see Hochman (2002); for Brazil, see Dillinger (2002); for Mexico, see Barrientos (2002); and for Russia, see Popov (2002). For a summary of Brazil, Mexico, and Russia, see Liu and Waibel (2006).
8. For an account of fiscal stress in Indian states, see Ianchovichina, Liu, and Nagarajan (2007). For the fiscal situation in China, see Liu (2008); for Colombia, see Liu and

Waibel (2006) and Webb (2004); for Hungary, see Jókay, Szepesi, and Szmetana (2004); and for South Africa, see Glasser (2005), Liu and Waibel (2008), and South Africa National Treasury (2001).

9. For example, Brazil's macroeconomic crises in the 1980s and 1990s were closely related to subnational insolvency (Dillinger 2002). In India, persistent imbalance in public finance is widely viewed as the most important challenge in macroeconomic management. About half of the general government deficit comes from states' fiscal deficits.

10. For example, China has been investing about 10 percent of its gross domestic product (GDP) annually in infrastructure since the 1990s, and subnational governments have taken up a large share of infrastructure investments, particularly in urban infrastructure. The majority of financing comes from proceeds from land leasing and public bank lending securitized on property and land valuation. Public infrastructure investment by Indian states has stayed below 3 percent of their gross state domestic product since the 1990s (Liu 2008). In Brazil, public investment by the general government (including for infrastructure) shrank about 50 percent between 1998 and 2006 to about 2 percent of GDP. In the United States, subnational infrastructure is financed predominantly by bonds raised in the private capital market (Liu and Wallis 2008).

11. However, borrowing to finance infrastructure can burden future generations with debt without corresponding benefits when infrastructure is badly planned and managed.

12. For a review of how the international rating agencies Standard & Poor's, Moody's, and Fitch access subnational creditworthiness, see Liu and Tan (2008).

13. *Rollover risk* refers to the difficulty of reprofiling debt when subnational governments encounter liquidity problems. The cost of rolling over debt increases dramatically. In some cases, debt cannot be rolled over at all. To the extent that rollover risk is limited to the risk that debt might have to be rolled over at higher interest rates, it may be considered a type of market risk. However, because the inability to roll over debt or exceptionally large increases in government funding costs can lead to, or exacerbate, a debt crisis—in addition to the purely financial effects of higher interest rates—such debt is often treated separately (IMF and World Bank 2001).

14. In establishing a framework for municipal finance borrowing after the fall of apartheid, South Africa clearly understood the benefits of competition in the subnational credit market. Its *Intergovernmental Fiscal Review* report states, "Active capital markets, with a variety of buyers and sellers, and a variety of financial products, can offer more efficiency than direct lending. First, competition for municipal debt instruments tends to keep borrowing costs down and create structural options for every need. Second, an active market implies liquidity for an investor who may wish to sell. Liquidity reduces risk, increases the pool of potential investors, and thus improves efficiency" (South Africa National Treasury 2001: 192).

15. See Liu and Waibel (2006) for a review of the subnational debt crisis in Brazil (1980s and 1990s), Mexico (1994–95), and Russia (1998–2000). Also see Dillinger (2002) and Webb (2004) for Brazil, Barrientos (2002) and Webb (2004) for Mexico, and Popov (2002) for Russia.

16. Although the economics literature approaches insolvency from the sustainability of fiscal policies, in a number of countries, specific legal definitions serve as procedural triggers for initiating insolvency procedures. In a legal sense, subnational

insolvency refers to the inability to pay debts as they fall due; however, details vary across countries. See Liu and Waibel (2008).

17. For China, see Liu (2008), and for India, see Ianchovichina, Liu, and Nagarajan (2007).

18. Such finance can take multiple forms, including direct borrowing as well as running arrears.

19. For how sovereign ratings affect subsovereign ratings, see Gaillard (2006). For how international rating agencies rate subnational creditworthiness, see Liu and Tan (2008).

20. This statement assumes, however, that economic growth translates into increased capacity to service debt, which may not happen if a subnational government is unable to exploit its growing tax base. Then, borrowing may still provoke a fiscal crisis, even when the proceeds have been put to good use.

21. Ianchovichina, Liu, and Nagarajan (2007) analyze key factors influencing subnational fiscal sustainability.

22. Revenue deficit is the amount of current expenditure (such as wages, pension outlays, subsidies, transfers, and operation and maintenance) net of total revenues. For more discussion on the state fiscal crisis in India, see Ianchovichina, Liu, and Nagarajan (2007).

23. From 1998 to 2001, at least 57 of 89 regional governments defaulted in Russia. In 2001, six years after the peso crisis, 60 percent of subnational governments in Mexico still struggled financially (Schwarcz 2002). One interesting difference is that subnational governments in Russia were allowed to borrow overseas, whereas such borrowing was prohibited in Mexico. However, subnational governments in Mexico were not insulated from foreign exchange risks, because the risks were transmitted through inflation and interest rates.

24. Taxless finance schemes finance infrastructure investments in a way so that revenues are not raised immediately to finance the project. For examples of how states in the United States used taxless finance schemes in the 19th century and the state debt crises in the early 1840s, see Wallis (2004). For implications of the U.S. experiences for developing countries, see Liu and Wallis (2008).

25. For a summary of hidden and contingent liabilities in several developing countries, see Liu and Waibel (2006).

26. Bonds were a major source of financing in São Paulo in Brazil.

27. See Weingast (2007) for a summary of the literature within the context of second-generation fiscal federalism.

28. This is a generic concern, irrespective of whether the borrower is a subnational entity. But this concern can be greater if the borrower is a subnational entity and its system of financial management and reporting is not transparent.

29. See Ter-Minassian and Craig (1997) for a summary of subnational borrowing control frameworks in more than 50 countries and Liu and Waibel (2006) for a review of ex ante regulations since the late 1990s in several countries. For comparative experiences of ex post insolvency mechanisms, see Liu and Waibel (2008).

30. The focus in this chapter is on demand-side regulation. On the supply side, various elements of the financial system, including competition and prudential regulations, come into play.

31. When South Africa restructured its legal framework for a municipal finance and management system in the postapartheid period, a clear objective was to nurture a

competitive private municipal credit market in which private investors play a dominant role (South Africa National Treasury 2001: 192).

32. If a bailout system exists, subnational governments are likely to share the national rating assigned by rating agencies. The subnational governments might thereby have easier and cheaper access to the capital market.

33. Insolvency law exercises a disciplining function (Paulus 2006).

34. The World Bank (2005) addresses creditor rights and insolvency standards in the context of corporate bankruptcy. Key principles apply to the subnational context, bearing in mind the differences between public and private bankruptcy.

35. The inability to compel holdouts to cooperate in a negotiated compromise motivated the passage of Chapter 9 of the U.S. Bankruptcy Code (McConnell and Picker 1993).

36. Chapter 11, the U.S. bankruptcy law for corporations, has significantly affected other countries. Similarly, Chapter 9 of the Bankruptcy Code has strongly influenced subnational insolvency frameworks in countries such as Hungary and South Africa.

37. Statutory controls on subnational borrowing have always existed in Brazil—controls on new borrowing and on the total stock of debt, expressed as percentages of revenue. But they had loopholes, and subnational governments had been creative in evading them. The regulations were strengthened in the late 1990s, leading to the unifying framework in 2000.

38. For a review of Brazil debt crises and remedies, see Dillinger (2002). For a review of fiscal responsibility legislations in several Latin American countries, see Webb (2004).

39. The constitutionally mandated Finance Commission convenes every five years to determine the sharing of revenues between the center and the states. Depending on its terms of reference, it may also recommend measures to improve state finances.

40. Short-term borrowing for working capital is still allowed, but provisions should be built in to prevent governments from rollover borrowing as a way of long-term borrowing for operating deficits.

41. The fiscal responsibility legislation in Brazil tightly controls current expenditure and aims for positive primary balance. India's 12th Finance Commission mandates that states eliminate revenue deficits (current expenditure exceeding total revenue), which implies that the borrowing is to finance capital expenditure only. The Colombian Fiscal Transparency and Responsibility Law (2003) specifies that the ratio of primary surplus over debt service be at least 100 percent. According to Peru's Fiscal Decentralization Law (2004), article 24, and General Debt Law (2005), article 51, borrowing is solely to finance infrastructure projects. According to the Russian Budget Law (1998), in provisions relating to regional governments, current expenditure may not exceed total revenues and borrowing may be used only to finance investment expenditures. The South African constitution prohibits borrowing for consumption expenditure (South Africa National Treasury 2001: 192).

42. The debt service ratio measures the capacity to service debt. Many national governments monitor the debt service ratio of subnational entities, but they define payment capacity differently. Brazil, in its Fiscal Responsibility Law, defines it as a share of current revenue net of transfers. Colombia, in Law 358 of 1997, records it as a share of operational savings. India defines it as the ratio of debt service payments over total revenues. Peru, in a 2003 law amending its Fiscal Prudence and Transparency Law, treats it as a share of current income including transfers, while Russia, in its Budget Code, denotes it as a share of total budgetary expenditures.

43. See note 22 for the definition of revenue deficit.

44. Law 358, passed in 1997, introduced a rating system for subnational governments by establishing indebtedness alert signals. These signals were based on two indicators: a liquidity indicator (interest payment/operational savings) and a solvency indicator (debt/current revenue). Subnational governments were classified into one of three zones. Governments in the red-light zone were not allowed to borrow, governments in the green-light zone were allowed to borrow, and governments in the yellow-light zone were allowed to borrow with the permission of the central government. Law 795, passed in 2003, eliminated the yellow-light category. Law 617, passed in 2000, established a ceiling for the ratio of discretionary current expenditure to nonearmarked current revenues. The implementing rules for Law 819, which was passed in 2003, added a third indicator to the traffic-light system by relating the primary surplus to debt service.

45. It is useful to note that the boundary between ex ante regulation and ex post insolvency is not as clear-cut. Fiscal responsibility regulation, for example, may incorporate elements of ex post consequences. For example, India's 12th Finance Commission mandates that states enact fiscal responsibility legislation and meet specific fiscal targets such as eliminating the revenue deficit. The commission also provides incentives to states, such as swapping high-cost debt with lower-cost debt for meeting fiscal targets. Such incentives can be interpreted as ex post consequences. Although Webb (2004) included transfer intercepts and lender control mechanism as part of ex post consequences, this chapter focuses on the insolvency proceedings themselves.

46. South Africa has three spheres of government: federal, provincial, and municipal. Provinces generally do not borrow from the financial market.

47. See Dillinger (2002) for a review of state debt crises in Brazil and debt restructuring packages.

48. Bankruptcy Act of 1938 ("Chandler Act"), 50 Stat. 654 (1937), amending the 1898 U.S. Bankruptcy Act. The 1938 act was the first legislation for municipal bankruptcy in the world, even though other countries had contemplated the introduction of similar mechanisms—for example, Switzerland did so in the second half of the 19th century (Meili 1885). In 1934, the U.S. Supreme Court had declared a previous version of this legislation unconstitutional (*Ashton* v. *Cameron County Water Improvement District No. One*, 298 U.S. 513).

49. The *mandamus* is a court order obliging public officials to take a certain course of action. For an excellent account of the mandamus and its motivation for Chapter 9, see McConnell and Picker (1993).

50. The enactment of the statute was one more step in a series of regulatory reforms on subnational borrowing since the first subnational debt crisis in the early 1840s. After the 1840s crisis, 12 states adopted new constitutions, and 11 of the 12 required that the state legislature adopt new procedures for authorizing state borrowing. Other reforms at the time included opening access for infrastructure finance and development and eliminating taxless finance (Wallis 2004). For implications of the U.S. experience for developing countries, see Liu and Wallis (2008).

51. The three states with conditions are North Carolina, Pennsylvania, and most prominently, New York.

52. In Chapter 9 of the U.S. Bankruptcy Code, *insolvency* is defined as the debtor either (a) currently not paying its debts as they become due, unless such debts are the

subject of a bona fide dispute, or (b) not being able to pay its debts as they become due. According to Hungary's 1996 Law on Municipal Debt Adjustment, the two central triggers occur (a) if the debtor has neither disputed nor paid an invoice sent by a creditor within 60 days of receipt or of date due if the due date is later or (b) if the debtor has not paid a recognized debt within 60 days of date due.

53. Only municipalities face a statutory requirement of insolvency. Section 109(c) imposes a procedural bar that is unique to Chapter 9 debtors: It requires prefiling efforts by the municipal debtor to work out its financial difficulties. The debtor must have reached agreement toward a plan or must have failed to do so despite good faith negotiations, or such negotiation must be "impracticable." Also, according to section 109(c)(2), municipalities need state authorization to file for bankruptcy.

54. See the Law on Municipal Debt Adjustment (Law XXV, 1996). Four years after the law was enacted, neither vendors nor banks petitioned for bankruptcy. According to Jókay, Szepesi, and Szmetana (2004), these creditors probably assumed that the local governments had few liquid assets and that operational cutbacks could not produce a cash flow sufficient for fully satisfying claims.

55. In the United States, the Contracts Clause of the U.S. constitution (article I. section 10, clause 1) puts the principle of good faith in contracts into constitutional form.

56. Cram-down involves court confirmation of bankruptcy plans despite opposition of certain creditors. Under section 1129(b) of Chapter 11 of the U.S. Bankruptcy Code, courts may thus confirm a plan if it (a) was accepted by at least one impaired class, (b) does not discriminate unfairly, and (c) is fair and equitable.

57. For more detailed case histories, see Kupetz (1995) and McConnell and Picker (1993).

58. Chapter II, section 9(3), of the Law on Municipal Debt Adjustment stipulates the financial trustee's independence.

59. Assets are distributed to creditors in the following order: (a) regular personnel benefits including severance pay; (b) securitized debt; (c) dues to the central government; (d) social insurance debts, taxes, and public contributions; (e) other claims; and (f) interest and fees on debt obligations incurred during the bankruptcy proceeding.

60. The U.S. experience suggests that in the absence of a bankruptcy framework, public entities in financial distress will use every possible technicality to challenge the validity of their outstanding obligations. Widespread challenges in a default wave during the 19th century led to the development of the bond counsel opinion, which certifies that the obligation is legal, valid, and enforceable.

61. For in-depth discussions and a review of the latest literature on intergovernmental fiscal systems, see Ahmad and Brosio (2006).

62. For how sovereign ratings affect subsovereign ratings, see Gaillard (2006).

References

Ahmad, Ehtisham, and Giorgio Brosio. 2006. *Handbook of Fiscal Federalism*. Cheltenham, U.K.: Edward Elgar.

Alam, Asad, Stepan Titov, and John Petersen. 2004. "Russian Federation." In *Subnational Capital Markets in Developing Countries: From Theory to Practice*, ed. Mila Freire and John Petersen, 571–92. Washington, DC: World Bank.

Bailey, Robert W. 1984. *The Crisis Regime: The MAC, the EFCB, and the Political Impact of the New York City Financial Crisis*. Albany: State University of New York Press.

Barrientos, Laura. 2002. "Subsovereign Defaults in Mexico." Moody's Investors Service, New York.

Dillinger, William. 2002. "Brazil: Issues in Fiscal Federalism." Report 22523-BR, Brazil Country Management Unit, PREM Sector Management Unit, Latin America and the Caribbean Region, World Bank.

Gaillard, Norbert. 2006. "Determinants of Moody's and S&P's Subsovereign Credit Rating." Paper presented at the 11th Annual Meeting of the Latin American and Caribbean Economic Association, Mexico City, November 3.

Gitlin, Richard A., and Brian N. Watkins. 1999. "Institutional Alternatives to Insolvency for Developing Countries." Paper presented at the conference Building Effective Insolvency Systems, World Bank, Washington, DC, September 29–30.

Glasser, Matthew. 2005. "Legal Framework for Local Government Insolvency." Paper presented at a World Bank seminar, Washington, DC, March 8.

Hochman, Steve. 2002. "Subsovereign Defaults in Argentina." Moody's Investors Service, New York.

Ianchovichina, Elena, Lili Liu, and Mohan Nagarajan. 2007. "Subnational Fiscal Sustainability Analysis: What Can We Learn from Tamil Nadu?" *Economic and Political Weekly* 42 (52): 111–19.

IMF (International Monetary Fund) and World Bank. 2001. "Guidelines for Public Debt Management." IMF, Washington, DC.

Jókay, Charles, Gábor Szepesi, and György Szmetana. 2004. "Municipal Bankruptcy Framework and Debt Management Experiences, 1990–2000." In *Intergovernmental Finances in Hungary: A Decade of Experience*, ed. Mihály Kopányi, Deborah L. Wetzel, and Samir El Daher. World Bank: Washington, DC.

Kupetz, David S. 1995. "Municipal Debt Adjustment under the Bankruptcy Code." *Urban Lawyer* 27 (3): 531–605.

Laughlin, Alexander M. 2005. "Municipal Insolvencies: A Primer on the Treatment of Municipalities under Chapter 9 of the U.S. Bankruptcy Code." Washington, DC: Wiley Rein & Fielding. http://www.wileyrein.com/publication.cfm?publication_id=11309.

Liu, Lili. 2008 "Creating a Regulatory Framework for Managing Subnational Borrowing." In *Public Finance in China: Reform and Growth for a Harmonious Society*, ed. Jiwei Lou and Shuilin Wang, 171–90. Washington, DC: World Bank.

Liu, Lili, and Kim Song Tan. 2008. "Creditworthiness Assessment of Subnational Governments." World Bank, Washington, DC.

Liu, Lili, and Michael Waibel. 2006. "Subnational Borrowing Notes on Middle-Income Countries." World Bank, Washington, DC.

———. 2008. "Subnational Insolvency: Cross-Country Experiences and Lessons." Policy Research Working Paper 4496, World Bank, Washington, DC.

Liu, Lili, and John Wallis. 2008. "Infrastructure Finance, Debt Restrictions, and Subnational Debt Market: Lessons from the United States." World Bank, Washington, DC.

Maco, Paul S. 2001. "Building a Strong Subnational Debt Market: A Regulator's Perspective." *Richmond Journal of Global Law and Business* 2 (1): 1–31.

McConnell, Michael, and Randal Picker. 1993. "When Cities Go Broke: A Conceptual Introduction to Municipal Bankruptcy." *University of Chicago Law Review* 60 (2): 425–35.

Meili, Friedrich. 1885. *Rechtsgutachten und Gesetzesvorschlag, betreffend die Schulexecu-tion und den Koncurs gegen Gemeinden.* Bern, Switzerland: Schmid, Francke & Co.

Noel, Michel, Zeynep Kantur, Evgny Krasnov, and Sue Rutledge. 2006. "Development of Capital Markets and Institutional Investors in Russia: Recent Achievements and Policy Challenges Ahead." Working Paper 87, World Bank, Washington, DC.

Paulus, Christoph. 2006. "Disciplining Function." Humboldt-Universität zu Berlin, Berlin.

Petersen, John. 2005. "U.S. Municipal Bond Market: Model or Maverick?" Paper presented at a World Bank seminar, Washington, DC, October 3.

Popov, Dimitri. 2002. "Subsovereign Defaults in Russia." Moody's Investors Service, New York.

Schwarcz, Steven L. 2002. "Global Decentralization and the Subnational Debt Problem." *Duke Law Journal* 51 (4): 1179–250.

Shah, Anwar. 2004. "Fiscal Decentralization in Developing and Transition Economies: Progress, Problems, and the Promise." Policy Research Working Paper 3282, World Bank, Washington, DC.

South Africa National Treasury. 2001. *Intergovernmental Fiscal Review.* Pretoria: South Africa National Treasury.

Ter-Minassian, Teresa, and Jon Craig. 1997. "Control of Subnational Government Borrowing." In *Fiscal Federalism in Theory and Practice*, ed. Teresa Ter-Minassian, 156–72. Washington, DC: International Monetary Fund.

Wallis, John Joseph. 2004. "Constitutions, Corporations, and Corruption: American States and Constitutional Changes, 1842–1852." NBER Working Paper 10451, National Bureau of Economic Research, Cambridge, MA.

Webb, Stephen B. 2004. "Fiscal Responsibility Laws for Subnational Discipline: The Latin American Experiences." Policy Research Working Paper 3309, World Bank, Washington, DC.

Weingast, Barry R. 2007. "Second Generation Fiscal Federalism: Implications for Development." Stanford University, Palo Alto, CA.

World Bank. 2005. "Creditor Rights and Insolvency Standard." World Bank, Washington, DC.

———. 2006. "East Asia Financial Sector Flagship Study." World Bank, Washington, DC.

Local Finance

7

A Local Perspective on Fiscal Federalism: Practices, Experiences, and Lessons from Industrial Countries

MELVILLE L. MCMILLAN

Diverse developments in various parts of the world have increased interest in the potential of local government. Notably, countries among the transitional economies and countries in the developing world often look to the experience of the industrial countries in their efforts to redesign and restructure government—particularly government at the local level. Also, local government in industrial countries is not static, because such countries, if not continually at least sporadically, are reassessing and experimenting with local authorities in search of improvement (see, for example, Danish Ministry of the Interior and Health 2005). The varying patterns, organizations, and intergovernmental relations found among industrial countries and the transitions that have occurred there offer many alternatives and potential insights for those seeking ways to structure, enhance, or reform local government.

The purpose of this study is to survey the fiscal structure of local government across the major industrial countries and to draw lessons from their practices and experiences. The approach is not to duplicate the many country-by-country studies (see Batley and Stoker 1991; Hesse 1991; and Shah 2006b, among numerous others).

In fact, the data used here, while affording valuable broad comparisons, fail to provide important details available only from careful country analyses. As a result, occasionally drawing from that literature is useful to illustrate notable practices and experiences relating to major features of local government, particularly the assignment of responsibilities and the funding of those activities. Many important nonfiscal features (for example, organization and structure) are not covered here.[1]

The chapter consists of two major components. One examines the expenditure side of the budget, and the other looks at the revenue side. Expenditures are considered from several perspectives. In particular, a distinction is made between core activities and social programs. Also, capital expenditures deserve special attention, and regulatory responsibilities need mentioning. The examination of revenues pays attention to alternative tax sources, nontax own-source revenue, and intergovernmental transfers. A summary with conclusions and lessons completes the chapter.

Expenditure Responsibilities of Local Government

What do local governments in industrial countries do? In particular, to what functions do local governments allocate their budgets, and in what proportions and in what amounts? The activities that are found in a broad selection of industrial countries are sketched herein, and the similarities and differences are highlighted.[2] The focus is almost entirely on the financial aspects—that is, the expenditures of local governments. The section begins by listing expenditure areas and by noting that their importance varies considerably among countries. The analysis continues with the consideration of expenditures in different contexts and from different perspectives.

Expenditures by Function

Examining the share of expenditures in common functional categories is a helpful start toward appreciating the expenditure responsibilities of local governments. Table 7.1 shows the distribution of local government expenditures across 10 major expenditure categories for 20 industrial countries. The average percentage shares over the 20 countries show that the major expenditure categories are education (18.6 percent), general public services (16.2 percent), social protection (16.1 percent), and economic affairs, predominantly transportation (13.5 percent). Each takes more than 10 percent of the average budget, and together they account for almost two-thirds of local outlays. Ignoring a residual "other" category,

TABLE 7.1 Local Government Expenditures by Function, 2003

Country	General public services (%)	Public order and safety (%)	Economic affairs			Environmental protection (%)	Housing and community amenities (%)	Recreation, culture, and religious affairs (%)	Education (%)	Health (%)	Social protection (%)	Other (defense) (%)	Total[b] (%)
			Transportation[a] (%)	Other (%)	Total (%)								
Federal													
Australia	21.1	2.4	24.9	5.3	30.1	8.4	14.9	15.3	0.4	1.6	5.7	—	100.0
Austria	17.1	2.3	—	—	14.5	2.7	3.4	7.4	17.2	17.1	18.2	—	100.0
Belgium	23.5	11.9	—	—	11.2	5.0	1.8	8.6	19.9	2.0	16.1	—	100.0
Canada	8.7	9.3	11.3	1.7	12.9	5.5	7.1	7.4	41.4	1.6	6.2	—	100.0
Germany	14.9	4.5	—	—	11.8	5.9	6.8	6.6	16.5	2.0	31.0	—	100.0
Switzerland[c]	15.7	4.6	7.1	1.6	8.7	5.9	2.5	5.4	23.0	19.2	14.4	0.5	100.0
United States[d]	5.8	10.8	6.1	1.1	7.1	...	2.1	3.4	44.2	8.7	7.5	10.5	100.0
Average	15.3	6.5	—	—	13.8	4.8	5.5	7.7	23.2	7.4	14.2	1.6	100.0
Unitary													
Denmark	4.2	0.3	2.7	2.1	4.8	0.9	0.7	2.8	13.7	20.8	51.8	0.1	100.0
Finland	12.2	1.6	—	—	7.4	0.8	0.9	4.9	21.4	27.5	23.3	—	100.0
France[c]	35.7	2.6	—	—	11.1	11.1	7.0	5.2	16.2	0.6	10.4	—	100.0
Iceland[c]	12.0	2.1	12.8	2.0	14.8	...	6.9	14.2	29.7	1.0	19.8	—	100.0
Italy	12.6	1.6	—	—	15.4	5.1	5.4	3.5	10.3	41.5	4.4	—	100.0
Luxembourg[c]	18.5	1.7	—	—	20.5	11.2	7.2	13.1	22.5	0.3	4.5	—	100.0
Netherlands	16.9	5.8	—	—	16.6	4.3	6.2	7.2	25.2	1.7	16.2	—	100.0
New Zealand	18.9	—	28.8	0.3	29.1	23.8	9.2	20.6	...	...	0.1	0.6	100.0
Norway	11.2	1.0	4.5	0.7	5.2	3.6	5.0	5.2	28.7	16.7	23.9	—	100.0
Portugal[c]	26.1	1.4	—	—	24.1	7.8	12.3	11.7	8.7	5.4	2.4	—	100.0
Spain[e]	35.1	9.5	8.4	3.9	12.3	9.6	12.5	9.8	2.9	1.8	6.3	—	100.0

(continued)

TABLE 7.1 Local Government Expenditures by Function, 2003 *(continued)*

Country	General public services (%)	Public order and safety (%)	Economic affairs			Environmental protection (%)	Housing and community amenities (%)	Recreation, culture, and religious affairs (%)	Education (%)	Health (%)	Social protection (%)	Other (defense) (%)	Total[b] (%)
			Transportation[a] (%)	Other (%)	Total (%)								
Sweden	10.7	1.1	—	—	5.3	0.7	2.8	3.2	21.5	27.3	27.3	—	100.0
United Kingdom[f]	4.0	12.3	4.9	1.2	6.0	...	5.4	3.1	28.7	—	32.5	8.0	100.0
Average	16.8	3.1			13.3	6.1	6.3	8.0	16.1	11.1	17.2	0.7	100.0
Overall average	16.2	4.3			13.5	5.6	6.0	7.9	18.6	9.8	16.1	1.0	100.0
Range													
Minimum	3.9	0.3			4.8	0.0	0.9	2.8	0.0	0.0	0.0	0.0	
Maximum	35.7	12.3			30.1	23.8	14.9	20.6	44.1	41.5	51.8	8.0	

Sources: Author's calculations from data in IMF 2002, 2004, and 2005.

Note: — = not available; ... = insignificant. Data are for 2003 unless otherwise indicated. There was a revision of classification as of 2001. Environmental protection was added as a separate category, social security and welfare were changed to social protection, and the "other" category was deleted. Other economic affairs include fuel and energy; agriculture, forestry, fishing, and hunting; and mining, construction, and manufacturing. The "other" category includes defense (for Denmark and the United Kingdom) and other expenditures. In addition to the countries reported here, Greece, Ireland, and Japan are classified as industrial countries by the International Monetary Fund (IMF); however, no data are available for those countries for this period.

a. Of those countries reporting transportation expenditures separately, 84.4 percent of economic affairs expenditures were for transportation.

b. Totals may not sum to 100.0 percent because of rounding and statistical discrepancies.

c. Data are for 2002.

d. Data are for 2000.

e. Data are for 2001.

f. Data are for 1998.

the remaining categories require from 4.3 percent (public order and safety) to 9.8 percent (health).

The countries analyzed are categorized as federal or unitary. This division was included because the existence of a middle tier of government in the federal countries might affect the pattern of expenditures. In fact, inspection of the averages of the two groups suggests modest differences. Although the ranking varies, education, general public services, social protection, and economic affairs are the major expenditure categories and account for over 60 percent of outlays for both groups. However, some differences are observed. Expenditures for public order and safety are relatively higher in federal countries (6.5 percent versus 3.1 percent of expenditures), and the share allotted for education is also larger. Meanwhile, local outlays for health and for social protection are somewhat larger on average in the unitary countries. However, the intercountry variation in these categories is large within both the unitary and federal groups.

The striking feature of table 7.1 is that the distribution of expenditures among functional areas across the countries is so uneven. The ranges in these percentage shares are shown at the bottom of the table. On average, the range across the categories is from a low of 1.3 percent to a high of 28.3 percent. Aside from the "other" category, the minimum absolute difference is 12 percentage points (that for public order and safety). The portion of local expenditures devoted to public order and safety, for example, is high in the United Kingdom and the United States, where local governments bear a large share of—or even full responsibility for—local policing, but is small (even nil in New Zealand), where policing is a provincial, state, or central responsibility as, for example, in Australia, Denmark, and France. Even the economic affairs category, which mostly comprises local road and transport services, varies from 4.8 percent in Denmark (figures are similarly low in Norway and Sweden) to 30.1 percent in Australia (with a similarly high percentage in New Zealand).[3] Most of the variation in the expenditure shares arises from differing local responsibilities for social programs—that is, for education (schooling), health, and social protection. These programs may account for essentially no local expenditures to 41.5 percent for health (Italy), 44.2 percent for education (United States), and 51.8 percent for social protection (Denmark). In a few countries (Australia, New Zealand, and Spain), local governments spend little on social programs, whereas in others— notably the Scandinavian countries—those programs represent the vast majority of local budgets.

This diverse array of expenditure allocations can seem confusing and can cause one to wonder whether any rationale exists for the underlying responsibility assignment or whether any lessons can be drawn from the experience of these countries. In fact, both an underlying logic and lessons do exist. The variation, however, demonstrates the range of possibilities and the need for appropriate fiscal design. To begin sorting out the problem, the chapter considers first the allocation of responsibilities among levels of governments.

Expenditures by Level of Government

The role of local government in the public sector and in the economy differs among countries. This situation is made explicit in table 7.2, which shows the share of government expenditures made by each level of government. Here, expenditures are attributed to the government that finally spends the public funds for goods and services regardless of whether those funds came from own-source revenues or from intergovernmental transfers.

Local government expenditures tend to be relatively more important in unitary countries than in federal countries. As might be expected, the presence of state or provincial governments diminishes the role of both central and local governments to some degree.[4] Across the federal countries, local government expenditures account for 17.8 percent of general government spending on average, while they undertake 29.9 percent on average in unitary countries. Still, there is considerable variation in the local role in both types of countries. Among the federal countries, local government accounts for only 6.8 percent of government expenditure in Australia but 25.8 percent in Switzerland and 26.2 percent in the United States. At about one-fourth of government expenditure, the levels in Switzerland and the United States equal or exceed the percentage represented by local government in 5 of the 13 unitary countries, where the local percentage ranges from 9.5 percent in New Zealand to 59.5 percent in Denmark. The overall range of 6.8 to 59.5 percent is huge, and though local governments in most countries fall into a 15 to 35 percent range, even that variation is large.

The size of local government relative to the economy also varies. Local government expenditure as a percentage of gross domestic product (GDP) is included in table 7.2. In the federal countries, local government spending amounts to 7.2 percent of GDP, but, at 14.0 percent, the amount is almost twice as large in the unitary countries. These differences (as do those among individual countries) depend on both the intergovernmental division of responsibilities and the role of government in the economy. Government in the unitary countries is somewhat larger than government in the federal countries, 47.1 percent compared with 40.9 percent of GDP.

TABLE 7.2 Relative Government Expenditures for Selected Countries

Country	Expenditure by level (%)			Government expenditure as a % of GDP	Local government expenditure as a % of GDP
	Central	State or provincial	Local		
Federal					
Australia	53.8	39.4	6.8	35.5	2.4
Austria	68.3	16.2	15.5	50.5	8.0
Belgium[a]	—	—	—	—	6.7
Canada	37.2	44.7	18.1	41.0	7.5
Germany	63.4	22.1	14.5	48.4	7.3
Switzerland[b]	40.1	34.1	25.8	37.4	9.8
United States[c]	51.0	22.7	26.2	32.6	8.8
Average[d]	52.3	29.9	17.8	40.9	7.2
Unitary					
Denmark[b]	40.5	n.a.	59.5	55.7	33.1
Finland	61.1	n.a.	38.9	50.9	19.5
France[b]	81.4	n.a.	18.6	53.7	10.2
Iceland[b]	70.8	n.a.	29.2	44.7	13.0
Italy	68.9	n.a.	31.1	49.1	15.4
Luxembourg[b]	86.0	n.a.	14.0	41.8	5.9
Netherlands	64.8	n.a.	35.2	49.2	17.4
New Zealand	90.5	n.a.	9.5	36.4	3.4
Norway	69.1	n.a.	31.1	48.8	15.2
Portugal[b]	85.7	n.a.	14.3	46.6	6.6
Spain[e]	63.9	n.a.	36.1[f]	36.9	6.5
Sweden	55.5	n.a.	44.5	58.7	26.0
United Kingdom[g]	73.9	n.a.	26.1	39.6	10.4
Average	70.1	n.a.	29.9	47.1	14.0

Sources: Author's calculations from data in IMF 2002, 2004, and 2005.
Note: — = not available; n.a. = not applicable. Data are for 2003 unless otherwise indicated. Expenditures are net of transfers to other governments.
a. Not all values were calculated because of a large statistical discrepancy.
b. Data are for 2002.
c. Data are for 2000.
d. Average of observations with data.
e. Data are for 2001.
f. Regional government in Spain accounts for 19.0 percent of the 36.1 percent.
g. Data are for 1998.

Local government expenditures in countries like Australia and New Zealand are small relative to GDP (2.4 percent and 3.4 percent, respectively) both because their assigned expenditure responsibilities are modest and because total government in those countries is relatively small (35.5 percent and 36.4 percent of GDP, respectively). In contrast, local government expenditure in

Denmark amounts to an extraordinarily large 33.1 percent of GDP, partly because total government spending there is large at 55.7 percent of GDP. Australia is exceptional even among federal countries because local expenditures in the other federal countries range from 6.7 percent to 9.8 percent of GDP. In the unitary countries, the range is larger, from 3.4 percent to 33.1 percent, and the percentages are more widely dispersed.

Social Programs and Local Government Finance

Responsibilities for social programs substantially affect local government budgets. As noted, those responsibilities are a major reason for the differences in the distribution of expenditures by function, and they affect the relative importance of local government in the public sector. The implications of the responsibilities for social programs (education, health, and social protection) are demonstrated in table 7.3. In that table, countries are grouped by local government expenditure as a percentage of GDP. Australia and New Zealand constitute the low group, with an average of 2.9 percent. Denmark and Sweden constitute the high group, with an average of 29.5 percent. The middle group is subdivided into countries with upper-medium and lower-medium budget shares. The upper-medium group is made up of 5 countries, with local expenditures as a percentage of GDP ranging from 13.0 percent to 19.5 percent and averaging 16.1 percent. The lower-medium group is the largest with 11 countries that have local expenditures ranging from 5.9 percent to 10.4 percent of GDP and an average of 7.9 percent. Local government as a percentage of total government parallels this classification, with averages across the groups (from low to high) of 8.1, 19.1, 33.1, and 52.0 percent. The absolute and relative size of local government corresponds to—and is essentially determined by—local responsibilities for social programs. Local government expenditures on social programs as a percentage of GDP across the groups average 0.08, 3.40, 9.46, and 24.18 percent. In contrast, the relative magnitude of nonsocial spending is much more homogeneous, with averages as a percentage of GDP of 2.8, 4.6, 6.6, and 5.3 percent.

Consider further the social expenditures by local government. First, because social programs are costly, they have a large effect on local budgets where local governments bear responsibility for such spending. Aside from the group with low budget shares (with an average of 3.4 percent), social spending averages 40.9, 58.3, and 81.2 percent of local government total expenditures. Among those three groups, the social expenditure share ranges from 11.0 in Spain to 86.3 in Denmark. Spain's share is low partly because its regional governments (which undertake 84 percent of spending on education)

TABLE 7.3 Social Programs in Local Government Finance, 2003

Country	Local government expenditure as a % of GDP	Local government as a % of total government	Local social program expenditure			Local government nonsocial program expenditures as a % of GDP	Local government budget transfer financed as a % of total budget
			As a % of local budgets	As a % of GDP	As a % of national public social expenditures		
Low budget share							
Australia	2.4	6.7	6.7	0.16	0.9	2.2	14.5
New Zealand[a]	3.4	9.5	0.1	0.003	0.5	3.4	9.3
Average	2.9	8.1	3.4	0.08	0.7	2.8	11.9
Lower-medium budget share							
Austria	8.0	15.5	52.5	4.20	12.5	3.8	21.0
Belgium	6.7	—	38.0	2.55	6.7	4.3	49.1
Canada	7.5	18.4	49.2	3.69	14.2	3.8	39.0
France[b]	10.2	18.6	27.3	2.78	7.7	7.4	41.7
Germany	7.3	14.5	49.5	3.61	10.4	3.7	32.5
Luxembourg	5.9	14.0	27.6	1.62	4.4	4.3	40.4
Portugal[b]	6.6	14.3	16.5	1.09	3.7	5.5	44.0
Spain[c,d]	6.5	17.1	11.0	0.71	2.9	5.8	38.4
Switzerland[b]	9.5	25.8	56.6	5.38	24.0	4.1	17.1
United Kingdom[e]	10.4	26.1	61.2	6.36	—	4.0	70.0
United States[f]	8.9	26.2	60.3	5.37	—	3.5	39.4
Average[g]	7.9	19.1	40.9	3.40	9.6	4.6	39.3

(continued)

TABLE 7.3 Social Programs in Local Government Finance, 2003 *(continued)*

Country	Local government expenditure as a % of GDP	Local government as a % of total government	Local social program expenditure			Local government nonsocial program expenditures as a % of GDP	Local government budget transfer financed as a % of total budget
			As a % of local budgets	As a % of GDP	As a % of national public social expenditures		
Upper-medium budget share							
Finland	19.5	38.9	72.2	14.08	40.5	5.4	26.4
Iceland[b]	13.0	29.2	50.5	6.57	26.4	6.4	9.3
Italy	15.4	31.1	56.2	8.65	29.6	6.7	41.2
Netherlands	17.3	35.2	43.1	7.46	26.3	9.8	61.1
Norway	15.2	31.1	69.3	10.53	31.3	4.7	34.6
Average	16.1	33.1	58.3	9.46	30.8	6.6	34.5
High budget share							
Denmark	33.1	59.5	86.3	28.57	47.3	4.5	37.1
Sweden	26.0	44.5	76.1	19.79	49.9	6.2	19.4
Average	29.5	52.0	81.2	24.18	48.6	5.3	28.3

Source: Author's calculations from data in IMF 2005 and other years as required.
Note: — = not available. Data are for 2003 unless otherwise indicated. Social program expenditures are those for education, health, and social protection.
a. Data are for 2004.
b. Data are for 2002.
c. Data are for 2001.
d. Spain's regional governments are not included.
e. Data are for 1998.
f. Data are for 2000.
g. Average of observations with data.

are not included with local government. Local government may or may not be responsible for a significant share of the national social expenditure. The striking feature here is that local governments with upper-medium and high budget shares account for one-fourth to one-half of national social spending (with averages of 30.8 and 48.6 percent of the total for the two groups). Among the countries in the other two groups, only Switzerland (where local government social spending represents 24 percent of total government social expenditure) approaches such levels. Elsewhere, local expenditures range from 0.5 percent to 14.2 percent and average 5.8 percent. Thus, in 40 percent of the countries examined (and those are predominantly Scandinavian), local government has a major responsibility for social programs, but in the other 60 percent, the local responsibility is typically quite small.

Because social programs usually involve significant redistribution and thus are not usually recommended as a local government financing responsibility, one might expect transfers to become more important as social expenditure represents an increasing share of the budget. Such is not the case. Although transfers from senior governments cover only 11.9 percent of expenditures in the group with low budget shares, transfers as a percentage of expenditures actually decline as the social expenditure share and level increase across the other three budget groups. Transfers average 39.3, 34.5, and 28.3 percent for the groups with lower-medium, upper-medium, and high budget shares, respectively. Differences in access to tax sources largely explain this situation, and further explanation must await that discussion.

Social expenditure responsibilities explain most of the large differences in the roles of local government among countries. Differences in the magnitudes of nonsocial expenditures are much smaller. As a percentage of GDP, nonsocial expenditures range from 2.2 percent in Australia to 9.8 percent in the Netherlands, but 17 of the 20 lie in the 3.5 to 7.4 percent range. Among those 17, the local governments in federal countries (where responsibilities are also shared with state or provincial governments) represent the lower end of that group, with values from 3.5 percent (United States) to 4.3 percent (Belgium). Thus, there appears to be a core set of responsibilities for local governments that is relatively common among countries. Details of these local core activities and of local social programs are provided in the next section.

Local Expenditures by Function as a Percentage of GDP

Further insight into and details about local government expenditures are provided in table 7.4, which reports expenditure by function as a percentage of GDP. Again, analyzing social and nonsocial spending separately is useful.

TABLE 7.4 Local Government Expenditures by Function as a Percentage of GDP, 2003

Country	General public services	Public order and safety	Economic affairs		
			Transportation	Other	Total
Low budget share					
Australia	0.51	0.06	0.6	0.13	0.73
New Zealand	0.64	—	0.98	0.01	0.99
Average	0.57	0.03	—	—	0.86
Lower-medium budget share					
Austria	1.37	0.18	—	—	1.16
Belgium	1.57	0.80	—	—	0.75
Canada	0.65	0.69	0.84	0.12	0.96
France	3.63	0.27	—	—	1.13
Germany	1.09	0.33	—	—	0.87
Luxembourg	1.09	0.10	—	—	1.21
Portugal[a]	1.72	0.09	—	—	1.59
Spain[b]	2.28	0.62	0.55	0.25	0.80
Switzerland	1.54	0.45	0.69	0.16	0.85
United Kingdom	0.41	1.27	0.50	0.12	0.62
United States	0.51	0.95	0.53	0.09	0.62
Average	1.44	0.52	—	—	0.96
Upper-medium budget share					
Finland	2.38	0.31	—	—	1.44
Iceland[a]	1.56	0.27	1.66	0.26	2.92
Italy	1.94	0.25	—	—	2.37
Netherlands	2.94	1.00	—	—	2.87
Norway	1.70	0.15	0.68	0.11	0.79
Average	2.10	0.40	—	—	1.87
High budget share					
Denmark	1.40	0.10	0.88	0.69	1.57
Sweden	2.78	0.29	—	—	1.38
Average	2.09	0.19	—	—	1.47
Overall average	1.59	0.41	—	—	1.23

Source: Author's calculations from data in IMF 2002, 2004, 2005.
Note: — = not available. Data are for 2003 unless indicated otherwise.
a. Data are for 2002.
b. Data are for 2001.

Environmental protection	Housing and community amenities	Recreation, culture, and religious affairs	Education	Health	Social protection	Other	Total
0.20	0.36	0.37	0.01	0.04	0.14	—	2.6
0.81	0.31	0.70	—	—	0.003	0.02	3.4
0.51	0.33	0.53	0.005	0.02	0.07	0.01	2.9
0.22	0.27	0.59	1.38	1.37	1.46	—	8.0
0.33	0.12	0.58	1.33	0.13	1.08	—	6.7
0.41	0.53	0.55	3.09	0.12	0.46	—	8.4
1.13	0.71	0.52	1.65	0.06	1.06	—	10.2
0.43	0.50	0.48	1.21	0.14	2.27	—	7.3
0.66	0.42	0.77	1.33	0.02	0.27	—	5.9
0.51	0.81	0.77	0.57	0.36	0.16	—	6.6
0.62	0.81	0.64	0.19	0.12	0.41	—	6.5
0.58	0.25	0.53	2.25	1.88	1.41	0.05	10.6
—	0.56	0.31	2.97	—	3.37	0.83	10.4
—	0.18	0.29	3.87	0.76	0.66	0.92	9.4
0.44	0.47	0.55	1.80	0.45	1.15	0.16	7.8
0.16	0.17	0.95	4.17	5.36	4.54	—	19.5
—	0.90	1.85	3.86	0.13	2.57	—	13.0
0.79	0.83	0.54	1.59	6.39	0.68	—	15.4
0.74	1.08	1.24	4.37	0.29	2.81	—	17.3
0.55	0.76	0.79	4.36	2.54	3.63	—	15.2
0.45	0.75	1.07	3.71	2.94	2.85	0.00	16.1
0.30	0.23	0.92	4.53	6.89	17.15	0.02	33.1
0.18	0.73	0.83	5.59	7.10	7.10	—	26.0
0.24	0.48	0.87	5.06	6.99	12.12	0.10	29.5
0.43	0.53	0.71	2.48	1.69	2.56	0.09	11.70

Beginning with social programs, Australia and New Zealand, which have low budget shares, stand out because local governments spend very little individually or collectively on education, health, and social protection (less than 0.2 percent of GDP in Australia and effectively nothing in New Zealand). In the group with lower-medium budget shares, education is the major social expenditure category.

Education is the largest of the three social programs in 7 (possibly 8) of the 11 countries and has the highest average at 1.8 percent of GDP. Education outlays are particularly large in the United Kingdom and the United States, where local government is fully responsible for schooling expenditure. Finance, however, can be quite different. In the United States, local school authorities finance about half of school spending from own sources, with the other half from (primarily) state transfers. In the United Kingdom, schooling is entirely funded by central transfers. In contrast, local authorities in France provide only the school infrastructure, and in Germany, the state governments provide the teachers. In Spain, education is the responsibility of the regional governments.

Within this budget group, local expenditure responsibilities for health care are small except for Austria and Switzerland, where they are in the 1 to 2 percent of GDP range. In the United Kingdom, health care is entirely a central responsibility and almost so in France and Luxembourg. Local spending on social protection actually averages 1.15 percent of GDP for this group, but the average is greatly affected by the high levels in Germany and the United Kingdom. The large percentage reported for the United Kingdom (3.37 percent) is not understood and is at odds with country reports (for example, King 2006). Social protection there is primarily housing assistance for various disadvantaged groups and is largely directed and funded by the central government. In Germany, local social assistance and housing allowances are determined and paid for by the federal government.

Thus, where local governments in this budget group become involved in spending for social programs, it is primarily for schooling. Even there— and more so for health and social protection—programs are directed or supervised by senior governments that commonly provide most of the funding if the level of expenditure is notable.

Local social program spending is broadly based in those countries in the groups with upper-medium and high budget shares. For the upper-medium group, education, health, and social protection expenditures average 3.71, 2.94, and 2.85 percent of GDP, respectively, while for the high group, the averages are 5.06, 6.99, and 12.12 percent. Still, there are some notable variations among countries. Local expenditures for health care are high (over

5 percent) in Denmark, Finland, Italy, and Sweden but very low (under 0.3 percent) in Iceland and the Netherlands. In Italy, health could be considered the only major area of local social spending. At 17.15 percent of GDP, expenditures for social protection are remarkably large in Denmark. Denmark's local governments are responsible for a broad range of social protection programs (including old-age pensions, child allowances, and welfare and employment programs) that are more commonly the responsibilities of senior governments. However, old-age pensions and child allowances are funded entirely by the central government, and the costs of welfare and employment programs are shared on a 50:50 basis. Growth in the size of local government relates directly to expansion in the size and breadth of social program responsibilities. That expansion is, however, typically accompanied by senior government direction and support.

Local spending in the nonsocial program areas is relatively uniform overall. As shown in table 7.4, the group averages of the levels of spending on general services, public order and safety, economic affairs (predominantly transportation), environmental protection, housing and community amenities, and recreation and cultural services are much more uniform than is the case for social programs. Still, the intercountry variations can be considerable. For example, spending on general public services, at 3.63 percent of GDP, is exceptionally high in France; spending on economic affairs is large in Iceland, Italy, and the Netherlands; expenditures for recreation and culture are relatively high in Iceland; and reported spending for environmental protection is low in the United Kingdom and the United States (but contrast with that indicated in country studies). The variation in expenditures for public order and safety relates to the assignment of policing responsibilities between local and senior governments. However, spending on environmental protection, housing and community amenities, and recreation and culture tends to be relatively consistent.

One country, the Netherlands, stands out. It consistently ranks first or second in the level of spending across the nonsocial functions and, for this expenditure class, has the distinctly highest level of spending at 9.8 percent of GDP (see table 7.3). Local government in the Netherlands has unique water management issues to address, which may explain the higher expenditures on economic affairs, but not the higher spending across the board. Toonen (1991) characterizes the situation in the Netherlands as the central government being too reliant on local government to carry out state affairs. That local government there generated only 31 percent of its revenues from own sources and still generates only 39 percent may support that argument. Stoker (1991: 18) summarizes the situation of Dutch local governments with the comment that they are both "over-ambitious and overburdened." Although anomalies exist, these data lend support to the existence of a relatively consistent set of core activities for which local governments are responsible in most countries.

In summary, the fiscal role of local governments varies widely among countries. The differences depend primarily on the expenditure responsibilities of local governments for social programs (schooling, health care, and social protection). Although local governments commonly have some responsibility for schooling, their responsibilities for health and social protection are more diverse. Responsibilities for and expenditures on the nonsocial program functions tend to be more uniform and, as such, they form a set of core responsibilities typical of and more common to local governments.

Regulation: Completing the Concept of Core Services

The preceding discussion of core services focused on expenditures. Attention concentrated on the significant budget demands of major services, such as transportation (for example, roadways and public transit); protection (for example, policing, fire, and emergency services); water and sewerage and drainage; waste collection and disposal; economic development; recreation and cultural facilities and services; and general administration (for example, council and tax assessment and collection). These largely physical services, sometimes referred to as *housekeeping activities*, are important for making a community functional and pleasant. Also essential is a second group of core services, which are largely regulatory. These services are the locally determined rules that promote safety (for example, traffic regulation, fire regulation, and building codes); promote the enjoyment of property (for example, regulation of development and of land use, noise, and waste); manage business (for example, business licenses and taxi permits); and generally control potential nuisances. These activities are not normally large within the local government budget and are only elements within the expenditure categories noted, so they are easily overlooked. Still, regulatory activities are important for creating a pleasant and safer local environment and so deserve recognition as part of the core activities of local governments.

Capital Expenditures

Local government is responsible for a disproportionate share of government capital—almost half the total. The International Monetary Fund's *Government Finance Statistics Yearbook* (IMF 2005) does not provide information on capital expenditures themselves, but it does provide estimates of the consumption of government-owned fixed capital, assuming normal use and obsolescence. Capital consumed must be replaced, so this measure of consumption reflects required replacement investment. Table 7.5 offers insight into local government's role in the consumption of this fixed capital. The table reports the consumption of total government capital by country for federal and unitary countries as a percentage of GDP. The overall average is 1.86 percent. The share of that from consumption of local government capital averages 47 percent. The average percentage is essentially equal for local government in both federal and unitary countries. Aside from Greece, where the local share is only 3.7 percent, the local shares range from 25 percent in Spain (but 48 percent if Spain's regional governments were included) to 65.8 percent in Portugal. On average, fixed-capital consumption is the equivalent of 13.6 percent of local government expenditure. The range here is broad, but the share tends to be larger where total local outlays are small (for example, Australia and New Zealand, at 21.1 percent and 20.3 percent, respectively) and smaller where local expenditures are large (for example, Denmark and Sweden, at 3.4 percent and 5.1 percent, respectively). Capital requirements are more closely associated with core services than social programs.

Local governments finance capital expenditures from a variety of sources. These sources may include own reserves (accumulated from taxes and user charges, for example); developer contributions or charges; capital grants; and debt. Senior governments usually control borrowing by local governments tightly. Normally, borrowing to finance capital expenditures is permitted, subject to controls, but borrowing to cover operating deficits is not allowed (except under very strict conditions). Hence, almost all borrowing is for capital purposes. Because borrowing to fund a portion of capital expenditures is common, local governments often run overall deficits. Net lending/borrowing as a percentage of revenues is reported in table 7.5. Only 6 of the 20 countries for which there are data were net lenders. The average net borrowing position was 1.8 percent of revenue. This finding means that local governments may accumulate debt. Total local government liabilities as a percentage of total revenue are also reported in table 7.5. Liabilities range from 23.7 percent to 78.9 percent of total revenue. Sources of funds vary among countries. In some (for example, the United States), local governments may borrow in private markets and even from foreign investors, although foreign borrowing is unusual and is typically relatively small. In other countries (for example, Australia and the United Kingdom), local governments may borrow only from senior governments. In many cases

TABLE 7.5 Local Government Consumption of Fixed Capital and Debt, 2004

Country	Total general government consumption of fixed capital as a % of GDP	Local government			
		Share of total consumptions of fixed capital (%)	Fixed-capital consumption as a % of expenditure by economic type	Net lending/ borrowing as a % of revenues[a]	Liabilities as a % of total revenue
Federal					
Australia	1.45	31.6	21.1	+0.9	46.2
Austria[b]	1.29	46.4	7.5	+2.2	32.1
Belgium[b]	1.57	47.9	11.2	−7.1	78.9
Canada	—	—	—	−3.3	71.1
Germany	1.59	58.4	12.5	−2.5	—
Switzerland	—	—	—	+2.6	—
United States	1.29	—	—	—	—
Average[c]	1.44	46.1	13.1	−1.2	57.1
Unitary					
Denmark	1.92	60.0	3.4	−2.2	23.7
Finland	2.38	55.0	6.8	−3.3	48.4
France	2.45	63.5	15.5	−1.1	70.8
Greece[d]	—	3.7	0.1	+1.8	—
Iceland[e]	2.08	30.2	5.3	−4.4	47.8
Italy[b]	1.33	62.1	5.8	−1.6	—
Japan[b]	2.76	—	—	—	—
Luxembourg	1.95	43.8	17.5	−2.5	40.4
Netherlands	2.49	64.6	10.1	−2.7	67.4
New Zealand	1.88	32.2	20.3	+5.0	64.4
Norway	1.96	50.6	7.2	−3.0	64.5[f]
Portugal[e]	2.13	65.8	25.3	−7.8	—
Spain[g]	1.43	25.0	7.0	−3.0	—
Sweden[b]	2.39	57.2	5.1	−1.0	45.1
United Kingdom	0.93	47.3	3.6	+1.0	—
Average[c]	2.01	47.2	9.5	−1.8	52.5
Overall average[c]	1.86	47.0	13.6	−1.6	53.9

Source: IMF 2005.
Note: — = not available. Data are for 2004 unless otherwise indicated.
a. If these data were unavailable, the cash surplus/deficit was used.
b. Data are for 2003.
c. Average of observations with data.
d. Data are for 2000.
e. Data are for 2002.
f. Specific value is for 2003.
g. Data are for 2001.

(most provinces in Canada), senior governments facilitate local borrowing and monitor it through special authorities.

Local Government Revenue

Local government revenues come from two main sources: own-source revenues and intergovernmental transfers. Own-source revenues are made up of taxes and nontax revenues. Nontax revenues come mostly from charges for services and privileges and from property and investment income. Although considerable variation exists among countries, on average taxes provide about 40 percent of local government revenue, nontax sources about 20 percent, and transfers about 40 percent. Before considering the distributions of these revenues among countries, one should examine taxes and tax sources.

Local Government Taxes

Local governments around the world use a variety of taxes. The spectrum of the main taxes used in federal and unitary countries is the main information reported in table 7.6.[5] Taxes on income and profits, on property, and on commodities and services (general sales, specific goods and services, and use) are the main sources of tax revenue. Most countries use more than one of these types of taxes. The figures in table 7.6 show the amount of local tax revenue from each source as a percentage of GDP. Total taxes, like expenditures, vary widely as a percentage of GDP: from levels as low as 0.6 percent in Ireland and 0.9 percent in Australia to levels as high as 16.5 percent in Sweden and 17.2 percent in Denmark.[6]

Property taxes and income taxes are the most popular local taxes. Property taxes are a source of revenue in 22 of the 24 countries included in the table, and they generate revenues amounting to about 1.1 percent of GDP. When used, property taxes may generate relatively little revenue (for example, 0.1 percent of GDP in Luxembourg), or they may be a major revenue generator (as is the case in Canada, Spain, and the United States, where property taxes represent from 2.6 percent to 2.7 percent of GDP). Local taxes on income and profits, reported in 16 of the 24 countries, are somewhat less common but generate more revenue (about 3.1 percent of GDP overall and 4.7 percent of GDP where used). Especially in the case of income taxes, these attributions require caution because, in some cases, the local authorities may have little (even no) discretion over the funds generated from the source. For example, revenue-sharing arrangements in which local governments automatically get a share of central income taxes qualify

TABLE 7.6 Main Taxes and Selected Other Own-Source Revenues of Local Governments in OECD Member Countries as a Percentage of GDP, 2003

Country	Income and profits taxes	Property taxes	General consumption taxes	Taxes on specific goods and services	Taxes on use	Other[a]	Total taxes	Nontax own-source revenue[b]	Total own-source revenue	Total expenditures[c]
Federal										
Australia	...	0.9	...	...	...	...	0.9	1.2	2.1	2.4
Austria[d]	1.4	0.4	0.9	0.2	0.1	1.0	4.0	1.6	5.6	8.0
Belgium[d]	2.1	...	0.1	0.2	0.1	...	2.5	1.6	4.1	6.7
Canada	...	2.7	...	...	0.1	0.1	2.9	1.3	4.2	7.5
Germany[d]	1.8	0.4	0.1	...	...	...	2.3	1.8	4.1	7.3
Switzerland	4.0	0.8	...	...	...	...	4.8	3.2	8.0	9.8
United States	0.2	2.7	0.4	0.2	0.2	...	3.7	1.8	5.5	8.8
Average[e]	1.36	1.13	0.21	0.09	0.07	0.16	3.01	1.78	4.8	7.2
Unitary										
Denmark[d]	16.0	1.2	...	...	...	...	17.2	4.0	21.2	33.1
Finland[d]	9.0	0.5	...	...	...	...	9.5	4.3	13.8	19.5
France[d]	...	2.4	...	0.3	0.1	1.6	4.4	2.0	6.4	10.2
Greece[d]	...	0.2	...	0.1	...	...	0.3	1.1	1.4	2.7
Iceland	7.7	1.3	0.9	...	...	...	9.9	1.9	11.8	13.0
Ireland[d]	...	0.6	...	...	...	...	0.6	2.1	9.3	—
Italy[d]	1.6	1.1	0.2	0.9	0.5	2.9	7.2	—	—	15.4
Japan	2.9	2.1	0.5	0.6	0.4	0.1	6.6	—	—	—
Luxembourg[d]	2.3	0.1	...	...	...	...	2.4	1.3	3.7	5.9
Netherlands[d]	...	0.8	...	...	0.6	...	1.4	2.9	4.3	17.3

New Zealand	...	1.8	...	...	0.2	...	2.0	0.9	2.9	3.4
Norway	5.7	0.6	...	...	0.1	...	6.4	3.2	9.6	15.2
Portugal[d]	0.5	0.5	0.4	0.6	...	0.1	2.1	1.5	3.6	6.6
Spain[d]	2.4	2.6	2.4	1.8	0.7	0.1	10.0	0.7	20.7	6.5
Sweden[d]	16.5	...	...	...	...	...	16.5	3.7	20.2	26.0
Turkey	0.6	0.4	0.6	0.1	...	0.1	1.8	...	—	—
United Kingdom[d]	...	1.7	...	...	...	...	1.7	2.4	4.1	10.4
Average	3.83	1.05	0.26	0.26	0.15	0.29	5.88	2.29[f]	8.79[f]	13.2
Overall average										
All[e]	3.11	1.07	0.27	0.20	0.13	0.25	5.04	2.12[f]	7.46[f]	11.2
All > 0[g]	4.66	1.17	0.64	0.51	0.27	0.76	5.04	2.45[f]	7.46[f]	11.2

Source: Author's calculations from data in OECD 2005.

Note: OECD = Organisation for Economic Co-operation and Development; — = not available; ... = insignificant.

a. For federal countries, this column includes social security contributions attributable to local governments (Austria) and some residual taxes, mainly on business (Austria and Canada). Also, in Austria, it includes payroll taxes (0.8%). For unitary countries, this column includes taxes at death (Portugal) and some residual taxes, mainly business (France and Italy).

b. Includes property income, sales, fines, and miscellaneous revenue.

c. Data are from table 7.2.

d. Payments to the European Union are excluded from these comparisons. EU countries are those that were members as of January 1, 2003: Austria, Belgium, Denmark, Finland, France, Germany, Greece, Ireland, Italy, Luxembourg, the Netherlands, Portugal, Spain, Sweden, and the United Kingdom.

e. Average of all cells, including those with zero or insignificant value.

f. Average of observations with data.

g. Average of cells having greater than 0 or insignificant value.

as "local" income taxes (OECD 2005: 303–4). Austria, Germany, and Spain are examples of countries with such arrangements. In contrast, local governments in Denmark and Sweden, for example, set their own income tax rates. The magnitude of local income taxes also varies considerably (from 0.2 percent of GDP in the United States to 16.5 percent in Sweden). The degree of local discretion in taxing is examined later.

Local taxes on commodities and services (represented in the columns on general consumption taxes, taxes on specific goods and services, and taxes on use) appear in some form in 16 of the 24 countries. Any one type of those taxes, however, is used in only 10 or 11 countries, and the revenue from each is more modest, averaging from about 0.3 percent to 0.8 percent of GDP when used. Taxes on general consumption are particularly important in Spain, where they amount to 2.4 percent of GDP in contrast to less than 1.0 percent elsewhere.

Other taxes encompass a mixture of less common taxes (see footnote a of table 7.6). They are typically minor sources of revenue, except in Austria (mainly social security contributions) and in France and Italy (mainly taxes on business).

Most countries rely primarily on a single major tax. For some, it is the property tax; for others, it is the income tax. Only a few countries use a more diverse mix of taxes. This pattern is demonstrated in table 7.7. It reports the tax composition for countries grouped into three classes: those that are highly property tax reliant, those that are highly income tax reliant, and those using mixed tax sources. Local governments in nine countries collect the majority of their tax revenue from property taxes. That percentage ranges from just over 50 percent in France and the Netherlands to 100 percent in Australia, Ireland, and the United Kingdom. For this group as a whole, property taxes represent almost 80 percent of local tax revenue. Note from table 7.6 that property tax revenues do not amount to more than 2.7 percent of GDP. Most of these countries also use some other taxes to generate revenue, and most choose some form of tax on commodities or services. Among this group of countries, only in the United States do local governments also raise revenue from income taxes. In France, the *taxe professionnelle* is levied on business (an "other" tax), and it generates just over one-third of local tax revenues.

Nine countries compose the group that is highly income tax reliant. For them, income tax revenues provide 88 percent of local tax revenue on average, with the share ranging from 74.7 percent in Germany to 100 percent in Sweden.[7] Personal income taxes dominate, except in Luxembourg, where all the local income tax comes from corporations. Taxes on corporations are nil or essentially nil in four countries. Elsewhere, they account for

TABLE 7.7 Composition of Local Government Tax Revenue in OECD Countries, 2003
(percent)

Country	Income and profits tax		Property tax	General consumption tax	Taxes on specific goods and services	Taxes on use	Other
	Total	From corporations[a]					
Highly property tax reliant							
Australia	...	...	100.0	...	...	...	...
Canada	...	...	93.8	0.2	0.2	1.8	4.1
United States	4.8	(0.8)	73.0	11.0	4.9	6.2	...
France	...	...	54.1	...	7.6	3.1	35.2
Greece	...	...	66.9	4.1	26.0	3.0	0.0
Ireland	...	...	100.0	...	...	...	...
Netherlands	...	...	56.6	...	1.5	41.9	...
New Zealand	...	...	90.4	...	1.1	8.5	...
United Kingdom	...	...	100.0	...	...	...	...
Average	0.53	(0.09)	81.64	1.70	4.59	7.17	4.37
Highly income tax reliant							
Belgium	86.5	(17.7)	...	2.2	6.9	4.1	...
Germany	74.7	(20.1)	18.6	5.5	0.5	0.5	0.3
Switzerland	83.3	(10.2)	16.4	...	0.2	0.1	...
Denmark	93.0	(1.9)	6.9	...	0.1	...	0.2
Finland	94.9	(7.4)	4.9	...	...	...	...
Iceland	78.1	...	13.0	8.9	...	...	...
Luxembourg	93.5	(93.5)	5.0	...	1.0	0.2	0.3
Norway	89.2	...	8.7	...	...	2.1	...
Sweden	100.0	...	...	...	...	...	...
Average	88.13	16.75	8.17	1.84	0.97	0.78	0.89
Mixed tax							
Austria	35.7	(6.1)	10.5	22.0	4.0	1.7	25.0[b]
Italy	22.1	(2.2)	15.1	3.0	12.5	7.3	39.9
Japan	45.2	(19.7)	32.2	7.3	8.5	5.8	1.0
Portugal	22.5	(14.8)	25.3	18.1	26.0	1.5	4.5
Spain	24.3	(1.7)	26.0	23.9	17.8	6.7	1.3
Turkey	32.5	(10.9)	18.8	34.1	6.9	1.8	6.0
Average	30.38	(6.15)	21.32	18.07	12.62	4.13	12.95
Overall average	40.84	(7.85)	39.01	5.85	5.24	3.99	5.21

Source: OECD 2005.
Note: ... = insignificant. Values may not sum to 100.0 percent because of rounding.
a. The percentage of total local tax revenue attributed to income taxes from corporations is shown in parentheses.
b. This figure comprises payroll tax (20.9 percent) and social security contributions (4.1 percent).

about 8 percent (Finland) to 27 percent (Germany) of the local income tax collections. Within this group, property taxes are the next most common tax, and overall, they generate the next largest amount of revenue (8 percent on average). Taxes on commodities and services amount to more than 10 percent of revenues in only one country, Belgium.

Six countries are considered to have a mixed set of tax sources. Within this group, no single tax accounts for more than 45.2 percent of local tax revenue (the income tax in Japan). Income and property taxes are used in all these countries and overall, represent about 30 percent and 21 percent of total tax revenue, respectively. Taxes on commodities and services are exceptionally popular with this group and raise about 35 percent of local tax revenue. Other forms of taxation are also more common with this group of countries, although they are the only major revenue sources in Austria and Italy. Other taxes in Austria are largely payroll taxes, and those in Italy are taxes on business.

One might note a geographic or cultural pattern to the tax grouping in table 7.7. The property tax group is dominated by countries having a British heritage. This situation was especially true a decade ago, before France and Greece, with expanded reliance on the property tax, moved into this group from the mixed-tax group. The mixed-tax group tended then to be predominantly southern European (with France and Greece and without Japan, which shifted to the mixed group with a decrease in the importance of local income taxes). The group that relies on income tax tends to be more northern European and especially includes the Nordic countries.

Property taxes

Property taxes can include taxes on a wide range of property. Of the countries most reliant on property taxes, these taxes are almost exclusively on immovable property (that is, land and structures). Where property is taxed elsewhere, taxes on immovable property are an important source of property taxes. In Norway and Switzerland, however, taxes on net wealth generate the bulk of property tax revenues for their local governments. Among the mixed-tax countries, taxes on financial and capital transactions (notably property transfers) account for significant shares of the property taxes in some countries (for example, Austria, Spain, and Turkey).

Taxation of immovable property is often recommended for local government. Reasons for its attractiveness include the following (Owens and Panella 1991):

■ Immobility of the tax base hampers evasion and permits interjurisdictional variation in tax rates.

■ Tax on immovable property is linked to benefits received because many municipal services benefit property.
■ It is visible.
■ The yield is predictable.
■ It is relatively easy to administer.

These reasons relate closely to Bird's (1993) characteristics of a good local tax: immobile base, adequate source of revenue, stable and predictable yield, fair, easily administered, not exportable, and visible.

Property taxes are not without problems. Assessments must be kept current with capital or rental values. Also, assessments must be fair, which is widely interpreted as being uniform. Assessment relative to market value is often noted to vary by type of property—low for agricultural and residential property and high for commercial and industrial property. In addition, where tax rates can vary, they, too, are often lower on agricultural and residential property. Clearly, there is a tendency to shift taxes to business property to at least obscure the incidence of the property tax, if not shift or export the property tax burden. Wide variations in (especially) the industrial tax base can create large fiscal disparities among local governments. Although property taxes may relate to certain benefits from local government, they may not relate as well to benefits from social services like schooling (or others with a more redistributive role). In addition, property taxes are often criticized as not relating well to current ability to pay. Hence, although attractive in many ways, property taxes may be inadequate in a number of situations.

Local income taxes

Local income taxes are a widely used and effective means of generating tax revenue. Income tax is really only a local tax if the local government gets to determine the tax revenue it can generate by setting the tax rate. Where rates are set centrally, are closely constrained, or are limited to a range where all jurisdictions essentially use the same rate (as in Norway and in the state of Maryland in the United States), the system becomes more a tax-sharing or tax-transfer system. Also, local income taxes operate best if they tax personal rather than business (that is, corporate) income. Japan's local governments can and do tax corporate income, but normally it is not permitted. The Scandinavian countries, after experimenting with local corporate income taxation and faced with a combination of equity and efficiency problems, abandoned their local corporate income taxes or (as in Denmark and Norway) replaced them with corporate income tax sharing. Piggybacking the local income tax on the central government's personal income tax minimizes administration and compliance costs. The central government defines the base and administers and collects the tax for the local authorities. Local governments commonly set a single low tax rate. Progressive rate structures are rare but exist (for example, in Japan). Commuters present a possible issue. In some places, they are not taxed, while in others they may be partially or even fully taxed. Local payroll taxes collected from employers are somewhat of an alternative to or a variation on local personal income taxes. Often with payroll taxes—and many times intentionally—no distinction is made between residents and non-residents. In addition, especially as demonstrated in many states within the United States, local income taxes can operate in environments where the tax mix is not uniform—that is, alongside other local taxes, such as property and sales taxes.

Local personal income taxes have a number of potential strengths. Among the advantages are the following:

- They can be a flexible and autonomous source of local tax revenue that is very visible to taxpayers.
- Administration and compliance costs can be low.
- Tax exporting can be minimal.
- The tax base is relatively immobile in that taxpayers must (as with the property tax) change their residence to avoid the local tax.
- More so than with property taxes, personal income tax revenue grows automatically with economic activity.

Major considerations are that they can generate relatively large amounts of revenue and that they can be seen as fair. Countries that are above average in terms of local tax revenues as a percentage of GDP predominantly are highly income tax reliant (and do not include those that are property tax reliant). They also tend to have high levels of expenditure responsibilities, with major responsibilities for social programs. In part, this arrangement works because, unlike other major local taxes, the local income tax results in a progressive distribution of the tax burden that is consistent with attitudes about fairness in financing social programs.[8] Hence, local income taxes enable an assignment of responsibilities that other taxes would not likely support. Their acceptance and success in such situations rely heavily on effective equalization to offset disparities in fiscal capacities among jurisdictions and to ensure relative uniformity in access to and levels of services across jurisdictions.

Local sales taxes

Local governments in most countries of the Organisation for Economic Co-operation and Development (OECD) levy some form of sales tax, but they are a major source of revenue in relatively few countries (notably those in the mixed-tax group). Japan, Spain, and the United States provide illustrations. Japanese municipalities and the regional prefectures levy a wide range of specific taxes, including taxes on products, ownership or use of light motor vehicles, automobile acquisition, tobacco, mineral products, light oil delivery, landholding, property acquisition, fixed assets, meals and hotels, golf links, spas, business offices, city planning, water utility and land profits, and hunting. The central government requires and administers some of these taxes. Individually, few generate significant revenue. Spain's municipalities and regional authorities also have an extensive list of taxes on items and activities. Again, some involve arrangements with the central government, so their local nature is questionable. In the United States, about 6,500 local authorities in 32 states levy local sales taxes. The tax is entirely a local option in 28 states. Local sales taxes are often piggybacked on the state general sales tax. In some states, special districts (for example, school and transit) as well as general-purpose local governments can levy a sales tax. A wide variety of local specific or selective sales taxes are also found throughout the country.

Local sales taxes can generate significant amounts of revenue and may be popular (as in the United States), but they have some drawbacks. One of the complications is that the tax base is typically very uneven across local governments. Hence, the revenue-generating potential varies greatly, making sales taxes less than a viable revenue source for all local governments. Also, depending on the concentration of retail activity, for example, interjurisdictional tax shifting may result. Nonresident contributions to local taxes are not a problem if local costs correspond to the tax, but if significant tax exporting occurs, equity and efficiency questions emerge. Border problems are of greater concern. Consumers are mobile, and shopping patterns near borders can be sensitive to differences in sales tax rates, thereby leading to inefficiencies in firm location and consumer shopping behavior. Various operating complications exist as well. Local sales taxes paid on business inputs are usually not or are only imperfectly deducted; hence, they augment costs and double taxation occurs when the outputs are sold. Goods are more commonly taxed than services, thus distorting relative prices. Relative to revenues, the costs of collecting some sales taxes (for example, some selective taxes) may be high. These various complications may contribute to the more limited reliance on sales taxes among OECD countries. They also contribute to making such taxes candidates for revenue sharing.

Business taxes

In a few countries, major local taxes are levied on businesses beyond the conventional property taxes or local income taxes. These taxes are notable in Canada, France, Germany, and Japan.

In France, the *taxe professionnelle*, a tax on incorporated and unincorporated businesses, generates about one-third of total local tax revenues. Since 1999, the base is the rental value of a firm's fixed assets only. Removal of the wage component was compensated for by a central subsidy. Even before that, the central government was estimated to be paying 30 percent of the tax because it contributed any amount of a firm's *taxe professionnelle* beyond 4 percent of value added. Local rates are restricted by the central government. In addition, an estimated 80 percent of the tax is exported beyond the taxing jurisdiction.

German local governments impose a trade tax that is based on corporate profits. The highest local rates are about twice the lowest. This tax generates about one-third of tax revenue and 15 percent of total revenue in the western portion of the country.

In Japan, local governments obtain about 20 percent of their tax revenues from corporations. The prefecture governments collect an enterprise tax, which is based (primarily) on corporate net income. Enterprise taxes provide about 26 percent of their tax revenue. The municipal governments get about 9 percent of their tax revenue from taxes on corporate income. The central government sets standard rates and allows very little variation. Corporations with operations in several jurisdictions allocate their taxes according to measures of business activity in each jurisdiction.

In Canada, special local taxes on business are permitted in most provinces. Those taxes once amounted to one-tenth of local taxes, but that figure is reported to have declined to only about 2.1 percent over the past decade.

Extensive use of additional business taxes appears to be part of a politically attractive effort to shift a larger share of the local tax burden to nonresident taxpayers and beyond the local community. Shifting and exporting taxes in this way masks the cost of local services and promotes excessive expenditures because local taxes do not properly signal costs.

Nontax Revenues

Nontax revenue refers to revenue from government sales of goods and services; property and investment income (for example, rentals, interest, and returns from enterprises); and income from fines and penalties.

Generating an average of 21 percent of revenue overall, nontax revenues are a significant source of revenue for local governments. Because local governments provide numerous goods and services for which prices or charges can be levied (for example, water and sewerage, public transit, refuse disposal, recreational facilities, and supplementary improvements such as lane lighting specific to select properties), many nontax revenues also have an important allocative efficiency role. Charges and fees for such services link benefits and costs and serve as a signal both to users and to the supplying local authorities. Well-designed charges can improve the decisions of consumers and governments alike. Bird (1993), for example, argues that local governments should pursue benefit-related finance, and the first step should be to levy user charges (and specific benefit taxes) where possible.

The contributions of taxes, nontax sources, and intergovernmental grants are reported in table 7.8. Across the countries reported there, nontax revenues of local governments average 2.04 percent of GDP and provide 21.55 percent of total revenue. With taxes accounting for about 42 percent of revenue, nontax sources generate half as much revenue as taxes do and are fully one-third of own-source revenues. The importance of nontax revenue varies considerably among countries. As a percentage of GDP, it is lowest in Spain at 0.70 percent and highest in Finland at 4.45 percent. Also, as a percentage of GDP, nontax revenue tends to be more important in the countries that are most reliant on income tax, where such revenues average 2.57 percent. However, as a percentage of total revenue, nontax revenues are more important for countries that are highly reliant on property taxes (averaging 27.34 percent). They are also a relatively larger share of own-source revenues in those countries (about 46 percent on average). For some countries in this group, nontax revenues actually exceed tax revenues (that is, Australia, Greece, the Netherlands, and the United Kingdom).

The relative importance of the various sources of nontax revenues is shown in table 7.9. Only the averages and the range are reported. Sales of goods and services account for about two-thirds of nontax revenues, with a range from 42.5 percent to 88.2 percent. Property income (for example, rents for government-owned property) is next most important, averaging 19.2 percent. Fines, penalties, and forfeits are a minor source, with an average of only 1.5 percent; most countries report no such income. Miscellaneous nontax income provides 13.8 percent. Miscellaneous income is relatively more important in the mixed-tax countries, and property income is relatively more important in the countries that are reliant on property taxes.

TABLE 7.8 Tax, Nontax, and Grant Revenue of Local Governments, 2003

Indicator	Percentage of GDP				Percentage of revenue		
	Taxes	Nontax revenues	Grants	Total	Taxes	Nontax revenues	Grants
Highly property tax reliant							
Australia	0.98	1.20	0.36	2.54	38.6	47.2	14.2
Canada	2.93	1.33	2.81	7.07	41.4	18.8	39.7
United States	3.74	1.79	3.67	9.20	40.7	19.5	39.9
France	4.48	2.00	4.15	10.63	42.1	18.8	39.0
Greece[a]	0.32	—	—	—	12.0	47.8	40.1
Ireland	0.62	—	—	—	—	—	—
Netherlands	1.49	2.95	11.66	16.10	9.3	18.3	72.4
New Zealand[b]	1.99	0.95	0.37	3.31	60.1	28.7	11.2
United Kingdom	1.68	2.42	8.26	12.36	13.6	19.6	66.8
Average[c]	2.03	1.81	4.47	8.74	32.23	27.34	40.41
Highly income tax reliant							
Belgium	2.35	0.95	3.27	6.93	33.9	13.8	47.2
Germany	2.60	1.87	2.38	6.95	39.2	25.8	32.7
Switzerland[d]	4.89	3.47	1.67	10.03	48.7	34.6	16.7
Denmark	17.23	2.79	12.41	32.95	52.3	8.5	37.7
Finland	9.43	4.45	5.15	19.04	49.5	23.3	27.0
Iceland	9.83	1.91	1.27	13.00	75.6	14.6	9.7
Luxembourg	2.12	1.30	2.78	6.18	33.8	21.0	44.9
Norway	6.37	2.71	5.26	14.34	44.4	18.9	33.7
Sweden	16.52	3.73	5.04	25.73	64.2	14.5	19.6
Average	7.93	2.57	4.36	15.02	49.07	19.44	29.91
Mixed tax							
Austria	4.50	1.58	1.68	8.15	55.2	19.4	20.5
Italy	6.87	1.83	6.57	15.14	45.4	12.1	41.9
Japan	6.56	—	—	—	—	—	—
Portugal[d,e]	2.22	0.92	2.91	6.12	36.3	15.0	47.5
Spain	2.77	0.70	2.23	5.73	48.3	12.3	38.9
Turkey	1.59	—	—	—	—	—	—
Average	4.09	1.26	3.35	8.79	46.30	14.70	37.20
Overall average	4.76	2.04	4.20	11.58	42.13	21.55	35.30

Sources: IMF 2005; OECD 2005.
Note: — = not available. Data are for 2003 unless indicated otherwise. Percentages may not add up to the total reported because of the omission of capital revenue and social security contributions.
a. Data are for 2000.
b. Data are for 1995.
c. Averages of observed data.
d. Data are for 2002.
e. Figures differ for the International Monetary Fund and the Organisation for Economic Co-operation and Development.

TABLE 7.9 Sources of Nontax Own-Source Revenue, 2003

Category of country	Average % of total nontax own revenue			
	Property income	Sales of goods and services	Fines, penalties, and forfeits	Miscellaneous
Highly property tax reliant	25.3	64.0	3.4	7.2
Highly income tax reliant	19.9	68.8	1.0	10.3
Mixed tax	10.7	62.0	0.2	27.1
All countries	19.2	65.5	1.5	13.8
Range	2.1–40.2	42.5–88.2	0–16.5	0–41.9

Source: OECD 2005.

Intergovernmental Transfers

Intergovernmental transfers are an important source of revenue for local governments in essentially all industrial countries. Transfers have a role when local own-source revenue is considered to be inadequate or inappropriate for funding the expenditure responsibilities of local governments. For the countries in table 7.8, grants average 35.3 percent of local government revenue. The averages are slightly larger (about 40 percent) for countries that are highly reliant on property taxes and somewhat lower (about 30 percent) for those countries that rely on income taxes. In the federal countries, transfers average a seemingly low 30.1 percent, but the range (from 14.2 percent to 47.2 percent) is still large. Beyond that, patterns are not obvious. The contribution of transfers varies widely among individual countries. At the low end are Iceland, New Zealand, and Australia (9.7 percent, 11.2 percent, and 14.2 percent of revenue, respectively). At the high end are the Netherlands (72.4 percent) and the United Kingdom (66.8 percent), but the next largest is Portugal at 47.5 percent. Obviously, a broad distribution exists, and countries are relatively evenly dispersed over all but the highest levels of the range.

Tax-sharing arrangements can complicate the distinction between grants and taxes. International Monetary Fund (IMF) and OECD criteria for designating shared tax revenues rely on having authority to impose the tax; having some ability to determine the revenue (for example, set the rate); and having control over use of the funds raised (IMF 2001: 50; OECD 2005: 303). An OECD tax policy study (OECD 1999) analyzes the taxing authority of subnational governments. It also reports the share of tax revenue generated from various taxes, including shared taxes. That information for local governments is the basis of table 7.10. One can see there that the OECD attributes the majority of local tax revenue in most countries to tax sources over which local governments have control of the tax rate, the tax base, or both (that is, they set the tax). Shared tax arrangements over which local authorities have limited (or no) control but that generate large amounts of tax revenue exist in only 4 of 15 countries: Norway, Austria, Germany, and Portugal (94 percent, 81 percent, 47 percent, and 37 percent, respectively).[9] Still, some caution is necessary because some difference of opinion may exist over these attributions. In the case of Japan, for example, the OECD designates 94 percent of tax revenues as coming from taxes set by local governments, but Mochida (2006: 164) argues that the failure of local governments to deviate from the nationally set standard tax rates implies that those taxes effectively approximate tax revenue sharing. Hence, to feel fully comfortable with the assignment between own-source revenues and transfers, one may need to assess for oneself the arrangements within individual countries.

Two sections follow. One reviews the purposes of transfers and provides illustrations. The second reviews the role of grants in the overall fiscal arrangements.

The purposes and types of grants

Intergovernmental transfers exist for both economic and political reasons. The economic reasons are (a) to close (vertical) fiscal gaps arising from local authorities' expenditure requirements exceeding their revenue-generating capacities, (b) to reduce (horizontal) fiscal disparities among local governments in their abilities to deliver public services, and (c) to correct for misallocations resulting from interjurisdictional spillovers (externalities).[10] In practice, grants typically do not fit neatly into these categories. Grants are normally categorized as *conditional* and *unconditional*—that is, grants that are designed or earmarked to be used for specific purposes and transfers that the recipient government is free to use as it sees fit. Transfers aimed at gap closing and equalization normally fall into the unconditional category, whereas those oriented toward correcting spillovers are classified as conditional. A cross-country comparison of grants by type has been made available only recently (Bergvall and others 2006). The analysis of Bergvall and others for local governments in most of the countries under examination here is reported in table 7.11.[11] Across the 15 countries in table 7.11, conditional and unconditional grants are equally important on average, with each accounting for half of total transfers to local governments. Again, however, wide differences exist among the countries. Conditional funding ranges from as little as 9.1 percent of total transfers to as much as 96.0 percent (and

TABLE 7.10 Local Government Tax Autonomy, 1995
(percentage of revenue by type of tax)

Country	Local government controls tax base or rates		Local government receives shared tax revenue			Central government sets tax base and rate
	Local government sets tax base and rate	Local government sets tax rate only	Revenue split requires local government consent	Revenue split fixed by national legislation	Revenue split part of central government annual budget	
Highly property tax reliant						
Australia	predominant					
Canada[a]	predominant			minimal		
United States	predominant			some		
France	predominant					
Netherlands	...	100	...	...	...	...
New Zealand	98	...	...	...	...	2
United Kingdom	...	100	...	...	...	...
Highly income tax reliant						
Belgium	13	84	...	2	1	...
Germany	1	52	47	...	...	...
Switzerland	...	97	...	3	...	...
Denmark	...	96	...	...	4	...
Finland	...	89	...	11	...	...
Iceland	8	92	...	...	...	...
Norway	...	5	...	1	94	...
Sweden	4	96	...	...	...	...

(continued)

TABLE 7.10 Local Government Tax Autonomy, 1995 *(continued)*
(percentage of revenue by type of tax)

Country	Local government controls tax base or rates		Local government receives shared tax revenue			Central government sets tax base and rate
	Local government sets tax base and rate	Local government sets tax rate only	Revenue split requires local government consent	Revenue split fixed by national legislation	Revenue split part of central government annual budget	
Mixed tax						
Austria	9	11	81	...	...	...
Japan	...	94	...	...	...	6
Portugal	49	14	...	...	...	37
Spain	33	51	16	...	...	...

Source: OECD 1999.
Note: ... = insignificant.
a. Characterizes general-purpose (municipal) government. Local school authorities in most provinces have little or no independent tax powers.

TABLE 7.11 Types of Grants Received by Local Governments

Country	Conditional				Unconditional				Total grants as a % of revenue
	Formal		Discretionary (%)	Total (%)	Formal		Discretionary (%)	Total (%)	
	Matching (%)	Nonmatching (%)			General purpose (%)	Block (%)			
Highly property tax reliant									
Australia	...	...	17.2	17.2	82.8	...	...	82.8	14.2
Canada	...	95.7	...	95.7	4.3	...	...	4.3	39.7
France	6.5	0.1	5.1	11.7	81.9	6.4	...	88.3	39.0
New Zealand	70.0	...	...	70.0	30.0	...	...	30.0	11.2
Highly income tax reliant									
Belgium	71.6	0.1	24.3	96.0	4.0	...	...	4.0	47.2
Switzerland	80.4	...	...	80.4	19.6	...	...	19.6	16.7
Denmark	66.6	0.5	2.6	69.7	30.2	...	...	30.2	37.7
Finland	5.7	...	3.4	9.1	16.3	74.0	0.6	90.9	27.0
Iceland	3.0	8.4	9.6	21.0	79.0	...	...	79.0	9.7
Norway	12.2	9.4	23.3	44.9	...	55.1	...	55.1	33.7
Sweden	...	...	28.8	28.8	71.3	...	...	71.3	19.6
Mixed tax									
Austria	42.8	42.2	1.2	86.2	13.7	0.1	...	13.8	20.5
Italy	...	...	75.5	75.5	24.5	...	...	24.5	41.9
Portugal	...	...	11.4	11.4	85.0	...	3.6	88.6	47.5
Spain	30.7	3.1	...	33.8	66.2	...	...	66.2	38.9
Average	26.0	10.6	13.5	50.1	40.6	9.0	0.3	49.9	29.6

Source: Bergvall and others 2006.
Note: ... = insignificant. Data are for either 2002 or 2003.

unconditional grants are just the opposite). No relationship exists between the level of conditional or unconditional funding and the importance of transfers in local government budgets.

Further detail is provided on both conditional and unconditional transfers. Grants can be divided into those that are provided entirely at the discretion of the granting government and those that are based on formal agreements (usually legislation and sometimes constitutions). As seen in table 7.11, discretionary grants are normally a small portion of total transfers, 13.5 percent on average. Italy, at 75.5 percent, is clearly an exception. Transfers for capital purposes make up half the discretionary transfers in these countries and the vast majority of all transfers for capital. The formal arrangements provide transparency and some certainty for as long as the arrangements last. Formal arrangements for conditional grants can require some portion of matching local funds, or they may be nonmatching but still require certain criteria to be satisfied to obtain the grant (for example, meeting certain service standards or other criteria besides spending on specified functions). Matching grants are a more important source of revenue than nonmatching grants, 26.0 versus 10.6 percent on average. However, both types display a tremendous range (from 0 percent to 80.4 percent and 95.7 percent for matching and nonmatching, respectively).

Unconditional transfers are dominated by formal arrangements providing general-purpose funding. Such grants account for over 80 percent of unconditional grants and 40.6 percent of total transfers in the countries table 7.11 reports on, but the differences among countries are huge. Bergvall and others (2006) include block grants with unconditional grants. However, because block grants are for broadly specified purposes (for example, education, social programs) and do not change relative prices to the recipient, they might equally well be considered nonmatching conditional grants. Norway, one of the only four countries shown with this type of grant revenue, might be an example. Nevertheless, considerable flexibility exists in the actual use of those funds.

Illustrations of unconditional and conditional transfers

UNCONDITIONAL TRANSFERS. Unconditional transfers are intended to close fiscal gaps or to provide equalization, and they typically embody elements of both objectives. Hence, identifying such grants with solely one purpose or the other is usually difficult. Revenue sharing and equalization grants illustrate. Revenue sharing can be viewed as a transfer primarily oriented toward closing a fiscal gap but normally allocated on an equalizing basis, whereas equalization grants are primarily aimed at equalization—although not uncommonly all or almost all local governments receive funds through the equalization program.

Revenue sharing—normally tax sharing—exists when senior governments assign a specific share of certain revenues to local governments. Several countries have such transfers. Some major cases serve to illustrate. In Austria, most of the major taxes are shared among federal, *Länder* (or state), and local governments. The sharing arrangements are renegotiated regularly. Shared income taxes provide Germany's local governments with over 40 percent of their tax revenues; about 5 percent comes from a share of the value added tax. Since 1990, Italy has experimented with a variety of dedicated or shared taxes to fund (primarily) health services through its regional governments. Since 2000, the regional authorities have shared 38.55 percent of the national value added tax and get the revenue from a 0.9 percent personal income tax surcharge. Japan's central government shares its revenues from personal and corporate income taxes, national consumption tax, and alcohol and tobacco taxes with its local governments. With local income tax rates at the maximum, the local personal income tax system in Norway is effectively a tax-sharing arrangement. The federal government in the United States had a revenue-sharing arrangement with local governments from 1972 to 1986. In Canada, some provinces share selected tax revenues with some or all localities, but the amounts are relatively small.

Although local governments overall may lack sufficient revenue capacity, individual authorities' requirements vary. Hence, shared revenues are normally allocated by formulas that take into account individual fiscal capacities and fiscal needs. The indicators vary depending on responsibilities and own-source revenues. Thus, the allocation of shared revenues is usually done on an equalizing basis.

Equalization grants are far more common than revenue sharing. Equalization transfers are directed to reducing fiscal disparities that arise among local authorities because of differences in revenue-generating capacity or expenditure needs. Ideally, good estimates of both fiscal capacity and expenditure requirements can be made, and the differences can be offset by the equalization grants. Examples of countries using such a method are Denmark, Japan, Sweden, and the United Kingdom. Equalization may be fraternal (that is, from rich to poor localities, as occurs in Denmark and Sweden) or, more commonly, paternal, with the equalizing transfer coming from a senior government. Often, equalization grants are funded from a pool of resources (not necessarily determined by capacities and needs) that is simply shared among local governments according to some formula. The factors in the sharing formula include population and other elements deemed to reflect fiscal capacity (for example, per capita tax bases) and need (for example, population, road length, area, or number of students). Examples of this type occur in Canada, the Netherlands, Portugal, and Spain. In some cases, the pool of funds for equalization may not be sufficient to meet fiscal deficiencies (if calculated), while in other instances it may be more than adequate. In some cases, Australia for example, all local governments may receive a basic or a minimum per capita amount from the equalization pool. In such instances, the program clearly goes beyond pure equalization and incorporates an element of fiscal gap–closing transfer.

CONDITIONAL TRANSFERS. Transfers to correct for spillovers can be important if public services provided by one local government afford significant benefits to residents of other jurisdictions. Transportation, schooling, recreational and cultural facilities, policing, and certain health services are examples. The failure to match well those paying with those benefiting can cause distortions (with the concern normally being undersupply). Grants can be designed to reduce such distortions. Usually, such grants are conditional (that is, for a specific purpose), and often they require some matching local contributions (reflecting local benefits at the margin).

Specific-purpose (conditional) grants dominate transfer programs in many countries. Canada illustrates this situation. In only 1 of 10 provinces do general-purpose transfers exceed the amount of specific-purpose transfers. As in many other countries, specific-purpose transfers tend to be concentrated on schooling and other social services and often represent a large share of their costs. Among core services, transportation is a major beneficiary of transfers. Transfers to fund capital projects are popular, but care must be taken in designing them to avoid distorting the allocation between capital and operating expenditures. Also, differing matching rates (not justified by differing spillovers) can distort expenditure choices among functions. This distortion was a reason for France's amalgamation of its capital grants into a single fund. A related problem is that conditional grants can proliferate and lead to a large and confusing array. In many countries, a multitude of specific-purpose grants have been considered unnecessary. For example, during the 1980s, Norway collapsed more than 200 specific-purpose grant programs into four block grants, each targeted to a specific broad function and with somewhat different distribution and performance criteria. In many cases, block grants have successfully simplified grant arrangements without sacrificing results.

An extreme version of conditional grants exists when the granting government provides essentially all the funding and dictates the grant's use. In such cases, local autonomy is essentially nonexistent, and the local government is really an agent of the senior authority hired to perform an activity. Such "transfers" are often hard to distinguish from payments or reimbursements for contracted services. The Danish arrangements for old-age security and selected other social services illustrate the local authority acting as agent.[12] Similar arrangements exist, but are more explicitly recognized as such, in Germany.

Summary, Conclusions, and Lessons

Local government may have a relatively small or a very large role in the government and the economy of a country. For example, among industrial countries, local government expenditures range from 2.4 percent to 33.1 percent of GDP. Four groups of countries appear: (a) 2 countries with low budget shares have expenditures averaging 2.9 percent, (b) 11 countries with lower-medium budget shares have expenditures averaging 7.9 percent, (c) 5 countries with upper-medium budget shares have expenditures averaging 16.1 percent, and (d) 2 countries with large budget shares have expenditures averaging 29.5 percent.

The magnitude of local government is explained primarily by its involvement in the delivery of social programs (that is, schooling, health, and social protection). Local governments almost uniformly undertake a set of core activities that include providing local roadways and walkways, fire (and often some police) protection, recreational and cultural facilities and programs, water and sewerage services, waste removal and disposal, and regulation of local activities (largely to enhance safety and enjoyment of property, to control nuisances, and to regulate business). Those programs typically require 3.5 to 7.4 percent of GDP. Spending on social programs, however, ranges from essentially 0 percent to 28.6 percent of GDP. Among social programs, some significant local expenditure responsibility for schooling is most common, with substantial involvement in health and social protection being more erratic. Local expenditures on schooling average 2.5 percent of GDP, and local authorities spend half of that or more in all but four countries.

Local governments must fund their expenditures from taxes, other own-source revenues, and intergovernmental transfers. On average, these sources account for about 42, 22, and 35 percent of revenues, respectively, but there is wide variation in the relative shares. Although a smaller share, the other nontax own-source revenues are important. Charges are a recommended source of funding where possible, and about two-thirds of this other revenue comes from sales of goods and services, with another one-fifth coming from property rentals and investment income.

Local governments commonly have access to property taxes, income taxes, and taxes on sales or use of commodities. Local governments in most countries rely primarily on one major type of tax, either property tax or income tax. The nine countries that rely heavily on property taxes obtain (on average) almost 82 percent of their tax revenue from property taxes. The nine countries that rely heavily on income taxes obtain (on average) about 88 percent of their tax revenues from income taxes. Sales taxes encompass a variety of taxes on sales and use, and in no country are these taxes the dominant revenue source. Countries that use sales taxes heavily also rely heavily on both property and income taxes and can be considered mixed-tax countries. Property taxes are levied on immobile land and structures, relate well to the benefits from core services, are widely recommended for local government use, and are used to some extent in almost all industrial countries (and have gained importance in some, notably France and Italy). Local taxes on personal income are widely accepted, can be applied easily when piggybacked on the personal income tax systems of senior governments, and have substantial (particularly relative to the property tax) revenue-generating power. Both property taxes and personal income taxes benefit from the relative immobility of residents. Taxes on corporate income and sales are more subject to exporting and reduced accountability and so are less conceptually appealing as local taxes. These problems contribute to their less widespread use and the wider appeal to intergovernmental revenue sharing of both (and especially corporate income taxes). Local taxes on business income are diminishing in importance. Local governments in the industrial countries have extensive tax autonomy. Local governments in about three-fourths of the countries get the vast majority of their tax revenues from tax sources that they control, usually by being able to set the tax rates.

At about 35 percent of revenues, intergovernmental transfers are important to local governments. Unconditional and conditional transfers are the two main types. Unconditional transfers address problems of fiscal gap (when expenditure responsibilities exceed reasonable expectations of revenue-generating capacities) and fiscal equalization (often without a clear distinction between the two objectives). Conditional transfers are better suited to correcting for spillovers (but, in practice, they sometimes embody aspects of gap closing and equalization). Across the industrial countries, grants are about half unconditional and half conditional. Conditional funding often involves matching contributions, whereas unconditional grants are nonmatching. Major conditional grants are often associated with the funding of social expenditures. Even then, they may be block grants without excessive strings attached. In cases where local authorities have little effective control in tax sharing, distinguishing between unconditional grants and tax sharing is often difficult. Formal agreements govern the vast majority of transfer arrangements. Although agreements do not ensure the stability of grants, agreements do make grants transparent so that their purposes and distribution are more apparent. Only about 14 percent of transfers are discretionary, and those transfers are mostly for capital funding purposes.

Capital expenditures and their financing deserve special mention. Local governments account for a disproportionate share of infrastructure—about half. Usually, the largest part of that amount is concentrated in the core local services, such as streets and roadways, public transit, water and sewerage systems, drainage, and recreational and cultural facilities. Infrastructure spending represents about 14 percent of expenditures. Capital expenditures are financed from operating revenues, reserves, and borrowing. Borrowing for capital purposes is almost the only borrowing that local governments are permitted to undertake. Even then, that borrowing is closely regulated and monitored, but senior governments typically assist or facilitate such debt.

In conclusion, the major observations and potential lessons for anyone interested in the fiscal design of local governments are highlighted:

- Effective performance by local government is not determined by size but by design. There is no single overriding assignment of responsibilities to recommend. Local governments may be small, undertaking only the essentially local core responsibilities, or large, depending on their roles in delivering social services. Social programs can benefit from local decision making, but they involve spillovers and redistribution calling for central engagement. As a result, responsibilities are often shared between senior and local authorities. Responsibility sharing can be done in many ways. On behalf of their citizens, senior governments have a legitimate interest in realizing at least minimum standards, if not uniformity, of schooling, health, and social protection programs. If local governments are responsible for delivering those programs, senior governments can ensure minimum standards by regulation and funding (providing grants or more adequate tax bases and grants). Experience indicates that there is considerable flexibility in the range of local tax and intergovernmental grant combinations that are workable for the local delivery and funding of social programs.
- Property taxes and user charges go far toward being adequate for the financing of core activities. For governments limited to core programs, grants for correcting for spillovers (for example, transportation) and for affording horizontal equity can be expected but are likely to be relatively

minor in the overall local budget. Social programs have high costs, and the evidence indicates that property taxes are not sufficient for funding them. For those governments limited to property taxes but responsible for significant social programs, transfers (usually designated specifically for the program) will be a substantial source of funds. Access to local income taxes greatly enhances local governments' abilities to finance programs—especially social programs. That source of funding, however, does not necessarily reduce the use or importance of transfers. Although tax revenues and social expenditures are typically larger (as a percentage of GDP) in countries with local governments having access to local income taxes, the choice between using local income taxes and using intergovernmental transfers seems somewhat arbitrary (often historically determined), and the mix is quite varied. Local access to income taxes does, however, provide the option of lower transfers when responsibilities are major. It does not, however, eliminate the need for grants. At a minimum, effective equalization is needed to ensure the capacity to provide comparable programs (especially social programs) across local authorities. The varied blends of property-related services and social services provided by local governments demonstrate how finance follows function. Designing a mix of taxes and transfers to provide those combinations efficiently and equitably is essential. Although the potential combinations are large, selecting the successful mix can be challenging.

■ Local own-source finances should fund the local services for which residents are willing to pay. Such finances need to be visible, have a close benefit-cost linkage, and be determined by local government. User charges are an initial choice. When benefits are generally available, however, taxes are necessary. Property taxes and local personal income taxes meet these and other requirements relatively well, and one or the other is the dominant local tax source in most industrial countries. Taxes on sales or use are less prevalent and, in all but a few countries, serve only as a supplement to other taxes. The potential for shifting or exporting sales taxes and corporate income taxes or special business taxes—and the exceptionally uneven distribution of their bases—make them conceptually less appealing as local taxes and more suitable for revenue sharing (that is, transfers rather than taxes). Regardless of the type and the range of taxes, a high degree of local tax autonomy is generally found in industrial countries.

■ Transfers are almost entirely provided through formal arrangements; that is, they are not at the discretion of the grantor. In addition, fully half the transfers are unconditional (primarily for meeting fiscal gaps and for equalization). Even many of the conditional programs (largely for addressing spillover correction) have modest restrictions (for example, block grants). Thus, while ensuring adequate services generating spillover benefits, local governments still enjoy a relatively high degree of fiscal autonomy. Transfers have a variety of important roles to play—especially when local governments have considerable responsibilities for social programs. In fact, they make the sharing of responsibilities for social programs workable. The appropriate design of transfers is vital.

■ Local governments have disproportionately large responsibilities for infrastructure. Financing infrastructure involves borrowing. Borrowing for capital expenditure purposes is usually the only permitted borrowing that local governments can do. Such borrowing is often closely regulated and monitored by senior governments but is commonly also assisted in one form or another. Important to note is that local debt is funded largely on a commercial basis whether through public or private agencies.

■ Although not specifically addressed here, essential to note is that the democratic nature of local governments in the industrial countries is their dominant and critical underlying characteristic (see Shah 2006a). This feature makes local authorities accountable ultimately to their electorate and, to greater or lesser extents, affords relatively substantial degrees of autonomy to what they do and how they accomplish it. The accountability and autonomy that accompany democratic institutions are central to successful local government.

Notes

1. This chapter is an updated but much abbreviated version of an earlier paper with the same title (McMillan 1996). Potentially dated but still valuable details and extensions are available there.
2. The group of industrial countries is based on those so identified in the International Monetary Fund's *Government Finance Statistics Yearbook* (IMF 2005).
3. In the case of environmental services (largely solid waste and wastewater services), the zero values reported for the United Kingdom and the United States are odd because local governments in both countries are responsible for such services and report expenditures on them (see, for example, King 2006; Schroeder 2006).
4. Government spending tends to be more decentralized in federal countries. About half of government spending is made by central governments in federal countries compared with an average of about 70 percent in unitary countries. Note that with central government expenditures amounting to about 40 percent or less of total government outlays, Canada and Switzerland are quite decentralized. In contrast, France, Luxembourg, New Zealand, and Portugal are quite centralized with over 80 percent of expenditures made by the central government, and the United Kingdom,

at 73.9 percent, is not far behind. Denmark stands out as an exceptionally decentralized unitary country, with the central government accounting for only 40.5 percent of government outlays.

5. The table reports on 24 countries. At the local government level, tax information is more common than expenditure information.

6. For reference, table 7.6 also reports nontax own-source revenue and total own-source revenue. Nontax own-source revenue averages almost 2 percent of GDP, and total own-source revenue averages 7 percent (somewhat less, 4.8 percent, in federal countries and somewhat more, 7.8 percent, in unitary countries). To allow ready comparison and to reflect the importance of intergovernmental transfers, the table also includes total expenditures.

7. Recall the need to be cautious about the attribution of shared tax revenues to local governments.

8. Hall and Smith (1995) demonstrate the potentially quite different distributional burdens of local income, property, and sales taxes. In their reasonable cases, the local income tax is progressive, the property tax largely regressive, and a local sales tax proportional.

9. Some general information has been added for countries examined here but not in the OECD study. In those countries, too, local determination of local tax revenue is predominant. See OECD (2002) and Darby, Muscatelli, and Roy (2003) as supplementary references.

10. Bergvall and others (2006) refer to these purposes as financing services, equalization, and subsidization.

11. The terms *conditional* and *unconditional* are substituted here for Bergvall and others' (2006) *earmarked* and *nonearmarked* grants. Also, *formal* here replaces *mandatory* in their article.

12. Under local government reform to be implemented in 2007, grants will replace certain reimbursements (Danish Ministry of the Interior and Health 2005).

References

Batley, Richard, and Gerry Stoker, eds. 1991. *Local Government in Europe: Trends and Developments*. New York: St. Martin's Press.

Bergvall, Daniel, Claire Charbit, Dirk-Jan Kraan, and Olaf Merk. 2006. "Intergovernmental Transfers and Decentralised Public Spending." *OECD Journal on Budgeting* 5 (4):114–62.

Bird, Richard M. 1993. "Threading the Fiscal Labyrinth: Some Issues in Fiscal Federalism." *National Tax Journal* 46 (2): 207–27.

Danish Ministry of the Interior and Health. 2005. "The Local Government Reform: In Brief," Ministry of the Interior and Health, Copenhagen.

Darby, Julia, Anton Muscatelli, and Graeme Roy. 2003. "Fiscal Decentralization in Europe: A Review of Recent Evidence." Department of Economics, University of Glasgow, Scotland.

Hall, John, and Stephen Smith. 1995. *Local Sales Taxation: An Assessment of the Feasibility and Likely Effects of Sales Taxation at the Local Level in the U.K.* London: Institute for Fiscal Studies.

Hesse, Joachim Jens, ed. 1991. *Local Government and Urban Affairs in International Perspective*. Baden-Baden, Germany: Nomos Verlagsgesellschaft.

IMF (International Monetary Fund). 2001. *Government Fiscal Statistics Manual*. Washington, DC: IMF.

———. 2002. *Government Finance Statistics Yearbook*. Washington, DC: IMF.

———. 2004. *Government Finance Statistics Yearbook*. Washington, DC: IMF.

———. 2005. *Government Finance Statistics Yearbook*. Washington, DC: IMF.

King, David. 2006. "Local Government Organization and Finance: United Kingdom." In *Local Governance in Industrial Countries*, ed. Anwar Shah, 265–312. Washington, DC: World Bank.

McMillan, Melville L. 1996; revised in 2001. "A Local Perspective on Fiscal Federalism: Practices, Experiences, and Lessons from Developed Countries." World Bank, Washington, DC.

Mochida, Nobuki. 2006. "Local Government Organization and Finance: Japan." In *Local Governance in Industrial Countries*, ed. Anwar Shah, 149–88. Washington, DC: World Bank.

OECD (Organisation for Economic Co-operation and Development). 1999. *Taxing Powers of State and Local Governments*. Paris: OECD.

———. 2002. *Fiscal Decentralization in EU Applicant States and Selected EU Member States*. Paris: OECD Centre for Tax Policy Administration.

———. 2005. *Revenue Statistics of OECD Member Countries, 1965–2004*. Paris: OECD.

Owens, Jeffrey, and Giorgio Panella. 1991. *Local Government: An International Perspective*. Amsterdam: North-Holland.

Schroeder, Larry. 2006. "Local Government Organization and Finance: United States." In *Local Governance in Industrial Countries*, ed. Anwar Shah, 313–58. Washington, DC: World Bank.

Shah, Anwar, ed. 2006a. "A Comparative Institutional Framework for Responsive, Responsible, and Accountable Local Government." In *Local Governance in Industrial Countries*, ed. Anwar Shah, 1–40. Washington, DC: World Bank.

———. 2006b. *Local Governance in Industrial Countries*. Washington, DC: World Bank.

Stoker, Gerry. 1991. "Introduction: Trends in Western European Local Government." In *Local Government in Europe: Trends and Developments*, eds. Richard Batley and Gerry Stoker, 1–20. New York: St. Martin's Press.

Toonen, Theo A. J. 1991. "Change in Continuity: Local Government and Urban Affairs in the Netherlands." In *Local Government and Urban Affairs in International Perspective*, ed. Joachim Jens Hesse, 291–332. Baden-Baden, Germany: Nomos Verlagsgesellschaft.

8

Decentralized Governance in Developing and Transition Countries: A Comparative Review

SEBASTIAN ECKARDT AND ANWAR SHAH

There is a growing consensus in both theoretical and empirical research that institutions and the quality of governance are important prerequisites for sustained economic growth and social development. If governance matters, so does the need for reliable and valid methodologies to meaningfully assess and compare the quality of institutions across different countries as well as the quality of single countries over time. Recent research and data collection efforts have focused on seemingly rigorous quantitative methods in evaluating governance and its effects. These approaches typically use statistical aggregation techniques to derive cross-country ordinal measurements and general governance rankings based on a large number of existing and often diverse perception-based data sets (see, for example, Huther and Shah 1998; Kaufmann, Kraay, and Mastruzzi 2005). The application of these methods has failed to identify robust, context-specific policy solutions.

This chapter suggests a simple diagnostic tool that has been designed to analyze selected aspects of governance in decentralized fiscal systems. Comparing governance systems across countries is a complex task. It requires identification of political incentives and of discretion on expenditure and revenue affairs at various levels of government as well as assessments of the result orientation that prevails in public organizations. Based on a concept of citizen-centered governance, the tool relies on a mix of qualitative indicators and specific descriptive features regarding both properties of organizational procedures and governance outcomes. The framework comprehends the fiscal and administrative incentives governments and bureaucracies face as well as the overarching political environment in which they operate. The tool allows comparison of countries, identification of strengths and weaknesses of particular systems, and monitoring of governance progress over time.

The remainder of the chapter is organized into two main parts. The first part outlines the conceptual underpinnings of the citizen-centered governance paradigm. On the basis of that background, the second part develops a measurement methodology and scoring system. The chapter then applies the scorecard to a sample of 26 developing and transition countries.

The Building Blocks of Citizen-Centered Governance in Decentralized Systems

Despite remarkable reform progress in recent decades, administrative systems in the developing world typically face a number of common obstructions. Limited resources; low internal capacity, both with regard to human resources and organizational structures; high degrees of centralization and monopolization; and poor evaluation and accountability mechanisms continue to constrain their performance. Reform efforts focusing on particular aspects—on participation, decentralization, or internal capacity building—have had limited effectiveness in solving these multiple issues in the past. More recently, citizen-centered governance has been suggested as a new comprehensive approach to the reform of public sector organizations. The approach is essentially based on the assumption that the most important change in the incentive environment of politicians and bureaucrats is to empower citizens to demand better results from governments (Shah and Andrews 2005). Cross-country evidence indicates a robust correlation between measures of openness of political processes and administrative performance even when effects of differences in the levels of per capita GDP are controlled for (figure 8.1).[1]

Under the citizen-centered governance paradigm, citizens are best described as having three roles in their relationship with the government: they are taxpayers, users of services, and co-deciders in policy decisions of the government. In turn, elected politicians and bureaucrats should face

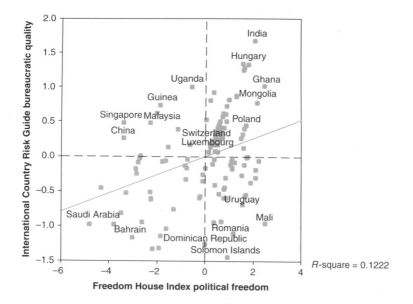

Sources: Freedom House 2002; PRS Group 2002; World Bank 2003d.

FIGURE 8.1 Political Freedom and Bureaucratic Quality: Partial Correlation Controlling for Per Capita GDP Log

positive and negative incentives to adopt policies and provide services that citizens signal as preferred. In a decentralized system, this result requires that fiscal, political, and administrative rules be aligned with one another to generate consistent incentive effects. For instance, the ability of voters to reward or punish incumbent governments at the polls creates an important accountability mechanism. However, in the presence of large vertical fiscal imbalances and continuous bailouts by the central government, bad performers may not be thrown out but rather may get reelected for their success in obtaining a larger share of other people's money. Moreover, to exert demand-side pressures, citizens need to have sufficient information regarding public budgeting and the achievement of results to be able to discern good from bad government performance and to attribute failures and successes of public policies to certain levels of government. This critical information can be disclosed only if applicable management procedures are in place. Because all these elements affect the incentives of governments, governance systems and processes need to be addressed in a comprehensive way. To analyze the governance environment in which governments work, the chapter distinguishes between two dimensions: (a) accountability and (b) fiscal responsibility.

Accountability

In contrast to earlier, more technocratic approaches toward public sector reform that tended to view its effects in isolation from the political and social pressures that prevail both inside and outside the government, citizen-centered governance gives greater emphasis to political institutions and the incentive effects they embed. Experience with decentralization reforms around the globe suggests that giving authority to local governments that are not accountable to their local populations may not improve outcomes. If accountability is incomplete, decentralization might in fact create powerful incentives for local elites to capture the local political process and divert public resources to match their own aspirations rather than those of the broader community. As Agrawal and Ribot (1999: 478) state, "It is only when constituents come to exercise accountability as a countervailing power that decentralization is likely to be effective." In a similar vein, *World Development Report 2004* places accountability succinctly at the center of public sector reform and public service delivery (World Bank 2003e).

Accountability systems broadly require that citizens have the ability to demand answers from public sector agents about proposed or executed actions and to impose sanctions in the event they regard performance as unsatisfactory (Manor 1997; Crook and Manor 2000; Khemani and others 2005; Shah 2004). Operationally, this power comprises mechanisms by which citizens select their political representatives; delegate authority to them; and hold them accountable through voting, checks and balances, and deliberative democracy—as well as informal ways of exerting control over the public sector, such as social capital and political pressure. Citizen-centered governance is most effective in representative systems of government.

Accountability systems are changing rapidly across the world. Alongside moves toward more fiscal decentralization, many countries have engaged in political devolution and have experimented with forms of electoral and representative democracy at both the national and the local levels. According to the Database of Political Institutions, the number of countries that are governed by freely elected governments (either executive or legislative, or both) increased from 60 to 100 between 1990 and 2000 (Beck and others 2001; Khemani and others 2005). This trend is replicated at subnational levels of government, which are increasingly subject to local political control through regular democratic elections. Whereas in 1980 only 10 of the 48 largest countries in the world had elected subnational governments, this number increased to 34 by 2000 (UNPAN 2000). Recent legislation on decentralization—such as the Philippine Local Government Act, which was enacted in 1991; the local government transition acts of 1993 and 1996 in South Africa; or the Indonesian laws on local governance of 1999 and 2004—typically spells out rules for the power and roles of elected representatives as well as basic accountability relationships at the subnational level.

Electoral incentives

Elections are important channels of accountability. They can be seen as both mechanisms to select capable political agents (prospective voting) and means to hold them accountable after they are elected (retrospective voting) (Fearon 1999; Kunicova and Rose-Ackerman 2001; Manin, Przeworski, and Stokes 1999; Przeworski, Stokes, and Manin 1999). How effective electoral incentives work in practice crucially depends on the design of electoral rules, the party system, intra- and interparty competition, voter awareness and turnout, political competition, and contestability. To minimize distortions caused by the strategic behavior of political agents, voters need to be well informed, political competition must be fair and open, and party platforms and lists must be based on broad representation. Conversely, under conditions of incomplete democratization—signified by restricted political competition, high volatility of voters and parties, and poorly defined public policy issues—the effectiveness of political institutions in mediating popular demands into policies is likely to diminish (Fearon 1999; Keefer and Khemani 2003). In addition, both theory and empirical evidence suggest that pluralist (winner-take-all) systems and proportional electoral systems vary in their political incentive structure (Kunicova and Rose-Ackerman 2001; Myerson 1993; Persson and Tabellini 2000; Persson, Tabellini, and Trebbi 2001). Individual accountability appears to be most strongly tied to personal ballots in plurality-rule elections, even though open party lists also seem to have some effect. The logic is simple: voting on individual candidates creates a direct link between individual performance and the probability of reelection, which creates incentives for politicians to refrain from rent-seeking. However, plurality-based electoral systems also have disadvantages. Under such systems, individual reelection-seeking politicians face stronger incentives for targeted transfers that have the characteristics of "private" benefits to their constituencies and, in particular, to swing voters who are more sensitive to electoral promises (Lizzeri and Persico 2001; Persson and Tabellini, 2000). As a consequence, pluralist electoral systems, although limiting public sector size and increasing individual accountability of elected representatives, skew public spending toward targeted transfers at the cost of broad-based public services. In contrast, under proportional systems, intraparty discipline creates incentives to favor broad-based policies that benefit larger party constituencies, although the accountability of individual representatives will tend to be more limited.

Checks and balances

Another important pillar of functioning systems of accountability is the existence of institutional checks and balances. In their relationship with the government, citizens often act indirectly through the competition and cooperation of their representatives and through the presence of permanently constituted, mutually recognized collective actors inside and outside the government that have the capacity and authority to monitor each other's behavior and to react to each other's initiatives (Schmitter and Karl 1991). In other words, power is controlled by dividing it. In practice, this system implies that if authority is delegated to one set of public agents, another set of public agents ("veto players") has the authority to block or amend decisions made by the first set of agents, to impose specific penalties, and to deauthorize them (remove them from office or curtail their authority). The presence of many such veto players—be they constitutionally based institutions, opposing political parties, or civil society organizations—constrains the ability of any one actor to change government policy. The mechanism is simple: ambition is checked by counterambition. With such an institutional design, incentives need to be designed so that they create countervailing interests among various subsets of agents. In private companies, managers are rewarded for increasing production, whereas controllers are rewarded for cutting costs and auditors for monitoring a manager's financial record.

Checks and balances with regard to government operations, including the separation of powers among the executive, legislative, and judiciary branches of government and departmental structures, follow a similar rationale (Persson, Roland, and Tabellini 1997). For instance, whereas local administrations are typically concerned with securing higher budget allocations, elected council members are more concerned with results and service performance. How these checks and balances work depends in practice on the effective powers of elected councils vis-à-vis the executive, including the capacity to appoint and remove executives (through votes of no confidence, impeachment, and so on); the power to get information from the executive (require reports, audits, and the like); the effective use of the power of the purse (the power of budgeting and funding); and a functioning committee system capable of knowledgeably monitoring and assessing executive branch behavior. It also depends on the incentives elected representatives face to fulfill their mandates. In systems with separate elections for the executive and legislative branches, incentives for supervision and oversight are typically stronger. Differential electoral incentives, however, have also been seen as creating undesirable gridlock, thereby reducing accountability by allowing the mayor and the council to shift blame to each other (Manor and Crook 1998).

In countries undergoing democratic transitions, representative structures and oversight mechanisms at both the central and subnational levels are typically weak, and government affairs remain dominated by the executive. This imbalance of power between the executive and legislative branches results from the executive's possession of an expanded workforce with technical and specialized knowledge. In addition to these capacity constraints, a singular chain of delegation and accountability from the community to elected representatives to the bureaucracy is only as strong as its weakest link. If electoral accountability of elected council members to the community is low and council members are primarily motivated by private interests, increasing horizontal accountability of the executive to the councils can even be counterproductive.

Community participation

Direct participation, in addition to elections and checks and balances, represents another means to exert political control over the public sector. Direct democracy empowers all citizens with the opportunity to directly participate in the decision-making process of their society; however, it also increases political transaction costs, because informed participation is costly to citizens. It includes formalized referenda on specific government policies and fiscal issues or the recall of elected or appointed officials from office, as well as more informal ways of participation. All these forms of participation reduce the accountability problem associated with political delegation by directly constraining the discretion of the public sector agents. Other alleged benefits of participation include informational advantages and civic education, greater legitimacy and acceptance of actions taken, and mobilization of additional resources—both financial and human. In practice, the use of direct democracy will not be feasible when the population is large or citizens are spread over a wide area. This finding is the essence of Robert A. Dahl's (1998: 109) "law of time and numbers": "The more citizens a democratic unit contains, the less citizens can participate directly in government decisions and the more they must delegate authority to others." Not surprisingly, subnational governments are widely assumed to represent the most suitable arena for deliberative democracy, because they are typically smaller. Although most modern political systems primarily rely on representative and electoral forms of government, there is a wide variance in which referenda and other forms of direct participation are used throughout the world. Indeed, the increasing importance of local governments has been accompanied by an upsurge of participative forms of decision making (Andrews 2005b). In addition, the advent of advanced information technologies that present new, cost-effective solutions for citizen participation has sparked new pressures for increasing direct-democracy elements in democratic systems (eDemocracy, electronic polls, and so on).

Fiscal Responsibility

The principle of responsibility, as it pertains to the citizen-centered governance paradigm, is simply that public management procedures—including the design of the fiscal system, internal financial management and auditing, managerial autonomy, and performance-oriented supervision—communicate and facilitate responsibility by the government to its citizens. Responsibility requires effective and transparent internal management and evaluation systems that ensure that the bureaucracy and service providers face incentives to be responsive to the demands of their citizen-clients.

Intergovernmental fiscal system

The design of the fiscal system, comprising the expenditure responsibilities of different levels of government and the means through which these responsibilities are financed, will crucially affect the incentives of governments. Both revenues and expenditure responsibilities should be assigned clearly to enable citizens to discern good from bad performance and to demand results from the respective levels of government. Fiscal decentralization has increased the responsibilities and public expenditures carried out by subnational governments around the world. Expenditure responsibilities of subnational governments typically include health, education, and infrastructure as well as welfare functions. Although the decentralization trend has prompted unprecedented change in the ways governments work, objectives, design, and outcomes of fiscal decentralization reforms vary significantly across countries. These differences in the institutional design of the intergovernmental system in a very real sense shape the opportunities and constraints for citizen-oriented service delivery at various levels of government.

With regard to revenue assignment, the way subnational governments are financed can distort their expenditure decisions and tax-raising efforts. To the extent possible, there should be a link between subnational taxes and public services to ensure accountable and efficient use of public resources. Taxes designed to cover at least marginal costs of local service provision, such as property taxes, user charges, and fees, should be assigned to local governments. Subnational governments must have control over the rates (or leverage rates, for that matter) of these taxes. Only by choosing to pay higher or lower taxes at the margin can residents of subnational jurisdictions choose the level of public services they want.

Besides the assignment of own-source revenues, fiscal systems rely to varying degrees on intergovernmental transfers to ensure resource adequacy at subnational levels. The design, allocation mechanisms, magnitude, and relative importance of fiscal transfers vary across countries. Whichever system is used, it should ensure certainty and predictability of transfers so that local governments can do appropriate fiscal planning. Fiscal transfer systems should also be designed to impose hard budget constraints on local governments to prevent opportunistic shifts of expenditure obligations to higher levels of government (Bird and Smart 2001).

Finally, borrowing and access to capital markets through municipal bonds can be used to finance capital assets and to impose fiscal discipline on subnational governments. However, the central government must put a proper regulatory framework in place that creates hard budget constraints (no central bailout in case of default) to prevent excessive subnational borrowing (Rodden 2000).

Administrative system

Although the devolution of political authority has empowered locally elected representatives in many countries, and although civil servants now report to councils or elected mayors, administrative decentralization has lagged because local-level civil servants remain accountable to higher levels of government and for career and other reasons prefer that status (Shah 2004). Autonomy in civil-service management is crucial in citizen-centered governance. A well-qualified and motivated bureaucracy is a key condition for high government performance and the delivery of high-quality public services. The skills and attitude of both administrative and "on the ground" civil servants, such as teachers and health care workers, are crucial for the efficiency and effectiveness of the public sector. Thus, civil-servant incentives, supervision, career development, and training need to be organized in mutually supportive ways. Only if subnational governments can control the size and structure of their civil service and can influence the career development of civil servants can they develop the administrative capacity necessary for effective public services and performance.

Result-oriented management

Management processes inside the administration should be designed with a clear focus on achieving results. A critical component of result-oriented management is a financial planning and accounting system that elicits information regarding the effective and efficient use of public resources. Conventional public budget accounts are designed for detailed control of inputs (salaries, procurement, operational costs, and the like), but they largely neglect whether spending accomplishes results. Establishing a link between stated policy objectives and budget plans has been a focus of reform efforts in public financial management in many countries, starting in institutionally more advanced countries of the Organisation for Economic Co-operation and Development (OECD) but increasingly also in developing countries (Andrews 2005a; Diamond 2003). Such result-oriented or performance budgets are intended to create greater accountability for results of both agencies and programs to their managers, to elected political representatives, and ultimately to the taxpayer and service user.

Meaningful result-oriented management requires a number of elements to be in place. Only if public policies and programs have clearly stated objectives that can be translated into measurable outcomes can associated costs and resources be allocated to meet those goals. In addition, conventional line-item accounting needs to be replaced by program- or service-based full cost accounting to generate information about the costs incurred in providing particular public programs and services. In simple terms, full cost accounting ties all direct and indirect costs to certain programs and services, thereby providing timely, accurate estimates and actual cost information for public programs or services. Accounting for direct costs is straightforward because these costs are, by definition, obviously and physically related to the provision of a service or program, such as purchased goods and services, contracted support, and direct civil-service salaries that are incurred at time of the delivery of the service or program. Accounting for indirect costs can be more difficult, because they cover a broad range of infrastructure and organizational capabilities that support multiple programs. These indirect costs need to be linked to a given service on the basis of usage, internal service charges, or allocation rules. In contrast to conventional line-item budgets, all institutional overhead costs, such as civil-service salaries, capital costs, and the use of infrastructure and support services, should be associated with benefiting programs. The use of full cost management, budgeting, and accounting promotes incentives for more cost-efficient administrative performance and greater accountability regarding the use of taxpayer resources. A result-oriented budget presents revenues and expenditures in a format that enhances community understanding of the services that the government will provide and establishes an informed basis for decisions on priority programs. Because the development of such budgeting systems is costly and accounting standards should be comparable across the country (and preferably even across countries), the central government—in particular, finance departments—typically plays an important role in the design and regulation of such systems. Subnational governments need to develop the capacity to execute their budgets within these frameworks.

A Simple Scorecard to Measure Decentralized Citizen-Centered Governance

Given the preceding conceptual considerations, the chapter next develops a scoring methodology to rank countries with regard to accountability and fiscal responsibility. The scorecard is purposely kept to a simple set of indicators designed to capture essential institutional differences in governance systems rather than make precise and absolute measurements. Although the aggregated scores for each of the dimensions broadly reflect strengths and weaknesses of particular systems, analyzing and interpreting the scores require careful consideration of the context in which the scorecard is applied.

This section applies the scoring system to a sample of 26 developing and transition countries. The sample is not random and was selected based on the availability and accessibility of necessary information. Although not representative in a statistical sense, the countries in the sample display a fairly wide range of different socioeconomic contexts. The real per capita gross domestic product (GDP) ranges from US$946.50 in Nigeria to US$15,614.80 in the Czech Republic. Country size varies by a similar magnitude, from India, with a population of more than 1 billion, to Albania, with a population of 3.2 million. Geographically, the sample is fairly widespread, including nine countries in Africa, eight countries in Asia, seven countries in Europe, and three countries in Latin America. The sample represents various types of political systems. Nine countries are commonly classified as federal systems, and 18 as unitary systems. Also, 5 parliamentary systems and 21 presidential systems are in the sample. Country scores are assigned on the basis of available research papers and country reports from various sources. The sources for each country are reported in table 8A.2 in annex 8A.

Accountability Scores

As can be seen from table 8.1, five indicators of particular institutional qualities are used to assess the level of accountability in the sampled countries.

The first two indicators simply record whether key officials in subnational governments are subject to regular elections. First, the scoring system looks at whether elected councils exist at subnational levels. A country receives a score of 3 if there are elected councils and a score of 1 if there are none. Second, the scoring system examines whether the heads of the executive of subnational governments are elected (directly through popular vote or indirectly through elected councils) or appointed by higher levels, assigning a score of 1 to countries that have appointed mayors and a score of 3 to countries that subject mayors to electoral control. The third indicator assigns scores according to the level of voter mobilization. Because no reliable cross-country data are available on voter turnout in subnational elections, the scorecard uses participation rates in the last national elections as a proxy for the general political mobilization that prevails in a given country. There are three possibilities for scoring this indicator. Countries receive a score of 2 if the turnout rate is in the range of half a standard deviation below or above the mean, a score of 1 if it is below that range, and a score of 3 if it is above. Fourth, a general measure of political freedom is included, based on the Freedom House index for 2002. Again, countries receive a score of 2 within the range of half a standard deviation above or below the mean,

TABLE 8.1 Accountability Indicators

Indicator	Scores
Elected councils?	Yes = 3
	No = 1
Elected key executives?	Yes = 3
	No = 1
Voter turnout?	High = 3
	Medium = 2
	Low = 1
Restrictions on electoral competition and political freedom?	High = 3
	Medium = 2
	Low = 1
Direct citizen participation in decision making?	High = 3
	Medium = 2
	Low = 1

Source: Authors' design.

a score of 1 below that range, and a score of 3 above that range. The last indicator assigns scores depending on the level of citizen participation (low = 1, medium = 2, high = 3). The information comes from country assessments based on the most recent available information. Overall scores are estimated as the sum of the individual scores divided by the number of indicators. Cumulative scores range from 1 to 3. Using the scoring system described, the accountability scores presented in figure 8.2 and table 8.2 are assigned.

Systematic information on the specific accountability systems at the subnational levels is particularly scarce, but scattered evidence suggests wide variation in the institutional setup with regard to both electoral systems and division of powers between councils and executive branches of government, thus leading to varying accountability outcomes. Not surprisingly, at the lower end of the spectrum are countries with relatively restricted political systems. In these systems, key executives in the local administration typically remain appointed by and accountable to the higher levels of government, and elections play only a limited ritual role in local government. In Mozambique, elected councils (*autarquias*) were established only in selected urban areas. Apart from these *autarquias*, all local authorities in Mozambique remain integral parts of the national government, with mayors nominated

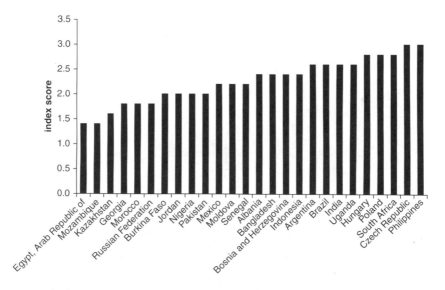

Source: Authors' assessment based on various sources as specified in annex table 8A.2.

FIGURE 8.2 Accountability

TABLE 8.2 Accountability Scores

Country	Score	Elected local council members	Elected heads of local government	Voter turnout (national elections percentage)	Political freedom (Freedom House Index)	Direct participation
Egypt, Arab Republic of	1.4	Yes	No	Low	Low	Low
Mozambique	1.4	No	No	Medium	Medium	Low
Kazakhstan	1.6	Yes	No	Medium	Low	Low
Georgia	1.8	Yes	No	Medium	Medium	Low
Morocco	1.8	Yes	No	Medium	Medium	Low
Russian Federation	1.8	Yes	No	Medium	Medium	Low
Burkina Faso	2.0	Yes	Yes	Low	Medium	Low
Jordan	2.0	Yes	Yes	Low	Medium	Low
Nigeria	2.0	Yes	Yes	Low	Medium	Low
Pakistan	2.0	Yes	Yes	Medium	Low	Low
Mexico	2.2	Yes	Yes	Low	High	Medium
Moldova	2.2	Yes	Yes	Medium	Medium	Low
Senegal	2.2	Yes	Yes	Low	High	Low
Albania	2.4	Yes	Yes	High	Medium	Low
Bangladesh	2.4	Yes	Yes	Medium	Medium	Medium

				High	Medium	Low
Bosnia and Herzegovina	2.4	Yes	No (Republika Srpska) Yes (Federation of Bosnia and Herzegovina)	High	Medium	Low
Indonesia	2.4	Yes	Yes	High	Medium	Medium
Argentina	2.6	Yes	Yes	High	Medium	Medium
Brazil	2.6	Yes	Yes	Low	High	High
India	2.6	Yes	Yes	Medium	High	Low
Uganda	2.6	Yes	Yes	High	Medium	Medium
Hungary	2.8	Yes	Yes	Medium	High	High
Poland	2.8	Yes	Yes	Medium	High	High
South Africa	2.8	Yes	Yes	High	Medium	High
Czech Republic	3.0	Yes	Yes	High	High	High
Philippines	3.0	Yes	Yes	High	High	High

Sources: Authors' assessment based on various sources as specified in annex table 8A.2.

by and accountable to the provincial governors. In Kazakhstan, legislative branches of oblast and rayon governments (*maslikhats*) are elected, but local and regional administrations are headed by centrally appointed executives (*akims*). The Russian Federation has experienced ebbs and flows of political decentralization: federal atrophy under President Boris Yeltsin's second term was followed by a renewed drive to recentralize under President Vladimir Putin, which in 2004 culminated in the replacement of gubernatorial elections in all of Russia's regions by the direct appointment of governors by Moscow (subject to nominal approval by local parliaments). Under such systems, local administrations often face opposing incentives and pressures from locally elected politicians and upper levels of governments, resulting in constrained direct local accountability.

Another class of systems with limited accountability is characterized by the presence of elected representatives whose influence on government actions is obstructed by countervailing institutions. In the medium group are countries that have established wide-ranging electoral control and accountability systems at subnational levels, but where institutions are still relatively weak. For example, Pakistan, while introducing elections at various levels of governments as part of its decentralization policy in 2001, has relied mostly on indirect elections for key officials in the local government. Mayors (district *nazims*) are indirectly elected by an electoral college made up of lower-level council members in the district. The indirect electoral system combined with a rather clientelistic electoral environment undermines the political accountability of *nazims*. Similar problems hold in Burkina Faso, where the mayor (*maire*) of the commune is indirectly elected by the *conseil municipal*, and in Indonesia, where the decentralization laws of 1999 empowered local elected councils (*Dewan Perwakilan Rakyat Daerah*) to appoint a head of regions (*bupati* or governor) and oversee the local administration. Under Indonesia's closed-list system, because citizens voted only for a party list of candidates in the 1999 general election, council members were primarily accountable to their parties (that decided the list places). Because these parties, in turn, largely lacked broad-based representative policy platforms, council members were mostly disconnected from their communities. Indonesia's recent electoral reforms in 2004 have introduced direct elections of the head of the executive, which are hoped to place the executive under more direct electoral pressure.

In the top group are countries that have experienced sustained democratization processes and established functioning representative structures at subnational levels. India's constitution provides for elected legislatures at the state level. States use different electoral systems; council members can be selected through a combination of direct election, indirect election, and nomination. The governors are indirectly elected by these councils. India has also had elected *panchayats* (councils) at various levels of substate government, but not until the 1990s did these councils gain constitutional status, making mandatory for all states a three-tiered (village, block, and district) system of *panchayats* with directly elected representatives. At the same time, these councils were provided with increased funding and increased responsibilities to support their communities. Although there are great cross-jurisdictional differences in the effectiveness of these institutions, they have proven to increase overall accountability during the past decade. Similarly, in the Philippines, local government acts introduced popular elections for both mayors and councils. Electoral competition and increased citizen participation made local authorities more accountable to citizens by increasing the political costs of inefficient and inadequate public decisions. As a result, local governments started enhancing local capacity for improved service delivery. In South Africa, a mixed electoral system is used at the local level, combining proportional representation and the "first-past-the-post" system. Half the seats in a municipal council are elected by proportional representation. Representatives from wards (subdistricts) fill the remaining council seats through election of individual candidates where the candidate who receives the most votes gets the council seat. Accordingly, each voter has two votes in the local government elections: one under the proportional representation system and one for the ward in which he or she lives. The elected council is responsible for developing policies and bylaws, approving budgets for the municipality, and electing the mayor. Although mayors in South Africa, as in Burkina Faso and Indonesia, are not directly accountable to the electorate, South Africa presents a counterfactual. It shows that the system of indirect accountability and continuous oversight can translate into higher accountability if electoral incentives and downward accountability of council members are functioning properly.

Overall, accountability structures are evolving in local governments around the world, predominantly in representative forms of local governance with regular electoral control. However, the political and electoral systems that are used at the local levels show significant institutional variation. Although most local governments do have some form of separation of powers between councils and mayors, the distribution of authority and the level of oversight, as well as the electoral systems used to constitute governments, differ widely. These essentially political incentives play a crucial role in structuring the environment of local administrations in a way that is conducive to citizen-centered governance and high service delivery performance.

Fiscal Responsibility Scores

As can be seen from table 8.3, five indicators of particular institutional qualities are used to assess the level of accountability in the sampled countries.

The first indicator is based on the subnational share in total public expenditures, a standard measure for the degree of fiscal decentralization used in the empirical literature. Although this measure does not fully reflect information on the distribution of decision-making authority between the levels of government, it provides a useful proxy for the relative level of countries' fiscal decentralization. Because the coverage of this indicator has restrictions, the measure partially relies on qualitative assessments based on country reports.

The second indicator captures variation in the assignment of authority for primary education, health, and infrastructure expenditures. The three sectors are treated in one indicator because most countries score equally with regard to all three. *Education* refers to primary education, and key responsibilities typically include authority over hiring primary school teachers and paying their salaries, determining curriculum, financing the program, and maintaining schooling infrastructure. *Infrastructure* deals with primary authority over local road construction—which level of government decides what roads are built and finances their construction. Three scores are possible,

TABLE 8.3 Fiscal Responsibility Indicators

Indicator	Scores
Subnational share in public expenditures?	High = 3 Medium = 2 Low = 1
Expenditure responsibility for education, health, and infrastructure?	High = 3 Medium = 2 Low = 1
Revenue-raising autonomy of subnational governments?	High = 3 Medium = 2 Low = 1
Administrative autonomy of subnational governments?	High = 3 Medium = 2 Low = 1
Result-oriented management system, including performance budgeting?	High = 3 Medium = 2 Low = 1

Source: Authors' design.

depending on the level of clarity in the assignment of functions to different levels of government. First, if authority resides primarily with the central government, the country receives a score of 1. Second, if authority is shared between the central and subnational governments, the score is 2. Third, if authority is primarily held by subnational governments, the score is 3.

The third indicator is about the level of revenue-raising autonomy of subnational governments (that is, whether subnational governments have the authority to raise their own resources either through local taxes and user fees or through access to capital markets). Again, three possibilities exist for scoring this variable.

The fourth indicator captures variation in the level of administrative decentralization, including the authority to hire and fire civil servants and to determine their salaries. The country scores 1 if these authorities are exclusively national, 2 if they are shared among levels of government, and 3 if they are exclusively vested in subnational governments.

The fifth indicator refers to the prevalence of result-oriented management frameworks at the subnational level. The country scores 1 if management systems are described as primarily focused on management of inputs and rule compliance. The score is 2 when transformation of subnational management frameworks increasingly emphasizes results in the preparation and implementation of local budgets and policies, but the general control environment still relies heavily on input and ex ante controls. The score is 3 when subnational governments successfully pursue modern public management techniques, with high levels of managerial flexibility and result accountability.

As with accountability systems, vast differences exist across countries in the way intergovernmental fiscal relations and administrative systems work. During the past two decades, many countries have witnessed major shifts in the assignment of expenditure responsibilities, and subnational governments are increasingly involved in providing public services in the education, health, and infrastructure sectors, but the level of decentralization varies significantly across the sample. The share of consolidated subnational expenditures in total public spending varies from 9 percent in Senegal to over 52 percent in Argentina. These differences are also reflected in the assignment of responsibilities in service sectors. Regarding basic education provision, for instance, at one extreme of the spectrum are countries such as Georgia or Mozambique that assign almost all tasks to the central government, whereas at the other extreme are countries such as Hungary that assign almost all tasks to local governments and schools (see figure 8.3 and table 8.4).

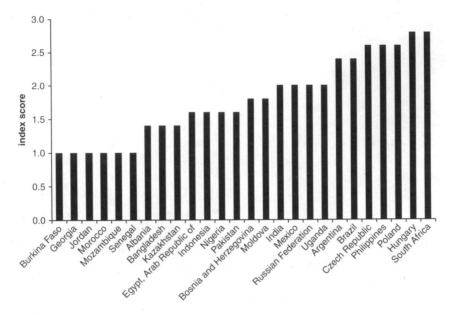

Source: Authors' assessment based on various sources as specified in annex table 8A.2.

FIGURE 8.3 Fiscal Responsibility

Also, on the revenue side, systems are characterized by different institutional arrangements. In a number of countries, subnational governments control significant revenue sources. In addition to property tax, South Africa has assigned significant nonproperty taxing powers to subnational governments, including a payroll and turnover tax—although subnationals hesitate to apply these taxes in practice—and has granted local governments some borrowing powers. In Uganda, local governments generate large parts of their revenue from a graduated personal tax. In Hungary, besides assigning own-source tax and nontax revenues to municipalities, the local government act of 1990 placed virtually no limits on municipal borrowing. Municipalities were able to borrow at whatever terms the council would approve. Because this system led to excessive borrowing and a series of municipal defaults and national bailouts, the Hungarian government in 1996 enacted a law on municipal bankruptcy and debt restructuring that allowed the national government to assume authority over municipal financial management in case of default.

In contrast, in many countries the assignment of adequate revenue sources has been lagging the decentralization of expenditures. Indonesia's

TABLE 8.4 Fiscal Responsibility Scores

Country	Score	Share of subnational in total expenditures	Subnational responsibility for education, health, and infrastructure	Revenue-raising autonomy	Administrative autonomy	Result-oriented management
Burkina Faso	1.0	Low	Low	Low	Low	Low
Georgia	1.0	Low	Low	Low	Low	Low
Jordan	1.0	Low	Low	Low	Low	Low
Morocco	1.0	Low	Low	Low	Low	Low
Mozambique	1.0	Low	Low	Low	Low	Low
Senegal	1.0	Low	Low	Low	Low	Low
Albania	1.4	Medium	Medium	Low	Low	Low
Bangladesh	1.4	Medium	Medium	Low	Low	Low
Kazakhstan	1.4	Medium	Medium	Low	Low	Low
Egypt, Arab Republic of	1.6	Medium	Medium	Low	Medium	Low
Indonesia	1.6	Medium	Medium	Low	Medium	Low
Nigeria	1.6	Medium	Medium	Low	Medium	Low
Pakistan	1.6	Medium	Medium	Medium	Low	Low
Bosnia and Herzegovina	1.8	Medium	Medium	Medium	Medium	Low
Moldova	1.8	Medium	Medium	Medium	Medium	Low
India	2.0	High	Medium	Medium	Medium	Low
Mexico	2.0	Medium	Medium	Medium	Medium	Medium
Russian Federation	2.0	High	Medium	Medium	Medium	Low
Uganda	2.0	Medium	Medium	Medium	Medium	Medium
Argentina	2.4	High	High	Medium	Medium	Medium
Brazil	2.4	Medium	High	High	Medium	Medium

(continued)

TABLE 8.4 Fiscal Responsibility Scores (*continued*)

Country	Score	Share of subnational in total expenditures	Subnational responsibility for education, health, and infrastructure	Revenue-raising autonomy	Administrative autonomy	Result-oriented management
Czech Republic	2.6	Medium	Medium	High	High	High
Philippines	2.6	Medium	High	Medium	High	High
Poland	2.6	Medium	Medium	High	High	High
Hungary	2.8	Medium	High	High	High	High
South Africa	2.8	High	High	High	Medium	High

Sources: Authors' assessment based on various sources as specified in annex table 8A.2.

decentralization policy, for instance, was primarily driven by the devolution of expenditure responsibilities, but the central government has retained control over all significant tax bases, including property taxes. Although the decentralization of expenditures allows subnationals some of the benefits of decentralization, such as lower-cost production, informational advantages, and matching of services with local demand, reaping substantial benefits from fiscal decentralization requires the devolution of the power to tax. If local tax rates are flexible, they can signal the costs of local services at least at the margin, and local residents can choose the level of services they desire. Moreover, if service delivery is more closely linked to local tax payments, citizens face greater incentives to monitor government performance and demand fiscal accountability from local governments.

Although all countries use transfers to finance subnational government operations, they use different institutional mechanisms to allocate funds across jurisdictions. For example, in India, Pakistan, and South Africa, allocations are based on the recommendations of periodic finance commissions, whereas Russia's, Indonesia's, and the Philippines' transfer systems rely on formula-based approaches. Both formula- and commission-based systems have in common that they attempt to insulate distributive decisions from regional political pressure for transfers. Although the experience shows that regional lobbyism will not vanish, but instead will focus on determining technical elements of the distribution (formulas), both mechanisms have the capacity to ward off frequent, politically motivated changes in the distribution. In contrast, in a number of countries with weaker institutions, transfers continue to be allocated on the basis of ad hoc methods with greater bureaucratic discretion. For example, in Senegal, the Ministry of Economy and Finance and the Local Government Bureau (Direction des Collectivités Locales) are responsible for the division of transfers to municipalities. These institutions determine the overall level of resources and mediate all pressures for transfers to subnational government. These ad hoc systems leave considerable room for debate and lobbying over the allocation as well as short-term adjustments, depending on the overall budgetary situation of the central government.

Information on subnational budgeting systems is scarce. Although a number of countries have initiated budgeting reforms moving toward more result- or performance-based systems, the overall picture suggests that these reforms are lagging. South Africa's reform policy, which is considered best practice for a developing country, was initiated through the 1999 Public Finance Management Act, which moved the system incrementally from line-item to program-based budgeting. In the Czech Republic, Hungary, and

Poland, compliance with the European System of Accounts 1995 regulations required a move from cash-based to accrual budgeting for all public organizations along with more result-oriented performance measurement. In the Philippines, performance indicators for government programs are linked to allocated budget envelopes, reported in budget annexes at the start of each budget year, and audited at the end of each fiscal year. Argentina has introduced similar reforms at the national level; however, subnational governments have been reluctant to adopt these standards because the federal constitution gives them authority to define their own budgets and accounting systems, leading to differences in public accounts across states. In other countries, reform attempts remain scattered, or countries simply lack the preconditions and capacity for planning, executing, and auditing to implement comprehensive performance-based systems.

Overall, Brazil, the Czech Republic, Hungary, the Philippines, Poland, and South Africa are in many respects the furthest ahead in implementing decentralized and result-oriented fiscal systems. These countries have successfully implemented fiscal decentralization reforms, increased the autonomy of subnational governments, and encouraged institutional reforms toward performance-based budgeting and greater civic participation. Subnational governments in these countries typically enjoy a great degree of authority over administrative matters and control the subnational civil service. In the medium range are countries that have sustained fiscal decentralization reforms but in which administrative decentralization has lagged and upper levels of government continue to control important matters, including substantial parts of the budgeting process and decisions to hire and fire personnel. A number of countries in this group, including Albania, Indonesia, and Nigeria, are making important efforts to catch up. In these countries, a combination of increased resources and authorities at subnational levels has resulted in higher levels of civic participation, which, in turn, increasingly brings a focus on results into government operations. In contrast, most countries at the lower end of the spectrum have only very recently begun to consider strategies for moving toward more decentralized and result-oriented fiscal systems.

Conclusion

This chapter has suggested citizen-centered governance as a new approach to public sector reforms. The paradigm is based on a comprehensive understanding of the incentive environment of public organizations, including institutions for political interest mediation, such as elections, representative government structures, and community participation, as well as fiscal incentives and result-oriented management systems. Among them, all these elements and interactions shape the incentive structure of governments and bring about performance outcomes. On the basis of these broad conceptual underpinnings, this chapter has developed a scorecard to measure specific institutional qualities of different governance systems. The scorecard purposely focuses on a simple set of indicators designed to capture essential institutional differences in governance systems rather than on precise and absolute measurements. This scorecard was applied to a set of 26 developing and transition countries.

The outcomes of this exercise are manifold. Although the past two decades have seen remarkable progress as a majority of countries have initiated reforms of their intergovernmental fiscal relations, significant differences across countries with regard to both fiscal systems and accountability institutions were revealed. Overall, the Czech Republic, Hungary, the Philippines, Poland, and South Africa are in many respects the closest to accountable, decentralized, and result-oriented governance systems. A number of countries that have started reforms more recently, including Indonesia, Nigeria, and Uganda, have made significant advances and are catching up. In contrast, in a small number of countries, including Burkina Faso, the Arab Republic of Egypt, Kazakhstan, and Morocco, reforms started much later and remain incomplete.

The scorecard also revealed differences in various elements of citizen-centered governance. Most countries have implemented wide-ranging reforms and have both fiscally decentralized and politically democratized their governance systems. Today, most local governments in the developing world have locally elected mayors and representative councils; they command significant fiscal resources and provide important services, including primary education, health, and infrastructure, to their communities. This authority has created increasing demand-side pressures and incentives for governments to be responsive as more organized and politically active communities turn to their local governments to demand public services. These processes are necessarily complex and far from complete in most countries because these institutions remain relatively weak; however, they are important changes that need to be applauded.

After the wave of fiscal decentralization and political devolution, a number of second-generation reforms have moved into focus. First, a typical weakness in a number of countries is incomplete administrative decentralization; subnational governments continue to lack the power to determine the size and structure of their civil service. Only if subnational governments have influence over the career development of their civil servants can those governments develop the incentives and meritocratic systems necessary for effective public services and performance at subnational levels. Second, result-based management systems are still lagging in most countries, with the notable exception of South Africa and the Central European transition countries. Given the subnational responsibility for managing increasingly large budgets, an important step to nurture citizen-centered governance would be reforms of subnational budgeting and auditing systems and practices toward performance-based systems that link resource allocations to outcomes.

Annex: Country Sample

TABLE 8A.1   Country Sample

Country name	GDP at purchasing power parity per capita (current international 2002 $)	Population size	Freedom House Political Freedom Index 2002	Voter turnout (last election reported 2005)
Asia				
Bangladesh	1,695.50	135.7	4	56
India	2,674.20	1,048.6	2	60.7
Indonesia	3,177.90	211.8	3	88.3
Georgia	2,254.80	5.2	4	60.6
Kazakhstan	5,896.90	14.9	6	64.3
Pakistan	2,017.60	144.9	6	41.8
Philippines	4,172.10	79.9	2	69.6
Africa				
Burkina Faso	1,109.70	11.8	4	38.3
Egypt, Arab Republic of	3,814.00	66.4	6	24.6
Jordan	4,224.20	5.2	5	29.9
Morocco	3,810.08	29.6	5	57.6
Mozambique	1,047.20	18.4	3	66.4
Nigeria	946.50	133.2	4	47.6
Senegal	1,591.80	10.0	2	42.6
South Africa	10,135.50	45.3	1	85.5
Uganda	1,403.20	24.6	5	50.6
Europe				
Albania	4,276.20	3.2	3	85.3

(continued)

TABLE 8A.1 Country Sample (*continued*)

Country name	GDP at purchasing power parity per capita (current international 2002 $)	Population size	Freedom House Political Freedom Index 2002	Voter turnout (last election reported 2005)
Bosnia and Herzegovina	5,762.20	4.1	4	82.8
Czech Republic	15,614.80	10.2	1	82.8
Hungary	13,920.50	10.2	1	64.1
Moldova	1,476.70	4.3	3	60.5
Poland	10,706.60	38.2	1	52.3
Russian Federation	8,308.80	144.1	5	55
Latin America				
Argentina	11,085.80	36.5	3	70.6
Brazil	7,776.50	174.5	2	47.9
Mexico	9,005.10	100.8	2	48.1

Sources: Various sources as specified in annex table 8A.2.

TABLE 8A.2 Sources for Country Sample

Country	Sources
Albania	Gurraj and others 2003; Mark and Nayyar-Stone 2002; World Bank 2003a
Argentina	Dillinger and Webb 1999; Tommasi, Saiegh, and Sanguinetti 2001
Bangladesh	Boex, Gudgeon, and Shotton 2002
Bosnia and Herzegovina	Jókay 2003
Brazil	Afonso 2002; Dillinger and Webb 1999; World Bank 2002
Burkina Faso	Ndegwa 2003
Czech Republic	OECD 2001a
Egypt, Arab Republic of	Sewell 2004
Georgia	Mark and Nayyar-Stone 2002; Shergelashvili 2003
Hungary	Fekete and others 2003; Kopanyi, Wetzel, and El Daher 2005; Mark and Nayyar-Stone 2002
India	Bahl and others 2005
Indonesia	World Bank 2005
Jordan	Sewell 2004

(continued)

TABLE 8A.2 Sources for Country Sample (*continued*)

Country	Sources
Kazakhstan	ADB 2001; USAID 2003
Mexico	Giugale and Webb 2000; Trillo, Cayeros, and González 2002; Webb and Gonzalez 2003
Moldova	Chiriac and others 2003
Morocco	Sarrouh 2003
Mozambique	Ndegwa 2003
Nigeria	Akindele, Olaopa, and Obiyan 2002; Alm and Boex 2002
Pakistan	Cheema, Khwaja, and Qadir 2006; Keefer, Narayan, and Vishwanath 2003; World Bank 2004
Philippines	Guevara 2004; World Bank 2003c, 2005
Poland	Kowalczyk 2003; OECD 2001b
Russian Federation	Martinez-Vasquez 2001
Senegal	Dickovick 2004; IMF 2005
South Africa	Smoke 2000
Uganda	Smoke 2000; World Bank 2003b

Note

1. Per capita GDP is positively correlated with both measures of political openness and measures of administrative performance. This result is not surprising. Governments in the industrial world are typically both more democratic and more effective.

References

ADB (Asian Development Bank). 2001. *Technical Assistance to Kazakhstan for Governance Study and Capacity Building for Administrative Reform*. Manila: ADB.

Afonso, José Roberto Rodrigues. 2002. "Decentralization and Budget Management of Local Government in Brazil." Brasília: Banco Nacional de Desenvolvimento Económico e Social.

Agrawal, Arun, and Jesse C. Ribot. 1999. "Accountability in Decentralisation: A Framework with South Asian and West African Cases." *Journal of Developing Areas* 33 (4): 473–502.

Akindele, S. T., O. R. Olaopa, and A. Sat. Obiyan. 2002. "Fiscal Federalism and Local Government Finance in Nigeria: An Examination of Revenue Rights and Fiscal Jurisdiction." *International Review of Administrative Sciences* 68 (4): 557–77.

Alm, James, and Jameson Boex. 2002. "An Overview of Intergovernmental Fiscal Relations and Subnational Finance in Nigeria." International Studies Working Paper 0201, Andrew Young School of Policy Studies, Georgia State University, Atlanta.

Andrews, Matthew. 2005a. "Performance Based Budgeting Reform: Progress, Problems, and Pointers." In *Fiscal Management*, ed. Anwar Shah, 31–70. Washington, DC: World Bank.

———. 2005b. "Voice Mechanisms and Local Government Fiscal Outcomes: How Do Civic Pressure and Participation Influence Public Accountability?" In *Public Expenditure Analysis*, ed. Anwar Shah, 217–48. Washington, DC: World Bank.

Bahl, Roy, Eunice Heredia-Ortiz, Jorge Martinez-Vazquez, and Mark Rider. 2005. "India: Fiscal Condition of the States, International Experience, and Options for Reform." Working Paper 05-14, vols. 1 and 2, Andrew Young School of Public Policy, Georgia State University, Atlanta.

Beck, Thorsten, George Clark, Alberto Groff, Philip Keefer, and Patrick Walsh. 2001. "New Tools in Comparative Political Economy: The Database of Political Institutions." *World Bank Economic Review* 15 (1): 165–76.

Bird, Richard M., and Michael Smart. 2001. "Intergovernmental Fiscal Transfers: Some Lessons from International Experience." Paper prepared for the Symposium on Intergovernmental Transfers in Asian Countries: Issues and Practices, Asian Tax and Public Policy Program, Hitosubashi University, Tokyo, February 21.

Boex, Jamie, Peter Gudgeon, and Roger Shotton. 2002. *Role of UNDP in Promoting Local Governance and Decentralization in Bangladesh.* New York: United Nations Development Programme.

Cheema, Ali, Asim Ijaz Khwaja, and Adnan Qadir. 2006. "Local Government Reform in Pakistan: Context, Content, and Causes." In *Decentralization and Local Governance in Developing Countries: A Comparative Perspective*, ed. Pranab Bardhan and Dilip Mookherjee, 257–84. Cambridge, MA: MIT Press.

Chiriac, Liubomir, Igor Munteanu, Victor Popa, and Victor Mocanu. 2003. "Local Government in Moldova." In *Stabilization of Local Governments*, ed. Emilia Kandeva, 290–349. Budapest: Open Society Institute, Local Government and Public Service Reform Initiative.

Crook, Richard, and James Manor. 2000. "Democratic Decentralization." OED Working Paper 11, Operations Evaluation Department, World Bank, Washington, DC.

Dahl, Robert A. 1998. *On Democracy.* New Haven, CT: Yale University Press.

Diamond, Jack. 2003. "Performance Budgeting: Managing the Reform Process." Working Paper 03/33, International Monetary Fund, Washington, DC.

Dickovick, J. Tyler. 2004. "Centralism and 'Decentralization' in Unitary States: A Comparative Analysis of Peru and Senegal." Woodrow Wilson School of Public and International Affairs, Princeton University, Princeton, NJ.

Dillinger, William, and Steven B. Webb. 1999. "Fiscal Management in Federal Democracies: Argentina and Brazil." Policy Research Working Paper 2121, World Bank, Washington, DC.

Fearon, James D. 1999. "Electoral Accountability and the Control of Politicians: Selecting Good Types versus Sanctioning Poor Performance." In *Democracy, Accountability, and Representation*, ed. Adam Przeworski, Susan C. Stokes, and Bernard Manin, 55–97. Cambridge, U.K.: Cambridge University Press.

Fekete, Éva G., Mihály Lados, Edit Pfeil, and Zsolt Szoboszlai. 2003. "Size of Local Governments, Local Democracy, and Local Service Delivery in Hungary." In *Consolidation or Fragmentation? The Size of Local Governments in Central and Eastern Europe*, ed. Pawel Swianiewicz, 31–100. Budapest: Open Society Institute, Local Government and Public Service Reform Initiative.

Freedom House. 2002. *Freedom in the World Report 2002.* New York: Freedom House.

Giugale, Marcelo M., and Steven B. Webb. 2000. *Achievements and Challenges of Fiscal Decentralization: Lessons from Mexico.* Washington, DC: World Bank.

Guevara, Milwida M. 2004. "The Fiscal Decentralization Process in the Philippines: Lessons from Experience." Graduate School of Economics, Hitotsubashi University, Tokyo.

Gurraj, Alma, Artan Hoxha, Auron Pasha, Genc Ruli, Qamil Talka, and Irma Tanku. 2003. "Local Government Budgeting: Albania." In *Local Government Budgeting, Part II*, 103–53. Budapest: Open Society Institute, Local Government and Public Service Reform Initiative.

Huther, Jeff, and Anwar Shah. 1998. "Applying a Simple Measure of Good Governance to the Debate on Fiscal Decentralization." Policy Research Working Paper 1894, World Bank, Washington, DC.

IMF (International Monetary Fund). 2005. "Senegal: Selected Issues and Statistical Appendix." Country Report 05/155, IMF, Washington, DC.

Jókay, Charles. 2003. "Local Government in Bosnia and Herzegovina." In *Stabilization of Local Governments*, ed. Emilia Kandeva, 90–140. Budapest: Open Society Institute, Local Government and Public Service Reform Initiative.

Kaufmann, Daniel, Aart Kraay, and Massimo Mastruzzi. 2005. *Governance Matters IV: New Data, New Challenges*. Washington, DC: World Bank.

Keefer, Philip E., and Stuti Khemani. 2003. "The Political Economy of Public Expenditures." World Bank, Washington, DC.

Keefer, Philip E., Ambar Narayan, and Tara Vishwanath. 2003. "The Political Economy of Decentralization in Pakistan." World Bank, Washington, DC.

Khemani, Stuti, Shantayanan Devarajan, Junaid Ahmad, and Shekhar Shah. 2005. "Decentralization and Service Delivery." Policy Research Working Paper 3603, World Bank, Washington, DC.

Kopanyi, Mihaly, Deborah Wetzel, and Samir El Daher. 2005. *Intergovernmental Finance in Hungary: A Decade of Experience 1990–2000*. Washington, DC: World Bank.

Kowalczyk, Andrzej. 2003. "Local Government in Poland." In *Decentralization: Experiments and Reform*, ed. Tamás M Horváth, 218–54. Budapest: Open Society Institute, Local Government and Public Service Reform Initiative.

Kunicova, Jana, and Susan Rose-Ackerman. 2001. "Electoral Rules as Constraints on Corruption: The Risks of Closed List Proportional Representation." Department of Political Sciences, Yale University, New Haven, CT.

Lizzeri, Alessandro, and Nicola Persico. 2001. "The Provision of Public Goods under Alternative Electoral Incentives." *American Economic Review* 91 (1): 225–39.

Manin, Bernard, Adam Przeworski, and Susan C. Stokes. 1999. "Elections and Representation." In *Democracy, Accountability, and Representation*, ed. Adam Przeworski, Susan C. Stokes, and Bernard Manin1–26. Cambridge, U.K.: Cambridge University Press.

Manor, James. 1997. *The Political Economy of Decentralization*. Washington, DC: World Bank.

Manor, James, and Richard Crook. 1998. *Democracy and Decentralization in South Asia and West Africa: Participation, Accountability and Performance*. Cambridge, U.K.: Cambridge University Press.

Mark, Katharine, and Ritu Nayyar-Stone. 2002. "Assessing the Benefits of Performance Management in Eastern Europe: Experience in Hungary, Albania, and Georgia." Urban Institute, Washington, DC.

Martinez-Vasquez, Jorge. 2001. *Russia's Transition to a New Federalism*. Washington, DC: World Bank.

Myerson, Roger. 1993. "Effectiveness of Electoral Systems for Reducing Government Corruption: A Game Theoretic Approach." *Games and Economic Behaviour* 5 (1): 118–32.

Ndegwa, Stephen N. 2003. "Decentralization in Africa: Emerging Trends and Progress." Finding Report 229, World Bank, Washington, DC.

OECD (Organisation for Economic Co-operation and Development). 2001a. "Fiscal Design across Levels of Government—Country Report: Czech Republic." OECD, Paris.

———. 2001b. "Fiscal Design across Levels of Government—Country Report: Poland." OECD, Paris.

Persson, Torsten, Gérard Roland, and Guido Tabellini. 1997. "Separation of Powers and Political Accountability." *Quarterly Journal of Economics* 112 (4): 1163–202.

Persson, Torsten, and Guido Tabellini. 2000. *Political Economics: Explaining Economic Policy.* Cambridge, MA: MIT Press.

Persson, Torsten, Guido Tabellini, and Francesco Trebbi. 2001. "Electoral Rules and Corruption." CESifo Working 416, Center for Economic Studies and Ifo Institute for Economic Research, Munich, Germany.

PRS Group. 2002. *International Country Risk Guide.* Rockville, MD: PRS Group.

Przeworski, Adam, Susan C. Stokes, and Bernard Manin. 1999. *Democracy, Accountability and Representation.* Cambridge, U.K.: Cambridge University Press.

Rodden, Jonathan. 2000. "The Dilemma of Fiscal Federalism: Hard and Soft Budget Constraints around the World." Massachusetts Institute of Technology, Cambridge, MA.

Sarrouh, Elissar. 2003. "The UNDP Role in Public Administration Reforms in the Arab Region." Paper prepared for the Expert Consultative Meeting on Public Administration and Public Accounting Development, with Stress on Electronic Tools, Beirut, July 1–3.

Schmitter, Phillippe, and Terry Lynn Karl. 1991. "What Democracy Is . . . and What It Is Not." *Journal of Democracy* 2 (3): 75–88.

Sewell, David. 2004. "Decentralization: Lessons from Other Middle Eastern Countries for Iraq." World Bank, Washington, DC.

Shah, Anwar. 2004. "Fiscal Decentralization in Developing and Transition Economies: Progress, Problems, and the Promise." Policy Research Working Paper 3282, World Bank, Washington, DC.

Shah, Anwar, and Matthew Andrews. 2005. "Citizen-Centered Governance: A New Approach to Public Sector Reform." In *Public Expenditure Analysis,* ed. Anwar Shah, 153–82. Washington, DC: World Bank.

Shergelashvili, Tenghiz. 2003. "How Fiscal Issues Can Turn into Fiction the Concept of Local Government and Decentralisation." Association of Young Economists of Georgia, Tbilisi.

Smoke, Paul. 2000. "Fiscal Decentralization in East and Southern Africa: A Selective Review of Experience and Thoughts on Moving Forward." Paper prepared for the Conference on Fiscal Decentralization, International Monetary Fund, Washington, DC, November 20–21.

Tommasi, Marino, Sebastian Saiegh, and Pablo Sanguinetti. 2001. "Fiscal Federalism in Argentina: Policies, Politics, and Institutional Reform." *Economia* 1 (2): 147–201.

Trillo, Fausto Hernández, Alberto Díaz Cayeros, and Rafael Gamboa González. 2002. "Fiscal Decentralization in Mexico: The Bailout Problem." Research Network Working Paper R-447, Inter-American Development Bank, Washington, DC.

UNPAN (United Nations Online Network in Public Administration and Finance). 2000. *Responding to Citizens' Needs: Local Governance and Social Services for All*. Stockholm: UNPAN.

USAID (U.S. Agency for International Development). 2003. *Supporting Local Government Reforms in the Republic of Kazakhstan*. Almaty: USAID.

Webb, Steven B., and Christian Y. Gonzalez. 2003. "Bargaining for a New Fiscal Pact in Mexico." Policy Research Working Paper 3284, World Bank, Washington, DC.

World Bank. 2002. "Brazil: Issues in Fiscal Federalism." Report 22523-BR, World Bank, Washington DC.

———. 2003a. *Albania: Fiscal Decentralization Study*. Washington, DC: World Bank.

———. 2003b. *Decentralisation Policies and Practices: Case Study Uganda*. Washington, DC: World Bank.

———. 2003c. *Philippines—Improving Government Performance: Discipline, Efficiency, and Equity in Managing Public Resources*. Washington, DC: World Bank.

———. 2003d. *World Development Indicators*. Washington, DC: World Bank.

———. 2003e. *World Development Report 2004: Making Services Work for Poor People*. Washington, DC: World Bank.

———. 2004. *Devolution in Pakistan*. Washington, DC: World Bank.

———. 2005. *East Asia Decentralizes: Making Local Government Work*. Washington, DC: World Bank.

Index

Boxes, figures, notes, and tables are indicated by b, f, n, and t, respectively.

academic institutions, tax on, 196–97
accountability, 293, 294–98, 302–7
accounting, 300–301
administrative systems, 299–300
    administrative decentralization, 309,
        311–12t8.4
    administrative federalism, 28, 31, 73
    and subnational insolvency, 227–28,
        238n51, 239n53
adverse selection, 220
adverse shocks, 102
agency, and debt markets, 220–21,
    236n28
Argentina, Convertibility Law, 110–11
Australia, 33, 74n2
    central bank structure, 47, 48t1.4, 52
    constitutional provisions of, 22t1.3
    coordination of fiscal policy, 128
    division of power in international
        agreements, 62
    internal economic integration, 20–24
    internal economic union, 17
    legislated fiscal rules, 124–25b3.1
    selected institutional features of,
        21t1.2
autarky, 24

bailout policies, 126, 233, 237n32
balance-of-payments deficit, 35
balance of power, 84
Bank of Canada, 55

Bank of England, 111–12
bankruptcies, 226, 230, 237n34, 237n36,
    239n56
    municipal, 227–28, 238nn48–51,
        239nn53–54
    United States, 223, 227–28, 237n36,
        238nn48–50
banks and banking, 116–18, 137n2
    Brazil, 111, 112–13, 116, 137n1
    and legislated fiscal rules, 126–28
    See also central banks
Belgian federation, 16–17
best practices, 10, 32
beta convergence, 149, 157, 159t4.5, 161,
    164t4.6
block grants, 280, 284
bond markets, 215, 234n4
bonds, 215–16, 234nn4–5, 236n26
borrowing, 112–13
    Australia, 128
    Brazil, 116–18, 131–32
    for capital expenditures, 261–63
    China, 134
    Germany, 127–28
    municipal, 310
    red–light zone, 224–25, 238n4
    Switzerland, 127
    See also subnational borrowing
Brazil, 131–32
    banks and banking, 111, 112–13, 116,
        137n1

coordination of fiscal policy in,
129–33
debt service, 225, 237n42
ex ante regulations, 223–24, 237n37
and fiscal rules, 224, 237n41
harmonization of interregional
transactions, 195–96, 210nn3–5
infrastructure investment, 235n10
insolvency mechanisms, 227
legislated fiscal rules, 124–25b3.1
monetary policy, 116, 137n1
off-budget liabilities, 225–26
regional income disparities in, 160–61,
173f4A.3, 173t4A.3
and use of ICMS, 97
VATs, 129, 130, 194–95, 210nn1–2
Brigitte Bardot (Canada), 61, 66
budgeting systems, 313–14
Bundesbank, 47, 49f1.4, 113, 128
Bundesrat, 128
Burkina Faso, 306, 307
business taxes, as source of local
government revenues, 272

Canada, 33, 35, 62, 281
Blanchard-Katz analysis of regional
issues in, 42–44
business tax revenues, 272
central bank structure, 47, 48t1.4, 52
constitutional provisions of, 22t1.3
economic union of, 28–29
federal VAT, 196–98, 210nn6–8
and fiscal federalism, 86, 88
fiscal policies of, 55–57, 74n5, 126–67
geometry of macro region problems,
36–42
gold-standard analogy for transfers,
35–36, 74n2
income disparities in, 149–52
internal economic integration, 20–24,
25–26
NAFTA, 11, 12t1.1, 67–68
provincial level taxes, 197–98, 210n8
regional-international interface,
11–14
selected institutional features of,
21t1.2

trends in regional income disparities,
171f4A.1, 171t4A.1
as unified economic space, 27
Canada-U.S. Free Trade Agreement, 11,
12t1.1, 27
capital expenditures, 260–63, 282, 285
capital markets
access to, 237n32
development of, 100
captive riders, 64–65
central banks, 74
Brazil, 116, 137n1
China, 116–17
independence of, 111–13, 118
and monetary policy, 47–53
and price stability, 111–12
See also banks and banking
central governments
expenditures of, 287–88n4
and international agreements, 61–64
centralization, 85, 108, 117, 137n2
central sales tax (CST), India, 205–8,
212n24
CenVAT, 202–3, 211nn13–17
charities, tax on, 197
checks and balances, 296–97
Chile, trends in income disparities,
163–64
China
fiscal management in, 133–35
and infrastructure investment,
235n10
monetary policy, 116–18, 137n2
regional income inequalities in,
167–68, 178f4A.8, 178t4A.8,
179t4A.9, 180f4A.9
cities, internationalization of, 12t1.1, 82
citizen-centered governance
building blocks of
accountability, 294–98
fiscal responsibility, 298–301
overview, 292–94, 318n1
conclusions concerning, 314–16
scorecard of
accountability scores, 302–7
fiscal responsibility scores, 308–14
overview, 301

citizens
  citizen voters, 64–68
  and consumer sovereignty, 14t1.1,
    64–68, 81–82
  empowerment of link to information
    revolution, 80–81
  and globalization, 64–68
citizens' rights, 66, 103
clearinghouse mechanisms, European
    Union, 198–99, 208, 210n9
coefficient of variation (CV), 144–46,
    150t4.1, 152, 153–54t4.2
  trends in federal countries, 157,
    158f4.3a
  trends in unitary countries, 155–57,
    161, 162f4.4a
Colombia, 226
  debt service, 224, 237n42
  and fiscal rules, 224, 237n41
Commission of the European
    Communities, 198–99, 210n9
commodities, 195–96, 266
common market, 24f1.1, 25
communities, participation in
    governance of, 297–98
compensating value added tax (CVAT),
    201–2, 210–11nn10–11
competition
  and intergovernmental transfers,
    97–98
  interjurisdictional, 121
  knowledge and international
    competitiveness, 82
conditional grants, 276, 279t7.11, 280,
    282–83, 284, 288nn11–12
CONFAZ. See National Public Finance
    Council (CONFAZ), Brazil
confederalism, 16–17, 64–68
constitutions, 2, 16, 19, 113
  Brazil, 129–32
  comparison of constitutional
    approaches to securing economic
    union, 28–30
  comparison of provisions of in mature
    federations, 22–23t1.3
  and conclusions concerning internal
    economic integration, 32–34

and coordination of fiscal policies,
    127–28
and division of power in international
    agreements, 62–63
and federalism, 71–72
and free trade, 95–96
institutional weaknesses in, 119, 137n3
and internal economic integration,
    31–32
jurisdictional issues of, 228
and revenue sharing, 237n39
tax issues, 202, 203, 204
consumer sovereignty, 14t1.1, 64–68,
    81–82
contracting systems
  China, 133
  and debt discharge, 230–31, 239n55,
    239nn59–60
convergence, 147–49, 169–87
Convertibility Law, Argentina, 110–11
core services, 260, 285
corporate taxes, 269–70, 284
costs, of result-oriented management,
    300–301
countervailing duty (CVD), 203, 211n15
Courchene, Thomas J., xix, 1–76
cram-down power, 230, 239n56
credit ceilings, 117
credit markets, 218, 2325n14
  facilitating local access to, 99–100
  and municipal borrowing, 235n14
  private municipal, 236–37n31
creditors' rights, 222, 226, 237n34
credit rating agencies, 218
credit ratings, 74nn5, 99, 226
cross-border issues, 59–60, 199–200
Crow, John, 52
CST. See central sales tax (CST), India
currencies
  European, 54–55
  separate currency solutions, 38–39
current-account deficits, 35–36
customs union, 24f1.1, 25
CV. See coefficient of variation (CV)
CVAT. See compensating value added tax
    (CVAT)
CVD. See countervailing duty (CVD)

Database of Political Institutions, 294
data sources, for trends in regional
  income disparities, 188–89A4B
DBCPT. *See* destination-based central
  purchase tax (DBCPT)
debt
  debt-deficit guidelines, 53–54
  debt discharge, 230–31, 239n55,
    239nn59–60
  debt service, 220, 232
  markets in, 215, 220
  and rollover risks, 218, 219, 235n13
debt restructurings, 222, 224
  Brazil, 131–32
  and insolvency frameworks, 229
  United States, 227–28, 237n50
debt service ratio, 224, 237n42, 238n44
decentralization
  and allocation of taxes, 53
  China, 117, 137n2
  and decision making, 108
  and fiscal equalization, 99
  fiscal federalism as boon to fiscal
    prudence, 120–22
  and glocalization, 85–86
  and intergovernmental transfers,
    97–98
  and international agreements, 61–64
  and preservation of internal common
    markets, 95–96
  of taxation, 100
  and transfer payments, 101
decentralized fiscal systems, 3, 5, 6, 129
  building blocks of citizen-centered
    governance in
    accountability, 294–98
    fiscal responsibility, 298–301
    overview, 292–94, 318n1
  and central bank independence,
    112–15
  and fiscal performance, 114–15t3.1,
    136, 136f3.3
  and monetary policy, 118
  products of, 113
  scorecard of citizen-centered
    governance
    accountability scores, 302–7

  fiscal responsibility scores, 308–14
  overview, 301
decentralized legislative federalism, 73
decision making
  centralization of, 108
  and citizen voters, 64–68
  community participation in,
    297–98
  consumer sovereignty and democracy
    deficits, 81–82
  and decentralization, 108
  localization and regionalization of,
    101–2
defaults, 222, 226
deferred payment system, European
  Union, 199–200
deficits, 218–19
  debt-deficit guidelines, 53–54
democracy deficits
  and consumer sovereignty, 81–82
  and global confederalizing, 64–68
  and global regimes, 103–4
destination-based central purchase tax
  (DBCPT), 209–10, 212n25
developing countries
  building blocks of citizen-centered
    governance in
    accountability, 294–98
    fiscal responsibility, 298–301
    overview, 292–94, 318n1
  scorecard of citizen-centered
    governance
    accountability scores, 302–7
    fiscal responsibility scores,
      308–14
    overview, 301
  trends in regional disparities,
    173–77f4A.3–4A.7,
    173–77tt4A.3–4A.7
diplomacy, paradiplomacy, 59–61
discretionary grants, 279t7.11, 280
divergence hypothesis, 147–49
division of powers, in federal nations,
  61–64, 88–90
domestic economic unions, 30
dual federalism, 89–90
dynamic efficiency, 10, 46–47

ECB. *See* European Central Bank (ECB)
ECJ. *See* European Court of Justice (ECJ)
Eckardt, Sebastian, xix–xx, 6, 291–322
economic affairs, expenditures for, 249, 255–60
economic development, advanced stage of, 158, 189n4
economics
  decouplings of global economy, 79
  and federal-state shared rule, 89–90
  international nature of, 69–70
economic union, 24f1.1, 25
  comparison of constitutional approaches to securing, 28–30
  impediments to, 92
  and regional equity, 95–102
  See also internal economic union; international integration
education, 82
  authority for, 308, 311–12t8.4
  expenditures for as share of GDP, 256–57t7.4, 258
elections
  and accountability scores, 302–7
  electoral incentives, 295–96, 297
employment growth rates, 42–43
EMU. *See* European Monetary Union (EMU)
endogenous growth, 10
environmental issues
  environmental dumping, 31
  expenditures for environmental protection as share of GDP, 255–60
  and international trade agreements, 83
  and macro federalism, 57–58
environmental services, 287n3
equalization programs, 91
  Canada, 42, 45
  fiscal equalization, 99
  grants, 280–82
EU. *See* European Union (EU)
Eurofed, 47, 52, 55–56, 57
Europe *1992*, 26, 27, 29–30
European Central Bank (ECB), 54
European Court of Justice (ECJ), 66

European Monetary Union (EMU), 17, 44, 55
European System of Accounts, 314
European Union Central Bank, 110, 111
European Union (EU), 81, 111, 123, 126
  central bank structure, 47, 50–51t1.4, 52
  and confederalism, 16–17
  coordination of fiscal policy in, 128
  deferred payment system, 199–200
  democracy deficits and globalization, 65
  division of power in international agreements, 63–64
  internal economic integration, 20–24
  and regional-international interface, 60–61
  stabilization of, 45–46
  and transfer dependency, 35
  VAT in, 198–200, 210n9
ex ante regulations, and subnational borrowing, 221–22, 224, 231–34, 236–37nn31–37, 237nn39–42, 238n44
exchange rates, 38, 45–46, 110
exclusive powers, 28
expenditures, 53
  of central governments, 287–88n4
  expenditure-revenue imbalances, 218
  subnational share of, 308–9, 311–12t8.4
  See also local government expenditures; subnational borrowing
exports
  DBCPT, 209–10, 212n25
  deferred payment systems, 199–200
  little boat model of dual VAT, 200–202, 210–11nn10–11
  tax on, 195
  See also trade
ex post insolvency mechanisms, 221–23, 226–31, 237n33, 237n36, 238nn45–46, 238–39nn48–56, 239nn59–60
  conclusions concerning, 231–34
external shocks, 83–84

federal constitutions. *See* constitutions
federalism. *See* federal systems
Federal Republic of Germany
(FRG), 149
federal-state shared rule, 89–90
federal systems, 1–2, 11, 107
categories of, 72–73
decentralized legislative
federations, 73
division of powers in, 61–64, 88–90
dual federalism, 89–90
and environmental issues, 58
fend-for-yourself federalism, 91–92
fiscal policy of, 53–57
income disparities in, 152, 155–57,
189*nn*2–3
intergovernmental fiscal transfers,
97–98
and local government consumption of
fixed capital, 261–63
and local government expenditures
by function, 248–50
by level of government, 250–52,
287–88*n*4
on social programs, 252–55
and local government revenues and
taxes, 263–72, 288*nn*5–7
and regional equity
securing economic union, 95–102
transfer dependencies, 94–95
regional-international interface, 11
as structure vs. process, 70–74
and tax harmonization, 197
trends in regional income disparities
and convergence, 157–60,
171–77*ff*4A.1–4A.7,
171–77*tt*4A.1–4A.7, 189*n*4
VAT in
Brazil, 129, 130, 194–96,
210*nn*1–5
Canada, 196–98, 210*nn*6–8
European Union, 198–200, 210*n*9
little boat model of dual VAT,
200–202, 210–11*nn*10–11
See also fiscal federalism; macro
federalism; mature federations;
nation-states; *specific country*

federations
central banking in, 47–53
comparison of constitutional
approaches to securing economic
union, 28–30
exclusive powers of, 28
legislative federations, 31–32, 56
monetary policy of, 47–53
and transfer dependency, 35
See also mature federations; *specific
country*
financial markets, 215, 234*n*2
access to, 221–22
benefits and risks of access to, 217–21,
235*nn*10–11, 235*nn*13–14,
235–36*n*16, 236*nn*18–20,
236*nn*22–24, 236*n*26
regulatory framework for, 221–22,
236–37*n*31
financial services, tax on, 196, 210*n*6
fiscal adjustment programs, 92
fiscal decentralization. *See* decentralized
fiscal systems
fiscal deficits, 218–19, 236*n*22
fiscal equalization, 96, 99
fiscal federalism, 3–4, 70
as bane of fiscal prudence, 119
as boon to fiscal prudence, 120–22
and division of fiscal powers, 88–90
fend-for-yourself federalism, 91–92
fiscal divide within nations, 90–91
and fragmentation of internal
common markets, 92
incentives for governance, 93
literature review, 9–10
overview, 86, 88
fiscal management, impact on fiscal
decentralization, 114–15*t*3.1, 129
fiscal policies, 53–57, 224, 237*n*41
Canada, 55–57, 74*n*5, 126–27
China, 133–35
coordination of, 91–92
in Australia, 128
in Brazil, 129–33
conclusions concerning, 135
in EU, 128
in Germany, 127–28

institutional setting for, 118–35, 137*n*3
See also legislated fiscal rules
fiscal responsibility laws, 123–25
fiscal stresses, 216, 218, 235*n*9
  and insolvency, 218, 235–36*n*16
  and regulatory framework, 218–29,
    236*n*18
fiscal systems, 220
  fiscal responsibility scores, 308–14
  intergovernmental fiscal systems, 220,
    298–99
  See also decentralized fiscal systems
fixed-capital consumption, 261–63
foreign direct investments, 101–2
France, 150–51, 272
free internal markets, 28
free trade, 95–96
free trade agreements (FTAs), 11, 12*t*1.1,
    24*f*1.1, 25
  and international integration, 26
  and role of nation-states in, 66
  See also specific agreement
FRG. *See* Federal Republic of Germany
    (FRG)
FTAs. *See* free trade agreements (FTAs)

gasoline tax, 210*n*8
gatekeepers, 121–22
GATT. *See* General Agreement on Tariffs
    and Trade (GATT)
GDP. *See* gross domestic product (GDP)
General Agreement on Tariffs and Trade
    (GATT), 18–19, 62–63
geographic space, 28
German federation, 17
Germany, 28, 56, 149, 281
  business tax revenues, 272
  central bank structure, 47, 49*t*1.4, 52
  constitutional provisions of, 22*t*1.3
  coordination of fiscal policy, 127–28
  and division of power in international
    agreements, 63–64
  economic union of, 28, 29
  selected institutional features of, 21*t*1.2
  subnational borrowing, 224, 237*n*40
Gini index, 146–47, 150*t*4.1, 153–54*t*4.2
  trends in federal countries, 157, 158*f*4.3b

trends in unitary countries, 161,
    162*f*4.4b
Global Environmental Facility, 80
globalization, 60
  and democracy deficits, 64–68
  and external shocks, 83–84
  impact of, 77–78
  impact on governance, 78–84
  and information-knowledge
    revolution, 11–15
  mitigating adverse consequences of,
    101–2
  See also glocalization
globalization of information. *See*
    information revolution
glocalization, 1–2, 70, 85–86, 87*t*2.1
  See also localization
GNP. *See* gross national product (GNP)
golden rule, 224, 237*nn*40–41
gold standard mechanism, 35–36
goods and services tax (GST), 97, 130,
    194–95, 210*n*2
  Canada, 196–97, 210*nn*6–8
  European Union, 198
  See also tax on circulation of goods
    and services (ICMS)
governance, 2–3
  and central banks, 113
  comparison of systems of, 291–92
  composition of, 119, 137*n*3
  and glocalization, 86, 87*t*2.1
  impact of globalization and
    information revolution on,
    78–84
  incentives for, 93
  local vs. state, 90
  multicentered approach to, 103–4
  resistance from state governments to
    local governance, 90
  See also citizen-centered governance
Government Finance Statistics Yearbook,
    260–61
government spending. *See* expenditures;
    local government expenditures
grants, 98
  as source of local government
    revenues, 273, 274*t*7.8

types and purposes of, 276, 279*t*7.11, 280, 282–83, 288*nn*10–12
See also transfer dependency; transfer systems
GRDP. *See* gross regional domestic product (GRDP)
gross domestic product (GDP), 110, 145
and infrastructure investments, 235*n*10
and local government expenditures, 250–51, 255–60, 283
and local government revenue sources, 273, 274*t*7.8
Ontario, 55
property tax revenues as share of, 266
relationship to political processes and administrative performance, 292, 293*f*8.1
social programs as share of, 252–55, 283
variations in, 316–18*tt*8A.1–8A.2
gross national product (GNP), 127, 133
gross regional domestic product (GRDP), 144, 150*t*4.1, 153–54*t*4.2
in federal countries, 157–60, 189*n*4
industrial countries, 149–52
growth, 10
GST. *See* goods and services tax (GST)
Gulliver Effect, 16

hard budget constraints, 222, 233–34
harmonization, 197
of interregional transactions in Brazil, 195–96, 210*nn*3–5
of interstate tax, 205
of taxes in European Union, 198–200
harmonized sales tax (HST), 197
health care
authority for, 308, 311–12*t*8.4
expenditures for as share of GDP, 256–57*t*7.4, 258–59
holdout problems, 222, 227, 237*n*35
home-country rule, 12*t*1.1, 17, 27
home-province rule, 27
horizontal fiscal imbalances, 99
hospitals, tax on, 196–97
housekeeping activities, 260

housing, expenditures for as share of GDP, 255–60
HST. *See* harmonized sales tax (HST)
Hungary
debt settlement, 230, 239*n*59
insolvency mechanisms, 227, 228, 229, 238*n*46, 238–39*n*52, 239*n*54

ICMS. *See* tax on circulation of goods and services (ICMS)
imbalance of power, 296–97
IMF. *See* International Monetary Fund (IMF)
imports
and DBCPT, 209–10, 212*n*25
and deferred payment systems, 199–200
little boat model of dual VAT, 200–202, 210–11*nn*10–11
tax on, 195
See also trade
incentives, electoral, 295–96, 297
income
gaps in, 83–84
See also regional income inequalities
income-support systems, 41
income taxes
Brazil, 131–32
as source of local government revenue, 263–68, 269–70, 288*n*8
independence rankings, 48–51*t*1.4, 52
India
debt service ratio, 224, 237*n*42
distribution of revenue from CST among states, 206, 207*t*5.2
fiscal deficits, 219, 236*n*22
and fiscal regulations, 238*n*45
and fiscal sustainability, 224, 237*n*39
legislated fiscal rules, 125*b*3.1
off-budget liabilities, 225
political decentralization in, 306–7
regional income disparities in, 160, 173*f*4A.4, 174*t*4A.4
taxation system, 202–8, 211–12*nn*12–24
Indonesia
political decentralization in, 306

regional income inequalities in,
166–67, 181*f*4A.10, 181*t*4A.10
Industrial and Commercial Bank of
China, 117
industrial countries
and regional income disparities,
149–52
trends in regional income disparities,
171–72*f*4A.1–4A.2,
171–72*tt*4A.1–4A.2
See also specific country
industries, tax on, 204–5, 211*n*21
inflation, 111, 117, 137*n*2
information revolution, 1–2, 13*t*1.1
and citizen empowerment, 80–81
impact of explosion of, 66–67
impact of governance on, 78–84
and international nature of
economics, 69
overview, 17–18
information superhighway, 67
infrastructure, 215, 216, 285, 287
authority for, 308–9, 311–12*t*8.4
finance of, 217–21, 235*nn*10–11,
235*nn*13–14, 235–36*n*16,
236*nn*18–20, 236*nn*22–24,
236*n*26
insolvency, 216–17, 235*n*9
conclusions concerning, 231–34
and fiscal stress, 218, 235–36*n*16
and subnational borrowing, 221–23,
226–34, 237*n*33, 237*n*36,
238*nn*45–46, 238–39*nn*48–56,
239*nn*59–60
institutional arrangements, 2
and allocation of funds across
jurisdictions, 313
Canada, 21*t*1.2
for equalization programs, 91
of federal systems, 72–73
for fiscal policy, 118–35, 137*n*3
impact on decentralization, 85
and intergovernmental fiscal systems,
298–99
and monetary policy, 110–18
and revenues, 310
insurance mechanisms, 45–46

integration
negative vs. positive, 24, 26
See also internal economic
integration
Intergovernmental Fiscal Review,
235*n*14
intergovernmental transfers, 34, 284–85,
286–87
and decentralization, 97–98
as source of local government
revenues, 275–83, 275*t*7.8,
288*nn*9–11
See also transfer dependency; transfer
systems
internal common markets, 3, 92,
95–96
internal economic integration, 20–24
conclusions concerning, 32–34
constitutional approaches to securing
economic union, 28–30
economic integration continuum,
24–27
international integration and internal
economic union, 30–32
internal economic union, 17,
30–32, 73
international agreements, 83
and division of powers in federal
nations, 61–64
and macro federalism, 59–64
international integration, 26, 30–32
International Monetary Fund (IMF),
122, 260–61, 275
interprovincial transactions, 197
interregional transactions, 195–96,
210*nn*3–5
interstate trade, 71, 201, 204, 208–10,
212*n*25
intrastate transactions, 205
IPI. *See* tax on industrial products (IPI)

Japan, 272, 281
job creation, 39
judicial procedures, and subnational
insolvency, 227–28, 238*n*51,
239*n*53
jurisdictional realignment, 16

knowledge, 13t1.1, 82
See also information revolution

labor force, 38, 41–42, 43
Law of Fiscal Responsibility (LRF), 116,
  132–33
legislated fiscal rules, 122–26, 131–32, 134
legislative federations, 31–32, 56
literature reviews, macro federalism,
  9–10
little boat model, 200–202, 209,
  210–11nn10–11
Liu, Lili, xx, 5, 215–41
loans, China, 116–18
local government expenditures
  capital expenditures, 260–63
  conclusions concerning, 283–87
  core services, 260
  by function, 246–50, 287n3
  by level of government, 250–52,
    287–88nn4
  social programs, 252–55
  See also expenditures
local government revenues
  conclusions concerning, 283–87
  intergovernmental transfers, 275–83,
    275t7.8, 288nn9–11
  nontax revenues, 272–75
  tax autonomy (1995), 277–78t7.10
  and taxes, 263–72, 288nn5–7
local governments, 5–6
  checks and balances in, 296–97
  democratic nature of, 287
  fiscal design of, 285–87
  resistance from state governments to
    local governance, 90
  taxation policies, 134–35
localization, 3, 84
  of decision making, 101–2
  facilitating local access to credit,
    99–100
  resistance from state governments to,
    90
  strengthening of, 79–80
  See also glocalization
LRF. See Law of Fiscal Responsibility
  (LRF)

Maastricht Treaty, 17, 53–57, 74nn4–5,
  123
macroeconomic management, 2
  institutional setting for monetary
    policy, 110–18
  overview, 109–10
  and subnational borrowing, 219
macro federalism, 10
  conclusions concerning, 68–74
  definition, 18–19
  democracy deficits and global
    confederalizing, 64–68
  international dimensions of, 59–64
management systems, result-oriented
  management, 300–301, 309,
    311–12t8.4, 314
Manaus Free Zone (ZFM), Brazil, 194,
  195
mandamus writ, 227, 237n45
manufacturing sector
  tax on, 195–96
  tax on industrial products, 130,
    194–96, 210n1
  tax on manufactured goods, 202–3,
    211nn13–17
MASH. See municipalities, academic
  institutions, schools, and hospitals
  (MASH)
mature federations, 35
  Blanchard-Katz analysis of, 42–44, 46
  central bank structure, 48–50t1.4
  comparison of constitutional
    provisions of, 22–23t1.3, 32
  environmental issues, 57–58
  fiscal policy coordination in, 122–28
  and free trade, 95–96
  free trade, 95–96
  selected institutional features of,
    21t1.2
  See also federal systems; specific
    country
maximum-to-minimum ratio (MMR),
  144, 150t4.1, 153–54f4.2
MBBs. See municipal bond banks
  (MBBs)
McKenna, Frank, 41–42
McMillan, Melville L., xx, 5–6, 245–89

Mexico
  credit rating system, 226
  debt crisis, 224
  regional income disparities in, 161,
      175f4A.5, 175t4A.5
  subnational borrowing, 219, 236n23
MMR. See maximum-to-minimum ratio
      (MMR)
MNCs. See multinational corporations
      (MNCs)
mobility, 15t1.1, 28–29
modified value added tax (Modvat),
      India, 202–3, 211nn13–14
monetary policy, 47–53, 110–18,
      137nn1–2
monetary union, 24f1.1, 25
money supply, 113, 114–15t3.1
moral hazard, and work-sharing
      programs, 41
multicentered governance, 2–3
multinational corporations (MNCs),
      12t1.1
municipal bond banks (MBBs), 99
municipal finance corporations, 100
municipalities, academic institutions,
      schools, and hospitals (MASH),
      196–97, 210n7
municipalities, tax on, 196–97

NAFTA. See North American Free Trade
      Agreement (NAFTA)
National Public Finance Council
      (CONFAZ), Brazil, 195, 210nn4–5
nation-states
  and central banks, 47–53
  conclusions concerning internal
      economic integration of, 32–34
  and confederalism, 16–17, 64–68
  and democracy deficits, 64–68
  and economic integration continuum,
      24–27
  and economic union, 28–32
  fiscal divide within, 90–91
  and glocalization, 85–86
  impact of globalization on, 77–78
  impact of new technoeconomic
      paradigm on, 18–19

international integration of, 30–32
  and international nature of
      economics, 69–70
  monetary policy of, 47–53
  reorientation of, 79–80
  See also federal systems
negative integration, 24, 26, 29
neoinstitutional economics, 108
new technoeconomic paradigm, 11–15,
      17–18, 66–69
New Zealand, 112, 124–25b3.1
nonindustrial countries, regional income
      inequalities in, 152, 153–54t4.2
nonprofit organizations, tax on, 197
nonsocial care, expenditures for as share
      of GDP, 255–60
nontax revenues, as source of local
      government revenues, 272–75
North American Free Trade Agreement
      (NAFTA), 11, 12t1.1, 67–68

OECD. See Organisation for Economic
      Co-operation and Development
      (OECD) countries
off-budget liabilities, 225–26, 232
Ontario, Canada, 55–57, 120–21
Organisation for Economic Co-operation
      and Development (OECD)
      countries, 160
  reliance on sales taxes, 271
  result-oriented management in,
      300–301
  tax-sharing arrangements, 275–76,
      277–78t7.10, 288n9
outmigration, 37–38, 39, 40–41
out-of-state transactions, 198–99
own-source finances, 286
own-source revenues, 299

Pakistan, 112, 176f4A.6, 176t4A.6, 306
paradiplomacy, 59–61, 67
paternalism, and regional equity, 94–95
People's Bank of China (PBC), 112,
      116–18
Peru, 223, 224, 225, 237nn41–42
Philippines, 165–66, 182f4A.11,
      182t4A.11, 307

pluralist electoral systems, 295–96
policies
    regional, 4, 34, 46–47, 102, 169–87
    and regional income disparities,
        147–49
    regional-international interface, 11
    See also decision making
politics
    and accountability mechanisms,
        294–95
    and accountability scores, 302–7
    political integration, 26
pork-barrel politics, 119, 124*b*3.3,
        126, 130
positive integration, 24, 26
price stability, 52, 53, 110–12
private capital, 215
privatization, and glocalization, 85–86
production, internationalization of, 11
production-distribution processes,
        194–95
profitability, 118
property rights, 66, 67
property taxes, as source of local
        government revenues, 263–69, 284,
        288*n*8
proportional electoral systems, 295
protectionism, 83
provincial finance corporations, 99
provincial issues
    banking, 117–18
    home-province rule, 27
    labor force, 40–42
    little boat model of dual VAT, 200–202,
        210–11*nn*10–11
    provincial taxes, 197–98, 210*n*8
    See also regional issues
provincial sales tax (PST), Canada, 197
PST. *See* provincial sales tax (PST),
        Canada
public functions, trilogy of, 109
public goods, supply of, 98
public policies, and regional income
        inequalities, 147–49
public safety, 249, 255–60
public services
    and creditors' rights, 226

local government expenditures as
        share of GDP, 255–60
Purohit, Mahesh C., xx, 4–5, 193–213
Putin, Vladimir, 306

QST. *See* Quebec sales tax (QST), Canada
Quebec, Canada, 74, 74*nn*5
Quebec Hydro, 61, 66–67, 74*n*5
Quebec sales tax (QST), Canada, 197

red-light zone, 224–25, 238*n*44
regime theory, 14*t*1.1
regional income inequalities, 3–4
    classification of convergence and
        regional development policies,
        169–87
    federal vs. unitary countries, 152,
        155–57, 189*nn*2–3
    industrial countries, 149–52
    measures of
        dynamic concepts of regional
            inequality, 147–49
        static measure of regional
            inequality, 144–47, 150*t*4.1
    nonindustrial countries, 152,
        153–54*t*4.2
    overview, 143–44
    trends in
        federal countries, 152, 157–60,
            171–77*ff*4A.1–4A.7,
            171–77*tt*4A.1–4A.7, 189*nn*2–4
        unitary countries, 152, 161–68,
            178–87*ff*4A.8–4A.16,
            178–87*tt*4A.8–4A.16, 189*nn*2–4
    See also regional issues
regional issues, 4
    Blanchard-Katz analysis of, 42–44, 46
    and decision making, 101–2
    and glocalization, 85–86
    institutional setting for monetary
        policy, 110–18
    internationalization of cities and
        regions, 82, 112*t*1.1
    interregional transactions, 195–96,
        210*nn*3–5
    policies for growth, 34
    policies for regional development, 102

regional convergence, 148
regional-international interface,
        11–14, 33, 46
    and decentralization, 61–64
    and international nature of
        economics, 69–70
    and paradiplomacy, 59–61
    research in regional policies, 46–47
    securing economic union, 95–102
    stabilization policies, 44–46, 120
    and transfer dependencies, 36–42,
        94–95
    See also internal economic integration;
        provincial issues; regional income
        inequalities
regulatory frameworks
    legislated fiscal rules, 122–26
    for subnational borrowing, 218–19,
        231–34, 236n18
        ex ante regulation, 221–23, 224,
            231–34, 236–37nn31–36,
            237nn39–42, 238n44
        insolvency mechanisms for, 221–23,
            226–31, 227n36, 237n33,
            238nn45–46, 238–39nn48–56,
            239nn59–60
    supranational, 16–17
relative mean deviation, 146, 150t4.1,
        153–54t4.2
residuary entry, 202, 203, 211n12
result-oriented management, 300–301,
        309, 311–12t8.4, 314
retail sales tax, Canada, 197
revenues, 88
    deficits in, 236n22
    distribution from CST among states in
        India, 206, 207t5.2
    expenditure-revenue imbalances, 218
    level of autonomy to raise, 309,
        311–12t8.4
    See also local government revenues
revenue sharing, 133–34, 237n39, 280–81
rollover risks, 218, 219, 235n13
Romania, 183f4A.12, 183t4A.12
Russia, 161, 219, 236n23, 237nn41–42
Russian Federation, 177f4A.7,
        177t4A.7, 306

sales taxes
    India, 204–5, 206t5.1, 211n19, 211n24
    as source of local government
        revenues, 271
schools, tax on, 196–97
seigniorage finance, 229
separation of powers, 307
services, as source of local government
        revenue, 263–72, 288nn5–7
service tax, India, 203
Shah, Anwar, xxi, 1–6, 77–106, 107–41,
        143–91, 291–322
Shankar, Raja, xxi, 4, 143–91
shared rule, 89–90
sigma convergence, 149
skills and skilled workers, 4, 102
social dumping, 31, 83
social issues and policies, 13t1.1, 18, 31,
        55, 83, 101
social programs, 286
    expenditures for as share of GDP, 249,
        255–60
    local government delivery of, 283
    local government finance of, 252–55,
        270, 288n8
    Ontario, 120–21
social risk, management of through
        transfers and social insurance, 101
social union, 24f1.1, 25
SOEs. See state-owned enterprises
        (SOEs)
soft budget constraints, 220
South Africa, 237n41
    and credit markets, 235n14
    debt discharge, 230
    insolvency mechanisms, 227, 228, 229,
        238n46
    political decentralization in, 307
Spain, income inequalities in, 150–51
specific-purpose grants, 276, 279t7.11,
        280, 282–83, 288nn11–12
spillovers, 276, 282, 287
Sri Lanka, 164–65, 184f4A.13, 184t4A.13
stabilization policies, 44–46, 55, 109–10,
        120
state governments
    resistance to local governance, 90

state VAT in
　Brazil, 194–95, 210n2
　India, 204–5, 211n19, 211nn21–23
　tax issues, 203, 204
state-owned enterprises (SOEs),
　117, 118
subnational bonds, 215–16, 218,
　234nn4–5
subnational borrowing, 5, 234n3
　benefits and risks of, 217–21,
　　235nn10–11, 235nn13–14,
　　235–36n16, 236nn18–20,
　　236nn22–24, 236n26
　China, 134
　conclusions concerning, 231–34
　ex ante regulation, 221–22,
　　236–37nn31–37, 237nn39–42,
　　238n44
　insolvency mechanisms, 221–23,
　　226–31, 227n36, 237n33,
　　238nn45–46, 238–39nn48–56,
　　239nn59–60
　overview, 215–17, 234nn1–6, 235n9
　rationales for regulation of, 221–23,
　　236–37nn31–36
subnational governments, 234n1
　and debt-deficit guidelines, 53–54
　impact of knowledge and international
　　competition on, 82
　international trade agreements, 83
subnational insolvency. See insolvency
subsidies, 39, 99–100
supranational issues, 19
　emergence of supranational regimes,
　　79–80
　and federalism, 74
　regulatory structures, 16–17
　social policies, 31
Swiss National Bank, 113
Switzerland, 127
　central bank structure, 47, 49t1.4, 52
　constitutional provisions of, 23t1.3
　division of power in international
　　agreements, 62
　selected institutional features of,
　　21t1.2
symbolic-analytic services, 82, 104n2

taxation, 313
　allocation of taxes, 53–57
　Brazil, 194–96, 210nn1–5
　Canada, 196–98, 210n6
　centralization of powers of, 88
　China, 133–34, 133–35
　decentralization of, 100
　erosion of government's capacity to
　　tax, 80
　European Union, 198–200, 210n9
　and GDP, 273, 274t7.8
　harmonization of interstate tax, 205
　India, 202–8, 211–12nn12–24
　and intergovernmental fiscal
　　systems, 299
　little boat model, 200–202, 209,
　　210–11nn10–11
　local vs. state, 90
　recommendations for tax on interstate
　　transactions, 208–10, 212n25
　as source of local government
　　revenues, 283–84
　tax harmonization, 96–97
　tax-sharing arrangements, 275–76,
　　277–78t7.10, 288n9
　tax-transfer systems, 45
　See also local government revenues;
　　specific tax
tax credits, 194, 203, 210n1, 211n16
Tax-for-Fee Program, China, 135
tax information exchange system
　　(TINXSYS), India, 208
taxless finance schemes, 220, 236n24
tax on circulation of goods and services
　　(ICMS), 97, 130, 194–95, 210n2
　See also goods and services tax
　　(GST)
tax on industrial products (IPI), 130,
　　194–96, 210n1
Thailand, 168, 185f4A.14, 185t4A.14
Theil index, 147, 150t4.1, 153–54t4.2, 157
　trends in federal countries, 157,
　　159f4.3c
　trends in unitary countries, 161,
　　163f4.4c
TINXSYS. See tax information exchange
　　system (TINXSYS), India

TNCs. *See* transnational corporations
(TNCs)
trade, 30, 95–96
and environmental issues, 83
interregional, 195–96, 210nn3–5
interstate, 70, 201, 204, 208–10,
212n25
See also specific trade agreement
trade-account deficits, 35, 74n2
training, 82
transfer dependency
geometry of macro region problems,
36–42
gold-standard analogy for, 35–36, 74n2
overview, 34–35
and regional equity, 94–95
term usage, 34–35
transfer systems
Brazil, 130–32
and macro federalism, 35–36, 74n2
to manage social risk, 101
regional, 45
and social expenditures, 255
See also intergovernmental transfers
transition countries
building blocks of citizen-centered
governance in
accountability, 294–98
fiscal responsibility, 298–301
overview, 292–94, 318n1
scorecard of citizen-centered
governance
accountability scores, 302–7
fiscal responsibility scores, 308–14
overview, 301
transnational corporations (TNCs),
12t1.1, 16, 80, 81
transparency, 225, 226, 232

UED. *See* union excise duty (UED)
ultramobility, 15t1.1
unconditional transfers, 276, 279t7.11,
280–82, 284, 288n11
unemployment insurance, 41–42, 101
unemployment rates, 42–43
unified economic space, 26–27
unified socioeconomic space, 24–25

uniformity, 33
union excise duty (UED), 202–3, 211n17
union governments, and CenVAT in
India, 202–3, 211nn13–17
Union List, India, 202, 203, 211n12
unitary countries
beta convergence results in, 161,
164t4.6
and economic integration, 26–27
income inequalities in, 152, 155–57,
189nn2–3
local government consumption of
fixed capital, 261–63
local government expenditures
by function, 248–50
by level of government, 250–52,
287–88n4
local government revenues and taxes,
263–72, 288nn5–7
trends in income inequalities, 161,
162–63ff4.4a-4.4c,
178–87ff4A.8–4A.16,
178–87tt4A.8–4A.16
United Kingdom
central banking, 53
and citizens' rights, 66
income disparities in, 149–52
subnational borrowing, 224, 237n40
United States, 58, 121, 126, 225
approach to regional disparities, 102
bankruptcy framework, 223, 237n36
Blanchard-Katz analysis of regional
issues in, 42–44
Canada-U.S. Trade Agreement, 11,
12t1.1, 27
central bank structure, 47, 50t1.4, 52
constitutional provisions of, 23t1.3,
28, 30
division of power in international
agreements, 62
Federal Reserve, 47, 50t1.4, 52
income disparities in, 149–52
infrastructure investment, 235n10
insolvency mechanisms, 227–29,
237nn48–50, 238–39nn52–53
internal economic integration, 20–24
and local sales taxes, 271

NAFTA, 11, 12t1.1, 67–68
and regional-international
    interface, 60
selected institutional features of, 21t1.2
subnational bonds, 215–16, 234nn4–5
subnational borrowing, 219–20,
    236n24
trends in regional disparities,
    172f4A.2, 172t4A.2
universalism, 119, 121
U.S. Bankruptcy Code, 223, 232, 237n36
Uzbekistan, 163, 186f4A.15, 186t4A.15

value added taxes (VATs), 4–5
    Brazil, 129, 130, 194–96, 210nn1–5
    Canada, 196–98, 210nn6–8
    China, 134
    European Union, 198–200, 210n9
    federal-state VATs, 130
    India, 202–8, 211–12nn12–14
    little boat model, 200–202, 209,
        210–11nn10–11

prepaid, 209
zero-rating of state VAT, 208, 209
vertical fiscal gaps, 88
veto players, 296
Vietnam, 165, 187f4A.16, 187t4A.16
von Bismarck, Otto, 64

wage rates, 37–39, 41, 83
wages, 37–38, 41, 43
Waibel, Michael, xxi, 5, 215–41
work-sharing programs, 41
World Development Report 2004, 294
World Trade Organization (WTO),
    68, 80

Yeltsin, Boris, 306

zero ratings, 197, 200, 210
    of sales, 195
    of state value added tax, 208, 209
ZFM. *See* Manaus Free Zone (ZFM),
    Brazil

ECO-AUDIT
Environmental Benefits Statement

The World Bank is committed to preserving endangered forests and natural resources. The Office of the Publisher has chosen to print *Macro Federalism and Local Finance* on recycled paper with 30 percent postconsumer fiber in accordance with the recommended standards for paper usage set by the Green Press Initiative, a nonprofit program supporting publishers in using fiber that is not sourced from endangered forests. For more information, visit www.greenpressinitiative.org.

Saved:
- 13 trees
- 9 million Btu of total energy
- 1,113 lb. of net greenhouse gases
- 4,620 gal. of waste water
- 593 lb. of solid waste